SECRET
SOLDIERS

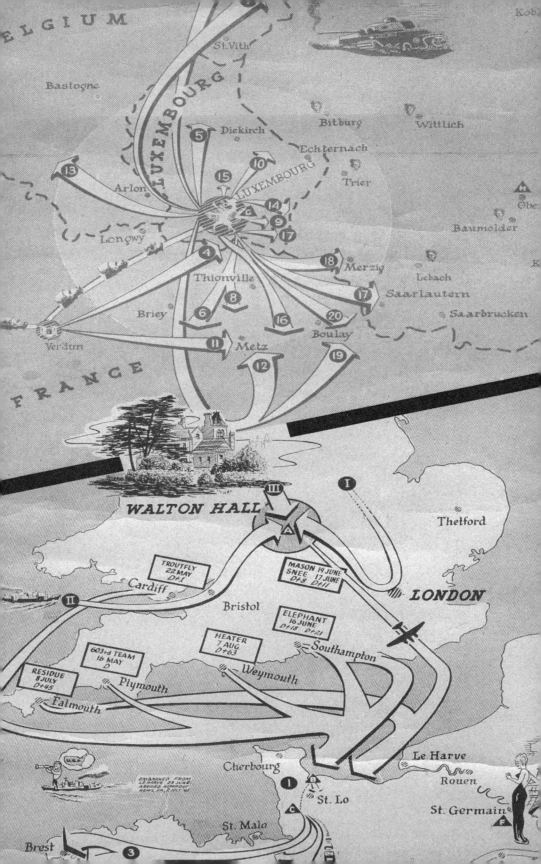

Routes and Operations
23RD HEADQUARTERS
Special Troops
7 APRIL '44 — 7 JUNE '45

BIVOUAC AREAS

WALTON HALL
15 May-16 Jun 44
(Near Stratford-upon-Avon, England. "Residue" stayed here through 8 July; HEATER stayed here through 7 Aug.)

NORMANDY
16 Jun-3 Aug
(Eubercy was an orchard just south of Trevieres, France. "Residue" joined ELEPHANT here. ELEPHANT had camped first in some fields near Ecrammeville west of Trevieres.)

LE FREMONDRE
3 Aug-23 Aug
(Orchard few miles north of Coutance. HEATER joined main body here.)

TORCE en CHARNIE
23 Aug-31 Aug
(Grounds of abandoned chateau between Laval and LeMans.)

MAUNY
31 Aug-7 Sep
(Hillside 25 miles west of Troyes.)

ST GERMAIN
7 Sep-20 Sep
(Napoleonic palace and military barracks near enough to Paris. Task force departed for Bettembourg Operation 4, 13 Sep. Rear Echelon came up to Verdun 20 Sept. Entire command reassembled in Luxembourg 25 Sep.)

LUXEMBOURG
25 Sep-13 Apr 45
(In the Italian Legation. Units in seminary and school. On 26 Dec units moved back to a caserne in Verdun while command remained in Luxembourg. On 10 Jan 45 units moved up to a caserne in Briey which was the rear base camp until 13 Apr.)

IDAR-OBERSTEIN
13 Apr-   Jun
(In Hotel Hermes. Units scattered throughout Saar-Palatinate-Moselle and out nearly to Czechoslovakia. All units eventually regrouped in fields outside Oberstein 21 May for POM staging.)

OPERATIONS

I.   ADVANCE PARTY ARRIVES AT GLASGOW VIA AIR 17 APRIL '44.

II. MAIN BODY ARRIVES IN ETO 15 MAY '44

III. 3132 SIG. SV. CO. (HEATER) ARRIVED ETO 11 JUNE '44.

1 ELEPHANT 1-4 July 44
2 BRITTANY 9-12 Aug 44
3 BREST 20-27 Aug 44
4 BETTEMBOURG 14-22 Sep 44
5 WILTZ 4-10 Oct 44
6 DALLAS 2-10 Nov 44
7 ELSENBORN 3-12 Nov 44
8 CASANOVA 4-9 Nov 44
9 KOBLENZ 6-14 Dec 44
10 KODAK 22-23 Dec 44
11 METZ I 28-31 Dec 44
12 METZ II 6-9 Jan 45
13 LEGLISE 10-15 Jan 45
14 FLAXWEILER 17-18 Jan 45
15 STEINSEL 27-29 Jan 45
16 LANDONVILLE 28 Jan-2 Feb 45
17 WHIPSAW 1-4 Feb 45
18 MERZIG 13-14 Feb 45
19 LOCHINVAR 1-11 Mar 45
20 BOUZONVILLE 11-13 Mar 45
21 VIERSEN 18-24 Mar 45

KEY

● ADMINISTRATION MOVES IN UNITED KINGDOM INDICATED IN ROMAN NOS.

♪ TACTICAL MOVES ON CONTINENT INDICATED IN ARABIC NOS.

⛵ ADMINISTRATION MOVES ON CONTINENT

◉ DISPLACED PERSONS' CAMPS

▲ BIVOUAC AREAS

Excerpts from Operations Map, 23d Headquarters Special Troops by T-5 George A. Martin, B Co., 603d Engineers and battalion photographer. Martin drew and hand lettered the map while in Europe. MAP COURTESY OF ROY EICHHORN AND GEORGE A. MARTIN.

SECRET SOLDIERS

THE STORY OF WORLD WAR II'S
HEROIC ARMY OF DECEPTION

Philip Gerard

DUTTON

DUTTON
Published by the Penguin Group
Penguin Putnam Inc., 375 Hudson Street, New York, New York 10014, U.S.A.
Penguin Books Ltd, 80 Strand, London WC2R 0RL, England
Penguin Books Australia Ltd, Ringwood, Victoria, Australia
Penguin Books Canada Ltd, 10 Alcorn Avenue, Toronto, Ontario, Canada M4V 3B2
Penguin Books (N.Z.) Ltd, 182–190 Wairau Road, Auckland 10, New Zealand

Penguin Books Ltd, Registered Offices: Harmondsworth, Middlesex, England

Published by Dutton, a member of Penguin Putnam Inc.

First printing, June 2002
10   9   8   7   6   5   4   3   2   1

 REGISTERED TRADEMARK—MARCA REGISTRADA

CIP data has been applied for.

ISBN 0-525-94664-0

Printed in the United States of America
Set in Transitional 521
Designed by Leonard Telesca

Art Credits

Frontispiece excerpts from Operations Map, 23d Headquarters Special Troops. Courtesy of Roy Eichhorn and George A. Martin.

Page 9: *Morning Winds*. Arthur Shilstone. Courtesy of Arthur Shilstone.

Page 60: Virgil Bragdon caricature. Jack Masey. Courtesy of Jack Masey.

Page 137: From *Sketches at Trévières*. George Vander Sluis. *Yank: The Army Weekly*. 20 August, 1944. Courtesy of Robert Dahl.

Page 147: *Landing in Normandy*. Arthur Shilstone. Courtesy of Arthur Shilstone.

Page 257: *Not Me, Please*. Harold Laynor. Oil/Masonite. 19" x 14". Courtesy of Gloria Laynor.

Page 262: *Young Soldiers Being Transported to the Front, Remagen, Château de Divonne, France*. 1945. Ink. 5 1/4" x 8". © Ellsworth Kelly. Photo by Jerry Thompson. Courtesy of Ellsworth Kelly.

Page 293: *Study for Guard Duty*. Harold Laynor. Watercolor. 9" x 17". Courtesy of Gloria Laynor. The Laynor Foundation.

For all the secret soldiers,
especially George C. Peddle,
Chester Pelliccioni, and
Thomas G. Wells, who made
the supreme sacrifice for
their country

Contents

ACT III: CLOSING THE SHOW

Chronology of Events

January 1936–1940   Hilton Howell Railey commissioned lieutenant, senior grade, U.S. Naval Intelligence Reserve, sent to Panama Canal Zone as consultant.

17 April 1941   Douglas Fairbanks Jr. commissioned lieutenant (jg), USNR.

April–June 1941   Douglas Fairbanks Jr. pursues secret mission to South America for FDR.

August–October 1941   Hilton Howell Railey conducts secret study of U.S. Army morale for *New York Times* and the War Department.

7 December 1941   Japanese attack Pearl Harbor: U.S. at war.

18 July–October 1942   Lt. Comdr. Douglas Fairbanks Jr. serves as special naval observer with British Combined Operations under Lord Louis Mountbatten.

25 August 1942   Joint Security Control established by the Joint Chiefs of Staff to oversee security, cover, and deception.

1942   Railey publishes *What the Citizen Should Know About Civilian Defense.*

22 September 1942–
4 October 1943   Lieutenant Colonel Railey serves as executive of the Secret War Department Planning Board.

October 1942   Lieutenant Commander Fairbanks makes his
                        pitch to Joint Chiefs of Staff for a deception
                        "pyramid."

27 October 1942   Field trial of seaborne sonic deception at
                        "Battle of Sandy Hook."

23 October–   Battle of El Alamein: General Montgomery
7 November 1943   wins by deception.

March–May 1943   Lieutenant Commander Fairbanks establishes
                        Beach Jumpers school at Camp Bradford, Va.,
                        and trains recruits.

27 May 1943   Army Experimental Station established at
                        Fort Hancock, N.J., with Lieutenant Colonel
                        Railey as commanding officer.

12 June 1943   Lieutenant Commander Fairbanks assigned
                        to Beach Jumpers' units in Mediterranean.

10 July 1943   Allies invade Sicily—Lieutenant Commander
                        Fairbanks participates.

9 September 1943   Allies land in Italy. Lieutenant Commander
                        Fairbanks participates in deceptive operations
                        with Beach Jumpers during invasion, awarded
                        combat Silver Star.

4 October 1943–1945   Lieutenant Colonel Railey promoted to colonel
                        and serves as president of the Secret War De-
                        partment Planning Board. Joint Security Con-
                        trol establishes blueprint for 23d Headquarters
                        Special Troops, acting on a report from General
                        Devers's Cover and Deception staff.

20 January 1944   23d Headquarters Special Troops activated.

February 1944   Army Experimental Station moves to Pine
                        Camp (now Fort Drum), N.Y. Allied planners

	begin drawing up cover plan for invasion of Normandy, called FORTITUDE.
6 June 1944	D-Day: Allies land at Normandy. First Special Troops ashore.
1–4 July 1944	Operation ELEPHANT (CERISY)
9–12 August 1944	Operation BRITTANY
15 August 1944	Allies land in south of France: Lieutenant Commander Fairbanks and Beach Jumpers conduct deceptive missions. Fairbanks awarded Legion of Merit with Bronze V for valor.
20–27 August 1944	Operation BREST
25 August 1944	Liberation of Paris by Allied forces.
12–22 September 1944	Operation BETTEMBOURG
4–10 October 1944	Operation WILTZ
2–10 November 1944	Operation DALLAS
4–9 November 1944	Operation CASANOVA
3–12 November 1944	Operation ELSENBORN
6–14 December 1944	Operation KOBLENZ
16 December 1944	Germans counterattack in Ardennes—the Battle of the Bulge begins.
22–23 December 1944	Operation KODAK
28–31 December 1944	Operation METZ I
6–9 January 1945	Operation METZ II. On January 7, Chester "Chet" Pelliccioni killed by a German hand grenade.

10–15 January 1944	Operation L'ÉGLISE
17–18 January 1945	Operation FLAXWEILER
27–29 January 1945	Operation STEINSEL
28 January–2 February 1945	Operation LANDONVILLE
1–4 February 1945	Operation WHIPSAW
13–14 February 1945	Operation MERZIG
February 1945	Colonel Railey visits sonic troops in Luxembourg at the close of the Ardennes offensive.
1–11 March 1945	Operation LOCHINVAR
11–13 March 1945	Operation BOUZONVILLE: George C. Peddle and Thomas G. Wells killed in action and fifteen wounded, including Harold Laynor.
18–24 March 1945	Operation VIERSEN: cover for Rhine Crossing by Ninth Army
29 March 1945	Lt. Gen. William H. Simpson issues a commendation letter to the 23d Special Troops.
11 April–28 April 1945	23d Special Troops manage and guard five displaced persons camps.
12 April 1945	Lieutenant Commander Fairbanks awarded French Legion d'Honneur in the degree of Chevalier and Croix de Guerre with Palm for actions on Elba and in the south of France in August 1944.
7 May 1945	Germany surrenders—Victory in Europe (V-E Day).

16 June 1945	23d Special Troops arrive at Camp Twenty Grand to prepare to go home.
23 June– 2 July 1945	USS *General O. H. Ernst* carries 23d Special Troops to Norfolk, Va.
7 July–7 August 1945	Thirty-day furloughs granted for 23d Special Troops before redeployment to Pacific Theater.
6 August 1945	First atomic bomb dropped on Hiroshima.
8 August 1945	Second atomic bomb dropped on Nagasaki.
14 August 1945	Japan announces unconditional surrender: Victory in Japan (V-J Day).
15 August 1945	3132d Sonic Company deactivated.
15 September 1945	23d Special Troops deactivated.
25 September 1945	603d Engineer Camouflage Battalion deactivated.
17 September 1945	Colonel Railey awarded Legion of Merit.
1 November 1945	Army Experimental Station closed.
5 February 1946	Commander Fairbanks released from naval service.
29 April 1946	Colonel Railey retires from active military service.
1 October 1948	Commander Fairbanks awarded Italian Military Cross for Valor for his actions at Salerno, Italy, in September 1943.

Introduction

23 March 1945. The war in western Europe had come down to this: Two of the greatest armies in history were facing each other across the Rhine River, preparing for the final battle.

It would begin with an Allied amphibious assault across the river. Supreme Commander Dwight D. Eisenhower said that the massive crossing by three armies was tantamount to a naval operation. The river crossing had to happen: there was no other way into the German heartland. For German intelligence, the questions were *where* and *when*.

Nine months earlier, on 6 June 1944, British and American armies had stormed ashore at Normandy and, in two months of bloody fighting, driven the Germans out of western France, liberated Paris, and routed the German army. By September, the Allies had chased the retreating Germans into the Rhineland, where they stalled against the Siegfried Line, a wall of fortified towns, pillboxes, and concrete gun emplacements guarding the German border. Just before Christmas, when the war seemed all but won, the Germans counterattacked in the Ardennes through Belgium and Luxembourg, catching the Allies totally by surprise and splitting the American line down the middle. The armored offensive separated the American armies, leaving U.S. First and Ninth Armies on the northern flank of the "Bulge" with the British and Patton's Third Army to the south.

By February 1945, after suffering tens of thousands of casualties in the cruelest winter fighting ever undertaken by American forces, the U.S. armies were again attacking through the German frontier. Ninth Army remained attached to the British command in the north, while Gen. Omar Bradley's two American armies, First and Third, punched through in the south.

On March 7, U.S. First Army forced a precarious bridgehead at Remagen and after two weeks of hard fighting in hilly terrain was at last ready to break out into open country. Farther south still, at Oppenheim, Gen. George S. Patton's Third Army crossed the Rhine on March 22.

But the key to victory lay on the northern Rhine plain. Three armies under Field Marshal Bernard Montgomery were massed on the western banks of the river. Then were poised to strike the sledgehammer blow Eisenhower had planned since D-Day, crush the remaining Wehrmacht armies, and occupy Germany. Canadian First, British Second, and U.S. Ninth Armies had moved into position opposite Wesel, a major rail and road junction on the northwestern edge of Germany, some thirty miles from the Dutch border. Already delayed a month by weather and German resistance, the big push would commence in the early hours of March 23.

No permanent bridges stood at Wesel; the three armies would cross in assault barges. Once on the east bank of the Rhine, equipped with fourteen hundred tanks and other heavy armor, they would roll eastward across some of the most perfect tank country in Europe under skies ruled by waves of Allied Thunderbolt fighter-bombers, envelop the Ruhr industrial sector, the heart of Nazi war production, and overwhelm the last defenders of the Third Reich. They could end the war in a matter of weeks.

But first they had to get across the river—the castle moat that, until 1945, invading troops had not crossed since Napoleon's had done so in 1806.

Waiting for them somewhere across that moat were eighty German divisions. Battered by four years of war and four million casualties, the German High Command had to resort to drafting boys and old men into *Volkssturm* brigades. But the best of them, the parachute troops and Panzer grenadiers and Waffen SS battalions, would fight tenaciously, using the familiar terrain of their home ground for cover. They had had four years to sight in their deadly 88mm guns and heavy mortars and Spandau machine guns, to turn the Rhine into a kill zone.

The Allied plan called for the infantry to cross first, dig in on the other side, and secure the bridgeheads. Then the combat engineers could move up and construct pontoon bridges under the protection of the infantry, and tanks could roll across the bridges in force before the defenders counterattacked.

Montgomery had been concentrating troops, vehicles, and matériel for months. He intended to strike with overwhelming force; casualty projections were enormous. If the Germans turned back this assault, it would be more long months before he could mount another offensive. Hitler was playing for time: time to perfect his V-2 rockets, mass-produce the Messerschmitt 262 jet fighters that already outflew the fastest Allied aircraft, and finish his program of Jewish extermination. By some intelligence estimates, Germany needed only four more months to produce enough jets to turn the tide of war and fight the Allies to a draw. Then they could negotiate a World War I–style armistice, leaving Germany essentially intact, allowing Hitler to turn his attention east toward the Russians.

Anchoring the southern flank of the assault, Lt. Gen. William H. Simpson's U.S. Ninth Army would launch two divisions across in the vanguard: the 30th "Old Hickory" Division and the 79th "Cross of Lorraine" Division. This assault wave of more than 20,000 men would secure the crucial bridgeheads.

To take the enemy by surprise, Ninth Army relied on a plan dreamed up by a charming southerner, Lt. Col. Merrick Hector Truly. Truly served as the executive officer of an unorthodox unit of secret soldiers: the 23d Headquarters Special Troops.

Most of the soldiers in the American army didn't even know the Special Troops existed—they never wore their own sleeve insignia, camouflaged their vehicles with the markings of other outfits, operated at night and in strict secrecy, and were under orders never to divulge the nature of their mission even to superior officers in their own army.

Comprising 82 officers and 1,023 enlisted men, they were unlike any outfit in the U.S. Army before or since. They were artists, actors, engineers, special-effects experts, architects, advertising layout men, electronic wizards, writers, and designers. Four units comprised the Special Troops: a sonic deception company, a special radio company, a company of combat engineers, and a battalion of camoufleurs. They answered directly to Gen. Omar Bradley, the American ground commander in Europe, through the Special Plans Branch attached to his 12th Army Group headquarters. Long before the D day invasion, Bradley had taken a hand in designing this special unit. They trained Stateside in the southern swamps, the western desert, the Jersey shore, and the north woods, then served under fire with four armies in five European countries during five major campaigns from D-Day until the end of the war.

Their overall mission was deception: optical illusion, sleight of hand, radio misinformation, bluff, sonic feints, disappearing acts—all calculated to fool the enemy into doing or not doing exactly what the Americans wanted. And they were good at it—their last disappearing act was to vanish from history.

Their mission on the Rhine was simple: to create a false "truth" for the enemy, an old-fashioned hoax to convince German intelligence that Ninth Army would not attack at Wesel but more than thirty miles south, near Düsseldorf. And not on March 23—in fact, not before mid-April at the earliest. Thus the Germans would not fortify the real bridgeheads. They would instead divert precious reserves to a place far from the planned battle, where they would be as harmless as if they had already been captured.

But the execution would prove anything but simple. It would require every man's best, every trick they collectively had learned in twenty previous "shows" in France, Luxembourg, Belgium, Holland, and Germany: a plausible script, superb acting, authentic costumes, realistic props, a cast of reliable extras, a sophisticated sound-and-light show, some old-fashioned courage, a dash of derring-do, airtight security, perfect timing, and a little luck.

They would employ their six principle means of deception: camouflaging real troops and tanks, artfully positioning dummy tanks and artillery to be photographed by enemy reconnaissance aircraft, firing off pyrotechnics to mimic artillery fire, projecting a remarkably realistic range of sound effects, transmitting bogus or "spoof" radio traffic, and employing special effects—which included everything from sewing on fake sleeve insignia to impersonating generals.

This is the story of that epic show on the Rhine and of all the preceding shows the Special Troops staged during their remarkable war of illusion against the Germans. While every other unit in the army was doing its best to avoid being shot at, the Special Troops deliberately drew fire on themselves in order to accomplish their mission. That mission was to save lives and help win battles.

Because the 23d Special Troops was organized out of existing units, its early history is not an easy linear chronology. Several army and navy programs that played a part in its evolution were going on at the same time in different places. At Camp Bradford, Virginia, near Norfolk, a seaborne deception outfit first deployed the sonic deception equipment that technicians from Bell Labs and the Stevens Institute of Technology pioneered while working at the Army Experimental Station (AES) at Sandy Hook, New Jersey. Later the AES moved up to Pine Camp, in northern New York.

The key personnel for the Special Troops came together in three principal locations: Fort Meade, Maryland, where the 603d Engineer Camouflage Battalion was organized and trained; the Army Experimental Station at Pine Camp, New York, where the 3132d Signal Service Company learned its trade of sonic deception; and Camp Forrest, Tennessee, where, before shipping out to the war, all the units except the sonic troops were brought together under the designation of the newly activated 23d Special Troops.

To follow the path of their training and subsequent role in winning the war, it is necessary to move among these locations, to see the units evolve first separately and then combined into a larger, cohesive, many-faceted deception force.

The need for such a force was not obvious at first to American military planners, though from ancient times generals had understood that deception is a crucial weapon on the battlefield.

"All warfare is based on deception," declared the Chinese war theoretician Sun Tzu in *The Art of War*, written probably in the fourth century B.C. "Therefore, when capable, feign incapacity; when active, inactivity. When near, make it appear that you are far away; when far away, that you are near. Offer the enemy a bait to lure him; feign disorder and strike him."

Deception fulfills two critical functions in war. First, it turns weakness into strength. An army possessing overwhelming numbers of troops or matériel would not have to resort to wiles. The underdog, however, must find an edge, what current military strategists call a "force multiplier." He must not just even the odds but change them in his favor by making his army seem more powerful than it is.

In 1943, the *Flat-Top*, the newsletter of the 603d Enigneer Camouflage Battalion at Fort Meade, recounted the Old Testament story of how Gideon issued trumpets and lighted lamps concealed inside crockery pitchers to each of his three hundred warriors. In the dead of night, concealed by darkness, as thousands of Midianites slept on the plain below, Gideon and his men stole upon their camp. Gideon blew his trumpet, signaling the attack. Each man simultaneously blew his trumpet and smashed his pitcher, so that they swooped upon the camp in a spectacle of noise and light that seemed to come from thousands of attackers and routed a far superior enemy.

"Weapons have changed since then, but men and resourcefulness remain as vital factors in warfare," the article concluded. "And Surprise, protected by smart Camouflage, is still the most potent of all."

All successful guerrilla leaders, from Robin Hood and the Swamp Fox to Pancho Villa and Ho Chi Minh, have resorted to guile and trickery in the face of overwhelming force.

The second enduring reason to deceive the enemy is to minimize casualties. Not only is this a humane motive, but it also preserves an army's striking power. It lifts morale among one's own troops, one's allies, and the home front, which must show political nerve in supporting the war. Especially in armies that rely on volunteers, spending the lives of soldiers needlessly can cripple an army, cause mass desertions, and spoil the will to fight.

In truth, no army has ever existed that did not resort to deception in one form or another. The Greeks used smoke screens to hide their troops movements from archers, while the Romans perfected the practice of letting forged treasonous letters, implicating key enemy commanders, fall into the hands of the enemy chief, thus causing confusion and mistrust in the enemy's ranks. They also feigned flight in order to draw the enemy after them into an ambush. So, apparently, did the invading Normans under William the Conqueror at Hastings in 1066.

Medieval princes, urged on by Machiavelli, an apostle of misdirection and trickery, became adept at all forms of deception. Their armies were usually loose associations of local nobles, backed by personal contingents of vassals and peasants. Thus, if they could force the surrender of a besieged castle by trickery rather than frontal assault, they had a better chance of keeping intact their own power base. A favorite ruse was to manufacture a show of overwhelming force surrounding the castle—noise and campfires enough for untold thousands. The garrison would lose heart and concede defeat. Or else, while the army was making a grand show outside the walls, sappers would secretly tunnel under the castle, set off explosives, and breach the wall. They might even insert secret agents into the castle to open the gates.

On All Fools' Day in 1403, a small band of Welsh rebels captured Conwy, the castle of King Edward I, by such a ruse. They sent a carpenter knocking on the gate, pretending that he had been summoned to perform routine work inside the castle. Once inside, he overpowered the guards and flung the gate open for his comrades. Hardly sophisticated but still effective.

During the American Civil War, the Confederates, woefully short of cannons, frequently constructed "Quaker guns" by painting logs and mounting them on wagon wheels. Using this simple ploy, more than once they bluffed Gen. George B. MacClellan, the timid commander of the Army of the Potomac, into waiting for reinforcements before attacking the thin Rebel line that stood between the Union army and Richmond.

Military planners distinguish among three kinds of deception: strategic, operational, and tactical. These mimic categories in regular military planning. Strategic planning occurs on a grand scale, involving a whole theater of operations—for instance, the deception plan to make the Germans calculate the wrong location for the Allied landings in Normandy on D day.

Operational deception occurs on a somewhat smaller scale, involving movements across large but limited sectors, such as the northern line on the Rhine River in the spring of 1945.

Tactical deception plays out at the local battlefield level, involving a squad (8–15 soldiers), a platoon (30–50 soldiers), a company (150–200 soldiers), a battalion (800–1,000 soldiers), a regiment (2,500–3,500 soldiers) even a whole division (10,000–15,000 soldiers). Thus it is often referred to as "battlefield deception."

The Special Troops most often staged tactical deception, sometimes combined with operational deception. And their final operation on the Rhine, as we will see, was part of a strategic deception whose ultimate aim was the conquest of Germany. Clearly, the categories can overlap.

Historically, deceptions take several recurring forms. A commander might conceal his numerical strength in order to mount a surprise attack or conceal his weakness by multiplying his forces through mock-ups like Quaker guns or pyrotechnics like Gideon's torches. The desired result is that either the enemy won't attack or will retreat when attacked. Other options are for him to make a *demonstration*, that is, attack merely to distract the enemy away from some other area; mount a diversionary attack to mask the main attack; pretend to prepare for an attack in one sector when in fact the attack will be launched in another; feign retreat in order to draw the enemy after him, usually into ambush; pretend to entrench while actually retreating through some carefully planned escape route; trick the enemy into revealing his position so he can be successfully destroyed; and perhaps most important, gain a crucial psychological advantage over the enemy.

Even the tall bearskin shakos Napoleon's Old Guard wore were a form of deception. Soldiers advancing under such large headgear appeared much larger and more formidable than ordinary soldiers.

The Special Troops, like most armies in history, combined several forms of deception in the same operation, concealing strength on one part of the battlefield, for instance, while concealing weakness on another.

In forming the unit, Americans relearned another old lesson: Not all soldiers are fond of practicing deception. Some American combat commanders in World War II instinctively resisted using deception, preferring to charge straight ahead like the old-style cavalrymen they were. Even for some in the Special Troops, such as Lt. Col. Clifford G. Simenson, whose task it was to train the tricksters and then plan combat operations, it posed a genuine moral conundrum and seemed to utterly subvert his West Point code of Duty, Honor, Country. Lying, even in a good cause, did not come easily to such men.

Others, such as Col. Harry Reeder, the commanding officer of the Special Troops, simply preferred conventional battle as a route to honor and glory. Traditionally for American officers, secret soldiering carried a whiff of dishonor; besides it was never written up in *The Stars and Stripes*.

America has a habit of forgetting the lessons of war during peacetime. Though the U.S. Army had fielded a talented camouflage corps in World War I and learned critical lessons from its British and French counterparts about the practical value of deception on the battlefield, by the time the United States declared war on Germany and Japan, it had all but forgotten them. The whole theory of deception had to be reinvented, and a new generation of men trained to put it into effect in a cataclysmic war.

Like many bold ideas, the notion of a specially trained battlefield deception unit grew out of unlikely beginnings, including weakness, failure, trial and error, and individual initiative. Because battlefield deception has always been more an art than a science, artists were the natural choice to carry it off, under the direction of professional military officers.

Thus, during the course of World War II, more than two thousand remarkably talented individuals lent their artistry, technical expertise, imagination, and hard work to the American effort at battlefield deception. You will meet a handful of them in this book. "Don't forget the enlisted men," one of them told me in an interview, and I have heeded his advice. Sergeants, corporals, and privates, led by young lieutenants, drew the hard, dangerous duty of putting into action the elaborate plans that captains, majors, and colonels devised.

In addition to Lieutenant Colonels Truly, who planned the Rhine operation, and Simenson, who trained the troops and planned many other operations, three dynamic men in particular, none of them a professional military man, helped turn a daring idea into a reality that worked on the battlefield. One was a young, Princeton-educated lieutenant in the Signal Corps named Fred Fox, who helped script the battlefield scenarios at Special Troops Headquarters. Before the war, he wrote radio scripts for NBC and aspired to be an actor. After the war, he found his vocation as a Christian minister. For him, deception was a moral imperative, a humane way to win a necessary war to preserve civilization.

Another was a high-society public relations man and journalist who delighted in cloak-and-dagger intrigue, Hilton Howell Railey. With extraordinary vision, he supervised the development of sonic deception at the Army Experimental Station.

The third was a swashbuckling matinee idol and real-life hero, Douglas Fairbanks Jr. He was serving aboard a battleship in the Atlantic when the news reached him that the Japanese had nearly wiped out the American Pacific fleet at Pearl Harbor, through an act of calculated deception.

Fairbanks, Railey, Fox, Simenson, Truly, and all the rest of their comrades, including and especially the enlisted soldiers, would not only learn the art of deception; they would refine it to a new level of sophistication and success. With their newfound expertise, they would help America win a world war.

ACT I
Rehearsal

ARTHUR SHILSTONE

ONE

THE SWASHBUCKLER
1941–1942

I have at times had to seem intrepid without when actually shaking within.

— Douglas Fairbanks Jr.

More than three years before the Special Troops staged their grand finale on the Rhine River, hundreds of sailors sat waiting in the chilly dark for a different kind of show to begin—on the afterdeck of the battleship USS *Mississippi* at a navy pier on the James River in Norfolk, Virginia.

The night was clear. The air temperature had dropped to the low forties, and a slight north wind made it seem even colder. The men's breath smoked in the damp river air. They had recently returned from Reykjavik, Iceland, so they were used to being outdoors in the cold. Officers and chiefs sat in rows of folding slat-seated chairs. Enlisted men sat cross-legged on the immaculate teak deck, slouched against the bulwarks, or perched atop the lower fourteen-inch gun turret, hanging their legs down the armored face. A sailor lounged astride each of the three massive gun barrels, leaning back against the cool steel slant of the turret, legs crossed or dangling on either side. Others leaned out of antiaircraft turrets, rubbing their gloved hands to keep warm.

As they waited, they smoked and joshed and some talked in more serious tones about the war. Little more than a week ago "Ole Miss" had been on station in Iceland, with her sister ship *Idaho*, when they got the incredible news: The Japanese had attacked Pearl Harbor. The USS *Arizona* was sunk, a destroyer and other vessels damaged. The U.S. was at war.

They knew little else. Strict censorship hid from them the devastating success of the attack. In fact five battleships had been sunk, nine other warships badly damaged, two hundred planes destroyed, and more than two thousand men killed. Only three American battleships remained of the entire Pacific fleet. Two days after Pearl Harbor, the two old battlewagons— *Mississippi* had been launched in 1917 during an era of warfare before air attacks—weighed anchor and steamed south for a brief refit here at Norfolk Navy Yard. In a few days, they would sail for Hawaii and the Pacific War.

But tonight's gathering wasn't about the war. A movie screen had been rigged from the crane on the fantail. The catapult holding the observation plane was rotated sideways—as if to launch the plane into the clear, starry night—to allow the screen to hang plumb. When it was full dark, the projector flickered, and all at once the screen came alive as a rectangle of light and moving images: the naval premier of *The Corsican Brothers*.

Before long, a familiar figure captured the screen—the larger-than-life image of Douglas Fairbanks Jr. Lean, darkly handsome, with wavy hair and piercing eyes, he grinned devilishly under his pencil-thin mustache. The Hollywood star was the very image of the swashbuckling hero: dark stocking cap, gold ear hoop, brace of pistols stuffed into his sash, sword flashing in his hand. He galloped across the screen on a bay charger, dueled for the lady's honor at the Paris opera, swept up the lovely Countess Isabelle in his arms for a long Hollywood kiss.

The men applauded and cheered and some of the officers hooted and jeered, and the one laughing loudest of all was Lt. (jg) Douglas Fairbanks Jr., USNR. He sat grinning with appreciation for his messmates, who had conspired secretly to get a print of the film to show their movie-star shipmate— the first time he'd ever watched his own picture. It was a fine birthday present—he was celebrating his thirty-second on the day they sailed from Reykjavik—and the sort of thing only good shipmates would do, a signal that he'd been accepted, taken seriously as a serving naval officer.

That hadn't always been the case.

For the next hour and a half, the hundreds of men gathered in the dark could forget they were about to head into battle on a distant, unknown ocean where already better ships than theirs lay shattered or sunk. Instead they could lose themselves in a spirited costume confection dreamed up by Alexandre Dumas, the same author who gave the world *The Three Musketeers*—also a tale full of disguise and trickery.

This movie was a festival of trompe l'oeil: Fairbanks played *both* brothers—stalwart hero and charming rogue. The two were Siamese twins separated at birth by a surgeon's scalpel after "their" parents were murdered. Mario is sent to Paris, where he is raised to become a gentleman, Lucien to the mountains of Corsica, where he grows up to be a bandit. In an inevitable twist of plot, the brothers are reunited twenty-one years later by that same doctor to avenge their parents against Baron Colonna, the murderous villain who took their lives and later grabbed power over all of Corsica. He's mistakenly believed that the brothers died at birth, when he burned down their parents' villa. The brothers meet at the graves of their parents and vow revenge against Colonna. They shake hands, and Mario wonders how they will ever be able to defeat the seemingly invincible baron. Lucien answers him slyly, "No one knows that there are two of us— that will be our sharpest weapon!"

Later, in a rare cinematic love triangle, Fairbanks vies with himself for the hand of the enchanting Countess Isabelle—played by Ruth Warrick.

What made the film spectacular was not the predictable coincidences of plot but the magical special effects.

In his double role, Fairbanks had to play scene after scene with *himself*— exchanging dialogue with himself, slapping himself, wrestling himself, fighting himself with drawn daggers. It was all done through tricks that fooled the eye: double exposure, back-projecting one Fairbanks character while the other acted for the camera, using split-screen editing to combine two images of Fairbanks shot in different costumes.

Artful cinematic deception.

Fairbanks explained the crowning stunt this way: "Finally the mystery of how I could possibly carry myself in my own arms is explained by my having a plaster life mask made of my face. This was transferred onto thin rubber and fitted onto the face of a double. I thus picked up the double with the mask of my face fitted onto his, and carried him in my arms."

His appearance both on the screen and in the shipboard audience doubled the joke again.

But it wasn't such a stretch for Fairbanks to be playing two very different roles at once. Almost a year before Pearl Harbor, convinced war with Germany was inevitable—and he *wanted* to fight the Nazis—he'd made up his mind to enlist. He considered the alternatives. Though he'd made a hit in 1930 as a war-weary World War I ace in *The Dawn Patrol*, he actually knew nothing about flying, so he rejected the Army Air Corps as a possibility. Likewise the army infantry and the marines—they both required too much walking. The Canadian navy would gladly have taken him, for it was in desperate need of volunteers and favored Americans. But Fairbanks wanted to fight in the American forces.

He wanted to enlist as an officer in the United States Navy.

It wasn't easy. His close friend and fellow actor Robert Montgomery, who had already done a stint as an ambulance driver in France, got them an interview with the commander of the 11th Naval District in San Diego. To be taken as an officer, he'd have to show proof of an advanced education. Not an easy task for a young man who had studied with a mixed bag of tutors and sporadically attended a round robin of private schools. Still working on the movie lot by day, he and Montgomery took some training classes at night and passed the first of many examinations. But it was slow going. Months passed, and he still wasn't in the navy.

Then, from a retired admiral, he learned the loophole that would change the direction of his entire naval career and give him the chance to play a significant role in the war: He wouldn't need to complete any further training until later if he enlisted directly into Naval *Intelligence.*

The irony was not lost on him. He and Montgomery enlisted immediately. On 17 April 1941, Fairbanks was commissioned a lieutenant, junior grade, in the U.S. Naval Reserve.

Now Fairbanks was a movie star *and* a naval officer—two roles often in conflict. Though he tried to keep a low profile, everywhere he went he was recognized. Not surprising, even discounting that he was the namesake of the most famous silent film star who ever lived. His most recent hit film, *Gunga Din,* was supposed to be just a colorful adventure yarn set in nineteenth century British India. In it, he played Sergeant Ballantyne, one of three wisecracking sergeant pals who—with the timely aid of their water boy, Gunga Din—thwart the plans of a fanatical cult of thuggees to massacre the garrison and overrun the country. Cary Grant and Victor McLaglen played his comrades.

But the audience was living in anxious times. Only the previous year, the British and French had caved in to Hitler's demand to take over Austria and the Sudetenland of Czechoslovakia, and now Nazi troops were massing on the borders of Moravia, Bohemia, and Poland, with whom the British had a treaty of mutual defense. President Roosevelt fumed because the United States wouldn't back the Allies more openly.

In the brutal tactics of the thuggees, the audience recognized Nazi thuggery. The three sergeants fighting gallantly beside their water boy turned into an emblem of noble British resolve to protect the native peoples of the Empire. When the movie opened at Radio City Music Hall in February 1939, it became something much more than an adventure yarn— it became a metaphor for standing up to Nazi aggression. *Gunga Din* became a blockbuster, a rousing call to arms against the Nazis, and before he'd ever even enlisted, Douglas Fairbanks Jr. became something of a war hero.

Almost immediately after Secretary of the Navy Frank Knox signed his commission in April 1941, Fairbanks left to undertake a clandestine mission at the personal request of President Roosevelt. He had first met Roosevelt when his father took him to the White House in 1918. Fairbanks senior, Mary Pickford, and Charlie Chaplin—the three greatest cinematic superstars of their era—were being honored for selling war bonds. Roosevelt was then assistant secretary of the navy.

Fairbanks junior later renewed the acquaintance—while he worked energetically for the William Allen White Committee to Defend America by Aiding the Allies, making radio broadcasts and public appearances to urge America to enter the war alongside Britain. From time to time, he quietly visited the White House.

From the end of April 1941 until June, Fairbanks toured five South American countries, gathering intelligence for the War Department. "This mission was ostensibly to investigate the effects of American motion pictures on Latin American public opinion," Fairbanks explained. "But the *real* objective was to get in touch with influential national groups who 'are now believed to be veering toward Nazi ideology.' I was to submit an analysis of their current and potential influence—in addition to proposals of what we could do about it. . . . And most important I was to find out if we would be welcome in that country if we needed to use its ports as possible emergency repair bases for our navy."

Obviously, then, Douglas Fairbanks Jr. was no ordinary fledgling officer.

When he was posted to his first regular navy assignment in October 1941, his celebrity created problems. His first orders were to sail on a supply ship from Boston to Newfoundland, en route to the fleet at Reykjavik. The other officers hazed him relentlessly, even assigning him to a pitching, airless berth in the bow of the ship, as he later recollected with wry humor: "I was well aware that the ship's officers had decided in advance that Lt. (jg) Douglas Fairbanks Jr. was a freak, and that it was quite in order either to stare, try to bait me on one subject or another, or ask silly questions about movies."

On arrival at Argentia, Newfoundland, his suspicions were confirmed. "As I was leaving, one of the ship's officers shook my hand and said, 'You're a better sport than we thought you'd be! The skipper was waiting to see if you'd complain about anything . . . he thought you'd be one of those rich, spoiled movie stars and make a fuss.' "

For the next three months, first on the destroyer *Ludlow* and then on the *Mississippi*, Fairbanks tried his best to prove he was no mere Hollywood pretty boy. He stood antiaircraft watches on the freezing open deck in all weathers, practiced navigation, learned to write detailed reports, took on every chore with enthusiasm and good humor, and won the respect of his shipmates.

So sitting on the deck of *"Ole Miss"* in Norfolk surrounded by fellow officers, all raptly watching his latest film and marveling at the optical illusions that let him be two men at the same time, must have been deeply gratifying. Fairbanks was a man who greatly valued male camaraderie. He was that rare sort of man whom women found irresistible and men felt drawn to for his nerve and male sense of adventure. Charming and self-deprecating, he made fast friends with men like Montgomery, Cary Grant, and David Niven, and he kept them for life. Before long he was to become a member of the most close-knit, elite male fraternity to which he ever belonged, a wartime fraternity based on deception.

Fairbanks never made it to the Pacific War—*"Ole Miss"* left Norfolk without him. Instead he was ordered to Washington, briefly; from there, the Navy Department sent him to England on a bona fide intelligence mission as a special naval observer. So in April 1942, a year after enlisting, Fairbanks arrived in London. He went out on the town with Vivien Leigh, Laurence Olivier, and David Niven, old cronies from the days when he'd lived in London, made films at a nearby studio, and conducted a torrid love affair with Marlene Dietrich at Claridge's Hotel. To protect her reputation, he used to sneak down the fire escape in the middle of the night and swing acrobatically to the ground. On one occasion, he was caught in the act by a bobby, who recognized him at once. "Trying out a new trick for your next film? Good idea now, with nobody about!" he said, and strolled off.

From England, Fairbanks sailed aboard the USS *Wasp*, which led a task force on a harrowing mission to deliver fighter planes to Malta, a beleaguered British island outpost in the Mediterranean. Then he served convoy duty to Murmansk through a U-boat wolfpack.

But routine active duty wasn't what he craved. He sought some special way to distinguish himself, the adventure of a lifetime. He'd grown up in the shadow of a father who, in his day, was perhaps the most recognized celebrity in the world, a star of electrifying personal charisma, the center of attention wherever he went. Fairbanks junior had spent his entire life deliberately cutting a different path. He cultivated a different look, a style of British nonchalance. And whereas Fairbanks senior was known for his athletic stunts in swashbuckling adventure films, for many years his son had resisted appearing in such roles, until pictures came along that were simply too tempting to pass up: *Catherine the Great* opposite Elisabeth Bergner, *The Prisoner of Zenda* with Ronald Colman and Mary Astor, and of course

Gunga Din with his old friend Cary Grant. Ironically, he was identified more strongly than ever with the legend of his father.

But Fairbanks senior, though a hero at selling war bonds during the First World War, had never served in uniform. In the navy, Fairbanks junior was out to make his mark. While his father had performed daredevil stunts only on the silver screen, Fairbanks junior would play his role on a real battlefield, with real bullets and shells whistling past, and he would become a real-life hero to the men with whom he served. Fairbanks exhibited more than a trace of the dashing romantic. His boyhood idols had been the Knights of the Round Table and the seagoing heroes of Robert Louis Stevenson's stories. He was captivated by the rough-riding cowboys and cavalry troopers depicted in the paintings and sculptures of Frederic Remington. He even painted and sculpted a bit himself. On his service record, he listed his civilian occupation as "Artist."

As an actor and producer, he had already spent almost two decades creating cinematic illusions, as well as moving among the elite "in" crowd of London, Paris, New York, and Hollywood. So it was probably inevitable that he found himself irresistibly drawn to the intrigue of special operations carried on under a veil of secrecy by elite men who shared the ultimate insider's knowledge.

One of those men was an old family friend, Lord Louis Mountbatten. Fairbanks knew him as "Dickie," and always remembered him fondly: "In his personal life, as the son of a famous admiral who had been politically martyred during the First World War, he had been motivated by a determination to excel. Although our circumstances were very different, Dickie said he recognized in me a 'similarity of spirit.' I was also the son of a once-famous world hero who was now reduced in rank. This was one of the reasons why, from the first, Dickie became almost a surrogate (though seldom seen) older brother and my own principal hero outside the theater."

Mountbatten was delving into a whole novel area of warfare—deception.

The British had learned from long and hard experience that fighting the good fight was not enough. Especially when the enemy was a disciplined industrial powerhouse producing modern tanks, airplanes, and cannons by the tens of thousands, with a colossal army already hardened by battles on two continents where they'd grown accustomed to winning. "Without sufficient force to overcome the enemy, the British had to concentrate on outwitting him," explained an American army European Theater of Operations report late in the war. The Brits needed an edge, and Mountbatten was searching for it.

In those early years of the war, the British military assumed a role toward its American counterpart much like Mountbatten's mentoring role toward Fairbanks. The Brits saw themselves as worldly and experienced in modern warfare, and their fear was that once an invasion was launched to recapture Europe, the guileless, naïve, but cocky Yanks would be outfoxed by the wily Germans—and then easily crushed. To survive and conquer, the Americans would need to approach the war with a realistic respect for their enemy. That meant learning how to lie, dissemble, fool, fake, feint, mask their intentions, and take their enemy by surprise.

To win, the Yanks would have to become experts in deception.

Mountbatten confided in Fairbanks enough to whet his appetite, and Fairbanks dropped repeated hints that he'd like to be included in Mountbatten's secret work. After all, Fairbanks had been sent to England to observe British naval operations, to learn all he could about their latest tactics. Like hundreds of American officers just like him, he was shadowing his British counterparts in every military department, but his celebrity gained him access few others enjoyed. In July 1942, Mountbatten invited him to join his Combined Operations command. "Combined Ops" meant amphibious operations, the key to getting Allied armies back on the European continent. They would be the crucial first battles to win back Italy, France, and all the other countries overrun by the Blitzkrieg—dangerous, in all likelihood bloody, and always at risk of failure.

During World War II, establishing a beachhead on enemy territory, from the sea or across a river, was enormoulsy difficult, especially since the Germans were masters of defending fortified positions against onrushing troops. To make a beachhead, troops must advance in the open, in boats, exposed to withering fire. Until they left the boats and moved off the open beach, they couldn't even defend themselves, let alone attack the enemy. Mountbatten was exploring every tactic his team could invent to increase the odds of success.

That meant dreaming up ways to deceive the enemy about when and where amphibious landings would occur.

Throughout 1942, Mountbatten borrowed ideas that were being tried out in the North African campaign, at that time the most active theater of the war, many of them conjured up by the aptly named Jasper Maskelyne, a third-generation career magician from a family of famous magicians. As a major in the British army working under Brigadier General Dudley Clarke's "A" Force, Maskelyne engineered many astonishing optical illusions. He even managed to make the entire strategically critical Suez Canal disappear every night through the use of concentrated, blinding "sparkle lights" projected upward at enemy bombers.

Perhaps his most significant work was a ruse that helped tip the balance at the Battle of El Alamein, the first major British victory of the war. Up to that point, the German army—like Baron Colonna in *The Corsican Brothers*—had seemed invincible. Maskelyne created dummy tanks, armored cars, and artillery batteries, placing them in the desert like pieces on a giant gameboard to be spotted by German observation aircraft, while coming up with ingenious ways to hide actual tanks and troops so they would remain invisible until the moment they struck. General Erwin Rommel and his Afrika Korps reserves prepared to defend the southern end of their line against the phantom armored divisions. Meanwhile, Maj. Gen. Bernard Montgomery's British Eighth Army, in a classic use of a stage performer's misdirection, actually attacked in the north and broke through.

Again like Baron Colonna, Rommel didn't know there were two armies—and that proved to be Montgomery's sharpest weapon. Winston Churchill lauded the victory on the floor of the House of Commons. "By a marvelous system of camouflage, a complete tactical surprise was achieved in the desert." From then on, the successful ploy at El Alamein became the touchstone for Allied deception operations in every corner of the war.

Months before the victory at El Alamein, Mountbatten was experimenting with one more new element of deception: sound effects. "All this evolved into an idea to deceive the enemy by projecting the prerecorded sounds of tanks and landing craft from a hidden distance—behind smoke screens," Fairbanks recalled. "They were testing the sounds of a moving squadron of armored cars, together with soldiers' voices and related noises. . . . The intention was for the enemy to adjust his local defenses to meet our nonexistent group."

The principle was simple and devious: create the sounds of real troops, real tanks, real landing craft, and force the enemy to counter the phantom attack with real troops—while the real attackers slipped in without opposition someplace else.

Not only that, such deception could save lives and insure a victory without the butcher's bill.

It was all wonderfully cloak-and-dagger stuff, exactly suited to Fairbanks's penchant for intrigue and romance. The members of the British secret unit lived at Achnocarry, a haunted castle in Scotland, and experimented with deception at a top secret base at nearby Ballantrae, across the North Channel from Northern Ireland. To Fairbanks's delight, this happened to be the setting for one his favorite Robert Louis Stevenson stories, *The Master of Ballantrae*. Occasionally the unit forayed offshore in motor torpedo boats to field-test their sound effects of multiple landing craft behind real fog or a smoke screen. The men loved careening through the cold waves with the salt spray on their faces, adrenaline pumping through their veins, the engines roaring in their ears, the bogus noise blaring out toward a mock enemy.

Unfortunately for Fairbanks, his celebrity again caught up with him.

His face was too well known, even in Britain, and everywhere he went he attracted fans. Mountbatten feared that too much public attention would threaten the security of the project. And according to Fairbanks, Mountbatten had another, even more compelling reason for sending him back to the States "He was very anxious that the U.S. Navy and Army develop their own special tactical deception operations, using all the new equipment we had been developing. He wanted me to be the emissary for the idea. But first I had to learn all phases and tactics of amphibious landing operations—which included real raids in the small landing craft and, later, the command of a flotilla of them at sea."

Those nighttime raids took him from a forward base on the Isle of Wight across the English Channel to occupied France. Unbeknownst to the Germans, Fairbanks and his comrades tried out their sonic tactics on them. They succeeded in drawing fire, forcing coastal troops to reinforce a beach where the "attack" was being reported. From time to time, they even went ashore and harassed German defenders, just to keep them off balance, keep them guessing where an invasion might occur. So by the time Fairbanks, recently promoted to lieutenant, returned Stateside in October 1942, he was one of a handful of American officers who had actually tried out tactical deception under fire. Nobody knew more about the current technology or how to apply it. Nobody was a more avid disciple of deception than the actor who had played two roles at once, competing with his own alter ego for the girl.

Fairbanks was barely ashore in Norfolk when he made his pitch to RAdm. H. Kent Hewitt, commander of the Atlantic Fleet's Amphibious Force, at his headquarters at the Nansemond Hotel at the mouth of the Chesapeake Bay. On the placid beaches nearby, hundreds of troops staged mock assaults, rushing out of landing craft into the surf and storming across the sand. Fairbanks knew it was a dress rehearsal for a real invasion to come soon, and it reminded him of the urgency of his mission.

Fairbanks was thinking big. His plan survives in an undated top secret memo he wrote for the U.S. Army late in the war, "Deceptive Warfare and Special Operations—comments on."

First, he proposed that the Pentagon establish a cover and deception agency at the very top level of planning. "On the very highest echelon of national decision, there should be someone charged with attending all planning meetings, having access to all ULTRA Intelligence files, enjoying proper status in and entrée to the State Department, the War and Navy Departments, the OSS, the FBI, the White House, and any specified government agency." That "someone" would report directly to the Joint Chiefs of Staff. ULTRA files contained the top-secret intelligence deciphered by British decoders, who had cracked the German ENIGMA code. "This section should submit plans designed to deceive or mislead actual or potential enemies as to our prospective intentions. This sphere of interest necessarily includes diplomatic and political fields as well as military."

Next, Fairbanks argued that the U.S. should institute a theater-wide agency that would coordinate with its British counterpart already in place, the benignly named London Controlling Section. The LCS handled everything from large-scale cover operations for invasions to radio misinformation to double agents, which it preferred to call "special means."

And third, on his "pyramid of deception," he wanted to immediately create a new, elite, amphibious combat unit to carry out deception activities during the landings that were sure to take place soon.

Though it was a grandiose scheme involving the planning, adminstrative coordination, and implementation of deceptive practices, Admiral Hewitt was surprisingly receptive. He himself had recently returned from a tour of Mountbatten's operations impressed by what he'd seen and was in the process of helping to plan Operation TORCH, the invasion of North Africa. He, too, was looking for an edge. He couldn't answer for the two high-level agencies Fairbanks suggested, but he gave a ready reply to his request to create his own special combat deception unit: Do it, Hewitt said—if you can get authorization from Admiral King. Admiral Ernest J. King was as powerful in the U.S. Navy as Gen. George C. Marshall was in the army: commander in chief, U.S. Fleet, and chief of naval operations. Eisenhower called him the "one-man navy." Fairbanks drafted his recommendations into a formal paper and left for Washington. What he didn't know was that King, at least in part, was one step ahead of him.

Once again, the impetus was partly chance. At a cocktail party months before Fairbanks returned from England, King had overheard some officers casually discussing details of the upcoming landings in North Africa—top-secret plans. The date for the assault had finally been settled. It would take place on 8 November 1942, and elaborate plans had been laid to transport American troops to three different landing beaches in Casablanca,

Oran, and Algiers. TORCH was to be the debut of U.S. amphibious operations against the Nazi-Vichy coalition, the first test of large-scale landing tactics and the first chance for American troops to prove themselves under fire in the European War. If it failed, there would be hell to pay—a lot of dead soldiers on the beaches and a serious setback to winning the war. The breach of security at the party infuriated Admiral King.

And not just King. As early as August 20, Marshall had issued a memorandum to the Joint Chiefs about breaches of security: "This has already reached a point which may seriously jeopardize the success of the operation."

In the navy, RAdm. C. M. "Savvy" Cooke Jr., chief of staff for planning, wrote, "The operation designation 'TORCH' is already so widely compromised, that in my opinion the only possible remedial measure is to cancel it, and to set up a substitute operation, ostensibly destined for some other area."

Security and deception were inextricably linked, as the British already knew and the Americans were finding out.

The original proposal to establish a security committee, as approved by the Joint Psychological Warfare Committee and presented to the Joint Chiefs of Staff, demonstrated that connection eloquently. Deception was not some separate entity, it argued, but intrinsic to waging war: "Surprise is essential to successful military operations. . . . The prospect of obtaining surprise may be greatly increased by a vigorous and imaginative psychological warfare policy of active deception, so that the enemy is lead [sic] to misconstrue even that true information which he does obtain."

And it offered a credo for all disciples of deception: "The essence of successful deception is truth which presents a false picture."

Admiral King lost no time in working out with his counterpart Marshall a way to control security at the top. By 25 August 1942, the Joint Chiefs had approved their proposal. The new office, Joint Security Control (JSC), would be the "someone" that Fairbanks had envisioned—actually a rear admiral (H. C. Train) and a major general (George V. Strong) with exceptional powers, who answered only to the Joint Chiefs. Among other more traditional responsibilities for security, General Marshall and Admiral King assigned JSC the tasks of concocting and overseeing cover and deception operations on land and sea—even those carried out by "nonmilitary" agencies—and controlling who was told what about new secret weapons.

So Fairbanks's three-part sales pitch fell on apparently deaf ears: He was a mere lieutenant, and the whole point of Joint Security Control was to limit to the essential few the number of people who knew about any particular plan, let alone the top-secret security agency itself. Hewitt's support, he wrote later with obvious disappointment, "failed to persuade the Joint Chiefs of Staff in Washington, the army, or even the navy that deception operations were anything more than a waste of time and money; they thought the idea just another set of wasteful silly tricks."

In fact, the Joint Chiefs were deceiving him.

When he made his pitch in October, one of the three levels of deception organization he was recommending had already been authorized for almost two months: That top-level deception agency was Joint Security Control. As for the second, Fairbanks came away with a green light to form a small unit to practice deception—the bottom-level or tactical component.

The third, middle-level organization—to handle theater-wide and operational cover and deception—would take a little longer to establish. It would also require its own hierarchy of planners within Gen. Omar Bradley's 12th Army Group and at General Eisenhower's Supreme Headquarters Allied Expeditionary Force (SHAEF). To implement the plans 12th Army Group devised, which would direct U.S. ground forces in Europe after D-Day, General Bradley would rely on the 23d Headquarters Special Troops to do just what Fairbanks had done in *The Corsican Brothers*: double itself by creating optical illusions, making a few seem like many, and making it possible for two armies—one real and the other fake—to be in different places at the same time.

There's every reason to suspect that the Joint Chiefs put Fairbanks's recommendations to good use.

As they finalized the mission of Joint Security Control, they gave it more and more of a mandate to create cover and deception scenarios for major operations. Certainly the final form the agency took in the months following that meeting bore a striking resemblance to the one Fairbanks designed. Either Marshall and King were already thinking along the same track, or they incorporated his notions comprehensively into their own plans. And they acted directly on Fairbanks's request to create an amphibious unit whose sole mission was battlefield deception, a brand-new idea for the American military. Since the Revolutionary War, each branch had handled its own deception plans in a rather ad hoc way, improvising as the need arose.

The following year, on 20 January 1942, the Joint Chiefs would create a land-based counterpart directly on his model: the Special Troops.

And by the time the Special Troops got to Europe, a theater-wide deception staff—the middle rung—would already be in place to fool the Germans about where and when to expect OVERLORD, the Normandy Invasion, and subsequent attacks.

So when all was said and done, by coincidence or deliberate adoption, Fairbanks's plan became the template for how the Americans handled deception in the European War. It would not be the last time a high-level plan of his would be adopted without his finding out until later. As a member of Hewitt's War Plans Section, he now carried what he called an "open sesame" letter from the admiral allowing him nearly unlimited freedom of movement and access. Mountbatten had provided him with a similar letter in England. Hewitt's read, in part, "It is particularly requested that those concerned will give him every possible assistance and appreciate that for security reasons he will not always be able to give full explanation of the duties he is performing."

Fairbanks could move freely, bypass much red tape, and not have to answer to any superior officer except Hewitt, the third most powerful admiral—after King and Cooke—in the Navy.

There wasn't time to outfit and train the new unit for the North African landings less than a month away, but Fairbanks was determined they would be ready when the time came to strike across the Mediterranean at Sicily, Italy, and the south of France. Once again the beguiling actor, for the remainder of the fall and through the winter of 1942–43, Fairbanks launched himself on a recruiting tour of select technical schools and universities around the country, playing his cloak-and-dagger role to the hilt. His call for volunteers posted at Notre Dame Midshipman's School conveyed the tantalizing flavor of his appeal to bold young men: "The navy is requesting volunteers for prolonged, hazardous, distant duty for a secret project." When he showed up on campus, he promised adventure, and he got all the volunteers he needed.

By the middle of March 1943, he had established a training base for his unit, called the Beach Jumpers, at Camp Bradford, Virginia. In time he would also stage mock assaults on Ocracoke Island, in those days an isolated barrier island on North Carolina's Outer Banks, an appropriate site for developing a new weapon: On the northernmost part of the Outer Banks, at Kitty Hawk, the Wright brothers had first taken to the air in a machine that would revolutionize warfare. And just offshore, Billy Mitchell had bombed a fleet of mothballed World War I battleships to demonstrate to benighted generals and admirals that the next war would be exactly the kind that Pearl Harbor proved it to be, a war of lightning surprise attacks from the air.

Soon the Beach Jumpers' base at Camp Bradford blossomed with two-man tents to house the first of the 180 officers and 300 enlisted men he was authorized to recruit, all of whom had to meet four requirements:

1. no seasickness,
2. experience in small boat handling,
3. enough electrical knowledge to fix a home radio, and
4. at least fundamental knowledge of celestial navigation.

At their disposal, the Beach Jumper trainees had six sixty-three-foot air-sea rescue boats. The idea was to move quickly and stealthily, create a diversion, then, when the enemy took the bait and came out firing, to get out fast. A crew of six manned each boat: skipper, first mate, antiaircraft gunner, boatswain, and two engineers. In combat, they would use motor torpedo boats and landing craft, just as Fairbanks had done under Mountbatten. Despite his low rank, Fairbanks functioned as officer in charge until the full complement of recruits arrived and the training commenced in earnest. As the training school grew, the navy replaced Fairbanks as head with a more senior officer, Capt. Anthony L. Rorschach. Rorschach had safely skippered the destroyer USS *Dale* out of Pearl Harbor under serial attack by Japanese dive bombers and commanded her in action across the Pacific, winning a Silver Star while repulsing the Japanese invasion of the Aleutians in the Battle of the Kommandorski Islands.

Fairbanks continued to run the training program according to the philosophy he had learned under Mountbatten: "No amount of indoctrination or textbook learning will in themselves develop more than efficient mediocrity. The problems of these operations *should* be handled with an ephemeral combination of force, subtlety, shrewdness, guile, and knowledge born of actual experience."

While a Hollywood special effects expert named Fletcher Stephens taught the Beach Jumpers how to simulate real explosions with flash devices, Fairbanks held seminars on the use of smoke screens, inflatable dummy "assault troops" nicknamed "gooney birds," and dummy paratroopers, which he helped to design and which were used to good effect in the nighttime hours before D-Day to help create panic among the German defenders. Fairbanks was now enjoying the role of the seasoned combat veteran whipping the new recruits into shape, a role that didn't always go over well with the more regulation-minded officers who shared the base for conventional training. They resented Fairbanks's dashing air. He affected a British style, for good reason. His old Combined Ops uniform was both comfortable and practical for "wet duty": a thick, warm, navy-blue version

Fairbanks (left) on antiaircraft watch aboard USS *Wasp*

of the army's Eisenhower jacket bearing a Combined Ops shoulder patch, a softer cap, and a commando dagger in his belt.

For more formal occasions, he wore tailored uniforms with brighter-than-regulation gold stripes on the sleeves, a change from his shipboard days when he had learned to drag his extra sleeve stripes, brass buttons, and shoulder-board braid overboard in a bag to turn them a salty yellow green, the signature of an old hand. Lieutenant Douglas Fairbanks Jr. was still very much the actor, and he had also turned into a first-rate naval officer. In both roles, he was the star of a new kind of show.

But go back and linger a moment in October 1942, a month of important coincidences and two critical tests for the theory of battlefield deception.

It was in October that Fairbanks had returned to the States to make his pitch for a deception unit and to float his master plan to the Joint Chiefs. In October also, Gen. Bernard Montgomery launched his decisive attack against Rommel at El Alamein, an attack that relied on surprise gained by deception. The textbook case.

Also that October, Fairbanks's interest in using sound to deceive the enemy coincided with another secret joint Army-Navy venture, Project 17:3-1: "The Physiological and Psychological Effects of Sound on Men in Warfare."

Division 17, a secret research-and-development arm of the National Defense Research Committee (NDRC), a scientific and technical board working on new weapons, was run by Harvey Fletcher of Bell Telephone

Labs. The project team included Harvard Medical School physiologist Hallowell Davis and theatrical sound engineer Vincent Mallory. It was directed by acoustical wizard Harold Burris-Meyer, theater and sound research director at Stevens Institute of Technology in New Jersey. He had made movie history by developing a new stereophonic system that made it possible for Walt Disney Studios to record the music for its groundbreaking film *Fantasia*.

The high-powered cadre of scientists and technicians carried on their experiments at Bell Labs and the Stevens Institute, beginning back in February 1942, while Fairbanks was still stuck in Washington in the Public Relations section itching to get into the war. The Joint Chiefs accorded sonic deception research such a high priority that, to oversee the project, they created a secret Planning Board of seven military officers and civilians, chaired by Col. Charles C. Blakeney, himself a member of the Joint Chiefs. The board reported directly to General Marshall himself.

As soon as Fairbanks returned from England in October 1942, because of his crucial experience, he was named naval liaison to the board. The executive officer of the board was a kindred spirit nearly as charismatic as Fairbanks. Lieutenant Colonel Hilton Howell Railey was a debonair specialist in public relations, the man who had discovered Amelia Earhart, had tried to raise gold from the sunken *Lusitania*, and served as Adm. Richard Byrd's expedition manager on his trek to the South Pole. Railey dressed in cavalry jodhpurs and carried a riding crop, peering out of his rimless spectacles with a steady eye, like an intellectual soldier of fortune. Charming and intense, he was always even tempered on the outside, but inside by turns maniacally energetic or darkly moody. He was smart—in many ways brilliant—and, most important, he believed wholeheartedly in the value of sonic deception.

Railey and the board had access to the best civilian technical experts. Fairbanks had the tactical experience. If those experts could build the deception equipment, he could show them how to use it. And then units such as the Beach Jumpers and Special Troops could take it back to the war.

Fairbanks had barely become acquainted with Railey when Division 17 staged a dramatic mock invasion that came to be known as the Battle of Sandy Hook. Railey and the board, including Fairbanks as naval liaison, watched the show from the luxurious Walgreen family yacht, the *Dixonia*. Railey, with typical theatrical flair, had procured the opulent vessel for the occasion through the Army Transport Service.

It was a long way from the armored hull of the *"Ole Miss"* to a millionaire's pleasure boat, and this time the show was even more thrilling. Just as Fairbanks and his fellow officers had gathered in the dark on the fantail of the old battleship to watch a movie, now an audience of board members, technicians, and VIPs gathered on another ship's deck converted to a nighttime theater. The *Dixonia* boarded her VIPs at Governors Island, then motored out of New York harbor through the Verrazano Narrows past Coney Island and south along the Jersey coast, as if she were the committee boat heading out to the America's Cup racing ground.

But on this night, 27 October 1942, she operated as flagship for the invading fleet of six landing craft, a Coast Guard cutter, and two converted Gloucester fishing boats while six airplanes roved overhead—three to launch illumination flares over the beach and three to lay a smoke screen offshore to cover the "attack." The *Dixonia* and the Gloucestermen mounted phonographs and loudspeakers to play boat motor noise on records mastered from commercial recordings mixed with original ones.

The *Dixonia's* equipment was rated at twenty-five watts. The two Gloucestermen, designated YP-254 and YP-257, were armed with five-hundred-watt Western Electric amplifiers and loudspeakers developed originally for use on the flight decks of aircraft carriers, so a skipper or air boss could project announcements above the roar of airplane engines. The mammoth speakers were called "heaters."

Cranked even to moderate volume, they could blow out matches.

The timing was propitious: In Egypt, the British attack at El Alamein was entering its fifth day. While British troops in American General Grant tanks slugged it out with Rommel's Panzers in a surprise offensive, the *Dixonia* task force was attempting a deception on a smaller and far less risky scale. On shore, three hundred infantrymen deployed along a three-mile strip of Sandy Hook's ocean beach to repel the invaders. The object of the game was to fool the troops ashore about where the landing would take place—distract and divert them with sound effects in the dark. If the ruse worked, it would prove to American planners that you could fool real troops with fake sounds—or more accurately with real sounds projected in a false context.

Truth which presents a false picture.

The storms that had caused the trial to be postponed the previous night had left behind a brisk offshore wind, degrading the quality of the sound transmissions and whipping away the smoke screen nearly as fast as the planes could lay it, so that the little fleet lay silhouetted under a full moon.

The sound boats would make two feints at the southern end of the beach, hoping to draw off troops from the northern and central sectors.

Cranking up their sonic equipment, the Gloucestermen moved south in company with the *Dixonia* and one of the landing barges, which wallowed in the heaving seas.

We can imagine the defending soldiers hunkered behind sandbags on the beach, straining to hear above the wind the noise of the seaborne invaders. They squint their eyes against blowing sand and smoke, cock an ear toward the slapping surf, flatten themselves against the beach under the searching glare of the illumination flares, scan the moonlit whitecaps with their binoculars. Pretty soon their eyes are seeing what their ears tell them to see.

At the first feint, the beach commander confidently committed his reserves to the southern end. Even though the heavy seas kept skipping the phonograph needles out of their grooves, the sound effects did the trick, convincing the "enemy" that he was seeing what he heard: a flotilla of landing craft roaring toward the south beach.

When the sonic boats made their second feinting pass, the motor sounds were more audible on the beach, even above the wind. The shore commander ordered all his troops from the northern and central sectors to double-time it down the beach and defend the southern end.

Meanwhile, the five amphibious barges landed on the northern end of the beach and three hundred invaders rushed ashore, completely unopposed. If it had been a real assault against an armed defender shooting to kill, scores of men—maybe as many as a hundred—would owe their lives to the deception.

For the sonic warriors, it was a major coup. From now on, the task would be to develop and test reliable field equipment, train smart troops to use it, and get it into the war.

Railey launched himself with a passion into sonic research and development, already forging his own legend, and Fairbanks went back to Camp Bradford to recruit and train his Beach Jumpers to wage a new kind of war—a theatrical form of war from which he would emerge as a genuine hero and have a combat Silver Star to prove it.

TWO

HILTON HOWELL RAILEY—

The P. T. Barnum of Deception
1942–1944

I seek a permanent connection in which the distillation of my whole experience may be employed to the advantage of those who honor me with their faith, and in whom, reciprocally, I can believe.

—Hilton Howell Railey

They would usually make the run at night.

The half-ton U.S. Army weapons carrier—a light truck painted olive drab—would slip out the gates of the Canadian Forces base at Kingston, Ontario, and head northeast along the ice-choked St. Lawrence River for fifteen miles or so to the new Thousand Islands International Bridge.

The winter of 1943–44 was the coldest in memory in upper New York state: snowstorm after snowstorm swooped in from the West. Motorists were stranded on highways, lost the road in the whiteout conditions, slid into ditches. Trains were halted in the middle of the countryside. Schools closed, opened, then closed again. Planes were grounded for days at a time.

In January, "mystery blasts" heard as far away as Long Island were explained by the Weather Bureau as unseasonal thunder from unusually violent storms.

In February alone, five people died of exposure.

The coal supply was dangerously low in the northern counties.

Long into April, snow would still be falling, the roads slick, visibility poor, the flakes sticking to the fogged windshield. Slow going, even on the highway. To ward off the freezing wind, the two-man detail would keep the canvas-and-isinglass side-curtains of the cab buttoned up. Their fragile cargo would ride in the back, protected from prying eyes by a canvas top and canvas flaps strapped to the tailgate.

The Canadian customs men would wave them across the long, slippery bridge.

At the far side, the U.S. Customs men would approach the cab. The driver would unfasten his side curtain. The customs man would peer in, recognize the U.S. Army uniforms, see the lieutenant riding shotgun, a .45-caliber Thompson submachine gun slung across his lap. The lieutenant would show his identification and orders from a classified post called the U.S. Army Experimental Station.

No civilians knew exactly what went on at the Experimental Station. Sometimes folks who lived in the towns at the edge of the military reservation would hear strange sounds in the night, always in the night: a sustained howling like sirens, or just a high-pitched whine that seemed to be coming from everywhere and nowhere.

In those years, it was better not to snoop around too much. All over the country, special installations had sprung up to work on secret weapons, and they always had deceptively ordinary names. But the barbed wire and armed MPs at the gate usually convinced the curious it was better not to get too close.

If the U.S. Customs man asked to look into the cargo box, the lieutenant would finger his weapon, say, "Well, see, this is all classified."

The customs man would say, "Pass on," and wave them into the darkness.

Another half hour or so would take them south along the empty highway toward Watertown, New York, to the crossroads where they'd turn east onto County Route 16 to Evans Mills, a stop on the New York Central Railroad, through town on LeRay Street, then east again on Route 26 past Wards Corners and through the thick woods and into the back gate of Pine Camp, a remote U.S. Army base on the Black River.

In the vast meadows of the mountainous camp, the snow was drifted high as a Greyhound bus.

The guard would pass them through, and just a short distance farther on, the weapons carrier would pull up to another gate: Section No. 11, a compound of sixty-two barracks and offices surrounded by a high barbed-wire fence. During the First World War, it had been the cantonment for a field artillery battalion.

The sign on the swing gate now read, in bold letters:

STOP
NO ADMITTANCE
Without Written Authority

of Commanding Officer
ARMY EXPERIMENTAL STATION

Again, the MPs would pass them through.

Driving slowly now, the weapons carrier would move among the wooden barracks, the storage sheds, and the mess halls, dogleg around the headquarters building, and pull up next to the chapel at the three-room base commander's hut. The lieutenant would sling his tommy gun and step out. He and the driver would draw back the stiff curtains and carefully unload their secret cargo: cases of bootleg Teacher's Scotch whisky.

Then carry it inside to Col. Hilton Howell Railey.

Bootleg Scotch was cheaper, of course, no excise tax, but that was probably not what appealed to Railey. By all accounts he was a man who cultivated an air of mystery about himself, who liked to get away with things, pull off ruses. He enjoyed deception as much for its own sake as for its practical value.

Railey was the brilliant and eccentric commander of the Army Experimental Station, which had moved from its cramped quarters at Fort Hancock on the Jersey shore to this vast encampment in the north woods of upper New York state in February 1944 to perfect the science—and art—of sonic deception. Here he would also train handpicked troops in the so-called Sonic Companies how to use it.

An urbane, sophisticated man, intimate with the wealthy and powerful in New York and Washington, Railey was rumored to have gone from civilian to lieutenant colonel in one day by President Roosevelt's personal orders. Additionally, Railey claimed exotic heritage: his great-uncle on his mother's side was Jefferson Davis, president of the Confederacy during the Civil War. On his father's side, he was descended from Sir Walter Raleigh, the English explorer who had first sailed into Ocracoke Harbor—near the Coast Guard station where Fairbanks's Beach Jumpers trained.

And like Fairbanks, Railey spent his early years trying to escape the shadow of an accomplished and overbearing father—and became an early adept at deception. "I began to keep my thoughts to myself," he wrote later, "—to have one reaction outwardly, quite another inwardly—and to develop the protective mechanism of which, in those days, I had great need. Father was so formidable!"

He would carry that habit into adulthood—brooding inwardly, outwardly appearing calm and composed. He rarely lost his temper. With no warning to his New Orleans family, he secretly ran away to sea at the age of seventeen, jumped ship at Panama, and signed on with the Isthmian Canal Commission—a job that took him into the jungle, down into the bowels of the Gatun Dam, inside the giant power stations that drove the locks.

It was an adventurous time, and his first taste of it whetted his appetite for more.

After Panama, he wrote for *The New Orleans American* as a police reporter out to expose corruption, until the politicians it had sought to indict forced it out of business. Railey left town toting an illegal pistol and fearing for his life. His crusading reputation won him a job on the War and Navy Departments' Commission on Training Camp Activities, determined to curb drunkenness and venereal disease among the hordes of soldiers mobilized for the First World War.

The minimum age for service was twenty-five. Railey, only twenty-two when he signed on, swore he was in fact twenty-seven years old. When his lie was later found out, he was enlisted into the army as a buck private, rose to sergeant, and was posted to New York. "There I took charge of a two-fisted, slugging law-enforcement squad whose tender task it was to make Manhattan safe and pure for gobs and doughboys stationed in the metropolitan area, and hundreds of thousands of others enjoying a last fling before shoving off to join the AEF," he reported. He and his squad raided brothels and clip joints, and he learned to wield a blackjack and a billy club, as well as his fists—though he didn't always win his fights. He finally earned a commission as a second lieutenant, but instead of going to war in France, he ended up at Camp Pike, Arkansas, raiding bootleggers' camps and finally quelling a race riot, a killing business in which it was not at all clear who was to blame. Railey left the army as a captain and went into public relations and fund raising, then on to international projects.

Railey was a member of the Explorers Club, founded by Arctic explorer Henry C. Walsh, and including such famous scientific pioneers as Robert E. Peary, Roy Chapman Andrews, and Teddy Roosevelt. In 1930, as manager and publicist, Railey used shortwave radio transmission to keep in touch with Adm. Richard Byrd's expedition to the remote Antarctic and to publicize it to the world. Mostly he raised money—lots of it. Of Railey, Byrd reported, "A better and more conscientious man I doubt if I could have picked."

Railey turned Amelia Earhart from an obscure aviation enthusiast into the most famous woman adventurer in history, then lived to regret it when her plane disappeared in 1937 in the Pacific somewhere south of Hawaii. Also in the 1930s, he raised and lost a small fortune trying to recover gold from the torpedoed liner *Lusitania,* a venture that outraged the British press. To them, the sunken wreck was an almost sacred national burial site. The costly misadventure caused associates to question his judgment, even his sanity. At the end of that debacle, while Railey was still in London cleaning up the mess, an emissary of the Third Reich tried to enlist him as Hitler's personal PR man in the United States. It would be a lucrative position and dig him out of his financial hole. He replied, with atypical understatement, that Nazi persecution of the Jews would make it impossible to put Hitler in a good light in the U.S. "Tell him also that no fee could induce me to tackle the task he has in mind if Germany's anti-semitic [sic] activities are to continue."

He wrote later, more dramatically, "In London I found my pot of gold—filled with Nazi Reichsmarks—and left it where it lay."

Railey worked at a furious pace all through the 1930s, and the work nearly destroyed his health. After two nervous breakdowns, he sought a long rest, partly to dry out. Instead of signing himself into an upscale sanatorium, as might be expected of a man of his social class, he voluntarily admitted himself to a camp for Depression transients run by the Temporary Emergency Relief Administration, a New Deal agency. There, without formal medical training, he ran the infirmary and even performed surgery. When he recovered, he was recruited to return to the Panama Canal Zone on a special assignment to prepare it for its crucial role in the coming war. He recorded the assignment in his résumé: "Commissioned lieutenant, senior grade, Intelligence Reserve, U.S. Navy (January, 1936, resigned, 1940), and made report on alien activities, Canal Zone."

So, coincidentally, he and Douglas Fairbanks Jr. shared experience in Naval Intelligence.

Railey was an impresario of unlikely causes, a fund raiser of extraordinary ability. Between 1925 and FDR's inauguration, H. H. Railey & Co., Inc., raised $40 million for "scientific, educational, and philanthropic institutions"—then dissolved in the Great Depression. He was widely read, eloquent, a man who could grasp both the big picture and the complex technical details. He was a native of New Orleans but spoke without a trace of southern accent. Most of his men assumed he was a blueblood Yankee and were startled to learn otherwise, usually years later. He was a Protestant but not devout, a Democrat critical of Roosevelt, an internationalist who put patriotism first, a married man who publicly declared himself a misogynist. His wife, Julia—herself a published novelist—was never seen at the Army Experimental Station, at either location, all during the war. Most of his officers didn't even realize Railey was married. Meanwhile he was rumored to be carrying on an affair with a married woman in nearby

Watertown. A writer, lecturer, man of opinions, particularly regarding the international scene—he had briefly served as the national director of the quixotic American League of Nations Association—he was witty but not a joke teller, charming but also intensely private.

"One of the things he liked to do was to get the unit all together— the Army Experimental Station staff combined with one of the units in training—and lecture them," recalls Darrel Rippeteau, at that time a strapping twenty-seven-year-old lieutenant, later captain. He was Railey's S3, army shorthand that means he was in charge of plans and training, one of a handful of officers who ran the station. He saw Railey every day, met with him weekly for staff meetings at Railey's spartan quarters. "He'd give a lecture about his life and some of his background. Stuff would surface from the book."

The book. Word had gotten around that Railey had published a memoir, and all the officers' wives had scrambled to obtain copies for their husbands— and themselves, to know what kind of a man was in charge of the station.

"And it was dramatic—he was a very dramatic guy," Rippeteau says.

Railey would stride into the recreation hall where the men were assembled in folding chairs. He would be dressed in impeccably creased cavalry breeches and boots, affecting the manner of General Patton, who was rumored to be a close friend of his. As he walked, with each step he'd absently whip a leather riding crop against his leg.

"Colonel Railey was perfection," recalls Tom Schwerin, then a technician who taught a compulsory course in motor generators at the station. "He was a very imposing-looking man. A proud man. Built with a good-sized chest on him. Very forceful."

Railey carried himself erect, every inch a soldier, and when he entered a room, everyone present instinctively turned toward him. He was just short of six feet tall, only a little more handsome than average, late forties, trim, with receding iron-gray hair combed neatly with Wildroot creme oil. Despite his average stature, like General Eisenhower he always seemed to dominate a physical space. By the time he was in his sixties he would complain of ill health, but during this period he was robust and energetic. He seemed both a scholar and a man of action.

In his presence, the men would rise to their feet automatically. "They stood up because they knew that's what they were supposed to do, not because they were scared soldiers in the army," explains Rippeteau, a prominent architect in civilian life and a career reserve soldier. "I believe I've put my finger right there on the attitude." These men, smart and recruited for their expertise, didn't kowtow to officers, yet they had a strong sense of decorum, of manners, and they respected Railey.

It wasn't army discipline, exactly—but it was probably better.

"At ease," Railey would say, and slap his riding crop gently against his leg. "Smoke 'em if you got 'em."

As Railey walked to the lectern, everybody would paw around in his blouse for a cigarette—smoking was a universal soldier's habit in those years—and Railey himself would pause to light a cigarette and smoke it elegantly as he spun off one of his captivating stories about Europe or the Panama Canal Zone or the Far East. His lectures were entertaining, informative, at times wryly humorous, most often tinged with patriotism. He talked without notes for forty-five minutes or so, relying on memory and his broad experience, boiling down the complex geopolitical situation with remarkable eloquence. He made points by brandishing his lit cigarette at the air, quietly tapping his riding crop against his leg.

The whole affair would be very informal, yet Railey was never tempted to walk out among the men, would never stray from behind the lectern. Rippeteau says, "The last thing he'd do would be to get into an unorganized, uncontrolled situation."

His was an oddly effective style. On the one hand, Railey cultivated an almost relaxed atmosphere at the AES. On the other, he would stand on his own version of ceremony. He wouldn't simply show up in the field in the middle of a training exercise. He'd wait until his officers had the exercise mastered and invited him to show it off. "It was gentlemanly—nobody ever got chewed out as is normal in a line outfit, where you've got very serious results if things go wrong," explains Rippeteau, who came to the AES from a field artillery outfit, where a mistake could get you blown up. "It was a gentlemen's setup—almost everybody was well educated and almost everybody was very temporary in the army and knew it."

Railey's leadership style provided a lesson to his subordinate officers: Don't wing it. Stay on top of the situation. Stay organized. Delegate, then rely on your subordinates. Stick with your plan.

He would wait till all the cigarettes were lit, everyone settled in his seat. Now that he had their relaxed attention, he might talk about his adventures during the Russo-Polish War.

"In August 1920, with credentials as a war correspondent, I set out for Poland," he wrote in his memoir, aptly titled *Touch'd with Madness*. "Those credentials were phony."

In fact, he was an emissary for the Polish minister in the U.S. and had visions of writing a book that would inflame American public opinion on behalf of the underdog Poles, who were in danger of being overrun by Russian Bolsheviks. He wound up a captain in the Polish army, another bit of masquerade, since he never commanded troops or fired a shot in anger. All he wanted really was carte blanche to get the inside scoop. He set out for the front in a Mercedes Benz convertible to watch Pilsudski rout the Bolsheviks at Novogrodek. His shadowy exploits in Poland ran him afoul of both British Intelligence and the American Secret Service. Railey later claimed that only Roosevelt's direct intervention saved him.

Some who knew Railey consider that memoir a wonderful novel, full of truth and also full of artful exaggeration, so that the reader is never sure which is the real Hilton H. Railey. He himself teases the reader to beware taking everything he says at face value: "By no means all of my experiences were so heroic as these fine words imply."

He had also spent many months in Europe before the war investigating international arms cartels for *Fortune* magazine—a project that never came to fruition but provided him with a wealth of stories of foreign intrigue, secret agents, shadowy meetings in hotel rooms, and governmental corruption.

"I hate institutions," Railey, for twelve years a military school cadet, confided in his autobiography. "I despise the indignity of regimentation." Yet he loved the army and all its ceremonial trappings. By the time he rejoined the wartime army, he had made a small reputation as a writer and a big reputation as a world-class public relations man—and a maverick. A maverick with a fondness for drink. At Pine Camp, his favorite haunt was the semibasement bar of the Hotel Woodruff. Railey would hand out minor promotions, awards for good conduct, right there at the bar. He bought many of his "boys" their first beers. Rippeteau: "I once said to my first wife, Donna, that if I drank half as much as he drinks, I'd be dead." Railey often started his day with two shots of Scotch with milk for breakfast. Sometimes he required a shot of B_{12} in the morning before he could function. Yet in public, in front of his men, he never appeared drunk, always retained an unshakable sense of dignity and decorum. He inspired fierce loyalty in his men, and he returned that loyalty with equal ferocity. "We were never called anything except 'my boys,' " recalls Dr. Edward Gilmore, one of the first enlisted men Railey recruited. " 'My boys' this and 'my boys' that."

Railey treated his "boys" with great affection, became a father figure to many. His attitude wasn't just sentimental. He had very specific convictions about how to lead men, and to him the key to leadership was to create and maintain high morale. To Railey, morale was not an abstraction. "Morale," he wrote, "is the cheerful, willing, and obedient performance of the most arduous duties under the most adverse circumstances." His last assignment before enlisting had brought him face to face with the issue in a way that would crystallize his convictions and form the core principles of his own leadership style at Pine Camp.

In the summer of 1941, while Fairbanks was wrapping up his covert tour of Latin America for the War Department, Railey had begun writing the most important story of his life—then or after—for *The New York Times*. A story that he agreed in advance might never be published, a story of vital importance to the army.

In 1940, already anticipating war, the U.S. Congress had passed its first peacetime draft in history, with a term of service set for just one year. So by the summer of 1941, the War Department was wrestling with the problem of losing nearly a million conscripted soldiers—more than two thirds of the army—when their enlistments expired in the fall. General George C. Marshall feared "the disintegration of the army." With pressure from Marshall and Roosevelt, Congress passed the Service Extension Act by a single vote. Now all those reserve officers, national guardsmen, and draftees, who had looked forward to going home in October, were automatically reenlisted for six more months. The result was a crisis in morale: if called on to fight the Nazis or the Japanese, large segments of the United States Army might balk—or worse, actually desert. One division started chalking the word *OHIO* on artillery pieces, cars, latrines: Over the Hill In October.

So reported *Life* magazine on 18 August 1941.

In stepped Arthur Hays Sulzberger, a stalwart supporter of FDR and publisher of *The New York Times*, for which Railey was then writing. "As I recall it, I told Railey that I thought this article had probably been written by a young fellow who didn't know Army life as Railey and I did from the first [sic] World War, that this chap had not recognized the fact that grousing was to be expected in a citizen army, and I asked him to make a thorough study of conditions, adding these words, 'I will tell you in advance that unless you can disprove the statement, we're not going to run the story.' "

Shortly after Fairbanks returned from his whirlwind spy tour of Latin America, Railey took off on a tour of his own, which also had a hidden purpose. He logged eleven thousand miles to seven U.S. Army forts and camps, interviewed more than a thousand officers and enlisted men, in barracks and on field maneuvers, observed their behavior in bars and on the training ground, even infiltrated a young assistant into their ranks—all purportedly to write a newspaper story. But he and Sulzberger both knew that he was also acting as a private agent for the War Department and the White House.

What he found was a disaster waiting to happen.

"The men feel they are superior to their officers in everything except rank," he wrote of the situation at Fort Meade, Maryland, typical of the whole army. "They find it difficult to take orders from people they regard as inferiors." Many National Guard officers admitted they were physically afraid of their own men.

It was difficult to create "an offensive spirit, a *win* spirit, in troops training under peacetime conditions without (from their viewpoint) a specific and inspiring objective. . . . *An abiding faith is lacking.*"

Morale-building in the army was limited to ball games, movies, and "leg shows." Nobody bothered to explain to either enlisted men or officers why their service was so crucial, where and against whom they might be expected to fight, why a citizen army was even necessary. They felt deceived by President Roosevelt, betrayed by Congress, trapped in a socially inferior job making twenty-one dollars a month while their friends in civilian life were all making real money and advancing their careers. The troops were in a surly mood. If it came to war, they could not be counted on to fight. And the colonels and generals who commanded them had no clue about the trouble—they remained aloof and physically remote from their own troops. How could this happen? "They are cheating at solitaire," an officer confided obliquely to Railey.

"Now it is obvious that an army is not truly fit to fight unless the men in it are inspired *by some belief in the things for which they are fighting.*"

Railey concluded, "With extraordinary uniformity . . . the morale of the United States Army, as I have sampled and verified it from the Atlantic to the Pacific, is not reassuring."

There was no question of publication—Railey himself recommended against it.

Sulzberger, for whom the war had for all intents and purposes started when Roosevelt signed the lend-lease agreement with Great Britain, wrote, "I, for one, did not propose to make Hitler a present through the columns of *The New York Times* of the fact that there was bad morale in the armed services." Railey and Sulzberger hand-carried the 72,000-word report directly to Washington and met with Roosevelt, and the President was mightily disturbed by it. "My visit, which might normally have lasted fifteen minutes," wrote Sulzberger, "was extended to an hour and a half."

Railey recommended stationing National Guard troops closer to home, creating a command school for National Guard officers, and mustering out men over twenty-eight years old, who usually were the worst malcontents. Most important, he maintained, it was essential to instill in all troops a sense of the principles for which they were being asked to risk their lives. Railey also personally delivered one of the five copies of the report to General Marshall, who reacted quickly to its recommendations. The army launched a major effort to improve morale in its citizen army by trying to get across to the men exactly what was at stake, why their sacrifice mattered, how much their country needed them at this hour of crisis. At first, this took the form of an orientation course—lectures, discussions, written pamphlets. Eventually it evolved into a more sophisticated orientation integrated into every unit's weekly training, including the "Why We Fight" series of films.

So if Railey were to accomplish nothing else for the war effort, he had already made his mark, and gained priceless experience in how to establish and maintain high morale. The most important lesson: No officer of any rank can afford to become remote from the men under his command. He took that lesson to heart.

Ed Gilmore, one of Railey's first recruits, recounts the time at Fort Hancock when, as a private, he was smitten by a terrible case of homesickness—though he thought he was physically ill—and Railey gave up his own quarters for him. "I slept in Colonel Railey's bed for three nights, 'cause I was sick. He took care of me—he was my doctor. He knew it was psychological."

"You heard from the colonel—he'd come around and talk to people," Rippeteau remembers. "Maybe that was why the morale was so good."

Though he'd already done his part, within twenty-four hours of Pearl Harbor, Railey volunteered for combat duty with Second Army, one of the units he had visited to make his report. He was turned down: at forty-six years of age, he was too old. In March 1942, he applied to another general with influence in the War Department. "Off the record, some days ago, you indicated that I might qualify for 'a tough job' in your Corps area. Tough jobs not only interest me but stimulate my sense of responsibility. Moreover, in this country and abroad, since 1917, I have successfully functioned as a trouble-shooter."

In short order he was reactivated at the rank of lieutenant colonel and joined the general staff at Governors Island, New York. There he served as chief of the Plans and Training Branch, helping to coordinate coastal defenses in a three-state area, including the "dimout" of city skylines. His efforts helped him produce a book on civil defense. When the War Department established its Planning Board in September 1942 to oversee the development of secret weapons, Railey was a natural pick. Probably because of his outstanding abilities as a writer—and his critical report on army morale, which had made him known to the Joint Chiefs—Colonel Blakeney made him secretary and executive officer.

Thus Railey was sitting at the table when Fairbanks walked in, preaching his gospel of battlefield deception. The Battle of Sandy Hook had Railey's stamp all over it: a secret and dramatic nighttime foray to put one over on officers and troops who were still thinking "inside the box." After that successful demonstration, the Planning Board ordered a prototype service model of the sonic equipment used to simulate boat motors for further field testing. The speakers and amplifiers used off Sandy Hook had been a conglomeration of three generations of equipment. Meanwhile the navy, prompted by Fairbanks, ordered thirty sonic units for the Beach Jumpers. The sonic unit was battery powered, capable of automatically activating itself at a preset time within twenty-four hours, then operating for thirty minutes before destroying itself.

At this early stage, a fundamental philosophical rift was already developing between the army and the navy. The navy wanted to train with the equipment previously developed, primitive as it was, and get it into combat as quickly as possible. Driving that plan was Fairbanks's missionary zeal. The army, however, wasn't satisfied with the equipment in its present state of evolution. The so-called heaters and the monstrous battery packs required to power them were far too large and heavy to mount on any sort of land vehicle. Likewise, turntables were tricky enough to operate on the relatively steady platform of a large boat, but they'd be useless in a moving jeep or truck. Furthermore, the systems had trouble projecting low frequencies—the rumble of tank engines, for instance—and nobody was quite sure how far any frequency would carry over land.

Did the weather affect how far the sound carried? Almost certainly—but how? Did temperature matter? Fog, rain, snow? Just how wide a spectrum of frequencies could be projected—and which ones would actually be heard, and from how far away?

So the acoustical engineers continued their work, addressing each problem in turn, many of them dividing their time between their laboratories and Camp Bradford, Virginia, where they helped train Fairbanks's sailors in seaborne deception. And the Beach Jumpers sent technicians north to Bell Labs for further instruction.

Whether Railey himself spent time at Camp Bradford is a matter of conjecture, but it's hard to imagine a man of his curiosity and adventurous temperament, charged with his responsibilities, not taking advantage of such a hands-on opportunity. The amphibious training base had become the field laboratory for both the navy and the army. Fairbanks continued to sit with the Planning Board, so in any case Railey had plenty of contact with him and the progress of his Beach Jumpers. Drawing heavily on his experience with Combined Ops in England, Fairbanks was writing the book on the tactics of sonic deception—tactics that Railey and his officers would adapt for use on land.

After a few months and probably at Railey's instigation, the army decided it needed a facility of its own. On 4 June 1943, it authorized the Army Experimental Station (AES)—and predictably chose as its commander Lt. Col. Hilton Howell Railey. After the war, he would write, "Warned by the War Department General Staff that only 1 new weapon in 8,000 ever reaches the blueprint stage, I accepted these odds and, as president of a TOP SECRET Army-Navy Board began development of those in which I had faith."

It's likely that Railey was initially drawn to the work of the secret Planning Board for the obvious reasons embedded in his character. He craved intrigue, was genuinely patriotic, loved to explore technological boundaries, felt he could use his experience and intelligence to help the war effort by developing secret weapons. He had social connections among the higher-ups at Bell Labs, and Dr. Davis, President of the Stevens Institute of Technology, had helped elect him director of the American League of Nations Association. But at some point, perhaps during the Battle of Sandy Hook, perhaps even earlier, he became committed to the cause of sonic deception in particular. Something about it fired his imagination, inspired him to extraordinary effort—as he had been inspired by the self-effacing young aviatrix Amelia Earhart, or the prospect not just of raising sunken treasure from an ocean liner but of creating a technological breakthrough that would revolutionize undersea exploration. As usual, once he was focused on a single mission, he achieved extraordinary results. Those results didn't come without a cost.

Railey was a tireless self-promoter. His instinct to trumpet his own achievements was always at war with his duty to be circumspect. Like Fairbanks, he courted recognition and craved celebrity, was a natural public performer, and was irresistibly drawn to the intrigue of top-secret work. It must have been maddening for both men not to be able to brag about their work in public. They could confide only in a secret fraternity, and perhaps that was one of the great satisfactions of the work. After all: the daily association with inventive minds solving complex problems with ingenuity and style and keeping it all secret from the outside world ought to have been enough to gratify even the grandest ego.

Railey set up shop at Fort Hancock, New Jersey, on the northen tip of Sandy Hook—the beach he had successfully "invaded"—in a spartan compound of old Civilian Conservation Corps barracks, including a lab, a recreation hall, and a dirigible hangar. His own quarters was a small board-and-batten house with a bedroom and an office. An orderly tended to his personal needs and looked after his red shepherd dog, Jerry.

Even in his routine private life he cultivated an air of mystery. He rode everywhere in a 1940 olive-drab two-door Army Ford, driven by a slim young sergeant everyone knew as Bill Railey, his son. The story was that Railey had personally walked Bill through the induction center at Grand Central Station, New York, and Bill immediately went to work for him, without ever having to undergo basic training, and was quickly promoted. Bill stayed with him all through the war, always at his side, even sharing his quarters. Bill remained aloof from the men and rarely spoke to them. "Any attempt to discuss something with Bill was just a dead end," Rippeteau recalls.

Railey alludes to Bill in his postwar résumé to explain why he turned down an offer of a full colonelcy on the general staff of Third Army, "proffered in the presence of Col. Dwight D. Eisenhower," while he was doing his morale study: "I declined, regretfully: Reason: my youngest son, Bill, only sixteen, needed his Dad."

Sergeant William D. Railey indeed appears on the roster of Headquarters and Headquarters Detachment, AES. But Railey had only two sons, John and Kenneth. Whoever "Bill Railey" really was—an adopted son or simply a protégé—his identity was one more small deception carried on by a man with a constitutional need to create and keep secrets. "He simply didn't want other people to know much about his background," Rippeteau says. "I think he lived his whole life afraid of being found out."

At any rate, Railey's first order of business at Fort Hancock was choosing the right men. Like Fairbanks, he recruited personally from a pool of extremely bright, competent young men. He first interviewed recruits who had tested high enough on their mechanical and mental aptitude tests to qualify for the Army Specialist Training Program—ASTP.

The Army Specialist Training Program was set up early in the war at the urging of Secretary of War Henry Stimson to identify young men particularly gifted in areas that might be useful to the military—smart guys who could handle math, engineering, writing, foreign languages, electronics, radio codes, radar, navigation, and so on. The ASTP was one of the most enlightened ideas to come out of the War Department in those days. It took advantage of native intelligence and special abilities that would become crucial to the war effort as weapons and tactics became increasingly sophisticated. Until needed, about 150,000 of these ASTP recruits, a number greater than the whole prewar army, were parked in colleges, universities, and special army schools to continue their studies while still privates in the U.S. Army.

Later in the war, anticipating casualties during the invasion of Europe, the army raided the program for infantrymen. So by the fall of 1944, as historian Stephen E. Ambrose observes, "the U.S. Army was feeding into its fighting force its best young men."

Railey interviewed candidates at Sea Girt, known as Camp Edison, since before the war it had been the estate of New Jersey Governor Thomas Edison Jr., and at Camp Wood, an annex of the Signal Corps base at Fort Monmouth, New Jersey. He saw them in groups of ten or a dozen, and went through some four hundred men before he chose just thirteen to join his initial cadre.

Ed Gilmore was one of those thirteen. He had taken a radio course in night school at Cornell University and joined the Signal Corps. At Camp Wood, he interviewed for ASTP and ten days later was still awaiting the results when he was summoned to the CO's office. There was Railey.

His first impression of Railey: "He was a very straight man—and I mean *straight*. Well spoken. Knew what he wanted and knew where he was going."

Though Gilmore had watched other candidates before him dismissed after only five minutes, Railey grilled him for nearly an hour, then looked him in the eye and asked one final question: "This is going to be a special outfit, a combat outfit. Are you willing to make a total sacrifice to our cause?"

Without hesitation, Gilmore responded: "Yes."

Railey said, "Follow my stars and you'll wear diamonds."

Jim Barrett, interviewed by Railey's assistant, a short, broad-shouldered major named Florian, had a similar experience. Florian said, "It's not a suicide squad, but it's going to be risky." Was he willing to make the ultimate sacrifice? Like Gilmore and the others who were selected, Barrett said, "Yes."

He didn't know at first he'd even been selected. As an ASTP candidate, he'd watched guys come and go, but every time he was scheduled to ship out from Camp Wood, they'd pull him out of ranks and say, "Not you— you're hot." At last he was put on a weapons carrier with other guys being shipped out as replacements for truck drivers. "I guess the party's over," he told himself. But at the gate to Camp Wood, a jeep intercepted their vehicle. "Guy named Barrett in there?" the driver called.

Soon he found himself hoisting his duffel bag into a six-by truck for the short ride to Fort Hancock with a gang of other men Railey had selected. As they approached the gate, they passed mammoth railroad guns. Crossing the tracks, they suddenly heard the shriek of a train whistle that jolted them from their seats in panic. "And we're all looking—but there's no train. They were projecting the sound of a train whistle." That was his introduction to sonic deception—Railey style.

Later, Railey expanded his search, recruiting from ASTP pools at Grinnell College, Iowa, and the University of Chicago, to fill out a complement of more than four hundred officers and enlisted men. Then he recruited civilians such as Theodore "Ted" Crabtree and Norman Stryker from Bell Telephone Labs. "All of the enlisted men and all of the officers were way above the ordinary army intelligence level," Rippeteau says. "These were a smart group of people."

They included Ellsworth "Bud" Haver, a semipro baseball pitcher; Ralph Caldwell, the company clerk, who his buddies say resembled Radar O'Reilly, the character from the television show *M*A*S*H*, complete with wire-rimmed glasses, knit cap, and superhuman memory; Robert Tanner, who went from Bell Labs into the army and directly to the AES with no basic training; Harry Robin, a second lieutenant who played the violin professionally and acted as an advisor on the quality of sound recordings; Lt. John Kiernan, who kept a Saint Bernard dog named Bonzo and acquired a legendary library of dirty limericks recorded on the top-secret sonic equipment; Kenneth Hailstone, a small man with piercing eyes, rumored to be an OSS man actually recruited to spy on the others; and Capt. George Melvin, Railey's soft-spoken exec, also suspected as a "spook."

When Colonel Blakeney, head of the secret Planning Board, was sent overseas, he recommended Railey for a promotion to full colonel to succeed him as president of the board. He wrote, "Lt. Col. Railey has shown tact, energy, ingenuity, and initiative far in excess of the call of duty."

Railey got his promotion.

From October 1943 on, most of the work of research and development would shift to the AES. The civilian experts would work side by side with handpicked troops. And Railey was now in charge of the whole army program.

The program now focused on several areas: creating a library of originally recorded military sounds that might be useful on the battlefield; developing a table similar to an artillery firing table to establish the necessary volume and direction of various frequencies so as to project them over a given distance in specific weather conditions; scaling down the equipment so it could be more mobile; and developing speakers that could project low-frequency noise.

During sound projection experiments, Jim Barrett worked twelve hours on, twelve hours off. His job was climbing up a ladder on the ninety-foot steel weather tower to take temperature, wind velocity, and relative humidity readings at thirty feet, sixty feet, and ninety feet no matter the conditions. He was a strong, agile kid and didn't think in those days how arduous the task was.

Railey's technicians quickly achieved one significant breakthrough: they successfully created the illusion of moving vehicles from stationary sound sources.

In night or fog or poor visibility, an enemy observer would hear the sound of tanks actually moving laterally across the battlefield in front of him. Rippeteau emphasizes how realistic the sound effects were: "There is no question that if you were there and it was dark or dusky or poor observation, a nighttime operation, you heard those tanks moving along, and you heard them trying to get up hills. And you heard them park. And you heard them backfire when they shut the engine off. There's no question—all that stuff happened."

But though the civilian scientists were making progress, in the beginning many of the enlisted men were not really sure what sort of mission they'd been picked for at Fort Hancock. They were not yet fully integrated into the program. "We really didn't know what the hell we were doing, what was even planned of us," Gilmore recollects. "We never knew that we were going to be in sonic warfare—we didn't find that out until we got to Pine Camp."

By regular army standards, discipline was lax. "It was just like living in a country club," Gilmore says. The AES worked civilian hours, with nights and weekends off, and the men received class-A passes into New York City. Only a handful of them turned out for the 5:30 A.M. reveille formation— the rest sacked out in their bunks. Physical fitness training consisted of an hour swim in the ocean at three o'clock every afternoon. When Railey organized war games, the first time, the men gleefully fired blanks at one another. But, Gilmore says, they quickly learned their lesson. "We found out how dirty the blanks made our rifles, and it was such a hell of a job cleaning them out afterward that nobody shot at anybody else after that—we just lay there and let 'em infiltrate!"

At this time there were twenty or so men at the station—the original thirteen plus a small corps of people Railey had brought with him. One was Hugo Buttino, who had been secretary to crusading New York district attorney Thomas E. Dewey. Others in the cadre recall that he used to lie awake at night and drive the rest of his barracks mates crazy making up bad poetry. "She laid on my white delectable body. . . ."

Railey spent a good deal of his time in showmanship—staging demonstrations, promoting sonic deception to visiting VIPs from the army and navy. He held nineteen such shows. The distinguished visitors included Fairbanks, now a lieutenant commander. But the Army Experimental Station was quickly outgrowing Fort Hancock. The sonic equipment had now been adapted for vehicles, and to test it, they needed more wide-open spaces than the crowded Jersey shore could offer. Also, as of December 1943, the AES would be charged with training combat units in sonic deception, which would need maneuver areas. In February 1944, the whole operation moved north to Pine Camp, in the thickly forested hills near the Canadian border.

On moving day, the men were roused at 3:00 A.M. This time nobody stayed in his bunk. They wolfed down a breakfast of steak and eggs. Fourteen half-tracks led by a command jeep started down the peninsula, picked up the Pulaski Skyway, and rumbled through the Holland Tunnel. Behind the half-tracks followed another twenty-odd trucks full of equipment driven by an all-black transportation contingent out of New York City, their two-and-a-half-ton trucks immaculately maintained and waxed to a high shine, putting to shame the grubby half-tracks the AES men drove. The convoy proceeded up the West Side Highway through Manhattan, Harlem, and The Bronx and into Westchester County on Route 9. A minor traffic accident with the lead jeep stopped them for an hour near Yonkers, then they pushed on to Utica, where they spent the night in the National Guard armory. The next day they arrived in Watertown, and drove through its snowy streets and on to Pine Camp, just beyond town.

Pine Camp had been founded on ten thousand acres along the Black River. Brig. Gen. Frederick Dent Grant, son of the Civil War hero and president, trained two thousand regulars and eight thousand militia there in 1908. The rugged training ground was so useful to developing and testing tactics that the army continued to buy up the land adjacent to it. In 1935, with war looming across the Atlantic and Pacific horizons, the army held the largest peacetime maneuvers in history here. Using Pine Camp as a nucleus of operations, 36,500 soldiers from all over the Northeast converged on the countryside of upper New York State and staged mock combat on a battlefield a hundred miles long, leased by the army for the occasion.

By 1944, when the AES arrived, Pine Camp had swelled to a hundred thousand acres, swallowing five whole villages and displacing more than five hundred families. Eight hundred new wooden buildings had been hastily constructed for the wartime army , including 240 barracks, 84 mess halls, 27 officers' quarters, and a hospital. General George Patton trained his 4th Armored Division there. One of his battalion commanders was Gen. Creighton Abrams, namesake of the M1 Abrams tank.

The AES men had a common first impression: "Cold damn place!" Gilmore remembers. Barrett, a North Dakota boy who had been enjoying the relatively balmy Jersey shore, thought glumly, *I'm back in North Dakota!* The frozen, packed snow snapped under their boots. They were immediately issued fleece-lined jackets and other arctic gear.

And new men started coming in—recruits for the 3132d Signal Service Company that would train under Railey, regular officers to manage the hundreds of arriving soldiers, and support staff, including cooks and MPs. The merging of regular army personnel and Railey's handpicked specialists made Pine Camp an especially interesting assignment for all parties—many of whom had unique backgrounds.

In the spring of 1944, Railey's eventual S3, Darrel D. Rippeteau, served as a forward observer for a field-artillery battery at Camp Campbell, Kentucky. He came from a heritage of wartime service. His grandfather, who had Americanized his surname to James Emory Rippetoe, along with several brothers and cousins, had served in Eli Lilly's 1st Indiana Light Artillery Battery during the Civil War. Rippeteau had earned his commission through four years in the Citizens' Military Training Camps program followed by ROTC at the University of Nebraska, where he graduated with a degree in architecture. Not an unusual career path in those days: between seventy-five and ninety percent of Army officers were ROTC grads.

Rippeteau was sitting under a tree at Camp Campbell with his forward observer group when a jeep skidded up with a courier summoning him to the adjutant's office. "What are you pulling?" the adjutant demanded.

"Nothing," he said.

"You're not by chance the grandson of the chief signal officer, are you?" Meaning, somebody high up is looking out for you. "You've got orders for the Army Experimental Station at Pine Camp."

"I don't even know where that is."

The adjutant laughed. "Here's how you get to Pine Camp," he said.

"Get on a train. Go to Syracuse, New York. When you get off the train, turn left, go ahead about three blocks. There will be a guy there who can rent you six dogs and a sled. You'll need only four dogs to pull the sled, but they'll eat a couple of the dogs. Then go up into the wilderness. If you get to a big river, that will be the St. Lawrence, and you've gone too far. Turn right before the river. There will be a place to turn in the dogs and the sled and get your money back."

When Rippeteau arrived at Pine Camp—by taxicab, not dogsled—he found a very different army than the one he was used to. "Basically these were just a bunch of artists, playactors, aesthetic-type guys, camouflage experts, electronics—as of that day—experts, and they were not military types. They weren't very anxious to wear the uniform completely at any given time. Falling out for reveille was really a joke. The whole thing was sort of like a boy scout camp."

He also caught up with Maj. Ivan Miller, an old friend from the Armored Force school at Fort Knox, where Rippeteau had taught tank destroyer tactics before joining the field artillery. Miller was the new executive officer, or second in command, at the station. "I guess I'm indebted to you, if that's the right word, for being called up here on duty," he told Miller.

Miller replied, "Well, I've been up here now several months, and I'm desperate. We've got to have some *military semblance* in this organization."

For squared-away officers like Miller and Rippeteau, the casual approach to army regulations took some getting used to. "I don't remember ever having a disciplinary problem—that's quite a thing," Rippeteau says. "But the reason we didn't have any was that there wasn't very much *discipline*. But the whole organization was moving technically in the same direction, and they all understood they were pretty unusual type people doing a very unusual military job. And from that standpoint you could say that the esprit de corps was fairly high."

Another ROTC officer who made the trek up to Pine Camp was Lt. Richard Syracuse.

Syracuse was a tall, muscular man with a flamboyant manner, a ladies' man, darkly handsome with thick, jet-black wavy hair. He grew a pencil-thin mustache to look older, and to this day his contemporaries who served with him still talk of him as an older brother, a mentor. A graduate of the City College of New York with a degree in chemical engineering, Syracuse was commissioned at the age of twenty in 1942 and sent south to Fort Blanding, Florida, to take command of the 81st Chemical Smoke

Generating Company—an all-black outfit. Syracuse recalls, "I spent fourteen–fifteen months in the South, both at Camp Blanding and Camp Seibert outside of Gadsden, Alabama, fighting Jim Crow in the army."

Usually a captain would be in charge of such a unit, a more mature officer with more experience. But Syracuse grew up learning to take charge on the rough streets of the South Bronx. He was the only non-Jew in a Jewish neighborhood, but it didn't matter, because he was a hell of a stickball player—and that's how they judged a kid, by how good a stickball player he was. He says matter-of-factly, "My leadership qualities developed—as I look back and I realize it—from being captain of a great stickball team in the South Bronx—and that required leadership."

That experience made him confident, even cocky, and it made him tough. Syracuse had learned that if you want guys to respect you, you have to perform. He ran track at Stuyvesant High School, and he knew that to perform well you had to cultivate discipline—winning didn't happen accidentally. You had to make your guys believe they could win, even when it seemed hopeless. You had to calm them down when they got nervous. And most of all, you had to stick up for them, no matter what.

On the train south to assume his command of the 81st, he traveled with two other white officers, each with his black cadre—a first sergeant and other sergeants and corporals who would organize their new units. At suppertime, after all the white passengers had been served, he took his men into the dining car. The three officers sat down together at a table and the noncommissioned officers chose seats nearby. The conductor started to hang a sheet between them, to separate the blacks from the whites.

"What the hell is this? What kind of shit is this?" Syracuse demanded.

The conductor said, "Well, sir, we're down below the Mason-Dixon Line, and white folks don't eat with black folks."

Syracuse was livid. "Buddy, you've got the wrong story here. These are black soldiers, and we are their officers, and we are going to war together, and we're going to eat together, and we're gonna eat on your goddamn train too!"

The conductor took down the sheet.

At Camp Seibert, Alabama, Syracuse ran into Jim Crow with a vengeance. "We were in the ass end of camp, we got the last buses into town, we had a crummy PX. Gadsden had a beautiful USO for white troops, and nothing for blacks. Black officers were segregated from the white officers—they had their own mess."

And he battled it. He was not insubordinate, just headstrong, with a well-developed sense of what was fair and right. In the civilian army, unlike the regular army, officers were not concerned with advancing their careers: "We just wanted to get the war over with as fast as we could so we could go home."

Just like in any army, an officer had to earn respect. Syracuse ate with his black second lieutenants in the colored mess. "They were a great bunch," he recalls. "We developed a wonderful esprit." Syracuse's company was a rough-and-ready lot—tough street kids from Detroit and Chicago, farmboys from Dixie, mill hands and factory workers from all over. They became a tight, efficient outfit. But his liberal ideas put him at odds with his CO, a Colonel Glazebrook.

Glazebrook ordered Syracuse to undergo company punishment—confinement to a special disciplinary tent—and Syracuse refused, demanding an official court-martial instead. Glazebrook backed down.

Since high school, Syracuse had planned on serving in the military, though not making it a career. In school, he'd been a great buff of the United States military and its history and had idealistic notions of what it meant to serve. "One of the things I learned and felt deeply about was that rank, while it had its privilege, also had its responsibilities."

His chief responsibility was the welfare of his troops—and what got him into trouble time and again was that he refused to comply with the segregation policy of the U.S. Army. "One of the things we did was to proselytize as much as we could to have black officers be placed in command positions. Up to that point, there were none. Finally the War Department did send down a directive. And guess who was one of the first white officers relieved?"

So one blizzardy February night in 1944, Syracuse stamped the snow off his boots and strode into Railey's office at Pine Camp to report for duty. His new assignment would be to lead a security platoon of half-tracks and jeeps armed with heavy machine guns and bazookas. His mission: to protect the sonic deception platoons and keep them and their equipment from falling into enemy hands.

After he had warmed up at the stove and they had chatted for a few minutes, Railey said, "Our mission is to draw fire from the enemy—you understand that?"

Syracuse replied, "Well, I come from New York, and I've been kicked in the ass a few times. But I reserve the right to kick some ass back."

Railey laughed and said, "I think it's cocktail hour—you like Scotch?" He brought out the ubiquitous bottle of Teacher's.

"I love Scotch," Syracuse said.

Railey filled their glasses, and they drank deep.

On the next nighttime operation, Railey drove Syracuse to the old ar-
tillery observation point atop a remote hill in the snowy north woods.
Thanks to Rippeteau, the woods would come to be known as Sherwood
Forest and the observation point "Railey's Roost."

Imagine: It's black wilderness, the only light the ground glow from the
snow. In the distance, Syracuse can hear grinding motors. They come
closer, and closer, and he stares into the darkness. The noise is loud now,
the groan of dozens of tank engines laboring up the hill toward them. He
strains to see, and then swears he does see the shadowy forms of tanks
emerging from the tree line. "Suddenly my ears are telling my eyes that
there are tanks out there," Syracuse recalls. "Is it possible for your ears to
tell your eyes to see something?"

In fact, it's not only possible, but psychologically inevitable, according
to the Bell Labs' "bible" on sonic deception, compiled from experiments at
the AES. "Another well-known psychological fact of interest in deception is
the association of stimuli received through several senses, for example,
sight and hearing. . . . An observer, under the strain of impending attack
and under conditions of poor visibility, such as moonlight or dawn, will
transform a suggestive noise, faintly heard, into a strong illusion of a concentration of enemy forces *and may firmly believe that he sees as well as
hears them.*" [italics mine]

The tanks never materialized out of the black tree line. Instead, all motor sounds abruptly ceased, and all at once a new sound came blaring out
of the woods—the opening strains of "I Dream of Jeannie With the Light
Brown Hair," Railey's favorite song.

THREE

CASTING CALL FOR CAMOUFLEURS
1942–1944

*Deception is an art, not a science. Those who practice it must
be adept at making something out of nothing.*
— Brig. Gen. Dudley Clarke

The art students had made a pact—they were all going to enlist together
into a special camouflage unit.

Early one October morning in 1942, Harold "Hal" Laynor strode purposefully with his father to the army recruiting center in Greenwich Village
near the Parsons School of Design, where he'd just completed the three-
year course of study in graphic art. The New York papers were full of reports of the siege of Stalingrad. In the Pacific, American marines were
slugging it out with the Japanese on Guadalcanal in a bloodbath that
would last another month. And even in New York, British general Bernard
Montgomery was grabbing headlines for his bold success at the Battle of El
Alamein in North Africa. But the secret research into sonic warfare going
on a few miles away in New Jersey didn't make the papers. There was no
mention of the work of Douglas Fairbanks Jr. or Hilton Howell Railey. No
dispatches from the Battle of Sandy Hook.

Hal's father, blond and blue-eyed John Laynor—who'd changed the
family name from Levinsky—owned a string of movie theaters in New York
and was something of a personality in the neighborhood. People on the
street often mistook him for the musical actor Danny Kaye.

Hal had the same arresting blue eyes, but his blond hair was heavily
tinged with red. He stood five foot ten, had the round, chubby face of a
twenty-year-old kid, and was prone to stockiness. Hal, too, was something

of a character. He'd waltz into a party and suddenly the room would come alive with his jokes and rich baritone voice, and all the girls would gather around him. In high school, he had sung in the chorus and played in the *Mikado* and other shows. He never missed a chance to perform for an audience. In those days, Hal never had a dime in his pocket, yet he always managed to find a party. He roamed the world of Harlem and north Manhattan with a pint of whiskey stuffed into the back pocket of his uncreased trousers, singing while he walked, telling jokes to anybody who would listen, putting on an air of cocky, devil-may-care worldliness. One day while he was still in high school, he had sat on the stoop of his family's apartment with Gloria Silberman, a neighborhood girl with a wonderful laugh who eventually became his sweetheart. "I can't decide if I want to be a famous artist or a great teacher," he said to her in all seriousness. "Maybe I'll do both—become a famous artist *and* a great teacher."

As a student at Parsons School of Design, he won a scholarship to study art in Paris. His head was bursting with ideas, images, techniques he wanted to try. Already he dreamed of mixing media, painting not just with brushes but with sponges, towels, his fingers. He had painted since the age of twelve, when he swapped his stamp collection for a set of oil paints and brushes.

That was 1934, the same year Cliff Simenson was graduating from West Point.

Stamps had taught Hal about geography, and now he was ready to explore the world beyond New York City. He had always dreamed of studying art in Paris, setting up an easel on a bridge above the Seine and painting in that remarkable and famous light.

But then the war intervened.

As he waited for his buddies to show up at the recruiting center, Hal chain-smoked—a habit he had picked up while prowling the city hustling work. For a time, he painted neckties for a small factory in Harlem—Statue of Liberty, hula girls, whatever they wanted. Then Gimbel's Department Store hired him as part of a team to paint bucolic landscapes. One guy painted the meadow, another guy the barn, another a haystack, and so forth. Hal painted the sky. Gimbel's sold the landscapes for thirty-five dollars apiece—a dear price in a nation still reeling from the Depression—and Hal got fifty cents per sky.

One day, one of his painter buddies complained, "Hal, you're taking way too long with that sky. At that rate, you're not going to make nothing."

After that, he learned to paint fast, to work anywhere under almost any conditions. He was not a snob about art; to him it was a craft and a discipline, as well as a calling. The word had gone out to all the art schools in New York that the army needed artists for special work in camouflage. As an artist, the idea of camouflage intrigued him. He could use his sense of color and form for the war effort. He and his buddies had talked it over and made their pact.

But not one of his gang of pals from Parsons showed up.

For one reason or another, they had all reneged. Hal didn't back out— he wasn't a man to go back on a promise, especially one made to himself. He shook hands with his father, swore the oath, and before long found himself in a barracks at the induction center at Camp Upton, New York, on his way to Fort George G. Meade, Maryland—a new recruit to the 603d Engineer Camouflage Battalion. There he would join hundreds of other artists, designers, and theatrical types to train in camouflage. But he had no idea he was enlisting for an unconventional brand of secret warfare. The ultimate mission of the camoufleurs would evolve into a much more sophisticated kind of deception.

On another day, across the river in Brooklyn, Victor Dowd listened to a visiting general address the senior class at the Pratt Institute. The general had been invited there by the director of the school, John C. Boudreau, himself a reserve officer who had completed an active tour of duty at the Army Engineering School at Fort Belvoir, Virginia. It was the same pitch Hal Laynor had heard: the army needed artists.

Dowd was the son of an Irish-American father and his French war bride, a soft-spoken kid with a subtle and quick sense of humor who aspired to be an illustrator. In grammar school, he'd been the class artist. He'd elected to attend Brooklyn Technical High School, not for vocational training, but because it was known for its superb art department. He studied the glossy magazines almost religiously—*The Saturday Evening Post, Collier's, The Ladies' Home Journal, The Women's Home Companion,* even the rotogravure sections of the Sunday newspapers—not for their stories, but for their pictures. He marveled at the lines, the color, how a stroke here or there could create a mood, a facial expression, a sense of movement. He had a hungry eye for pictures, couldn't get enough of them, studied technique and style and perspective, then tried them out for himself, learned what kind of illustrations each magazine favored.

His particular talent was drawing people—figures, faces, men, women, people working, moving, standing, singly or in groups. His instructors at Pratt had been working illustrators, and they had introduced him to more in their profession at the New York Society of Illustrators. Dowd could see his career opening before him. But before he could embark on his profession, of course there was the war. Enlisting was not a difficult decision, volunteering not so special. "Everybody was in the service," he recalls. "In my old neighborhood, the one or two people who got out because of a trick knee or a punctured eardrum were looked down on by the rest of us."

Less than a year into America's war, the cost was already coming home. "There wasn't a neighborhood that wasn't touched by wounded and deaths. In my neighborhood, the kid across the street got killed, the kid next door lost his leg, and on and on. A friend of mine was a pilot—he was lost, and nobody knows what happened to him."

Dowd was first assigned to the 84th Engineer Camouflage Battalion, the only such unit in the army, commanded by a twenty-four-year-old West Point straight-arrow major, Julian V. Sollohub. After Pearl Harbor, the unit was stationed at Fort Totten, New York, to work on Atlantic coastal defenses—at the same time that Colonel Railey was engineering how to make the Manhattan skyline disappear from the hunting periscopes of German U-boats. In those days, the War Department still feared sabotage, naval attacks, even aerial strikes from hostile bases in Norway. Roosevelt had bluntly warned the American people to expect to be bombed.

But in April 1942, Sollohub was ordered to select a cadre from the 84th and form a new battalion at Fort Meade—the 603d.

Dowd was instructed to report to Fort Meade as part of Sollohub's new unit, in D Company. He found out he had a knack for counting cadence during marching drills and quickly moved up to corporal. His sergeant was a tough veteran of the Wilkes-Barre steel mills who enforced strict discipline. Once when Dowd carried out a maneuver differently from the way he had been ordered, the sergeant called him on it. Dowd tried to explain. "But, Sergeant, I thought—"

The sergeant cut him off. "You ain't s'posed to tink—I'll do the tinking in dis-here platoon."

Eventually Dowd earned his own sergeant's stripes.

Bill Blass had visited the World's Fair in New York City when he was sixteen and knew at once and with great certainty that the city was the only place for him.

A year later, he moved to Manhattan alone to make his fortune. He was used to acting independently. His father had committed suicide when he was only five years old, leaving him to help his mother after school in the family dressmaking business. He dreamed of becoming a fashion designer and was scraping out a living on Seventh Avenue doing sketches, trying to make a name for himself, when the war came along.

"I think we almost all of us in that age group felt obliged to enlist," he recalls. Though he'd never had the slightest interest in a military career, with his design expertise, when he heard through the art-world grapevine about the army's call for camouflage specialists, he joined up. "You see, it was a common cause," he explains. "While the Depression caused people to become more insular, the war brought us all together. We were all in the same position. I cannot imagine how one would have felt being a civilian during those years."

Since he'd already been on his own for a couple of years in the city, he didn't suffer the kind of homesickness that afflicted many of the raw recruits, most of whom were still living with their parents right up to the moment they went into the army. Blass settled into barracks life with remarkable ease, even though it meant giving up privacy and, to some extent, individuality. "You became serial number 12147747, and that was that. You were no longer a personality, a bon vivant or whatever you thought you were in your other life," he says. "You sublimated all that to becoming part of a group, of the unit. You lost individuality—individuality was something that was not acceptable, nor was it necessary. You had to work as a unit, not as an individual."

But far from stifling him, the barracks life opened up a whole new world for him—teamwork and shared hardship with other men on the drill field and out on bivouac, shared accomplishment, and always the lively good talk in the barracks at the end of the day. He says, with some nostalgia, "It was the closest thing to male bonding of family that I've ever found."

He had grown up surrounded by his mother and sister and their female friends, and now he had a barracks full of brothers, some of them older and wiser. For Blass, the camaraderie of the 603d would become the college experience he never had, and he would make the most of it.

Some took a more roundabout route to the camouflage battalion at Fort Meade than others.

William Flemer III—son and grandson of nurserymen in Princeton, New Jersey—was finishing up his junior year at Yale, when he volunteered. His father was already engaged in camouflage for the army, which had installed big coastal guns on either side of the Delaware Bay. His job was to plant shrubs over the soil disturbed by the heavy construction to disguise them from aerial observation. He heard about the new camouflage battalion and urged his son to apply for it.

And so he did. Flemer was inducted at Fort Devins and billeted with the tough Yankee infantry division—not the camoufleurs. He called his father, who made some calls of his own, and pretty soon Flemer, too, found himself in a barracks at Fort Meade. That first morning, he woke to the strains of a Stradivarius violin playing the Meditations from the opera *Tais* and knew he'd left the rough-tough Yankees behind for good. "I couldn't believe my ears," he recalls. "It was a wonderful outfit."

He was listening to Herman "Judge" Poole, an older-than-average recruit with some legal training who helped out with the rare court-martial—one of many barracks musicians: guitarists, drummers, piano players, even accordionists.

The 603d was split between artists, many from New York, and tough regular engineering troops.

"The army did one thing that in my opinion was very clever—and the army didn't do many clever things," Blass recalls. "In order to strengthen the unit, they took from the ranks of coal miners and bartenders, a whole contingent of a different sort of man, from a different sort of sociological background than the New York characters that the unit already consisted of. I mean, we had country music at one end of the barracks and philharmonic classical at the other end, and somehow it all went together."

To Blass, it was a reprise of Teddy Roosevelt's strategy half a century earlier when he forged the Rough Riders by throwing Harvard men in together with cowboys to instill a hybrid vigor, equal parts intellect and action. Vic Dowd became pals with one of the more colorful nonartists, Albin Smolinsky, a Polish-American kid from Fourth Street and Avenue B in New York. "You had to call him 'Lefty'—a real Damon Runyon character," Dowd says. "He sang beautifully and he had this thick New York accent, and to hear him sing like Frank Sinatra with 'da boids got together to choip about the weatha' was hilarious. He was a good guy and he had his own code of ethics. If he liked you, he would back you to the hilt. But if he didn't like you, you'd better watch out."

Lefty Smolinsky corresponded with some real characters from the neighborhood, some of whom were in jail, Dowd says. "They signed their letters, 'Your pal, the Eel.' Or 'Henry the Ape.'" Smolinsky would earn a Certificate of Merit for service in Normandy.

On another occasion, returning from a punishing twenty-mile forced march and ready to drop from exhaustion, Dowd and his platoon wearily trudged upstairs to their second-floor barracks—all the while hearing a strange rumbling sound over their heads. They entered the barracks room, where all the bunks had been shoved against the wall, all their footlockers piled into corners. And they saw at once the cause of the rumbling sound:

"This great big cook—he must have been six foot three, strapping big guy—was roller-skating back and forth across the wooden floor, bare-ass naked, wearing just his shoes and roller skates, dangling in the wind. It was kind of obscene and ridiculous at the same time."

Some of the artists made their entrances with more panache than others. Stanley Martineau, a wealthy twenty-seven-year-old sculptor from New York, arrived in a chauffeur-driven limousine. "That was rather a blow," Blass recalls with a smile. "His chauffeur brought his clothes in, and his valet unpacked him." Martineau would disappear for days at a time, on a pass cleared at the highest levels.

The mystery was solved when the *Fort Meade Post Enterprise* announced, "Fort Meade Soldier-Artist Carves Thirteen-Foot Bust of President." It turned out that Martineau was visiting Roosevelt at the White House, in order that Roosevelt could sit for him. New York mayor Fiorello La Guardia unveiled the four-ton sculpture on the steps of the General Post Office at Thirty-third Street and Eighth Avenue to open the national birthday ball in the "Miles of Dimes" crusade against infantile paralysis.

Martineau, the guest of honor, spoke briefly at the ceremony. "It has always been the mission of the artist to perpetuate in song and stone the common aspirations of man for a better world," he said. "What could be more noble and more beautiful than the dedication of ourselves to alleviate suffering in whatever form it may be?"

Blass had a little society cachet of his own. The first time he reported for KP duty, the mess sergeant lit up with recognition: "Mr. Blass!" Turns out he was the former butler of some of Blass's New York friends. Soft duty that day.

Blass stood six feet tall and had a broad, grinning face. In nearly every photograph taken of him during the whole war, he's smiling big, as if he's having the time of his life. Handsome, blond, appealing, a guy anybody could talk to easily, and in his Brooks Brothers–tailored uniform, he set the standard for style for the whole battalion. "We had to fall out every morning at five o'clock in our fatigues," photographer and artist George Martin recalls. "And sleepy-eyed Bill Blass would come out—what he did with those fatigues! He did something special, he had a foulard—he always looked a hundred percent better than we did."

Everyone took Blass for a suave New Yorker, but he'd grown up in Fort Wayne, Indiana. As a kid, he spent every minute he could at the movies watching divas like Greta Garbo and Marlene Dietrich slink across the screen in gorgeous gowns. Already he was captivated by women's clothing— his school books were full of doodled sketches of beautifully dressed women lounging on penthouse terraces, cocktail in one hand, cigarette holder in the other.

Since leaving home for the New York fashion world at seventeen, he had deliberately created a new identity for himself: He wasn't about to be taken for a hick from Indiana. In New York, he peddled pencil sketches of fashion ideas for twenty-five dollars apiece, already imagining a future for himself on the fashion runways of New York and Paris. This was his dream, to leave an indelible mark, and like many of his fellows in the "artists' army" of camoufleuers, his dreams had the force of talent and determination to make them come true. Like many of his buddies, Blass was already in the habit of carrying a spiral notepad in his pocket. In it, he sketched designs for dresses, jackets, and hats, along with notations of money he owed and ideas that occurred to him in the long idle hours of waiting between actions.

Jack Masey's caricature of the 3d
Platoon's Virgil Bragdon

Blass was assigned to B Company, which, like the others, was full of artists, as he quickly discovered:

Hal Laynor, already nicknamed "Kingfish" because he was such a big operator, always at the center of things, organizing variety shows.

George Martin, who designed the covers of sheet music in Tin Pan Alley and soon became the battalion photographer.

Jack Masey, a graphic designer and gifted caricaturist fresh out of Manhattan's High School of Music and Art, thrilled to find himself among so many more accomplished artists.

Bob Tompkins, a sketch artist headed for a distinguished career in advertising, who would become Blass's best friend throughout the war.

And George Vander Sluis, a brilliant watercolorist who at once became a model for some of the younger artists. Arthur Shilstone, already an accomplished illustrator on the verge of a stellar career in national magazines, would adopt his technique of drawing with a fountain pen—using his thumb to smudge lines for a shadowing effect, licking his thumb and smearing the page to lighten the contrast. According to Blass, "Shilstone was sleek and he had a subtlety about him," and Blass admired his sense of style.

The other companies were also full of talent: A Company had sculptor Olin Dows, painters Robert Nisely and Ellsworth Kelly, and Martineau. C Company included Howard Holt, who had painted showcards for movie theaters, wrote songs, and aspired to be an advertising designer; art student Jim Laubheimer; and Art Singer, soon to be the most famous painter of wild birds in North America. In D Company were Dowd, sculptor Harold Dahl, and cartoonist Ray Harford, who drew the "Captain Marvel" comics. Headquarters and Service Company had Richard Morton, another Pratt graduate and aspiring commercial artist. And there were dozens more.

The evening barracks bull sessions covered an eclectic mix of subjects: the usual army grousing and scuttlebutt about the war, talk about baseball and girls, and also conversations about mixing oil paints, the latest soirée at Toots Schor's, whether a martini was preferable to a sidecar, whether Art Deco would ever come back into fashion. And their favorite subject: what they would all do after the war.

A few had problems adjusting: a rich young dress designer moped about the barracks eating chocolates and writing forlorn letters home. Another tender recruit earned a psychological discharge—a "Section Eight"—after pulling one crazy stunt after another and remaining constipated for two weeks.

"A lot of these guys spent most of their time trying to beat the system," says Ed Biow, a Pratt graduate assigned to drive a truck. He recalls a stunt by his buddy Hirschel Rabinow. "We went on a hike with full field pack, forty to forty-five pounds, big bulky damn thing. Hirschel decided he wasn't going to carry that damned pack. He filled his pack with toilet paper so it would look full and was light." But the first sergeant caught on to the sham.

The 603d was full of highly educated guys who didn't always have patience with some of their working-class sergeants and officers. Dowd knew of two guys in his own platoon who had IQs of 150.

During basic training, Shilstone sat listening to an officer deliver yet another orientation lecture. The officer began, "Between you and I—"

A recruit raised his hand and interrupted. "Sir, you said, 'Between you and I,' but it should be, 'Between you and *me*,' because *between* is a preposition and takes the objective case."

The officer didn't miss a beat. "Well, then," he went on, "between you and *me*, private, it's time for you to put on your full fucking field pack and jog around the parade ground until I tell you to stop!"

During the standard VD lecture, the sergeant said, "Whenever you're tempted to go with a prostitute, think of your mother and your sister." A Kentucky roughneck shook his head and drawled, "Sarge, if I think of my mother and sister, I get horny!"

On another occasion, Shilstone was sitting in his barracks sketching one of his buddies, while a group of guys watched. The bell rang for chow and they all disappeared, but Shilstone kept working. Suddenly, between him and the guy he was drawing stood his platoon sergeant, a tough character named Max David, staring down at him with clear admiration. "You mean," he said, "you can just sit there and do that fuckin' shit?"

Shilstone, now famous as a magazine illustrator and watercolorist, says, "That's probably the most eloquent compliment I've ever had in my life."

Ellsworth Kelly took almost six months getting to the 603d .

He remembers with crystal clarity the family gathered around the radio listening to the news bulletin about the attack on Pearl Harbor. "It's hard to capture the emotion we felt—even then, my older brother and I said, 'Ah—we're going into the army.' " He didn't think twice about it. But there was one big hitch: he suffered from a bad back, and the doctors told him it would disqualify him from military service. "I had to get into the army," Kelly says. "It would have ruined me if I'd been 4-F. Isn't that amazing? I just had to get in."

He was a tall, good-looking kid with a sudden, infectious grin that went on like a light bulb and then disappeared just as suddenly. But usually he kept to himself, was the kind of kid nobody much noticed. His father sold insurance, and the family had moved several times, eventually landing in Oradell, New Jersey, across the Hudson from New York City, a town so small Kelly had to be bused to Englewood for high school. He remembers being painfully shy in those days. "I was extremely shy because I had a speech problem," he says, with any trace of a speech impediment long gone; rather he speaks now with quiet eloquence. He was so invisible growing up that his mother used to joke, "Where's my third boy?"

He spent a lot of time alone—roaming the New Jersey woods along a reservoir behind his house, accessible only by a little-used dirt road. He started to notice birds. When he was twelve or thirteen, he spotted a red start, glossy black with a startling red patch on the wings. "I was transfixed," he says. It was the beginning of a lifelong fascination with color and form in the animal world. "I was always involved with nature—and with the abstraction of nature."

He began to pay attention to the distinctive patterns of warblers and tanagers—the contrast of bright, vivid markings against dull bodies. He didn't draw or paint the birds then, but he made extraordinary use of those patterns later when he turned to abstraction and earned an international reputation for his groundbreaking hard-edged paintings.

When a new science teacher announced he wanted to take the class birding, he inquired if anybody knew of a good spot. Kelly volunteered to guide the class around the reservoir—to him, familiar territory. So the next morning all his classmates gathered, the teacher scouting the treetops and foliage with binoculars, trying to spot birds. But even without binoculars, Kelly could easily point out all his favorites. "There's a black-throated blue warbler in that tree," he would announce, amazing the teacher with his keen eyesight.

The teacher never caught on that it was a kind of trick. Kelly had been studying those birds for many months.

He took up sketching and painting naturally. John James Audubon, who had captured wild birds on beautiful, accurate full-color plates in *The Birds of America*, became an enduring hero and influence. "Audubon is one of the artists I feel I owe a lot to," Kelly says. By his late teens, his artistic talent was clear. When the war came, it made sense to figure out a way to put it to use. He was then enrolled at Pratt, where he ran across an article on the camouflage battalion. "Working with camouflage meant working with perception," Kelly says. "I've always been interested in perception—as a visualist, a lot of my work is about understanding what I see. It's an investigation of what we see. The camouflage experience heightened it."

So he wrote to the adjutant of the camouflage outfit at Fort Meade, Lt. William McKinley Spierer, who took his name and address and instructed him to join the army. "We'll find you," Spierer promised.

So Kelly managed to hide his back ailment from the army doctor and enlisted, then spent a frustrating month at Fort Dix, New Jersey, waiting to be assigned to the camouflage unit. New recruits came and went, and still Kelly waited to be "found." At last his name was called. "Some general had requested me—some general that I didn't know. He must have had me mixed up with another Kelly." Kelly was shipped to Camp Cooper Hill near Leadville, Colorado, to train with an elite ski corps.

He had never skied in his life.

So despite an ailing back, he learned to ski among tough mountain troops, which of course included Olympic champions and guys who had practically grown up on skis.

He found the army strangely conducive to his development as an artist, for very practical reasons. "The army was taking care of me—I didn't have to worry about how I was going to make a living," he explains. "Being in the army allowed me the freedom of thought without the pressure to earn a living with it." Later, the GI Bill would continue that freedom, allowing him to attend a real art school in Boston.

And after only a few months in the army, he reached a life-changing decision. "I decided while I was in the ski troops that I didn't want to be a commercial artist. I wanted to be an artist just for me."

It happened one night when he couldn't sleep.

He was standing at a window, just staring out into the snowy night. The other guys in the barracks were all asleep, snoring, tossing around, or lying quiet after a hard day of training in the mountain cold. He doesn't know even now what was keeping him awake or what it was he saw out the window that inspired him, but something surely did. "Looking out a window, I had this strange epiphany: I said, *I want to be an artist*.

"It might have happened anywhere, but it happened there."

After more than two months training with the ski troops—and becoming a proficient skier—Kelly was finally "found" by the 603d, just as Spierer had promised. His commanding officer was reluctant to let him go, since his elite unit had a very high esprit de corps. "You don't want to leave," the CO cajoled him.

"Yes, I do," Kelly said.

At Fort Meade with the 603d, Kelly was the quiet, reserved guy among a bunch of performers. When he introduced himself to Blass, Blass said at once, "Ellsworth—that's a pretty long name. I think I'll call you 'Worth,' " after the fashion designer of that name.

One of the jobs the 603d undertook was to produce posters for training and morale purposes—to teach and inspire and warn. "Out of all the guys, they chose me to make posters," Kelly says, "because I immediately caught on: we were abstracting nature." Patterns of color against neutral fields, in forms meant to teach soldiers how to camouflage.

Kelly made it a habit to visit the National Gallery in Washington, D.C., and to take in classic shows on Broadway in New York: Katharine Cornell in *Three Sisters*, Laurette Taylor in *The Glass Menagerie*, Paul Robeson in *Othello*.

Kelly didn't draw attention to himself, often would go off alone to sketch or paint, so unobtrusively that many of his comrades, who themselves were sketching and painting in every spare moment, never even noticed.

But with every sketch, every drawing, he was coming one step closer to becoming what he aspired to be: an artist for himself.

• • •

Fort George G. Meade, named after the Union victor of the Battle of Gettysburg, lies about twenty-five miles from Washington, D.C., and about thirty-six miles from Baltimore. During the war years, its cantonments contained more than a thousand buildings spread across more than five thousand acres. During the war, some two hundred army units—three and a half million soldiers—trained on its ranges and maneuver areas, now part of the Patuxent Wildlife Refuge: infantry divisions; tank and antitank battalions; ordnance, signal, and engineer companies; even surgical hospital units.

The 603d joined more than fifty thousand soldiers training at Fort Meade—which Colonel Railey had described only the previous year in his secret morale report as a "whore house," due to the Wild West nature of the honky-tonk boomtown at Odenton Station, near the east gate, and the unruly troops stationed there.

Things had changed dramatically during that year. The nation was at war, and now Fort Meade was a disciplined training post going about the business of preparing draftees for a shooting war. Diversion could be found at three movie theaters, each showing two pictures daily. There were the usual service clubs, swimming pools, baseball fields, even a golf course for the officers.

The athletic director for the 603d was Sgt. "Red" Sonnenfeld, a tall, powerful three-sport letterman at Penn State who organized company leagues in softball, basketball, and touch football. Enlisted men played alongside officers, unusual in an era when such "fraternization" was frowned on. Sonnenfeld left the 603d to go to Officers Candidate School—one of very few who did, even though nearly all the men were qualified because of army intelligence test scores or schooling. They were not ambitious to rise in the army hierarchy. They would rather stay with the outfit. Out on the ranges, slogging through the winter rains or sweltering in the humid Maryland heat, the men would watch the trains go by on the Pennsylvania Railroad line and envy the passengers silhouetted in the windows of the dining car or the club car, racketing toward New York or Washington. On weekends they themselves would swarm aboard trains already mobbed with soldiers from Fort Belvoir and other camps, sprawled on the swaying floors, sleeping in the wooden overhead racks on the night journey to New York and back again in time for 6:00 A.M. reveille.

Julian Sollohub, the young commanding officer of the camoufleurs, was disappointed with his new assignment at Fort Meade, even though it had come with a promotion to lieutenant colonel.

Not bad enough that he had logged all that time with the 84th Camouflage Battalion safely hiding coastal defenses. When his transfer orders came, he had hoped to take command of a combat engineering regiment, go to the war, do what he had trained for at West Point. His whole life had been leading up to a combat assignment. He had become a boy scout back in Springfield Center, New York—a town of just two hundred—partly because he loved the military-style uniform, the excitement of adventuring into the wilderness on a mission, the feeling of being part of a team. Both his parents died when he was fourteen, and he had no choice but to become self-reliant. By sixteen he had graduated high school and was ready for West Point.

But the minimum age for a West Point cadet was seventeen. Undaunted, he applied for and won a New York State Scholarship to Cornell University and spent a year studying civil engineering. Then he got his appointment to West Point. After graduating sixteenth in a class of 298, he cut his teeth for two years in the Philippines with the legendary Philippine Scouts.

"We were building roads with mules and slip scrapers," Sollohub recalls, still incredulous at how primitively equipped the U.S. Army was when the Japanese attacked. "We were not ready for war." Out of a 329-man battalion, the Scouts would lose 309 killed before the war was won.

Sollohub was a gangly five foot eleven, had good physical endurance and an engineer's methodical mind. All he had ever wanted was to be an army engineer—a combat engineer. His career was a fast-track model: second lieutenant for three years, first lieutenant for three months, captain for three more months, major soon after Pearl Harbor, and after only a year of war, lieutenant colonel. Eisenhower himself was only a full colonel on the regular army list.

Get in early, move up fast, he thought. But camouflage?

"This is almost a confession, I guess, but I was not interested in camouflage," he says. He was always a straight shooter, and his men without exception looked up to him—hardly realizing that he was barely older than most of his troops, and younger than many. "Camouflage was not of interest to me. In fact, I resented being assigned to it."

His real interests were booby traps, tank obstacles, mine laying and detection. He imagined himself building critical roads under fire so the armor could advance, laying down prefabricated Bailey bridges for the first wave of assault troops.

And there was another concern. "Some of them were enthralled with getting into camouflage—they said, 'We're *artists*.' I began to worry about people wanting to get into camouflage when I didn't. If they *wanted* to get into camouflage, they must be peculiar people—probably gay people and all that sort of thing." He laughs now about his own naïveté, but back then he was wary of all those arty New York types.

In fact, a number of the camoufleurs were gay, but among their peers their status was a kind of open secret. The U.S. Army in World War II was a brutal place for homosexuals. As historian Stephen E. Ambrose notes, "They were stripped of all insignia, drummed out of the service, given long sentences in the stockade, disgraced without mercy."

But not in the 603d. "There was quite a lot of homosexuality in the unit," William Flemer says. "It was very active, but fairly covert. But there wasn't a great stigma attached to it. We thought it just went with the artistic temperament."

One of the more flamboyant was Benno de Terry, the Anglo-Hungarian son of the director of the State Museum for Fine Arts in Budapest. He had studied art and economics in Italy, France, and Berlin and spoke five languages. When he admired something, he would say, "Simply faaaabulous!" and wave a cigarette in a long holder. After the war, he would visit Harold Dahl, the sculptor and art appraiser, boasting, "I had everything in my bed including a snake and a second lieutenant, and of the two the snake seemed less dangerous!"

What kind of attitude would such men bring to the army?

But Sollohub was first and last a loyal soldier. He put his reservations aside. As long as he was in it, his attitude was: *It's my outfit, and I'm going to make it the best outfit I can.* "We had only one responsibility," he says, "and that was getting ready."

He put his troops through their paces. First, basic training: lots of marching, twenty-mile hikes lugging full field packs, close-order drill with heavy 1903 Springfield rifles, endless calisthenics. Then the obstacle course: scrambling up and over high board walls, monkey-swinging under a horizontal ladder, swinging on ropes across mud pits, high-stepping through a maze of old tires, crawling under barbed wire while machine gunners sprayed live ammo over their heads.

He took them to a remote range and made them dig foxholes in the frozen ground—deep ones—then ran tanks over their heads so they would know what armor sounded like right up close, how it could crush you if you didn't stay put.

Surprisingly, the artists took it all in stride. "We had an awful lot of really rugged basic training to get through," Blass reflects. "But it wasn't a feat—surprisingly not, considering our outfit was *not* made up of people who had been playing football the season before."

Sollohub was impressed with the performance of his men. "I was always pleased and happy with this unit," he says.

He knew at the time that he had two big advantages: First, most of these guys were volunteers for the camouflage corps. They didn't dare screw up enough to get reassigned to the infantry. Second, there was a war on, and that created a certain urgency, a seriousness of purpose. "It was an easy time to be a commander," Sollohub admits. "They all recognized they had a responsibility—even the youngsters were aware of that."

After physical conditioning came marksmanship—making sharpshooters out of guys who had never seen a rifle, let alone a machine gun, except in the movies. Qualifying day was raw, windy, and rainy, terrible shooting weather. A shooter had to keep a steady grip on a slippery wooden rifle stock, sight through blowing rain, and allow for windage. One by one, platoon by platoon, the men took their places on the firing line.

And one by one, the guys in C Company "boloed"—army slang for failing to qualify.

Jim Laubheimer, a Baltimore kid who had joined the army with only a year of night school in art under his belt, had a natural eye for drawing whatever he saw. Like many of the guys in his outfit, he carried his sketch pad everywhere. The guys mostly knew him for his piano and guitar playing. He could play "Stardust," "Body and Soul," all the jazz standards, by heart. He could sit in with a barracks combo and just swing all night long.

But he always struggled with his rifle. He could take the damned thing apart, all right—he just couldn't seem to get all the pieces back together. When his turn came, the instructor bawled at him, "Get that arm up! Flatten your feet! Keep the goddamned thing pointed downrange!"

Laubheimer also had a blind spot in his right eye.

"SQUEEZE that trigger!" the instructor yelled. Laubheimer squinted and the bull's-eye all but disappeared. He recalls, "So it was that I stood on the firing line in the wind and rain, made none of the allowances that I had learned about, and simply blasted away to get the whole thing behind me."

He outscored every man in the whole company, missing "expert" by only one point and winning a three-day pass.

Colonel Sollohub took them out on bivouac, hiking them through the rugged country of western Maryland in the dark, to camp in the open under the stars. He sent a soldier to climb a peak miles away with orders to strike a match—and the troops were astonished they could spot a match flaring bright as a muzzle flash from that incredible distance. It was the best kind of lesson—not words, but a visual sensation that imprinted itself on their memories and that could save their lives later in combat, when they craved a smoke.

Only then could he begin to train them as camouflage engineers.

Camouflage was a technique that carried an ancient legacy.

When the Romans assaulted Syracuse from the sea in 212 B.C., they stormed ashore onto a false beach constructed out of straw by the Greek defenders. The "beach" collapsed and the Greeks slaughtered the Romans as they floundered helplessly in the deep water.

The notorious Trojan horse was disguised as a gift. In reality, as Homer recorded, it was an assault vehicle.

In medieval times, outnumbered armies constructed sham battlements out of canvas and wood to appear stronger than they were.

The British had stumbled upon camouflage as early as 1846, when the colonial Indian Guides dyed their white uniforms the color of mud—"khaki," from the Urdu word for "dust." By the late nineteenth century, British units in India had adopted khaki, and by the turn of the century, khaki uniforms were standard issue for all British troops, who expected to fight not in France, as they did in World War I, but in colonial deserts.

But the real father of the modern camoufleurs was an eccentric American figure painter named Abbott Handerson Thayer.

Thayer had studied in Paris, then returned to Dublin, New Hampshire, where he zealously embraced a new vision of American art—epitomized by an 1893 painting, "A Virgin," in which his eldest daughter, Mary, leads her younger siblings by the hand. The children are robed in classical style, and a pair of billowing clouds form angelic wings behind Mary's back. The effect is of ethereal, tranquil beauty. Thayer's kindred spirits in this new vision included James McNeill Whistler and Augustus Saint-Gaudens—whose son Homer formed the first American camouflage corps and remained the leading expert on camouflage in the U.S. until the outbreak of World War II.

A small, wiry, bullet-headed man, Thayer dressed year-round in a tatty Norfolk jacket and long woollen underwear, cutting the legs off shorter and shorter as the season gradually warmed, and herded his family outdoors to camp in subzero temperatures. Richard Meryman, whose namesake father served as a second lieutenant in the American Camouflage Corps in World War I, wrote, "An Emersonian transcendentalist, he found in nature an unsullied form of the purity, the spiritual truth, and the beauty he sought in his painting."

In the 1890s, through his field studies as a naturalist, Thayer became obsessed with the natural camouflage of birds. His 1909 treatise, *Concealing-Coloration in the Animal Kingdom,* introduced the modern theory of camouflage. Creatures—like armies—either *blend* into their environments, effectively disappearing, or they *disrupt* their forms, appearing to be something they are not. Their most potent defense against predators, Thayer argued in his classic treatise, was *countershading:* a bird's top feathers and crown, for example, are colored dark, its undersides a contrasting lighter shade. "In the case of a great many birds and beasts, including virtually all those which have become famous for their power of hiding in plain sight, such as rabbits, quails, partridges, etc., it is developed to an exquisitely elaborate degree," wrote his son and collaborator, Gerald. "By its aid they are often virtually obliterated, in that the eye judges them as spaces through which the background is seen."

Countershading was a blending mechanism. The opposite effect—bright or extravagant patterns, such as the brilliant plumage of tropical birds or a zebra's stripes—disrupt an object's form and render it invisible.

Thayer perfected his treatise by studying some fifteen hundred bird skins he had collected personally on local hikes up Mt. Monadnock and on excursions farther afield in the eastern United States, Europe, and South America. He was fond of inviting natural history "experts" to view a demonstration of decoy birds—either stuffed specimens or models painted with his countershading—arranged in the open against their natural habitat. Then he would challenge them to find the birds, hidden in plain sight. They rarely could.

As the great powers turned to war in 1914, Thayer became an obsessive apostle for camouflage, tirelessly promoting his treatise to the British and the French, who were the first to apply his theories seriously on the battlefield. When America entered the war in 1917, other prominent artists presented their ideas for camouflaging warships, including Gerome Brush, Louis Bouché, Thomas Casilear Cole, and William Andrew Mackey. Thayer pleaded with Assistant Secretary of the Navy Franklin D. Roosevelt not to accept the secondhand perversion of his theories. "It will be disastrous if, after all, they dabble in my discoveries," Thayer wrote. "I beg you, be wise enough as to try accurately, mine, first."

Whether a perversion or an application of his theories, soon American and British warships were painted with experimental "dazzle" camouflage—striking and disruptive geometric patterns, often painted in brightly contrasting blues, oranges, and whites. The object was not so much to hide the vessel—which was nearly impossible on the open sea—but to distort its image, confuse the enemy as to what size and kind of ship it was and in which direction it was heading.

Soon dazzle camouflage became the rage, for seagoing ships and "ships" of the land: tanks. Dazzle colors were laid on in patterns mimicking the bloom of foliage, the face of rock. Inside the Fort Meade Museum, a type of dazzle-painted World War I tank stands on display, its machine-gun-scarred hull splashed with garish orange, blue, yellow, and white splotches painted exactly as the originals were by the secret camoufleurs at Thetford, England, in 1916.

Later, as the war took to the skies, airplanes were similarly painted—the elaborately decorative lozenge patterns utilized by the Austrians and Germans are primary examples of colorful geometrics.

Thayer had long argued that the use of animal skins and feathers, even the elaborate tattooing of certain indigenous tribes in South America, Africa, and the Antipodes, were not merely based on magic or superstition but on the practical need to remain hidden from enemies. But camouflage was often both at once—practical *and* magical.

Dazzle soon attracted a superstitious following. Though many scientific experts remained skeptical, sailors insisted their ships be painted in dazzle, believing that the strange camouflage would magically ward off U-boat attacks. By the end of the war, more than three thousand British merchantmen had distorted their hulls with brilliant-colored dazzle. One officer reported that sailing in a convoy of dazzle-painted ships was "like being in the middle of a floating art museum."

And somehow the peculiar magic worked: U-boats sank fewer than one percent of American ships painted in dazzle camouflage.

European troops marched into the maw of the First World War attired in bright tunics and flashy headgear. Before long, though, the Germans were melding into the monochrome of the trenches in field-gray, the French in horizon-blue, which appears flat and indistinct at dusk and dawn, the hours of most attacks. Long before war's end, the French had even discarded their traditional *pantalons rouges*.

Some observers have compared the changing color fashions of armies to the European movement from Romanticism (bright, distinct colors) to Impressionism (indistinct and fading pastels) to Cubism (jungle "tiger-stripes," splotchy woodland camouflage browns and greens). In World War II, for the first time, soldiers experimented with uniforms that actually fragmented the human form.

In Thayer's terms, they began wearing concealing coloration.

Though camouflage had been practiced for as long as warfare, the term *camouflage* first came into use during World War I—a corruption of *camouflet*, a small mine used to collapse an enemy's tunnel under your lines or to throw up smoke and conceal troop movements. Even that term derived from a practical joke: one lights a paper cone and holds it under a sleeping victim's nose. The smoke flutes into his nostrils at the broad part of the cone and he awakes coughing. The word comes from the Old French *camoufler*, smoke.

Camoufler evolved a new meaning that resonates with the mission of the Special Troops: to disguise, make unrecognizable, or conceal the true nature of. Probably that usage originally applied to theatrical makeup.

The French experiment with camouflage also began in World War I. Credit is usually given to Guirand de Scévola, who first devised netting to hang over artillery pieces to hide them from aerial observation. In 1915, the French high command authorized the formation of a camouflage section headed by de Scévola, who explained, "In order to totally deform objects, I employed the means Cubists used to represent them. Later this permitted me, without giving reasons, to hire in my section some painters, who, because of their very special vision, had an aptitude for denaturing any kind of form whatsoever."

In World War I, the French alone fielded a camouflage contingent of 1,200 officers and enlisted men, many recruited from the École des Beaux Arts in Paris, supported by 8,000 women who painted, sewed, and constructed camouflage devices in factories behind the front lines.

Camouflage could be hazardous duty, according to camouflage historian Guy Hartcup: "The camoufleur was required, for example, to crawl out into no-man's-land at dawn or dusk and record the enemy field of fire by sitting with his back to the German lines to sketch the landscape."

Naturally, the French headquartered their training center for camoufleurs in Paris. Eventually the French camouflage corps included 190 painters—including noted Cubists Jean-Louis Boussingault, Charles Dufresne, and Jacques Villon—six sculptors, five architects, and five cartoonists, along with carpenters, mold makers, and assorted technicians. Appropriately, the French camoufleurs chose for their insignia a chameleon.

Georges Braque, whose Cubist technique inspired Ellsworth Kelly, was not a camoufleur but served in the French army. "I was happy when, in 1914, I realized that the army had used the principles of my cubist paintings for camouflage," he commented after the war. "Before cubism we had Impressionism, and the army used pale blue uniforms, horizon-blue, atmospheric camouflage."

Scores of well-known French, British, and American artists worked in camouflage schools and training centers throughout the First World War, lending camouflage a certain artistic cachet—so it's not surprising that when the Second World War came along, American artists and designers enthusiastically signed on. The 603d Engineer Camouflage Battalion at Fort Meade was, in fact, a distant offspring of the old World War I "Camouflage Corps," also composed of artists. When Gen. John "Black Jack" Pershing arrived in France with his American Expeditionary Force in 1917, he observed British and French camouflage sections already in full swing: covering gun batteries from aerial observation, screening roads, building hollow steel tree trunks to hide observers and snipers, even using rows of pop-up plywood soldiers to simulate an attack.

Pershing wanted an American Camouflage Corps, and he got it. Homer Saint-Gaudens, son of the renowned sculptor Augustus Saint-Gaudens, rallied to the cause a distinguished band of three hundred other sculptors, painters, advertising men, designers, and architects. For practical help in constructing camouflage devices, he also recruited technical specialists— electricians, carpenters, machinists, even Hollywood set designers and prop men. They trained at American University in Washington, D.C., before going "over there."

At their university proving ground, like their descendants in the 603d, they learned to erect "flattops" from actual fishnets. Later nets were designed specifically for camouflage from a variety of rope and wire materials. "Fishnets" would remain the staple item of camouflage for the rest of the century.

The insignia of the American Camouflage Engineers in World War II, like the French Camouflage Corps of World War I, also featured a silver chameleon crawling invisibly across a silver branch on a red shield, under which a banner proclaimed: "We Conceal Our Might."

After weathering a few artillery barrages in Normandy, some wits in the 603d modified their motto slightly, to read: "We Conceal Our Fright."

During their training classes at Fort Meade, the camoufleurs of the 603d studied the British methods. At El Alamein, Montgomery created fake railheads, bogus armored columns, and battalions of "Chinese soldiers"— literal straw men—to draw enemy bombardment away from his real troops. He moved his columns at night, then covered them from aerial reconnaissance with elaborate camouflage, as he did his stockpiles of gasoline and ammunition. The resulting surprise attack drove the legendary "Desert Fox," Gen. Erwin Rommel, from his stronghold in North Africa.

On the home front, the British created fake aerodromes, factories, even fleets to draw off Luftwaffe bombers. In nearly every village, pillboxes disguised as shops, cottages, even bathing cabins, awaited Nazi invaders.

The American camoufleurs mastered basic engineering, then tackled more sophisticated camouflage projects.

"I was not a desk commander," Julian Sollohub, their leader, says. Beginning at eight o'clock every morning, the men would tackle field problems, and Sollohub would patrol the area, checking on their progress. Once they had to build a log bridge over a creek down near the Chesapeake Bay, then trust it enough to drive their own trucks across it. More often, to camouflage vehicles or gun emplacements, they raised "flattops": horizontal wire grids strung twelve feet off the ground between stout posts, double-guyed with more twisted heavy-gauge wire pegged into the ground using nine-pound mauls. They'd stretch fishnets over the wire, then weave strips of painted osnaburg, a kind of linen sackcloth, "garlanding" the net, to camouflage the top. It was heavy work.

The enlisted men held contests against their officers to see who could erect a thirty-six-by-forty-four-foot flattop the fastest. A team from A Company held the record: twenty-six and a half minutes.

They also learned silk-screening techniques to create signs and posters. Flemer and his buddy, Alan Wood-Thomas, invented canvas-and-wood decoys of tanks, trucks, and howitzers.

After a few months of classroom instruction and fieldwork, they were good enough to start teaching courses in camouflage to regular troops. Some wrote and acted in radio plays to drive home the value of camouflage. A model-making unit constructed scale reproductions of camouflage installations for use as teaching aids in seminars and public displays.

Some of the men—Blass, Shilstone, Laynor, and Flemer among them—were detailed to Long Island to camouflage giant railroad guns. "The first time the guns went off, the nets came down over everybody," Shilstone reports, laughing out loud at the memory. "I mean, it was like a school of fish—everybody trying to get out! So we were the 'experts.'"

But other demonstrations were more effective.

One of their favorites was to hide a dozen guys under camouflage in an open field. They'd march a company of infantry or tankers out there and say straight out, "This field is full of soldiers—find 'em!" The recruits never believed it. They'd wander about, and one by one the camoufleurs would pop up out of their hiding places, rifles leveled, scaring the hell out of them.

"They're looking for *people* out there," Jim Laubheimer explains. "We weren't *people*—*weeds* would suddenly stand up and confront you with a rifle."

When Sgt. Chester Piasecki—who was supposed to do it—succumbed to stage fright, Dowd served as ringmaster for their biggest demonstration, a camouflage show for a thousand troops, including WACs and nurses.

And there were the bizarre assignments.

One day a colonel showed up and asked, "Can anybody fly a kite?" They were all savvy enough by now to be wary of volunteering for anything in the army, but Laubheimer couldn't resist: he raised his hand, as did a few others. They trucked the volunteers down to the airstrip and gave them a huge white box kite with a large camera attached. The idea was to be able to conduct unmanned aerial reconnaissance. For a solid week, Laubheimer and his pals roared up and down the airstrip in their truck, having a ball, trying to get the contraption airborne. Time and again the kite would swoop and stall and crash back to earth. They never did make it fly—but it was better duty than digging foxholes and pounding in flattops. So next time, when they asked for volunteers who could paint and letter, Laubheimer jumped right in. He says, "I spent a weekend painting 'Edible' and 'Nonedible' on trashcans."

Hal Laynor began to slim down. The army was toughening him.

On leave to New York one night in June 1943, he took Gloria Silberman on a horse-drawn hansom cab ride around Central Park and proposed to her. He was broke, but he gave her a two-carat diamond ring. The diamond had come from his grandfather's stickpin. It was so conspicuous, she was afraid to wear it on the subway, so she hid it under a glove.

In October 1943, they were married. They honeymooned for two nights together at the Park Central Hotel in New York. He used to come home to her every chance he got, avoiding his family, though—his overprotective mother, Gussie, couldn't leave her only child alone with his wife, so he sneaked home and glided through his old neighborhood like a ghost.

He and Gloria celebrated New Year's Eve 1943 together at Fort Meade, in her hotel room, which cost two dollars a night. Hal sneaked in through a window, so they wouldn't charge for the extra person. Between them, they shared a Coke and a hamburger. But he didn't complain, nor did she. The way he saw it, they were together. "For the rest of our lives," he told her, "we'll always have more than we have right now." They talked and laughed half the night. They were just kids, too full of romance to worry about the future.

• • •

After nine months, at the beginning of 1943, Colonel Sollohub's transfer came through—once again, a disappointment. Instead of shipping out for the war, he moved down the road to Fort Belvoir, Virginia, to teach camouflage, demolition, and mine warfare at the Engineer School. He would languish there for two more years, in the inexplicably named Department of Natural Resources.

His troops were sorry to see him go. Richard Morton, a graduate of the Pratt camouflage course who worked in headquarters company and saw him often, summed up his commander this way: "Very sharp, lean, intelligent, fair minded, and well liked."

His replacement was one of his old subordinates from the 84th, Maj. Otis Fitz.

Sollohub considered Fitz a fine officer, and Fitz believed wholeheartedly in the camouflage mission. At forty somewhat older than Sollohub, he was a stout New York reservist who got along with everybody. Louis Porter, a department-store display man out of New Iberia, Louisiana, remembers that Fitz wasn't quite the West Point paragon that Sollohub was. "He was a kind of scholarly-looking fellow, civilian with a little mustache. A little rotund, with a buoyant personality. Cleaning his pistol in his office, he fired through the floor one time. He also wrecked his jeep one time. He was kind of a bumbler."

Fitz was popular, but he had a harder task than Sollohub. The camoufleurs were beginning to lose their edge. They had trained hard for nine months, and now all they were going to do was train some more. Nobody seemed to have a mission for them—except doing the same old thing over and over. They had expected to use their genius in design, to invent and create, and instead they were performing basic engineering tasks.

For diversion, they staged variety shows. Laynor pulled his stand-up comedy routine, impersonating celebrities and mimicking Jewish and Irish dialects. "Last night they had a variety show," Harold Dahl wrote home. "Only two things were any good: one, our Elliot Atkinson, who plays piano so well, and the other is a new fellow in our company, named Levinsky [Laynor], who did slapstick pantomimes that rolled us over in the aisles. He is a funny looking bird to start with and is very clever on the stage."

Another artist, Paul Seckel, performed a wild Hitler burlesque. At the B Company beer party, Fitz even chimed in with a Rudyard Kipling song. The unit did go on maneuvers in the swamps of Louisiana, where the troops wallowed in mud and mosquitoes, slept in hammocks strung between trees, and kept a sharp eye out for deadly coral snakes, but it was another whole year before the army figured out what to do with them.

• • •

In the early summer of 1943, there was not a single Allied soldier fighting on the continent of Europe.

The British, Americans, and French were solidly entrenched in North Africa. The next obvious step was to get troops onto the continent somehow—either across the Mediterranean into southern France or Italy, or across the English Channel into northwestern France.

In England, there was some confusion about command.

Lieutenant General Jacob Devers, USA, commanded the European Theater of Operations—ETO. As yet, no supreme allied commander had been appointed to oversee the war in Europe—since in effect there was no ground war in Europe. But in anticipation of the invasion of France, there had been named a chief of staff of the supreme allied commander (COSSAC), British lieutenant general Frederick E. Morgan, who was now in charge of all future planning until a supreme allied commander was appointed. He in turn created a Cover and Deception staff of naval, air, and army officers.

Once the Combined Chiefs of Staff of Britain and the U.S. determined that the Allies simply weren't ready for a cross-Channel invasion, the focus turned to the Mediterranean: they would invade Sicily in July and then move on Italy. In the East, the Russians were facing 160 German divisions, nearly two and a half million men, now closing in on Stalingrad. To draw troops away from the intended landing sites in Sicily—and also to help relieve the tremendous pressure on the Russian forces—Morgan's Cover and Deception staff concocted an elaborate scheme, called COCKADE. Its aim was to make the Germans believe the Allies were in fact preparing to invade Norway, the Brest Peninsula, and the Pas de Calais area—not Sicily.

Dummy landing craft, called BIGBOBS, were assembled at strategic ports, dummy aircraft arranged on Scottish airfields; real gliders were lined up on dummy airfields and real aircraft maneuvered in such a way as to draw attention to their activity. Meanwhile, real troops conducted training and embarkation exercises in England, and Allied agents and double agents—"special means"—disseminated false information to the enemy. The plan failed miserably.

The Germans didn't take the bait, didn't move a single soldier or tank from Sicily or Italy or the Russian front to counter the phantom threat. In fact, by the time of the landings on July 10, they had actually moved some of the few troops they could spare *out* of northwest France to reinforce Italy.

Deception had backfired, and but for the Russians tying up all those Panzer divisions in the East, the effect could have been disastrous.

A top-secret War Department report on the European Theater of Operations concluded, "The lesson learned by the Americans concerned was that, to succeed, a cover operation must be in scale with the facts. The notional COCKADE assault was wildly out of proportion to the real forces available." In other words, the feint was simply implausible.

Deception works best when it reinforces what the enemy already believes—what is possible and therefore likely. Since the Germans knew the Allies had only begun building up troops and materiel in England, they could not be persuaded to turn their beliefs a hundred and eighty degrees overnight.

Fortunately, a second deception would prove far more successful. A team of young, brazen officers from British intelligence had concocted a scheme to costume a corpse in the uniform of fictional Combined Ops officer, then set is adrift in a partially deflated life raft in the Mediterranean off the coast of Spain, where it would surely be discovered. Just as surely, the fascist authorities would allow the Germans to examine the body—and any papers it carried. Handcuffed to the wrist of "Major Martin" was a briefcase containing carefully forged dispatches, including one which left no doubt that the Allies planned to bypass Sicily and invade Greece and Sardinia simultaneously. As then-lieutenant commander Ewen Montagu, one of the instigators of the plan, recounts in *The Man Who Never Was*, the Germans took the bait and relaxed their vigilance in Sicily.

As the invasion armada headed for Sicily, the COSSAC planners had no way of knowing whether either deception plan had succeeded.

On board the USS *Monrovia*, RAdm. Kent H. Hewitt's flagship, Gen. George S. Patton Jr., wearing his famous brace of ivory-handled revolvers, sought out Lt. Comdr. Douglas Fairbanks Jr. in his cabin. Patton had written an inspirational message for his assault troops, and he wanted Fairbanks to tell him if it would "play." It's a strange scene to envision: the gruff, profane, legendary combat general nervously shifting from foot to foot as the suave young actor-officer reads his script with a critical eye.

The long, bellicose message read in part, "WHEN WE LAND WE WILL MEET GERMAN AND ITALIAN SOLDIERS WHO IT IS OUR HONOR AND PRIVILEGE TO ATTACK AND DESTROY. MANY OF YOU HAVE IN YOUR VEINS GERMAN AND ITALIAN BLOOD, BUT REMEMBER THAT THESE ANCESTORS OF YOURS SO LOVED FREEDOM THAT THEY GAVE UP HOME AND COUNTRY TO

CROSS THE OCEAN IN SEARCH OF LIBERTY. THE ANCESTORS OF THE PEOPLE WE SHALL KILL LACKED THE COURAGE TO MAKE SUCH A SACRIFICE AND REMAINED AS SLAVES."

Overwhelmed by the famous general's overbearing presence, Fairbanks hardly knew how to respond. It would play.

Fairbanks took an integral part in the Sicily landings, staging offshore diversions of sonic programs and pyrotechnics with his PT boats to draw enemy troops away from the two British and three American landing sites.

On 10 July 1943, nine Allied divisions swarmed ashore in landing zones on the southern and southeast coasts of Sicily. Montgomery commanded the Eastern Task Force, made up five divisions of the famous British Eighth Army, and Patton commanded the Western Task Force, made up of U.S. Seventh Army. Under cover of a fleet of battleships, cruisers, aircraft carriers, and destroyers, 1,839 landing craft ferried the assault troops to the beaches.

In spite of COCKADE's failure, the invasion succeeded brilliantly. The Germans were waiting for the invasion, but Field Marshal Albert von Kesselring, in command of German and Italian forces in Sicily, had guessed wrong about where the landings would occur. He massed his most powerful forces on the western coasts, where in fact an earlier Allied plan had called for embarkations. Fairbanks and his Beach Jumpers, projecting the sounds of invasion, staged diversions on the western flank of the British assault, and this no doubt helped Kesselring guess wrong. The fact that Allied planners had changed their minds eight different times about where and how their armies would assault Sicily probably also contributed to the German field marshal's error. If even the Allies couldn't decide where to land, how was he to predict the landing sites?

Luck and tactical deception, not the cover plan COCKADE, had carried the day. Allied planners would learn from their dangerous mistake. When in February 1944 they began to concoct an elaborate deception plan to cover the D-Day invasion in Normandy (code-named FORTITUDE) they strove to make it plausible. They waited until enough American troops and matériel had been amassed in Britain to make an invasion now seem possible. Then they took advantage of the fact that the Germans already *believed* that the best route for an Allied attack lay across the Pas de Calais—not through the rough water off Normandy. The Allied deception plan merely reinforced that false belief.

However good the new cover plan, it was clear that better means to carry out deception had to be invented if there was to be a cross-Channel invasion against the heavily fortified Atlantic Wall—Hitler's coastal defense line of concrete bunkers, marine minefields, and heavy guns along the coast of France—and then to forge onto Germany. General Devers, who as commander but not planner had been left holding the bag for the failure of COCKADE, appointed his own Cover and Deception staff and directed them to study the problem.

The result: "This study recommended to General Devers that the War Department be requested to activate, equip, and train a field deception unit capable of simulating one corps, consisting of one infantry and one armored division, by means of prefabricated portable dummies together with appropriate radio communications."

Back in Washington, Joint Security Control—the agency corresponding to the top level of Fairbanks's original pyramid plan—acted on the recommendation. By October 1943, it had designed such a deception unit, enlarged at the suggestion of General Bradley to be able to mimic three whole divisions. Bradley was Supreme Commander Eisenhower's choice to command 12th Army Group once enough American divisions were ashore in France, and its Special Plans Branch would direct the activities of the new deception unit. It would be built around the 379-man 603d Engineer Camouflage Battalion and incorporate a sonic deception company to take advantage of the work being done at the Army Experimental Station. Thus would be activated the 3132d Signal Service Company Special, 8 officers and 137 enlisted men.

Also included were two other units. The first was the 244th Signal Operations Company, a radio communications outfit. Since it would be performing "spoof" radio scripts to mislead the enemy as well as handling actual battlefield communications, 100 new radio operators were added, giving it a total strength of 11 officers and 285 enlisted men. The new unit was designated the 23d Signal Company Special.

Finally, in order to protect the deception troops from both the enemy and unauthorized civilians and friendly troops who were not to know their secrets, the Joint Security Control plan called for combat engineers— Company A of the 293d Engineer Combat Battalion, which had recently been training at Patton's vast and rugged Desert Training Center at the current site of Joshua Tree National Forest near Indio, California.

This seasoned and disciplined force was renamed the 406th Combat Engineer Company Special: 5 officers, including its tough commander, Captain George A. Rebh, and 163 enlisted men.

In order to give it the best chance to work with a variety of combat units in the field, Army Ground Forces selected a cadre of headquarters officers from each of the combat specialties: infantry (Simenson), armor (James W. Snee), field artillery (John W. Mayo), antiaircraft (Frederick E. Day), and signals (Charles H. Yokum).

These officers, all lieutenant colonels, would act as liaisons with combat units in the field when planning a particular deception operation. Curiously, though specified in the unit's table of organization, no engineer officer was appointed. Likely the commander of the 603d was expected to fill that role.

All the pieces were coming together. Thus on 20 January 1944, the 23d Headquarters Special Troops was born. Its strength, including the headquarters staff, was 82 officers and 1,023 enlisted men. One of the most revered officers would be a thirty-six-year-old lieutenant colonel named Cliff Simenson.

The camoufleurs at last got their orders to move out. But instead of going overseas, they headed by train to Tennessee, to join Simenson at Camp Forrest, where they would learn the tradecraft of deception.

FOUR

ARTISTS OF RAZZLE-DAZZLE
January–May 1944

The essence of successful deception is truth which presents a false picture.
          —Joint Psychological Warfare Committee, 2 May 1942

At last, Lt. Col. Cliff Simenson was out in the field.

He'd been chained to a desk in Washington on the general staff of Army Ground Forces for the last two years. He was the conscientious officer who had pulled all-nighters, sorting out which divisions were ready to go to North Africa. As a mere captain among colonels, he had written the definitive—and controversial—minority report urging the army *not* to adopt a plan for mechanized infantry divisions, a decision that would save the army countless casualties in Normandy. He had helped sort out the mobilization of an army that had ballooned from fewer than 150,000 men the year he graduated West Point to more than seven million.

Now on a January day in 1944, Simenson was soaring along high above the airborne training school at Fort Bragg, North Carolina, inside the drumming fuselage of a C-46, getting ready to jump out of a perfectly good aircraft.

He'd just arrived at Fort Bragg after a short training stint at Fort Leavenworth, and he was eager to get on with it. This morning he had sat chatting with the airborne commander, Lt. Col. Chet Degarve, over coffee. Simenson was saying how he didn't see why he had to do all that jumping-off-tables stuff—ground school—just to learn how to parachute out of an airplane.

"When do you want to jump?" Degarve asked.

"Anytime."

"How about one o'clock this afternoon?"

Now when the green light flashed and he felt the jumpmaster's pat on the back, he leapt into the wild blue yonder and immediately felt the winter air slam into his body. He tumbled in the high-altitude wind, not knowing which way was up. The force of the wind pressed his eyelids shut, and for a long time he couldn't get his bearings. Breathing came hard—he almost blacked out. Then, with deliberate calm, he got his breath, forced open his eyes, righted himself, checked the risers on his parachute, and began steering himself toward the landing zone. He enjoyed the ride down under beautiful Carolina blue skies and landed squarely—and safely—on his ass.

It was his first and last jump. He won his airborne certificate and the coveted *P* insignia, which he was authorized to wear, he claims, only on his pajamas.

He landed, gathered his chute, and jeeped back to headquarters. The next day, he got a call from General Riley Ennis, an old friend and colleague from the general staff of Army Ground Forces, which assigned officers to various units. General Ennis ordered Simenson to report immediately to Camp Forrest, Tennessee, as plans and operations officer for a new outfit called the 23d Headquarters Special Troops.

"What did I do wrong?" Simenson asked him.

"I can't tell you—it's security," Ennis said. "But you'll find out."

Simenson was chagrined. He had put in his time, paid his dues, and instead of going to war he was once again being sidetracked to a stateside billet. "I didn't like the assignment," he admits. "I really would have liked to get an infantry battalion, because that was what I was qualified for and that was what I'd hoped for."

Simenson was a trim career soldier, five feet ten inches tall, his sandy hair close cropped. He was West Point class of '34, and looked it. His blue eyes were steady, focused, his nimble brain always at work analyzing, interpreting, judging what he heard, separating the irrelevant details from genuine intelligence. He smiled easily, liked to laugh at a good joke. Spoke softly but with insistent confidence.

In his wildest imagination, he had never dreamed he would be fighting the war like this. He'd always thought he would be commanding infantry, charging right at the enemy—not beating him with lies, tricks, masquerade, sleight-of-hand, deception.

Simenson had not started out seeking a military career; he just wanted to go to college. He was born in 1909 in Valley City, North Dakota, a town of about five thousand. In his small high school, he was president of both the junior and senior classes, as well as quarterback of the football team. He yearned to break out into a bigger world. For a time he attended the University of North Dakota, but he couldn't afford the tuition to stay in college. Resourceful in a way that would mark him for the rest of his life, Simenson took the entrance exams for the United States Military Academy and the Naval Academy and won appointments to both, but there were no openings that year. An uncle in Fort Wayne, Indiana, intervened, and Simenson entered West Point from Indiana to take the place of a cadet who had flunked out.

Handicapped by his small-town schooling, he struggled at West Point, but he won over his instructors, who wouldn't let him fail, and he graduated in the middle of his class. Almost immediately he married the daughter of a military science instructor at the University of North Dakota, Evelyn Schillerstrom. "You wouldn't class her as a beautiful person— except as you got to know her, her character outshone everything else," Simenson remembers. "Dark eyes, lively, pleasant smile. She was outstanding among the southern belles, who liked to sit around in their white gloves and have tea in the afternoon and not learn anything. Evelyn was a trouper who would go with you anyplace, anytime. This is the type of a young lady who makes a wife permanently."

The marriage would last fifty-two years, until her death.

The first place he took his new bride was the Zamboanga, an outpost more than five hundred miles from Manila, where he trained with the Philippine Scouts, just as Julian Sollohub had done. Less than a month before Pearl Harbor, he was ordered back to the States and a desk on the general staff of Army Ground Forces. Because he worked with the general staff at the outbreak of the war mobilizing seven million men, because he performed constant miracles of organization and logistics, he counted among his friends many of the senior field commanders who would wind up in Europe. They called him Cliff.

And Simenson had learned how to listen—especially to his troops. He understood that valuable ideas often percolated up from the level of the company, the platoon, even the squad. He was a quick study, and he didn't much care who got credit for a good idea, so long as it was put to good use. Like Sollohub, he was ready to do what he had trained for. But he had missed action once, and now, bound for Tennessee, it seemed he would miss the whole war.

• • •

Camp Forrest was named for Confederate general Nathan Bedford Forrest, a fierce and wily soldier who, after the South's defeat, founded the Ku Klux Klan. Like many gargantuan World War II training posts, it had been hastily constructed in the middle of nowhere, where land was cheap and available—in this case eighty-three thousand acres of cantonments, gunnery ranges, and maneuver areas. The nearest town, Tullahoma, would soon be overwhelmed with servicemen. But when Simenson arrived at Camp Forrest to meet Col. Harry L. Reeder, his new CO, the camp was almost deserted—just the two of them and fifty-seven enlisted men. "That's where we assembled and hoped somebody would tell us what to do," Simenson says. "But nobody ever did."

Simenson struggled with another problem. He took seriously the pledge of "Duty, Honor, Country" he had sworn at West Point. Deception seemed less than honorable. He would have to lie, not just to the enemy, but to friendly troops who couldn't be let in on the deception. It seemed sneaky, unfair, downright unmanly, to fight a war of make-believe using ruses, feints, misdirection, and masquerade.

He wasn't just splitting hairs. The rules of international warfare under the Geneva Convention of 1868 specifically outlawed certain kinds of deceptions. It was forbidden, for example, to use a flag of truce to set up an ambush, or to feign surrender in order to attack by surprise. To broadcast news of an armistice or surrender, when in fact such was not the case, would be counted as treachery. Use of enemy uniforms and insignia was also forbidden. And though there was no provision governing the use of friendly uniforms or insignia to mislead the enemy, army regulations specifically forbade impersonation of a higher rank or a different unit. On the battlefield, you could tell certain lies and not others, make use of some pretenses but be condemned for others. Deception was a complicated business, straddling the fine line between acceptable trickery and treachery against the rules of civilized warfare. Simenson fretted about it a lot.

But like Sollohub, Simenson was a true soldier. If such tactics could save American lives, then he would practice them.

Colonel Harry L. Reeder, the commanding officer of the Special Troops, was an old tank soldier, one of the first graduates of the French tank training school in Paris. He'd campaigned against Pancho Villa with the Maryland National Guard on the Mexican border in 1916, served in the army of occupation in Germany after the last war, saw duty in Panama, and most recently commanded the 46th Armored Infantry Regiment of the 5th Armored Division. For him, this assignment was a clear demotion from significant command.

And it may well have been. Vic Dowd, one of the artist-camoufleurs, recalls, "We used to refer to him as the oldest colonel in the United States Army."

Simenson didn't really want to be there. Reeder didn't want to be there. And neither one had any previous training or experience in deception. Simenson admits candidly, "I felt incompetent."

The 603d Engineer Camouflage Battalion, the core of this new unit, had been formed by a commander who wasn't interested in camouflage—though he had done a smart and thorough job of training his troops to handle any camouflage problem that came their way.

Colonel Julian Sollohub had taught them, "Our primary mission is to avoid becoming a target—that's camouflage."

Now that mission had been turned on its head: becoming a decoy target was exactly what they *were* going to do. Camouflage was now only part of their mission. From now on, they were going to perform battlefield deception, which they had not trained for. Which nobody had even defined yet, at least not in the American army. They didn't even have their equipment yet—the pneumatic tanks and artillery pieces that would constitute the props for their "shows."

The plain fact was that a land-based deception unit was a novelty in the army, and there really wasn't anybody to tell them what to do or how to do it; they would have to write the book on battlefield deception themselves. Luckily, the sonic deception units would bring with them valuable tactics developed by Fairbanks and refined by Railey—but until January 1944, Simenson had never even heard of sonic deception. And he wouldn't meet up with the sonic troops until they all shipped out overseas.

While Reeder grumbled, Simenson got busy. Using his common sense, he invented field problems for each company. They learned to dig in, conceal themselves, move at night, set up decoy tanks made of canvas and wood. Many of the camoufleurs worked twelve-hour shifts for weeks on end constructing the decoys, which they would never actually use in combat.

But they learned the basic tricks of placing the tank decoys in realistic locations, learned how to camouflage dummy artillery emplacements a little less expertly than they'd been trained to do, coordinated with radio units sending out false traffic. Captain Irwin C. VanderHeide, the commanding officer of the radio company, knew his stuff, and that helped.

Lieutenant Colonel Merrick Hector Truly joined the Special Troops as exec to Reeder. He and Simenson became friends almost immediately. Truly was West Point class of '31, a tall, affable, gregarious southerner who never met a stranger and used to sit on the wooden porch of his quarters in a favorite rocking chair. "Always rock with the grain, never across it," he liked to say cryptically. Simenson says of Truly, with genuine affection, "I viewed him as the mainstay of our unit." His friends called him Hector.

"All Trulys are tall, lanky, walk with hands clasped behind their back, in a sort of amble," explains his daughter, Jeanne Truly Davis. "He told a tale of walking down the platform of a railroad station in the Deep South going to catch a train, and a redcap came up from behind him and said, 'Excuse me, sir, but are you a Truly from Fayette?' Swore it was true."

Truly had started out as a pilot in the Air Corps, until an ear problem forced him into the infantry. Like Simenson, he had served in the Philippines. After his wife and two children were evacuated by order of General MacArthur, Truly trained Filipino guerrillas and got out just ahead of the Japanese attack. Since the Revolutionary War, a Truly had served in every conflict fought by the American armed forces. Truly's own son, Merrick H. junior, would follow his father to West Point.

Simenson was also lucky to have the services of Fred Fox, a young Signal Corps lieutenant. Fox was a physical lightweight—tall but lean, brown hair, glasses—not a rugged, gung-ho soldier. He looked like a young assistant professor of English, or like a scriptwriter, which he had been before the war. Fox aspired to be an actor and had gone to work for NBC radio with precisely that ambition in mind, for he had acted in Triangle Club shows at Princeton. But they assigned him to write scripts instead. Now he would learn to write a whole different kind of script. Fox was always full of new ideas, constantly writing new memos—stage directions, really. Stop thinking like army drones and start thinking like you're in show business, he urged the other officers.

If Fox weren't so easygoing with such a wry sense of humor, he might have had trouble with Reeder. Instead he found him simply amusing. Fox got along well with everybody, seemed to know just how hard to push, when to break the tension and ease off. Fox had the gift of being able to make other men laugh. He lit up a room with his energy. Hannah Putnam, whom he met while stationed at Camp Forrest and later married, recalls that Fox could enter a roomful of strangers and in half an hour make friends for life. Simenson admired him and listened to him. Fox was the smart guy who had a knack for coming up with the answer and making it seem like somebody else's idea.

In addition to his ready sense of humor, inexhaustible energy, and innovative imagination, Fox had a deeply spiritual side. He was considering joining the ministry after the war, and always pondered the moral and ethical side of his actions and the actions of others. He also had an abiding passion for history.

Fox, who conjured much of the doctrine for employing battlefield deception out of common sense, imagination, and a passion for the theater, enjoyed telling the following story to illustrate the core principles of the mission of the Special Troops, as he and his fellow officers developed them, first at Camp Forrest, then in action on the European battlefield:

It was the day after New Year's, 1777, a raw January afternoon with a bitter wind sweeping down the Delaware River. George Washington surveyed the bleak landscape just south of Trenton, New Jersey: low river country, sparsely wooded, the fields scabbed with frozen snow. His 5,000 ragged colonials had been chased into a trap, backs to the broad, ice-clogged river. Between them and Lord Cornwallis's professional army of 7,500 lay only a narrow creek, the Assunpink—not much of a natural defensive barrier.

Once he had the rebels cornered, in the face of Washington's cannons Cornwallis halted his pursuit. He would rest his troops and attack at his leisure. He bragged of "bagging the fox" in the morning. Well-fed, well-rested British "lobsterbacks," augmented by mercenary Hessians still smarting over their Christmas defeat at Trenton, would close on the miserable rebels in disciplined ranks, their cavalry sweeping across the Assunpink, their infantry volley-firing as they advanced. The Americans didn't stand a chance. By sundown tomorrow, the colonial army would be crushed, the Revolution finished.

Washington had other plans. He guessed that when the British marched on him in the morning, they would leave a garrison ten miles north at Princeton. He issued his orders.

At nightfall, all but four hundred of his troops moved out in absolute silence, iron wagon wheels and gun wheels muffled in heavy cloth, following a road that led south, then east, and finally swept north, detouring around the left flank of Cornwallis's army.

Meanwhile, the four hundred troops left behind dug trenches, stoked the campfires, talked and sang, and generally made as much noise as possible all night long, mimicking the camp sounds of five thousand men preparing to receive the enemy. British sentries stationed just 150 yards away reported great campfires of cedar rails blazing all along the front, the clatter of rebel patrols scouting the lines on horseback, the thud and scrape of entrenching tools.

Shortly before dawn, the four hundred men of Washington's rearguard also slipped away down the back road.

As the morning sun glimmered weakly behind a gunmetal sky, Cornwallis's troops advanced into the American camp and found it abandoned. At almost precisely the same hour, up in Princeton, the tired and footsore colonials surprised two regiments of British reserves and, after a bloody battle lasting just forty-five minutes, killed or wounded some four hundred and completely routed the rest.

Washington had saved his army, with such style that Cornwallis later complimented him on his ruse. He paid the compliment when he surrendered to Washington at Yorktown.

Fox loved the story of Washington's daring maneuver at the Battle of Princeton. He especially delighted in the coincidence of names: Cornwallis habitually referred to Washington as "the Fox," not because he admired his wily tactics, but because he expected to run him to ground after a merry chase. In the rout at Princeton, Washington was reported to have rallied his men personally, shouting, "It's a fine fox chase, my boys!" To Fox, Princeton was a classic use of "razzle-dazzle"—his term for the deceptive antics of the Special Troops, American slang for a "flashy display meant to confuse, bewilder, or deceive."

"What we did was cover and deception," Cliff Simenson says of their exploits. "Cover—we make the enemy believe our actions are harmless. And deception—we try to make the enemy do something or not do something we want."

As Simenson and Truly and Fox developed the doctrine for the Special Troops, they came to understand that Washington's ruse demonstrated the six irreducible elements of a brilliant deception:

First, it had a focus or *target*. The audience was not merely a spy or a reconnaissance patrol but ultimately an enemy *decision maker*: Lord Cornwallis, who could actually order his forces to act or not act in a certain way.

Second, the operation was designed to achieve a specific *objective*—to cause the target adversary to take or not take a particular action. In this case, to convince Cornwallis to proceed with his obvious plan to attack where he thought Washington's army was—but where it was no longer.

Third, the deception was governed by *centralized control*—directed and with overall command by a single leader, in this case, Washington. The Special Troops would eventually learn just how crucially important this principle is.

"All deception begins with an intimate knowledge of the commander's intentions. Where does he want the enemy? What specific mistakes does he desire the enemy to make?" wrote Lt. Col. Ralph Ingersoll and his colleagues in a report prepared by Special Plans Branch at the end of the war. "During a deception operation it is as if there were *two* armed forces in the field—the real and the fictitious. The fictitious, as well as the real, deserves to be—and *can* only be—commanded by the senior commander."

Fourth, the operation enjoyed total *security*. No spies reported to Cornwallis that the Americans were marching out of the trap, no unauthorized noise gave away the plan, no civilians stumbled into camp and then wandered off to alert the British.

In World War II, planners compartmentalized knowledge on a "need-to-know" basis to limit the number of people who could let slip critical information to a spy or collaborator, or anyone who might betray a plan under torture. Security often interfered with communication: when a commander of a real unit didn't know a deception was going on in his area of operation, he could attack on deadly ground. Planners needed to strike a difficult balance between communicating with all those who truly needed to know the details of the deception and keeping it absolutely secret from the enemy.

Fifth, it was *timely*. A deception requires preparation time and time to work on the mind of the adversary. The second of these is crucial since deception is psychological in nature. An additional benefit of deceptive practices is that they cause the enemy to delay action. "It is a basic limitation of deception that it cannot be employed as a last-minute resort," warned the Special Plans Branch report. "This is not only because of limitations imposed by the enemy's communication with his agents, but also because the basic pattern of his thinking must be tampered with and he cannot be expected to commit himself to important decisions as a result of isolated snippets of intelligence."

It also must come off at exactly the right moment. Washington executed his plan at the perfect moment to be effective—while Cornwallis was smugly convinced that the Americans, having retreated from New York down the length of New Jersey, were hopelessly trapped. Washington's army needed only the afternoon to prepare, and the deception needed to last only until daybreak, when the light would give them away to British sentries.

Sixth, the deception was *integrated* with the battle plan. The rearguard of four hundred acted in concert with the march around the flank. Either action without the other would have proved futile.

In addition to identifying these six basic principles, contemporary deception planners define two basic kinds of deceptions. They have merely given formal terms to the tactics adopted and refined by the Special Troops. Any deception plan is a calculated ruse, as the army manual defines the term: "Ruses are tricks designed to deceive the enemy to obtain an advantage. They are characterized by deliberately exposing false information to enemy collection means." The first of these two basic deceptions is "A-Deception," by which the deceiver gives the enemy so many choices that he is paralyzed about how, where, and when to respond. As one historian explains, "The idea is to give your target a kaleidoscope to play with, and then let him use it as a looking glass."

Creating legions of fake troops and tanks would bewilder the enemy with difficult choices. Every army has finite resources, and the decision about where, when, and how to commit troops and tanks was the unglamorous nuts and bolts of the European campaign. Committing them in the wrong place—against a phantom enemy conjured out of sound effects, radio traffic, and rubber dummies—could dangerously weaken the army elsewhere and allow a breakthrough. Overestimating the enemy's strength could be just as disastrous as underestimating it.

Washington's audacious ruse, like Montgomery's at El Alamein, was a classic case of what army planners now call "M-Deception" or *misdirection*— a stage term Fairbanks and others borrowed from the magician's trick of "Now you see it, now you don't." "The strategy of misdirection is clear: to make the enemy very certain, very determined, and completely wrong."

Misdirection was by far the most frequent kind of deception the Special Troops staged: pretending that specific armored units were positioned where they weren't, that attacks were staging far from an actual corridor of attack. They played a kind of shell game on a very large scale, performed a stage play in the grandest theater imaginable—a theater of war big as a continent.

Every deception begins with a *story.*

"The deception story," explains the army field manual on Battlefield Deception, the bible of combat ruses refined from the original doctrine developed and revised by the Special Troops, "is that information conveyed to the target which will cause him to form the desired perception." As the manual makes clear, the point is to inject false truths into the enemy's decision-making process. Those false truths persuade him to act in certain ways advantageous to the deceiver.

Usually the story takes the form of a "concept of operation" statement, a synopsis of the false truth being sold to the enemy. The synopsis of Washington's "story": "My cold and hungry army is played out and trapped, so we will dig in and make our final fight on the ground behind the Assunpink Creek." In order to formulate such a statement, and to conceive such a plan, several other steps and several other points must be kept in mind.

A good deception story creates a *desired perception* in the mind of the target: a view of the battlefield that the target must hold if he is to act as we, the deceiver, want him to—and one that presents either a threat he must counter or an opportunity he may exploit. To succeed, the deceiver has to honestly answer three questions:

1. Who must hold the desired perception? Answer: Cornwallis.
2. What is the perception about? Answer: The ground where the colonial army will make its stand.
3. When and for how long must the perception be held? Answer: From nightfall until dawn.

To fool the enemy, the story must embody four qualities:

First, it must be *believable*. Does it gibe with the enemy's previous military experience about us, the deceiver? Would we really do what the story portrays? Forced into a trap by a superior force, the conventional strategy would have been to dig in and wait for the fight to come to you—as Washington did—since defenders always enjoy the advantages of cover and prearranged order. No European army of Cornwallis's time would attack with an inferior force.

Second, the enemy must be able to *verify* it. Those British sentries acted, in effect, as intelligence gatherers for Cornwallis, as well as unwitting agents for Washington. They confirmed that the rebels were staying put and digging in, exactly as expected. Had the sentries reported odd noises in the dark, or the lack of noises, or that all the fires had guttered out, the story would instantly have ceased to be plausible.

The Special Troops used German observers, reconnaissance patrols and aircraft, and civilian collaborators against the enemy in the same way.

Third, the story must seem *consistent* with all the other facts the target knows about the deceiver. Washington's troops *were* worn out, half-starved, beaten down by sickness and cold, and often unreliable as a fighting force. Faced with losing most of his Continental soldiers when their enlistments ran out on New Year's, three days before the battle General Washington had offered each of his men a bounty of ten dollars to remain in the field for another six weeks. Cornwallis had already defeated the Continentals in one engagement after another, so it was entirely consistent that they would fall into yet another trap and be defeated once more, this time for good.

He knew they had retreated behind Assunpink Creek, for he had watched them go.

Fourth, the ruse must be *executable*—that is, the deceiver's forces must be physically able to carry it off.

Marching exhausted troops in total silence ten miles over uncertain roads in pitch blackness in the dead of winter was a remarkable gamble. In those days, a well-rested, healthy army was doing well to cover ten miles in daylight on a good, familiar road, and no commander in his right mind would expect them to fight at the end of such an arduous march. At any moment, an alert British sentry might hear a wagon wheel creak or a soldier curse the cold or a horse falter, and then Washington's army would be sitting ducks, strung out in the open along a country road, cannons limbered and not ready to fire, commanders unable to organize their troops in the dark against a well-planned ambush.

There were other risks. It's easier to desert an army while on the move, and desertion had already dangerously whittled away Washington's struggling army. In the dark, men could get lost, horses go lame, stragglers stop to rest and get separated from their units and be captured by enemy patrols. The whole army, for that matter, could find itself suddenly lost. And in the morning, men who had been marching all night after the extreme physical exertions of the previous day's battle would be dead on their feet. How could they be expected to attack fresh troops and win?

Deception requires a gambler's eye for the main chance.

"One does not conduct deceptions merely to deceive," the manual reminds us. It is a kind of game, but a game played in deadly earnest for compelling reasons and with dangerous consequences.

A deception operation is essentially a con game, which always plays most effectively when the target has to work a little to be fooled. It exploits his own nature against him. Cornwallis was cocky and craved a warm fire, a glass of brandy, and a good night's sleep before battle; Washington was willing to endure a night of bitter cold in the open, stealing a march as the British general dreamed.

Deception turned British strength into weakness, and American weakness into strength.

Like any good lie, a deception contains as much truth as possible. The deceiver uses what the enemy "knows" to be true against him. In a certain sense, the target *wants* to be fooled. Like those British sentries, he's looking for the target to confirm what he already believes to be true. At that stage of the war, Cornwallis had little respect for Washington. He was just a colonial farmer, not a professional military man, so he could not be expected to come up with a dashing plan. The British sentries confirmed this "truth."

And even if Washington did, by some miracle, concoct a daring plan, his troops didn't have the discipline or ability to carry it off. Cornwallis knew Washington's army was in poor condition, so the logical conclusion was that it would not perform brilliantly. Except at Trenton, where the colonial army had faced groggy Hessians, not British regulars, it had always retreated.

And Cornwallis's own sentries—*not* a conveniently captured deserter who happened to carry marching plans in his pouch—did the final convincing. What they observed was no surprise. In fact, they observed exactly what they were looking and listening for. As the deception manual makes plain, "It is important that the enemy sees what he expects to see."

Targets, like a con man's mark, tend to expect the ordinary, not the extraordinary. They tend to dismiss unlikely events as impossible events. For example, the German high command figured that the Allies were unlikely to land at Normandy. The seas were too rough, the weather too unpredictable, the landing sites too far from the ports of embarkation in England for an invasion fleet to cross the English Channel in fighting order undetected.

It is also true that in many ways a war is a contest of stories—the narrative myth that defines who we are and why we fight. That was Hilton Howell Railey's contention when he investigated the abhorrent state of army morale in 1941: soldiers didn't know that story, or if they had heard it, didn't believe it. Railey knew that victory comes to the story that stands up strongest under the duress of national sacrifice and the violent clash of armies. Ultimately, with two armies more or less equally matched, the side that believes hardest in its own story will triumph. Even Sun Tzu and Clausewitz, the Prussian expert on nineteenth-century war, understood this; they called it the "moral" factor of war. Railey called it "morale": a soldier's implicit belief in his country's war aims, boiled down into straightforward narrative terms.

Though the story must contain an irreducible core of truth, some of that national story is fiction—exaggeration of the virtues of one's country, glossing over severe faults, encapsulating the complex into a simple story line that rings true and inspires the soldier with a sense of larger meaning to his sacrifice. World War II in Europe was a battle of the story of democracy against the story of fascism. The American soldier's story: We, the descendants of a free people, fight to liberate our allies from under the Nazi jackboot.

And with that story came a kind of implicit boast, part deception, because it simply was not true at the outset of the war, and came true only after many staggering defeats: Our army is bigger, stronger, better equipped, braver, and cannot lose. Patton stressed this part of the story in every message to his troops before sending them into battle: The American fighting man is the greatest and best equipped in the world. America is a nation of winners.

That was another crucial component of the effectiveness of American deception operations—they fit within the larger context of the overall story of Allied superiority. Each time, the Special Troops added to the plot with a new local twist, a story to impart caution, even fear, to the enemy: We have more tanks, guns, and troops than you do. You don't stand a chance. Do you still believe your story—that it's your destiny to rule the world for a thousand years?

Every good deception attempts to make the enemy stop believing in the story of why he's fighting and his story's assumption that he will win. When a nation surrenders, it has stopped believing its own story. Now it believes the story of the victor, which has come true. To achieve plausibility and ultimate success, there were—and remain—other important matters to consider when planning a deception. The longer, more complex the deception, the greater the need for sound planning:

Complete the deception story. Fill in the details of "character" and "plot." What troops exactly are playing which roles? Where are they positioned on the "stage"? What specific actions will they perform?

A relatively simple deception, like Washington's, required merely improvisation of familiar tasks. Radio deception, on the other hand, required a carefully edited script so that all the "dialogue" remained consistent with the plot and movement of characters. In every one of its deception operations, each unit of the Special Troops received detailed written plans covering every aspect of the ruse: specific radio messages to send, maps outlining the placement of dummy tanks and support vehicles, the timetable for and specially produced programs of sonic projection.

Identify the deception means. At Assunpink Creek, Washington used reliable troops and basic implements at hand: picks and shovels, fires, cloth to muffle iron wheels, silence, and a road known only to locals. The Special Troops used sonic gear, motorized vehicles, real tanks, dummies, flash bombs, spoof radio, and other special effects.

Develop the deception event schedule. A one-night march, a three-day fake artillery display, a coordinated and timed sonic projection, and so on. The order of events matters. If German observers were to spot dummy tanks *before* they heard them rumble into position, the ruse would become ludicrous, the hoax obvious. In deception as in life, timing was all.

Identify the deception feedback channels. How will we know if our deception is working? Is anybody watching, listening?

In Washington's case, no news meant good news. No alarm was raised, no shots were fired from ambush, and his scouts reported no enemy activity on his line of march. He might fail yet; Cornwallis might be waiting for him at Princeton. But Washington was in desperate straits. If he were discovered, he would be forced to surrender—exactly the end game he had already faced at Assunpink Creek. He would have lost nothing. A high roller with much to win and little to lose, he bet the house—and won.

Once overseas, staff officers like Simenson routinely observed the "show" the Special Troops were staging from church towers, hilltop observation posts, even aircraft, to see if it looked convincing—if it "played." The Special Plans Branch interrogated prisoners, examined reports from agents and recon patrols, pored over captured German documents and maps to discover where the Germans thought a particular American division was located, and most of all observed what the enemy actually did on the battlefield in reaction to the show. They even interviewed nearby friendly troops to learn whether *they* were fooled.

Finally, *develop the termination concept*—when is the show over and how do you wrap it up? And what do you do if it is compromised? One way or another, Washington's ruse would end at Princeton at daybreak. On that cold January morning in 1777, his exhausted troops faced not just a small garrison guard but two regiments marching to reinforce Cornwallis. The Continentals defeated them only by the bold action of an advance guard of 350 Virginians led by Gen. Hugh Mercer, who was mortally wounded in the attack.

For the Special Troops, the problems were more complicated and "termination" timing could be dicey. Once a flash-bomb battery of fake artillery had attracted counterbattery artillery fire from real enemy artillery, the usual smart move was to get the men the hell out of there as quickly as possible—not always easy. A ruse discovered could lead to a deadly counterattack, which would easily overrun the thin line of Special Troops at the front. Even if the ruse worked, the consequences could be dire. In World War II, armies maneuvered more quickly than in 1777. The Germans attacked behind waves of Panzer tanks, communicated by radio, infiltrated spies, photographed and then bombed positions from the air. They could also at any moment shower advancing Allied troops with heavy shells or mortar barrages from miles away, unseen. And when they did, it was no use taking cover under a rubber tank—though instinctively, the camoufleurs often did and joked about it nervously afterward.

The Special Troops most often closed out their shows by fading away in the night under radio silence and by daylight "infiltration," trickling away from the area of the operation in small groups, then reassembling the cast in a new locale, like an outlaw gang splitting up after a heist and meeting back at the hideout.

But for all the meticulous planning it required, all the risks of backfire, all the uncertainty, deception remained a cheap and effective way to cause the enemy to waste his efforts. Cheap because it risked fewer lives, and demanded almost no fighting equipment and only minimal supporting units. Effective because it achieved what the army calls "economy of force": a very small unit could tie up large numbers of enemy infantry, armored vehicles, and artillery pieces so they couldn't affect the outcome of the battle.

Fox called the Special Troops an "Instant Army," and always intended to publish an account of its exploits under that title. They could conjure into being whole divisions with a few strokes of an air pump, a handful of radio messages, and a convincing sonic broadcast. And though they couldn't quite do it instantly, they came close

What is also important to remember is that the Germans were particularly ripe targets for the deceptive practices the Special Troops trafficked in. The German military in World War II had developed sophisticated ways to gather information about the Allies—networks of spies and collaborators, radio interception, infrared aerial reconnaissance, whole staffs devoted to finding and analyzing every scrap of new information that came their way. They were watching closely and listening hard. Sometimes an enemy's or a mark's own wariness or paranoia can be exploited.

Current doctrine confirms this view. "The truth is that the greater the collection capability an opponent has, the greater the opportunity to feed him specifically designed false information." It turned out to be much harder to deceive the Japanese, whose intelligence capabilities were far less extensive, and whose commanders rarely reacted to fresh information— real or bogus—conditioned as they were to proceed with a preconceived plan unless given direct orders to the contrary.

Deception in war is a two-edged sword. Not only can a badly executed deception fail to help, it can actively harm the troops in a real attack by tipping off the enemy to the real plan.

At Camp Forrest, as they concocted field exercises in emplacing dummy equipment and sending out phony radio traffic, Simenson, Truly, and Fox began to learn how to put themselves in the enemy's place, to imagine they were watching the show from his point of view. The enemy was not just an adversary—he was the audience. It required a maddening kind of schizophrenia that came naturally to actors, to theatrical directors, to painters, but not always to soldiers.

Their real education would come in Europe, when they played in earnest in front of the Wehrmacht.

At Camp Forrest, training was even more strenuous than at Fort Meade. The troops noticed a sense of impending deployment to the war. In their few off hours, the camoufleurs sketched the Tennessee countryside or drew portraits of each other. Richard Morton and his pal, *Louisville Times* cartoonist Walter Arnett, drew caricatures of the officers and posted them on barracks bulletin boards. One of Morton's masterpieces was a group caricature of the 603d marching along in disarray, Major Fitz in the lead, singing out cadence to the tune of *"Frère Jacques"*:

> *Six-oh-third, six-oh-third*
> *Camoufleurs! Camoufleurs!*
> *Happy little morons, Happy little morons!*
> *Six-oh-third. Six-oh-third.*

Bill Blass and Bob Tompkins used to hang out together. They both loved to sketch. Tompkins and his new bride, Bunny, rented rooms in a house full of "mountaineers" and kept their own car, and once all three of them drove thirty miles north to McMinnville for dinner at a place that turned out to be a cathouse. They sat on the porch and talked about what they wanted to be after the war.

"I want to be an art director at a big advertising firm," Tompkins said.

Blass said, "I plan on being a world-famous fashion designer."

Neither man doubted the other would accomplish exactly what he set out to do.

There were dances every Friday night at the service clubs, the usual morale-building movies and lectures, four chaplains to conduct religious worship, eight thousand well-thumbed books to read at the post library, and jazz or country combos playing nearly every night in one barracks or another. The frozen winter mud gave way to glutinous spring mud, and at last there was a rumor of movement.

Vic Dowd got the news obliquely, when his popular company commander, Capt. Howard S. Raynor, called him into his office. Raynor was an easygoing CO, smart and quick to laugh. He sat behind his desk smoking a cigar. "Sergeant Dowd, you're from New York, right?" he asked.

"Yes, sir," Dowd answered, wondering where this conversation was leading.

"I've got a job for you. I want you to go to Washington, D.C., and pick up Kennedy, who is AWOL, being held in the army hospital. Bring him back. But you *are* from New York, right?"

Dowd caught on. Raynor was really telling him, *Here's your opportunity to go to New York and see your folks, because we're about to go overseas.* So Dowd retrieved Kennedy, but first he spent a couple of nights in New York saying good-bye to his family. For the others, there were no furloughs.

They had been well briefed on the need for secrecy. Sculptor Dahl wrote his sister in New Jersey, "Another thing—see to it, even if you have to explain it to whoever reports news from Towaco, that nothing gets in the paper if and when we leave. And you and Mother & the others must take it as part of your burden not to so much as tell anyone that I have gone until I get there and mail comes back to you. And *then*, if you get an idea where I am, *don't tell anyone*, no matter who. This thing we are doing might be suspected if it gets out that the 603d is gone—we must be simply forgotten— until after our job is done."

The Special Troops traveled by train to Camp Kilmer, New Jersey, then, on the night of 2 May 1944, embarked on a train-carrying barge for a tow up the Hudson to the Forty-sixth Street pier, in later years the permanent berth of the aircraft carrier USS *Intrepid*. Shilstone could look out over the river toward Weehauken on the bluffs of the Palisades and see a light burning in the house where he was born.

Fred Fox had made a date to take his fiancée, Hannah, to the circus with his parents, but he never showed up. That's how she found out he was shipping out for the war. Just before going overseas, Fox wrote to her, "As you know, it will be harder for me to practice caution. I am traveling into a violent world where timid men are a liability. . . . If I don't come home, please don't think that I am the only one with whom you could have lived the most wonderful life in the world."

Ellsworth Kelly remembers his feelings as the Special Troops quietly filed aboard the liner USS *Henry Gibbons*. They boarded well after midnight, the city's wartime skyline dimmed out, no fanfare or well-wishers to see them off. "We knew we were going to war. When we left New York, we were very fatalistic—we thought we weren't coming back."

The 603d Engineer Camouflage Battalion had trained longer than most units in the army, but for most of that time they were training for the wrong mission. They weren't ready.

FIVE

DECEPTIVE FIDELITY— THE SONIC CAMPAIGN

1944

What you got was a panorama of sound in motion—but the only thing moving was electrons and sound waves.

—Roy Tucker

Under cover of night, the assault troops paddle across the dark, misty river. Once across, they open fire in a fierce surprise attack and overwhelm the startled defenders. The Germans weren't expecting them here—five miles upstream from a fixed bridge the Americans have already captured and are holding tenuously with a few companies of infantry, waiting for their tanks to come up. The critical news reaches the German commander by telephone at his headquarters in a stone château behind the lines: "They have two bridgeheads, sir—both are being successfully contained," reports his aide.

"All that means is that they're across the river," the general scolds him, left fist cocked on his polished black belt in a stiff Prussian pose. "Having them contained doesn't interest me! I want those bridges eliminated. Where are they?"

His aide leads him to a wall-sized tactical map and briefs him on the situation. An American armored division is reported closing in on the river down a road that leads to the fixed bridge—the logical place for them to cross. But there's a wrinkle: Another road runs along the river on the American side and can put the tanks in position to take advantage of the new bridgehead upstream as well.

At dawn, the Germans will have to decide which bridgehead to counterattack, where to commit their tank destroyers, which are, at the moment, strategically assembled between the two bridgeheads.

It's imperative they get more intelligence—quickly.

Before long, a civilian "line crosser"—a local spy—reports that a jeep bearing the bumper markings of the 66th Armored Division has arrived in his sector, near the new upstream bridgehead. A major general and his staff are setting up a command post there.

"Is he trustworthy?" the general asks archly.

The intelligence officer replies, "I don't trust any of these line crossers, sir—but this one's been right before."

The German general is not convinced. "Maybe they'd *like* us to give them some attention up there—well, we won't." He puffs his cigarette dramatically. "Yet."

But as the night wears on, the picture clarifies. A listening post upstream reports sounds of bridge building, while the listening post miles downstream at the fixed bridge reports hearing a column of tanks veer off the road before reaching the bridge, detouring upstream along the river behind a screen of dense trees and darkness.

Other listening posts concur. The tanks are counted as their treads rumble across a wooden bridge, still heading upstream. Another listening post counts them again as, one by one, they gear down to climb a hill. A third listening post farther on confirms the count as the sound of exhaust cuts out momentarily when they crest the hill and skid down the other side. The observers can't *see* any tank movement—but they've got ears. They're close enough to the river to pick up every move the Americans make, purely by sound. Finally, the listening post that reported the sounds of bridge building now reports that the racket of steel-on-steel hammering has ceased. A new sound has taken its place: tanks forming up and idling, then shutting down their engines.

Now there is no doubt. The prefabricated bridge upstream is finished. The American tanks will advance across it, trying to outflank the Germans. The general makes the decision that will seal their fate. "Proceed as planned!"

The German tank destroyers, the lethal 88s that can punch through the flimsy armor of the Sherman tanks and incinerate them in their own gasoline, move upstream for the kill, to be waiting at dawn for the crossing. Strung out on that bridge, the Shermans will be as vulnerable as targets in a shooting gallery. If only the Americans knew how their noise gave them away.

But somehow, during the night, something has gone radically wrong. The tank destroyers deploy upstream and wait, but no tanks attempt to cross the river there.

Instead, at dawn, battalions of American tanks roll across the fixed bridge downstream, break through the unsupported defense there, destroy the unprotected German artillery, and pound the Germans into a rout.

But there weren't supposed to be any American tanks left downstream. At the château headquarters, the general's aide is shouting into the telephone. "They're coming down the *lower* bridge? Did you say tanks?" The general grabs the phone. "What's all this nonsense about tanks? How did it happen?"

In a dugout on the verge of being overrun, the listening post observer who first reported that the tanks had veered away from the fixed bridge now screams into his field phone, "How the hell do I know how it happened?" And is obliterated by an exploding tank shell.

The battle just described never took place. It was staged for a top-secret training film scripted by Darrel Rippeteau, shot on location at Pine Camp, produced at the Signal Corps studios in Fort Monmouth, New Jersey, starring B-movie actors and real sonic soldiers, and featuring a cameo appearance by Hilton Howell Railey.

The film was propaganda—not against the enemy, but to be played for field commanders, to convince them just how useful such a tactical ruse could be on the battlefield.

The sonic deception it portrayed was very real.

The American major general and his staff were impersonators, costumed in the appropriate uniforms, deliberately playing for an audience of local spies. At strategic points across the river, invisible behind thick forest, stationary sonic cars played programs of sound effects specifically produced to create an impression of tanks moving up the river.

First, the sonic car upstream began playing the sounds of bridge building. Then, as the real tanks stopped short of the fixed bridge downstream, another sonic car switched on its sounds of tank engines. At intervals, each new car stationed farther upriver switched on its program—tanks crossing a wooden bridge with loose boards, tanks climbing a hill, tanks descending, tanks assembling at the new bridgehead and then shutting down to wait for the assault. The cars downstream one by one shut down, and the sound magically "moved" along the river upstream.

The sonic soldiers had rehearsed exactly such a scenario on the wooded Black River near Pine Camp. The objective: to force the enemy to repel a sonic attack and thereby be caught unawares by the real one.

Throughout the spring of 1944, Col. Hilton Howell Railey was perfecting the sonic deception program at Pine Camp and training the men of the newly formed 3132d Signal Company Special how to use it. Just as Fort Meade became a magnet for artists seeking an assignment in camouflage, the Army Experimental Station at Pine Camp continued to draw men with technical expertise to its peculiar specialty.

Walter Manser, a slightly built, mild-mannered, bespectacled kid from a farm in the Midwest, never imagined himself a soldier, never dreamed he would wake up one day in the middle of the biggest war in history. He grew up during the Depression in Hinckley, Illinois, building radios from junked parts that he scrounged out of other people's trashcans, and he became something of a genius with vacuum tubes and radio crystals, electromagnets and complicated circuitry. He spent many long afternoons during his boyhood climbing into his cousin's attic and reading old stacks of *Popular Mechanics* and *Popular Science*, studying the complicated diagrams, tracing out the circuitry, figuring out how to build crystal sets, amplifiers, and speakers.

He couldn't afford to buy ready-made radios, or even commercially available kits. "As a kid in the Depression, money was damned tight," he remembers. "I learned from junk—not only radio and electronics, but also mechanics."

In grade school, his parents gave him a dollar watch for Christmas. "I popped off the back, took off the front," he remembers. "I thought, *There's a screw I can take out. There's another one.* Pretty soon I took out too many screws, and the thing fell to pieces. I learned a lesson from that: I learned that, before you take anything apart, you look at it real carefully first—then take off one thing at a time." Before long, he could disassemble a watch—and almost anything else—and put it back together in working order.

His family's farm was two and a half miles across the fields from town, and when they held a Saturday night dance there, he could listen to the music on the forty-watt loudspeakers clear as anything right in his own backyard. So using bits and pieces he patiently collected from every refuse heap in town, he built his own ten-watt sound system and walked out into the fields to find out just how far away he could go and still hear it, and he discovered he could go pretty far away. Sound would just travel amazingly far across those low fields. Sound made sense to him. He had an intuitive sense of how it all worked, could practically see the electrons racing along the thin wires, the waves oscillating through the air. He could turn broken parts, discarded junk, into a beautiful working wireless that could tune in the world.

He didn't have grand ambitions to travel to exotic lands or pursue great adventures. He liked working with his hands and his head. He figured he would take a course in radio repair, open his own shop someday, settle down in a small town like the one where he grew up. But eleven days before Pearl Harbor, he got drafted into the Signal Corps. The army said, "You'll be in for a year." Then, after the war broke out, everything changed. "You're going to stay in for the duration—that was the attitude—you don't have to like it," he says. Duration plus six months. It wasn't just Manser. The War Department was grabbing every able-bodied young man and not letting go.

At first, he got his wish. The Signal Corps sent him to radio repair school at Fort Knox, Kentucky—home also to the Armored Forces School, a coincidence that would work to his advantage later. He put in for Officers Candidate School, earned his commission. "After that, the supply of second lieutenants caught up with the demand," he says wryly. The Signal Corps needed supply officers. The army didn't give him any choice. It was going to make a supply officer out of him and sent him to one supply school after another. He mastered the subject easily enough—materiel, procurement, requisitions, depot maintenance. But his heart wasn't in supply.

During his training, he managed to talk his way into a course in electricity, taught by a philosophical sergeant. "The army is big enough that you can get anything you want, if you go about it the right way," the sergeant said. "If you try for something and don't get it, back off a little and go at it from a little bit different direction." Manser tucked away the advice in the back of his mind.

When Manser was finishing up his last supply course, the major in charge called him into the office. "Well," he told Manser, "you've been through every supply course the Signal Corps has to offer—what kind of assignment do you want?"

Manser still stubbornly clung to his original ambition. He said, "Sir, I want a technical assignment."

The major threw up one hand in exasperation. "You'll never get it." But somewhere in the pile of papers on the major's desk was an evaluation of Manser's performance in that electricity course. One of only four students without a degree in electrical engineering, he had finished first in a class of forty. His evaluation read, "Very satisfactory."

The major looked again at the card and said, "But I'll put you in for it." And sent him to the army Experimental Station—as laboratory supply officer.

Railey had other plans for him.

Before long, the army was letting Manser play with the most expensive, top-secret, state-of-the-art equipment it had ever built.

• • •

The whole notion of sonic deception evolved out of a failed idea.

When the Stuka dive bombers had come roaring out of the skies over Warsaw and Dunkirk, what terrified troops on the ground more than anything else was the signature screaming whine caused by a siren deliberately designed into the aircraft. Even though the Stuka soon proved inferior to other warplanes of the era, it instilled a paralyzing panic in those on the ground.

To the American engineers of Division 17 of the National Defense Research Committee, the lesson was clear: sound could terrify soldiers.

So they decided to take the concept to the next level and develop a sonic "bomb."

Harold Burris-Meyer, the *Fantasia* wizard and a member of Railey's secret Planning Board, decided to test the idea by lobbing bottles out of an airplane toward an observer on the ground. The theory was that the falling bottles would produce a high-pitched whine, similar to the Stuka siren, that would terrify those on the ground, inducing panic, flight, even surrender.

His accomplice, Vincent Mallory, former sound engineer for the Federal Theater in New York, stood waiting on the dock of a remote lake, scanning the sky. In due course the small plane banked into view, and as the pilot made his run, Burris-Meyer flung out the beer bottles. But the only terrorizing effect on Mallory was the one induced by the silent plummeting bottles threatening to brain him.

The idea of a sonic "bomb" never quite panned out, so the engineers shifted their work toward battlefield deception. There must be other ways to scare enemy troops, or at least manipulate them. By the time the Army Experimental Station moved to Pine Camp, they had made several important strides.

First, they had developed a smaller version of the 500-watt naval system used in the "Battle of Sandy Hook," called the "junior heater." Instead of a stack of a dozen metal "driver" horns gridded into a metal case, the new 250-watt system projected sound effects through six fifteen-inch "direct radiator" Jensen speakers mounted in a weatherproof wooden box with flaring sides to focus projection. At 40 pounds apiece—240 pounds total, plus the box—they were still much lighter than the horns.

What's more, they could project lower frequencies, such as tank engines—the second big stride.

This kind of speaker would become popular in the civilian world after the war in stereo hi-fi systems and as studio monitors because of one significant, and novel, virtue: *presence.* Earlier speakers, including the horns favored for use by navy beachmasters trying to establish order on a landing zone, were basically public address speakers—aptly called *loud-*speakers. They could project sound, especially voices, across distance, but they couldn't mimic the subtlety or range of frequency and timbre of real sound.

Presence is the reason your dog will bark at the sound of strange voices on a high-end stereo speaker, but not at the same voices projected through a tinny television speaker. The cheap TV speaker has no presence, and the dog is not deceived.

Presence, sometimes referred to as "acoustical intimacy," takes advantage of our binaural hearing. That is, we hear out of two ears, two channels of sound input. That sense of hearing is imperfect and can be fooled, especially when other senses, such as sight, are also involved. We do not hear in the precise way an oscilloscope measures sound waves. How and what we hear depends on context, both physical and emotional.

Presence emerged as a complex result of improvements in several key components of the sound recording and playback system. First, the recordings themselves were purer, clean of masking sound or obtrusive background noise. Second, the individual sound effects were mixed into multiple channels and then played back through multiple speakers, both on a single vehicle and on vehicles separated by hundreds of yards. The psychoacoustical effect was that, as sound moved between speakers, the listener heard a phantom sound, a sonic illusion, but one that did not jump from one sound source to another. Rather it lingered in the space between the two speakers, creating a sense of spatial reality for the sound. Even a sound played at a low volume could thus seem to be "large," fully developed and realistic.

Third and perhaps most important, the speaker itself evolved from a rigid metallic horn that gave off volume but sounded tinny and flat, like a megaphone. Now a larger, flexible speaker came into play. Its fifteen-inch diameter allowed it to handle "bass" or low-frequency sound waves. It was essentially a linear motor: driven by positive and negative polarity magnets, a large, flexible cone with a smaller voice-coil mounted at the center oscillated at various frequencies, responding to positive and negative waves from the amplifier, which itself had been improved to handle more nuanced sound. The in-out, pistonlike motion of the cone alternately compressed and expelled the mass of air in front, generating waves of sound.

Because of the increased size and flexibility of the cone, frequency response was richer. That is, the flexible speakers could produce a range of high, middle, and low sounds and preserve their *timbre*, or the natural harmonics of a sound, sometimes called *overtones*, that lend richness and realism. To the human ear, those overtones, which resonate at mathematically predictable frequency intervals, are not usually audible as separate sounds. Nevertheless, taken together they create an aural impression of authenticity. The horns had always been good at projecting higher-frequency metallic noises, but they flattened out harmonics. Combined with the new heaters, they could now create a complex of sound that the human ear would take for true. As in a high-quality contemporary home stereo system, the listener would have the impression that the sound was coming not just from the speaker itself but also from beside it and behind it. In a field situation, where the speaker itself was not visible, a listener would not be able to exactly pinpoint the source of a sound from any single sonic car.

"Thus, military acoustical devices were not just copies or minor physical modifications of existing instruments," reported Bell Labs, "but rather basically new designs."

Third, the engineers did away with the cumbersome battery, one of the heaviest and least mobile components of the whole system. Instead they powered the new system with a portable Kohler gasoline generator, designated PE 75, which put out two and a half kilowatts of electrical power.

Finally, the engineers at Bell Labs had solved the problem of the skipping phonograph needles—perhaps the most crucial problem of all. They did it not with radical innovation in new technology but by dusting off old technology: the magnetic wire recorder.

The device had originally been patented by Valdemar Poulsen of Denmark in 1899. "Poulsen had a truly radical idea, to magnetize steel wire and then play back the original message without any physical change in the recording material," explains Allen Koenigsberg, longtime publisher of *The Antique Phonograph Monthly*. The device was already in fairly widespread use. In fact, unbeknownst to the Allies, by the 1930s, Hitler's propaganda ministry was using the wire recorder to play prerecorded speeches by the Führer on the radio and pass them off as live broadcasts to deceive listeners and potential enemies as to his whereabouts.

Bell Labs, working with the Brush Development Company of Cleveland, Ohio, set to work improving on this old technology. Together they came up with a much more rugged and simplified version of the machine that would stand up under battlefield conditions, the KS-12009 Magnetic Recorder-Reproducer. All the components were fitted with weatherproof cases—including a "depot spares" box of vital replacement parts. Then they were connected by flexible cables with weatherproof plugs at each end, color-coded and sized differently so that, in the dark of the battlefield, it would be impossible for a nervous operator to plug any wire into the wrong receptacle.

By our twenty-first-century standards, the technology was primitive. The eight hundred pounds of rugged gear—with all its vacuum tubes and stainless-steel wire spools that could play just thirty continuous minutes of high-fidelity sound—today could be replaced by a digital minidisk recorder the size of a cigarette pack and an integrated circuit amplifier pushing sound through a pair of bookshelf speakers in an unending loop.

But in those days, it was cutting edge stuff. Roy Tucker, a sonic operator for the second company to train at Pine Camp, the 3133d, says, "For a moment, we were pioneers."

As ordered, Walter Manser, who had wanted to work in electronics but had been sent to one supply school after another, reported to Railey at the Army Experimental Station at Pine Camp in March 1944 and was immediately impressed during his initial interview. "I thought that the man had a tremendous amount of knowledge and understanding," Manser says.

Manser told him he'd done his basic training at Fort Knox and stressed his experience in radio school there.

"Then we can use you," Railey said at once, ignoring Manser's orders designating him a supply officer. "You'll be in charge of a group going to Fort Knox next week."

At last and all at once, by Railey's fiat, Manser was out of supply.

He started for Fort Knox with a contingent of eight enlisted technicians in a convoy of four vehicles: a K-53 radar box van housing the recording equipment; a two-and-a-half-ton truck to carry the power generator, baggage, and assorted other gear; a military station wagon; and a brand-new Plymouth army staff car for himself. Railey's representative would travel in style.

At Fort Knox, Railey had already greased the skids. He had told Manser that if he ran into any trouble whatsoever, he was to call Railey immediately. Railey would then call his old friend General Henry in Washington—the former commandant of the Armored Board that ran Fort Knox. "They knew we were coming," Manser says, "and they cooperated very well. Gave us everything we asked for."

As a mere second lieutenant on his first assignment, Manser had at his disposal a whole armored company—eighteen tanks plus supporting vehicles and almost two hundred soldiers—and two expansive maneuver areas from which all other activity was banned. Airplanes were not even allowed to fly over.

First, they set up their recording studio in a maneuver area near the Salt River. A tripod-mounted microphone—an off-the-shelf commercial studio brand—was the key. They affixed to it a wire basket covered in burlap to screen out wind noise. Cable snaked along the ground to the radar van, a hundred or so feet away. Inside the van, two technicians manned the turntables, on which a worm gear drove a recording head, etching grooves into a sixteen-inch glass-based transcription disk, the same kind used by radio and recording studios, thereby recording the input from the outside microphone.

It was a slow, painstaking process.

As the needle scored the glass disk, one technician peered through a microscope at the recording head to make sure that the sound input was not so loud that it caused the stylus of the recording head to cut across one groove into the next and spoil the recording. The other kept a sharp eye on the oscilloscope, the glowing TV-like monitor that showed sound frequencies as moving waves on its cathode ray tube, offering a real-time picture of what they were recording. The technician could watch for spikes in volume and adjust the levels accordingly.

Other technicians outside tended the microphone and monitored the power supply. Manser acted as director and executive producer, guiding the Sherman tank commanders this way and that, and ultimately taking responsibility for the quality of the recordings.

To record starts, idling, and backing up, the tanks were kept a hundred feet from the mike. For maneuvering, he'd direct them farther and farther away, have them return, then order them to circle again and again.

Circling around the fixed microphone was a key maneuver, as the Bell Labs engineers pointed out. "In this way, the collective sound of motor vehicles of the required type and number is obtained continuously and at high level, free of the revealing Doppler effect."

The Doppler effect describes the phenomenon of a sound being heard at a different frequency when it moves toward or away from the listener— such as the pitch of a train whistle seeming to "fall" as the train moves down the track. In practice, it meant that if all vehicle sounds were recorded moving past the microphone in a straight line, first sounding louder and then fainter, then projected later over a great distance, they would sound fake because the frequencies would rise or fall in a haphazard fashion. It would be impossible to project a continuous sound located in space. This was the biggest problem of commercially available recorded sound effects, and the main reason the army had to create its own library of tactical sounds.

Manser ran the tanks over bridges, up and down hills, assembled them into ranks, and told them to cut their engines.

That first day, he hit an unforeseen snag.

Just as his crew had all their gear set up, the tankers coached and beginning their first maneuvers, the recording stylus grooving the disk, a strange sound began to overwhelm the oscilloscope—not tank engines, not even wind noise or airplanes.

Frogs.

March was mating season, and as if on cue, thousands of frogs started a din of burping and croaking. Manser recalls, "The frogs started to courting and singing, and all of a sudden you'll be recording and you'll hear these frogs break in. You throw those platters away, and you start over again."

Fortunately, the other maneuver area, on higher ground, was free of amorous frogs, and Manser's crew could finish their work. For weeks, they recorded Shermans and smaller Stuarts and anything else they could think of, until their oscilloscope broke. Without that basic instrument to monitor the quality of the recordings, they were out of business. Manser took the broken oscilloscope to the post repair facility.

"You've got a C-priority here," the indifferent sergeant told him. "That means we'll do your scope in two weeks."

Manser turned to his own sergeant. "You stay here—we're going to have that scope this afternoon."

Using the savvy he had learned as a supply officer, Manser came up with paperwork giving it a much higher priority, then returned. "If you don't get that scope repaired today," Manser told the sergeant, "General Henry will know about it in Washington tomorrow morning." General Henry, who had once commanded the Armored Forces School at Fort Knox, now carried heavy clout in Washington.

They got their scope.

Toward the end of their stay at Fort Knox, Manser was offered a look at a new top-secret tank. Since it wouldn't be mass-produced for combat, there was no point in recording it. But didn't he want to see it anyway? He says, "As long as it was secret and I had no need to see it, I turned down the offer." The habit of secrecy was already ingrained in him, as it was in all of Railey's men. It was partly a phenomenon of the times, a willingness not to ask too many questions. And the War Department had developed elaborate structures to confine military knowledge to those who needed to know. "The compartmentalization of knowledge for security certainly reached perfection in the U.S. Army during World War II," Rippeteau explains. He himself has always kept a yearly diary—the volumes fill several shelves of his Florida home—but he did not write one word during the war, because he, like all the AES men and the Special Troops, was ordered not to.

Manser's team wrapped up their recording session after three weeks. Manser reported to the commandant, told him he was taking his contingent back to Pine Camp. "Lieutenant," the commandant said, "when you get back and see your colonel, tell him not to write a letter thanking me. Tell him to write a letter to General Henry and tell *him* that we cooperated!"

When Manser reported this to Railey, he declared magnanimously, "I shall write a letter to both."

Back at Pine Camp, Manser's team recorded additional sound effects: the metallic clatter of bridge building, truck and jeep noise, soldiers' voices, artillery tractor engines, bulldozers grading roads, any military activity that could possibly be useful in mounting a deception. Then they selected sound effects for specific training exercises and dubbed them from the fragile glass disks onto the more rugged stainless-steel wire. One of Manser's team was Ted Cruz, who had ten years of experience working with NBC radio in New York. His special talent was to remember where on any given disk was located a particular track they wanted. He could grab a platter and slip the needle into the groove precisely on the desired sound effect.

At the Army Experimental Station, they worked in a studio above the airplane hangar. But they could also create sonic programs in their mobile studio, which contained three turntables off which they could dub sound to four wire recorders apiece. Thus, preparing for action, they could tailor a dozen wire spool recordings at a time to the particular mission of deception, mixing armored noises with voices, bridge building, and so on. Each program was unique, to keep the enemy from picking up on the ruse.

Because the weather played such a critical role in the performance of the sonic equipment, Manser also had two weathermen working under him, borrowed from the Air Corps. With their mobile weather station, they could measure air temperature, barometric pressure, wind direction and force, and humidity. They could also independently formulate weather forecasts adapted to the local terrain where they would stage an operation. Weather forecasting was crucial to determining the optimum angle of projection, the direction, and the volume.

All through March 1944, specially selected men continued to arrive at Pine Camp to form the 3132d Signal Service Company Special—the first sonic deception unit ever used in the army.

In order to utilize the recorded sound effects in the field, they mounted each bank of specialized equipment on an M3 half-track. It was a perfect vehicle for this sort of work, a fast and rugged hybrid. The front end rode on two heavy-duty truck tires, the rear on rubber-tired caterpillar treads. The driver's compartment was shielded from the sides and front by armored panels with slits for seeing the road ahead. Behind it was a turret mounting a .50-caliber machine gun, one of the most lethal and reliable American weapons of the war.

Behind the turret, the bed of the vehicle was a roofless five-by-seven-foot armored box protected by steel sides three feet high, with bench seats running fore and aft, filled with sonic gear. When not in use, the gear was covered by an olive-drab tarpaulin for security against spies.

Under the floors were stowed packets of plastic explosive—CC-3—wired to a detonator handy to the driver. If they were overrun and threatened with capture, it would be the driver's job to blow the half-track. The explosives were arranged to assure nothing would be left of the vehicle or the sonic gear.

In a matter of minutes, the sonic operator who commanded the track could strip off the tarpaulin and crank the "coffee grinder" and the enormous wooden case holding six forty-watt Jensen speakers would rise on a rotating bracket. It could be angled for maximum effect, according to distance from the enemy, weather conditions, and the kind of program to be projected.

The recorder held two wire magazines. Each magazine in turn held two spindles and a take-up reel inside a weatherproof box the size of a typewriter case, weighing fifty pounds. Each spool contained two miles of .006-inch stainless-steel wire, which played thirty minutes of "music"—military sound effects—through a 250-watt amplifier into the bank of fifteen-inch speakers, which could project the sounds for up to fifteen miles. When one spool was almost out, the operator would start the other spool, then rewind the first, so they could soundcast a continuous loop all night long.

The whole apparatus was powered by a Kohler gasoline generator.

Major Charles Williams commanded the company. By all accounts, he was a popular and trusted CO. By April 1, 7 officers and 139 enlisted men were learning their tradecraft at the AES. At full strength, the unit would field 10 officers and 192 enlisted men, organized into three operating platoons, each with six half-tracks, called "sonic cars"; a reconnaissance and security platoon; and a supporting administrative platoon. They learned how to maneuver the M3 half-tracks in rugged terrain, position the "heaters," operate the wire recorders, load and change magazines, and repair all the equipment.

Sonic operator Harold Flinn recalls how they were taught to repair the stainless-steel magnetic music wire if it broke. "Light a cigarette, hold the lit end to the wire, and solder it." Tom Schwerin, who had tinkered with automobiles all his life and would operate successful dealerships after the war, taught the guys how to operate and repair the gasoline-powered generators. Without electricity, all their sophisticated sonic gear would go silent.

Then, on field maneuvers in the dark wilderness of Sherwood Forest, they put all their training into practice, cranking up the speakers and playing their music. "We called it 'cooking,'" Roy Tucker says, "'cooking' a problem."

The sonic troops quickly ran into one technical problem. At too high a volume, the powerful amplifiers would often melt the paper voice coils at the center of the new radiator speakers. Obviously, it was not practical to carry along a bunch of spare forty-pound speakers. Instead, they carried a box of fifty spare coils—so light a man could lift the whole box with one hand. Whenever a coil burned out, they could then shim and glue a new one into place in a matter of minutes.

But there was a second, more ominous concern: "Because of undue delay in the delivery of special equipment, the 3132d Signal Service Company was afforded only three weeks of training with the equipment," Lt. Robert Gaskins, Railey's adjutant, reported. The optimum training time: three *months*.

Even as the sound engineers were training troops for combat deception, they were constantly testing the equipment.

One day Ellsworth Roosevelt Haver, a fireballing semipro pitcher everybody called "Bud," was testing a microphone—not realizing it was feeding live to a loudspeaker outside the building. Haver was a comic impressionist, and today he was doing his well-known shtick on the President: "I hate wahh. Eleonah hates wahh. My little dahg Fallah hates wahh. And we will not send one of yaw sons to fight! No! We will send AWL of yaw sons to fight!"

For once, Railey was not amused.

The top-secret equipment found other unauthorized uses. Captain John Kiernan recorded a legendary hour and a half of dirty limericks on the glass disks. One of the station favorites:

> *There were two old maids from Birmingham*
> *It is a strange tale concerning them*
> *They lifted the frock and tickled the cock*

of the bishop as he was confirming them.
Now this bishop, he was no fool
He pulled down his britches
and pickled the bitches
With his twelve-inch episcopal tool.

Kiernan also kept a Saint Bernard named Bonzo, whom he liked to take out on maneuvers. One particular night in the dead of winter, the temperature had dipped well below zero and snow was drifted all around the bivouac of pup tents. "Sanitary discipline in a snow camp is always a big problem," recalls Rippeteau, who planned the bivouac to give the sonic soldiers experience in cold-weather operations, which he knew they would need in Europe. He also knew the men so far lacked field experience working around machinery in the pitch dark. In the morning, the whole bivouac area was spotted with yellow holes.

"We didn't do that," the men explained innocently. "That was Bonzo."

But mostly serious work was carried on at the station. Perhaps the most important tests were the ones supervised by Ted Crabtree, the Bell Labs civilian technician: sound ranging. The goal was to develop a set of firing tables, just like the ones used by artillery crews, to tell exactly how far they could "shoot" a given sound under specific conditions. This would boil down the highly technical data, all the complex calculations, into a simple formula that any reasonably smart sonic operator could use with precision on the battlefield to project the right volume of recorded noise in the right direction, with perfect deceptive fidelity.

"The sound level received at the enemy's position is of vital importance to successful deception," the Bell Labs engineers noted. "If the sound is too loud, there is greatly increased possibility that it will be recognized as a recording, while if it is too low, it will not be heard at all."

Crabtree and his team set up transmission and receiving stations in every conceivable variation of landscape, distance, and weather. They tested a whole range of sounds. They barged a half-track out to Bass Island in the middle of Lake Ontario and used its bumper winch to erect a ninety-foot tower, then sailed a converted power yacht offshore at night to transmit and receive high-frequency sound to and from the tower—the sirenlike wails that spooked the locals. They transmitted in snow and rain, through dense foliage and across open fields, up hill and down. They measured such arcane factors as frequency decay, dispersion, and humidity loss, the masking noise of wind and surf.

They made some important discoveries.

For instance, they noted, "Experience has indicated not only that few people are conscious of the true characteristics of familiar sounds, but also that sounds are deceptive even to the trained ear." In other words, men often couldn't recognize a familiar sound heard in a strange context.

It also turned out that, because of the use of multiple tracks and the complex dynamics of sound interacting from several sources, a listening enemy, even with electronic ranging equipment, would find it impossible to locate a single sonic car so long as several were projecting sound simultaneously. So it would be difficult for enemy gunners to zero in on any particular half-track. This was reassuring news for the sonic crews.

They also discovered that under optimum conditions—in clear weather over water at night—they could project realistic sound effects up to fifteen miles.

"Sound propagation over distance is much better at night," Rippeteau explains, "because there tends to be an inversion layer, which makes the sound waves bend toward the earth. The inversion usually extends from the earth up to about ten feet. It's what's called 'inversion fog,' which you often see in early mornings on the highway."

In practice, the sonic units would rarely try to project their music beyond six thousand yards—about three and a half miles—the optimum distance for ranging accuracy. And they would target listeners between five and thirty-five feet above the transmitting vehicle. The sound-ranging tables covered the three types of battlefield most ideal for sonic deception: flat open terrain, flat lightly wooded terrain, and flat heavily wooded terrain. The AES engineers emphasized a useful fact: "Again it should be noted that all experiments prove that these meteorological and terrain conditions affect sonic operations in *exactly the same manner that they affect actual operations.*"

The AES engineers tackled two other unusual projects. The first was a so-called "water heater"—a twenty-one-foot-long torpedo that could be fired from a submarine, travel by gyroscope to a preset distance, then deploy according to a timer. When the timer went off, a loudspeaker would pop out of the floating nose and project sound effects from a wire recorder, then arm or destroy itself at the end of its program. The water heaters were perfected too late to be used in the war.

The second project was even more bizarre.

The word came down to develop a very specific deception to use against the Japanese. Rippeteau remembers it well. "They said it had developed through research that the Japanese infantry soldiers, being peasants, were very superstitious. And one of the superstitions that signifies impending death is the barking of a dog." So Rippeteau supervised the recording of dogs barking—big dogs, little dogs, lone dogs, dogs in packs.

"So then somebody said, 'This is going to stand out like a sore thumb! You're going to have all these barking dogs, and there's no other sounds of the countryside,' " he says. By "countryside," they all erroneously assumed "jungle." So the AES sent a crew to Panama and recorded three disks full of birdcalls and animal noises. "Then they skillfully melded the jungle sounds in with the dog sounds so that it sounded like we had barking dogs in the jungle."

Like the beer-bottle sonic bomb, the barking-dog deception went unused.

Backing up all the sonic training was a more lethal kind of training. The recon and security platoon, led by Lt. Dick Syracuse, practiced two things: finding their way around any terrain in any conditions and mastering weapons. Syracuse took to his new assignment with gusto. He had good men, and for once he had superior officers—Williams and Railey—whom he respected. "These guys were all smart and the enlisted men were all capable and reliable," he says. "We organized, trained, and went overseas in three and a half months—that was unheard of."

While the crews of the sonic cars would have orders to avoid combat under almost any circumstances, Syracuse's job was the opposite: His platoon would have to scout out positions, often in hostile territory, and had to be ready to defend themselves against ambush. And once his platoon had led the operating platoons into position, they must be prepared to defend the sonic crews with their lives.

"I didn't know what we'd get into, so I got my gang fast and skillful with weapons, instilled a sense of unity and morale," Syracuse recalls. "My men were all experts in every weapon." He himself carried a Thompson submachine gun and hand grenades. His men carried an assortment of carbines and machine guns. The jeeps each mounted a .30-caliber machine gun, the half-tracks .50 calibers—the same big gun used on Flying Fortresses. They also carried bazookas and lots of rockets.

"Haba-haba," he would tell a guy when he wanted him to get cracking, then give him a quick light jab in the shoulder. It was just a saying he had picked up from his black first sergeant back in Alabama. "Haba-haba" meant look alive, get with it, don't let me down. And the jab said, stick with me, kid, you're on my team, I'll watch your back.

The recon and security platoon quickly became a crackerjack outfit. "I said, if that's what we're going to be, then we're going to be the best," Syracuse says. Before going overseas, he and his men put on a demonstration for Railey and a corps of visiting dignitaries. "Oh, that was some demonstration!" Syracuse recalls. "The brass loved it! Weapons, commando-type exercises, hand-to-hand combat. Right out of Hollywood—with live ammunition!"

Like Fairbanks and Railey, Syracuse was a born showman. He says, smiling, "We were Cecil B. DeMille warriors."

One of those warriors was Bill Brown from Salina, Ohio—a guy who is still kidded about his remarkable resemblance to Van Johnson, the heroic leading man in so many Hollywood World War II films. He'd been attending Indiana University when the war broke out, volunteered, passed radio operator school and code school, and was studying in the army ASTP program at Grinnell College when Railey's personnel scouts found him.

As with all the guys in the sonic program, unbeknownst to him the FBI had already interviewed his family and canvassed his old neighborhood, checking out his background, his politics, whether he had any record of criminal activity.

He was then recalled to Fort Monmouth, the Signal Corps Headquarters, and from there put on a train to Pine Camp. "The night we got there, it was thirty-five below zero and we had no arctic equipment," he says. "They had trucks backed up to the train, and there was a voice yelling, 'Get these guys back to the barracks as fast as you can!' " It was Railey.

Brown sat in the barracks for ten days with the other new men. One by one, they were called out for interviews. One by one, they returned to the barracks, sworn to secrecy about the interview. Then it was Brown's turn to go before Railey and Williams. "They asked me where I was from, my whole background. Did you like your father? Did you like your mother? What kind of life did you have? Did you go to high school? Did you play any sports? Your whole life, really. Then they said, 'Thank you,' and that was it."

Brown returned to the barracks and waited. After all the guys had been interviewed, an officer came to the barracks and called out a list of names—Brown's wasn't on it. "Pack up, you guys," the officer said. "You're leaving."

The remainder, Brown's contingent, was trucked over to the base movie theater, guarded by MPs. The men filed in and there was Railey to welcome them to sonic deception. They got their first lecture and watched a movie about how it all worked.

Brown became a gunner and radio operator in first half-track, first platoon,

3132d Signal Services Company Special. "We were always right behind Major Williams's jeep, so we always knew where we were going," Brown says. Claude Zachary was the driver and Sgt. Donald Davey, one of Railey's original cadre of thirteen, sonic operator and track commander. The three would serve together throughout the war.

"We didn't tell anybody what we were in," Brown recalls. "To be honest about it, they kind of threatened us."

If word got out that the Americans were developing sonic deception, the Germans would be alert for the ruse and would be harder to trick. Deception could always backfire. Principally, the need for deception arose from weakness. Therefore anytime the Germans found out the Americans were using it, they could rightly assume they were vulnerable to attack. And right here at home, spies might try to capture or sabotage the equipment. The FBI even interrogated the young women who worked as civilian switchboard operators in Watertown, grilling them about the content of calls to and from the AES.

What Railey used to tell his troops was simple and clear. "If you shoot off your mouth, you'll be liable to fall off the back of a truck some dark night and I'll have to file an accidental death report on you."

By late spring one important member of the sonic team had yet to arrive. Lieutenant John Walker started his army career fighting the war in the suburbs of Los Angeles, in the placid San Fernando Valley, home of the mammoth Lockheed and Vega Aircraft factories and the strategically important Los Angeles Air terminal.

His chemical troops would wait with torches at the end of a residential street. Walker would check one more time that everything was set.

The day would be clear—typically fine southern California weather. Bombing weather.

The chemical troops would have spent the last few days digging little pits in the front yards of houses—here and for miles around—placing thirty-gallon smudge pots and filling the pots with fuel oil. Some residents raised a fuss when they saw the soldiers spading into their lawns; others whose houses were skipped declared they were patriotic, too, and wouldn't the lieutenant *please* put a smudge pot in their yard? Then, on Walker's signal, the chemical troops would rush down the street, touching their torches to the line of several hundred smudge pots. Within seconds, gouts of oily black smoke would plume into the clear, dry air, spreading out in a cloudy black billow above the houses, the streets, the air terminal. Before long the smoke would obscure an area of twenty-five square miles.

For days, residents would choke and cough on the oily haze. The thick petroleum smoke screen would hover in the bowl of the mountains with nowhere to go. Coating cars and windows and the siding of houses with a greasy film, it would block out the sun and turn the horizon into a yellow-gray smudge. But it would protect them from Japanese dive bombers.

Every time a Japanese sub was reported, or an unidentified blip showed up on radar, or some reliable rumor about invasion came along, streetcars would grind to a halt in downtown L.A., electrical power would shut down, and Walker and his chemical troops would send up their smoke screen to obscure the aircraft factory from waves of enemy bombers that never came.

Walker says, "I tell people jestingly now that I created the first real smog in the San Fernando Valley."

From the summer of 1942 until New Year's 1943, he did this at least once a month.

Thus Walker started the war—not as a sonic soldier, but as a chemical officer whose job it was to create artificial cloud cover and hide big things from attacking airplanes. Walker bore a striking resemblance to the tough-guy movie actor Jack Palance—the same intense, brooding eyes and resonant baritone voice—though he was, and remains, a gentle, thoughtful man.

Before the war, Walker was a chemistry major at Penn State. He stood six foot five, and the basketball coach tried to recruit him, but he was spending forty hours a week in classes and labs and just didn't have the time. He never drank or smoked—a rarity in the army—and overseas he usually gave away his monthly Army-issued gin and Scotch bottles and cigarette rations to the guys in his platoon. His wife, Margie, was waiting back home. They had a single good year together before he went in the service.

Temperamentally, he was the exact opposite of Dick Syracuse, the flamboyant leader of the "haba-haba" recon platoon. But besides a degree in chemistry, the two shared a similar experience in fighting against racial bigotry. Walker, too, was assigned to command an all-black smoke-generating company, the 84th, at Camp Seibert, Alabama, on his circuitous route to Pine Camp.

Walker, too, ran afoul of the southern gang of officers who ran Camp Seibert—Walker was that big damned Yankee causing all the trouble. And the guy who had it in for him was Syracuse's old nemesis, Colonel Glazebrook. Walker says, "He didn't like the fact that I thought my men were equal, which I knew they were, and I believed it, and they knew I believed it, and they would produce anything for me."

At Glazebrook's instigation, for some purported infraction or other, he was summoned before the camp commandant, Brig. Gen. Hank Shekejian. When he entered and stood at attention, the brigadier was slouched in his chair puffing on a stogie and his deputy commander, Col. Frank Post, was pacing behind him. "Lieutenant, we're going to give you company punishment," the general announced.

"What for, sir?"

"Well, you were ordered to do some things in this company and you didn't do them."

Walker, a conscientious soldier, had seen this coming. He didn't fit in with the good old boys who ran things around here—that was his only infraction. He looked the brigadier straight in the eye and said, "No, sir."

The general leaned forward. "What do you mean, 'No, sir,' Lieutenant!"

"No, sir. I demand a court-martial—that's my right."

Post interjected, "Lieutenant, do you know what you're saying to the general?"

Walker remained at attention. "I want a court-martial for the charges, sir, or drop 'em."

Nothing more was said about charges. But the command cabal got him back in another way. Walker had spent months preparing his troops to go to Europe, and now he was relieved of command. His troops would go into action without the commander who had trained them. It was a blow—one that could ruin whatever army career he had left.

Walker got on the phone to some friends in Washington, who offered him a job as a POM (Preparation for Overseas Movement) officer at Pine Camp.

"But that's a signal company," Walker objected. "I'm a chemical officer."

"You got a company ready to go to Europe once, you can get one ready to go again."

So Walker joined the 3132d Signal Service Company Special to get the men ready for combat. He was twenty-three years old.

The new assignment proved challenging and rewarding, especially because of the high caliber of men with whom he was working. "Nobody could volunteer for our unit," he explains. "You had be picked by standards imposed from above. You had to meet certain criteria."

When the word came down that the sonic company would leave for a port of embarkation on 25 May 1944, Railey called two men, one at a time, into his office. The first was Jim Barrett, one of his original thirteen AES men from Fort Hancock. One of the drivers in the sonic company was sick and wouldn't be shipping out. Railey said, "It's up to you—you don't have to go. But if you want to go over there and see what this is all about, you can go."

Barrett could have stayed behind in Pine Camp for the rest of the war, weekends off, safely out of harm's way. But of course, he didn't.

The next guy he called in was Walker. As POM officer, his duties were coming to an end. He had meticulously planned the sonic unit's embarkation, and had procured all the spares they would need for their equipment and made arrangements to ship them.

Walker greatly admired Railey. "You didn't think about Pine Camp as just a place—it was *Railey's* place," he recalls. "He was so dominant in his personality, and his knowledge encompassed everything. With my background, I respected him greatly because he was also a realist. He should have been about a five-star general right then."

Railey's question was simple. "Don't you want to go with them?"

"Hell, yeah, I want to go," Walker said.

"They'll need a supply officer."

So on 30 May 1944, when the sonic troops drove their half-tracks aboard the SS *Exceller* at Bush Terminal, Pier 2, in New York—Williams, Brown, Davey, Manser, Flinn, Zachary, Syracuse, and all the others—Walker and Barrett were with them.

In an unguarded moment just before the sonic company departed Pine Camp, Railey mused out loud to Manser, "What do you do when somebody has been telling you that everything has been done, everything is fine, and you find out that it isn't?" Then he regained his composure. "Ah," he said, "but that's my problem, not yours."

Railey's boys had trained with their sonic equipment for only three weeks. In the film, their ruse against the enemy had worked with scripted perfection. But like the 603d, they weren't yet ready to face real Germans across the river.

SIX

DRESS REHEARSAL AT STRATFORD-UPON-AVON

May–July 1944

If all the knights and ladies of old together with Robin Hood and his Merry Men were to come marching out of the forest, you wouldn't be a bit surprised.

—Richard Morton

No one was allowed up on deck until the ship was far out to sea.

The USS *Henry Gibbons* steamed with all running lights blacked out in a convoy of 150 ships, the largest convoy yet to cross the Atlantic, formed on the cruiser USS *Cincinnati* at the center. The *Gibbons*'s station was on the extreme right front flank—so-called "coffin corner" because of its vulnerability to U-boats, which usually attacked from ahead of a convoy. But the luck of the Special Troops held—uncanny luck that would desert them fatally only three times during the whole war.

While the escort corvettes, sirens blaring, darted in and out among the formation chasing phantoms, and even sporadically launched depth charges, no torpedo attacks came. But in their cramped bunks belowdecks, the men listened in apprehensive silence to the thudding reverberations of the depth charges. "Everyone became quiet as though the enemy would be able to detect talking through the hull of the ship," Jim Laubheimer wrote.

The *Gibbons* was a clean, well-appointed ship, modeled after the American President liners, and the officers were served regular hot meals in her spacious dining saloon.

The troops, as usual, enjoyed far less luxury—four thousand soldiers stacked into five-high pipe berths on the airless lower decks. They stood in chow lines for hours on end, so that by the time they finished one meal, it was already time to line up again for the next. The mess served only two meals a day, slopped onto tin plates. "You'd pass by the windows of these great dining halls for officers and look in, and they're sitting at tables with white tablecloths being served regular dinners," Richard Morton, the caricaturist from headquarters company, recalls. "The contrast was just awful!" The enlisted men ate standing or squatting on deck while scores of seasick soldiers lined the rails and vomited overboard.

It turned out that some of the merchant seamen who ran the galley were hoarding food. Laubheimer forked out seventeen dollars for a loaf of bread. Other hungry soldiers bought candy bars by the box for a similar price. Later, in England, there were accusations that some of the food stores that should have fed the troops were sold onto the black market.

Many of the guys had never been on any sort of boat in their lives and remained seasick for the whole crossing—all thirteen days. Laubheimer recalls, "Surprisingly, even though the ship was moored to the docks, some of the guys got seasick before they reached their bunks."

Some, like Laubheimer, who had grown up sailing boats on the Chesapeake Bay and was immune from seasickness, volunteered to man the antiaircraft batteries. From a turret at the stern of the ship, he enjoyed four hours a day of fresh air and a panoramic view of the convoy—as well as first call in the chow line.

Many of the artists spent as much time on deck as possible simply to sketch with pencils, fountain pens, and charcoal. They drew figure studies of other soldiers, tableaux of sailors at the guns, seascapes of ships passing around them in the convoy. Like many of his classmates who came out of the commercial art program at Pratt, Morton had learned to work on the spot. He says, "Pratt told us we should always continue our artwork. Wherever we go, whatever we do—be an artist."

For some, the highlight of the crossing occurred several days out when a majestic liner steamed past on the horizon—the *Queen Mary*, now transporting troops. Fast enough to outrun U-boats, she sailed alone through the convoy and was soon out of sight. Arthur Shilstone, among many others, captured her in his sketchbook.

At night, they staged deck shows—stand-up comedy, scenes from Shakespeare, song-and-dance routines. But the ship was so crowded, many of the guys never even knew the shows were taking place. Instead they played poker. For some, the war would become one long poker game interrupted by missions, and a staggering amount of money changed hands.

Fred Fox followed an evening ritual. Each night before bed, he would stand at the bow of the ship. "The wind, the stars, the restless sea and reassuring convoy have all been described before," he wrote. "The sight makes me feel alternately like a king emperor and somebody's pet mouse."

With his spiritual bent, he was continually pondering the deeper questions of the war: the fate of the Jews, the habit of violence now deliberately ingrained in a generation of young men, the future of democracy after the war. He read voraciously and wrote the first of several hundred letters home to his fiancée, Hannah. He befriended Capt. Tom Wells, an equally lovelorn officer from Chicopee Falls, Massachusetts, with whom he would often share quarters in the campaigns to come. "Capt. Wells and I have an awfully nice game which we play every morning at breakfast," Fox wrote to Hannah. "I ask him how his wife (Barbara) is and he asks me how *you* are. Sometimes you've just come back from his house and have some interesting stories about his baby or the state of his kitchen. Sometimes they come over to see us."

Their whimsy may strike us, in these jaded times, as sentimental, but these men understood they were going to be away from their loved ones a long time—many months, perhaps even years—with no assurance of ever coming home. In such shared reveries and in long, intimate letters, they did their best to ward off loneliness, to soften the anxiety of the precarious present by daydreaming about an idyllic future.

Fox had already assumed duties as censorship officer for the headquarters staff. "I find that their profession of love isn't much different than mine," he wrote. "It's probably a pretty ordinary thing. No more unusual than a glass of water."

Rounding the coast of Northern Ireland into the notorious Irish Sea, the *Gibbons* was slammed by a violent storm. Laubheimer wrote, "From my seat in the turret, sometimes the sea was forty feet below and then it would be forty feet over my head." Louis Porter recalls, "Ships were disappearing between the waves. First time I'd seen anything like that." The storm was actually perfect protection against U-boats.

On the night of May 15, the *Gibbons* steamed up the Bristol Channel while the port city was being pounded yet again by heavy bombers. "We could watch the searchlights and hear the booming of the antiaircraft guns, feeling trapped on our little 'island of steel,' " Laubheimer reported.

But once again the luck of the Special Troops held, and the troopship arrived unscathed at the Bristol dock under the protection of barrage balloons.

Shilstone was struck by the coincidence. His last sight before leaving New York had been that solitary light across the Hudson, shining from the house where he grew up, and now he was stepping onto the same dock from where his grandfather had embarked generations ago to seek his fortune in America.

Most of the staff officers, including Simenson and Reeder, had flown over to England ahead of the troops. Next morning, Reeder greeted his troops on the wharf and boarded them onto the London, Midland, and Southern Railroad for the seven-hour journey up the Severn and Avon Rivers to Stratford-upon-Avon. From there it was five miles farther by truck to Walton Hall. The troops called it "The Castle," but the officers quartered in its luxurious rooms nicknamed it "Moldy Manor." The mansion carried a scandalous history.

Albert Edward, Prince of Wales, played a tawdry role in the deception. Harriett, Lady Mordaunt and mistress of Walton Hall, was entertaining lovers while her husband, Sir Charles, attended Parliament down in London.

When she bore a child with diseased eyes—probably the result of venereal infection—she was overcome with guilt and confessed to her bewildered husband, "Charlie, I have been very wicked. I have done very wrong." She named at least five men she had made love to, "often and in open day," who might have fathered her child, including the heir to Queen Victoria, the future King Edward VII. He of course denied it and remained aloof from what the London tabloids quickly trumpeted as "The Warwickshire Scandal."

But the deception was compounded far beyond mere adultery—even flagrant and multiple affairs—into something infinitely more tragic.

When Sir Charles Mordaunt, who traced his lineage back to William the Conqueror, sought a divorce, Harriett's Scottish father intervened. Divorced, she would lose her title and her share of Sir Charles's fortune, which her greedy family counted on. He claimed his daughter was a victim of "moral madness," symptoms of which included blatant promiscuity and heightened sexual appetite. By wile and trickery and the help of some unscrupulous doctors, he had his daughter declared insane. Under English law, a man could not divorce a wife not in her right mind.

Harriett dutifully if naïvely played her part in the charade, feigning madness to keep her fortune.

The ruse worked all too well—at least for a while.

Against her wishes, the court locked away twenty-three-year-old Harriett in a lunatic asylum, and her family kept her share of the fortune. At last, years later, the law allowed Charles Mordaunt his divorce. But by then, living among the mad, Harriett herself had gone truly insane. She remained shut away for thirty-five years, until her death in 1906.

Sir Charles married again, a granddaughter of barons named Mary Louisa Cholmondeley, nicknamed "M'aimée," loosely from the French for "beloved." Less than ten years later, Charles was killed in a carriage accident in Scotland. For the next half century, Maimée remained at Walton Hall dressed in mourning black.

She was still mistress of Walton Hall, a semiinvalid after a fall from a horse and confined to the north wing, when the Special Troops arrived in May 1944.

Walton Hall was a massive stone structure, solid as a fortress, with cloistered walkways, an imposing neo-Gothic facade, a labyrinth of cellars, and more than a hundred rooms. Two sets of arched double doors ten feet high opened into the main entry, where the eye traveled up banks of stained glass windows depicting the Mordaunt legacy of arms to a vaulted ceiling thirty feet high supported by marble pillars. Life-sized oil portraits of the various Mordaunt ancestors, including Sir Charles, adorned the paneled walls. Off to the left, a magnificent curving staircase led upstairs to the splendid suites and bedrooms where the careless Lady Harriett Mordaunt had sported with her lovers—now posh quarters for officers such as Simenson, Truly, Reeder, and Lt. Fred Fox.

Fox, the scriptwriter and radio analyst, described his new quarters with obvious delight. "Picture me wrapped up in a gray RAF blanket in the tower of a huge English manor house. From one window I overlook a medieval court with a four-sided clock which strikes every quarter hour and a tiny dungeon where they used to hang the venison. From the other window I look down lovely green lawns, a slow-moving lily-covered stream (with perch and eels), and gorgeous trees which pretend to be wild but have been groomed for centuries."

The spacious grounds encompassed stables and a coach house, barns and workers' cottages, even a free-standing stone chapel and a graveyard. But it was not such a grand billet for the line platoons. Some of the troops were lucky enough to be housed in prefabricated galvanized tin "Nissen huts" erected on patches of hardstand. Most bivouacked in pyramidal canvas tents in the meadows below the Bath Woods, bordering Jubilee Drive, which led from the Kineton Road up to the main house. The lime saplings that Sir Charles Mordaunt had planted along the lane in 1897 to celebrate the queen's jubilee had grown into mature shade trees.

"We are living in tents like real soldiers now," Morton reported. "Since being in England we have been living out of doors, and even tho it's midsummer, are wearing wool underwear (long) and our ODs, but the weather has been pretty nice altho not what we would classify as summer at home."

The men enjoyed their bucolic surroundings, but the chill summer weather took its toll—many of them caught colds. Bill Blass ended up in the hospital with pneumonia.

Their levels of comfort differed radically. When they weren't in London working out plans at European Theater of Operations, United States Army (ETOUSA), headquarters, the officers held grand parties in the main hall at Walton, sipping vintage Cognac, while the men congregated at local workingmen's pubs. But for all of them, Walton Hall was a fitting billet. Steeped in lies, intrigue, and infidelity, haunted by the ghost of a young, beautiful woman who had become the worst victim of her own and her family's deceptions, it was a story as much as a place: a perfect cautionary tale of how deception can go terribly wrong.

A mile down the Kineton Road lay Wellesbourne, a picturesque Midlands village of timber, stucco, and thatch that had already sent most of her sons and fathers off to war in the Territorial Army. Many local women had enlisted as auxiliaries and nurses. Dozens of families had taken in children evacuated from nearby Coventry after it was firebombed for a second time in November 1940—an ordeal that lasted for eleven straight hours. Coventry residents used to wander miles out into the countryside at nightfall, knocking on farmers' doors to be taken in for the night, or else they would sleep out under the hedgerows until the bombers were gone. But there was danger even here. One of the evacuees, a little boy, had fallen between a tractor and the plow it was towing right on Jubilee Drive and been killed.

Walter Arnett, the cartoonist, visited Coventry cathedral on a pass. Like the whole town, the cathedral had been bombed to ruins by German nighttime raids. He gathered up shards of stained glass, which he fashioned into a cross in remembrance of the destruction he had seen. Wellesbourne had also seen its share of death and sorrow. Wellesbourne lads had already fallen on battlefields as far away as Iraq. Scores of RAF fliers billeted in local homes were lost in missions over Germany, or crashed in the frequent fogs that blanketed the region. The bodies of German fliers shot down in the vicinity rested in the churchyard.

Rationing had already been in force for almost four years, and fresh food was scarce. A fresh egg was a "cracking treat." Gray "wartime" bread—baked with mystery ingredients—replaced white bread. Blackout curtains from Overbury's drapery shop blanketed every window in the village. The gas streetlamps had been extinguished for the duration. Headlamps of automobiles were hooded with metal shields with three narrow slits for light to shine through. Driving was precarious even in daylight—fearing Nazi invasion, the local authorities had years earlier removed all signposts from the roads.

Workmen carried rubber-smelling gas masks in cardboard cases along with their dinners. At night, air raid wardens patrolled the streets. Even before Coventry was hit, Wellesbourne and Walton were bombed. Then, when the airfield was completed, the village was bombed again on four successive nights, driving residents once more into their cellars. After the raids, kids collected dud incendiaries, unscrewed the tops, and set fire to the magnesium for amusement, then saved the bomb cases for souvenirs.

Parachutes were precious finds—the silk made fine undergarments to replace the ones no longer available in shops.

Even the gentry made sacrifices. Manor houses like Walton Hall had been commandeered by the military in order to disperse unit headquarters from London throughout the countryside and make them less vulnerable to bombing. The country-club set gave up the steeplechase. Eleanor Zonik, a teenager at the beginning of the war, recalls what became of the horses: "Quite incredibly, in a war which was to end with the atomic bomb, within twenty-four hours of its declaration, the remount officers arrived and commandeered everybody's hunters, to pull the guns in France!"

Major Stuart, the Walton Estate agent, led the local Home Defense Volunteers, in his Harris tweeds and plus-fours. His boys and old men practiced gunnery with .22 rifles and thrust their bayonets into meal sacks. On Sundays, the church bells remained silent. If they tolled, it would mean only one thing: Nazi invasion.

The Special Troops entered a community at war, a place already layered in a history of danger, scarcity, and sacrifice, and the reality struck them at once. Fox wrote, "We just returned from our first visit to town. I took along an orange to give to the first child I met. He was very happy and said he had never seen one before."

The Special Troops were not the first soldiers to settle in at Walton Hall. Before them had come legions of British, Belgian, and Czech troops. In the village, "colored" troops were billeted in the garages of the old gasworks. At night outside the Talbot and King's Head pubs, they used to slug it out with drunken white Yanks. Lady Elizabeth Hamilton, whose husband Sir Richard inherited the Walton estate, recalls that their brawls provided entertainment for the villagers: "The local lads would turn out and watch."

Italian and German prisoners of war were lorried to outlying farms, where they would labor alongside local men till almost midnight in the "double summer time" light. The little Christmas-card village was crawling with troops and POWs, loaded with airplanes, guns, and ammunition. By this late date in the war, the British were growing weary of boisterous Yanks, who immediately made themselves at home, romanced the local girls, and, in a country deprived of even basic amenities, always seemed to have stockpiles of luxuries such as food, chocolate, cigarettes, and nylons. "It's just that they were cold," Laubheimer recalls. "The fact that we were there to help them—they didn't seem to care. They'd just as soon we stayed away. I don't blame them, really, because we were all over their property and their life."

Still, catering to the troops was something of a local cottage industry. One village woman, Hettie Perkins, used to collect dirty laundry from the officers at Walton Hall and return the uniforms cleaned and pressed. "The best part," a local historian reports, "was in addition to being paid there would be a large tin of Spam or other food sent as well." On days when no passes were issued to the troops, Hettie's son Ron would carry up bottles from the Stag's Head Pub in Wellesbourne and sell them in the tent camp.

When the officers of the Special Troops departed Walton, a Wellesbourne woman who worked as secretary in the house was astonished at the bounty they left behind. "The Americans left in a hurry," Lady Hamilton says. "When they went, they left behind everything. The fridges were full of food—just bursting with fresh eggs and everything."

But the enlisted men enjoyed little fresh food. Their diet consisted of whatever could be shipped from America in tins or cartons. In their letters home, they clamored for hard candy, chewing gum, jam, hot chocolate mix, Hershey bars, Planter's peanuts. Anything sweet or salty. Kid food. They craved ice cream sundaes, but there was no ice cream to be had. And from now on, they would also crave a sunny day on which to eat it—and would mostly find overcast skies, damp chill, rain, and snow.

The Americans were impressed with the manicured beauty of the countryside and the quaint, storybook aspect of the village. Sculptor Harold Dahl wrote, "I'm greatly impressed with the English towns, which are beautifully clean and tidy—and I rather like their conservatism. It's way better than Tennessee." But after a while, the local charm began to wear thin: "There are some lovely spots—all a bit too reminiscent of a seed store calendar, though," he wrote wryly. Dahl was one of the few enlisted men who managed a visit to London, where he hooked up with family friends, was treated to dinner at the Ritz, took in *Arsenic and Old Lace*, and toured the sights.

Waiting for the equipment, the troops could do little training, so passes were frequent and liberal. They found plenty of diversions right in Welles-bourne. The Women's Institute held Saturday night dances featuring a combo with saxophone, accordion-piano, and drums. The King's Head and the Talbot served good British stout until nine or ten o'clock. The lone movie theater was currently playing *Dixie*, starring Bing Crosby. The men played almost daily games of baseball on the sheep-cropped lawns or went canoeing on the River Avon. And always, there was poker.

It was an in-between time, the suspended moment between training and action. They filled it with sketches and paintings, sightseeing bicycle tours, and lots of talk about the future.

"The feeling over here is very optimistic and I suppose it is the same at home, what with the generals predicting an early end of the War," Dahl wrote. "Goodness knows it is hard to see how the Germans hold out against the pounding they are getting from all sides." His comrades shared his optimism.

But in spite of the dances, baseball games, and sightseeing, it was also a time of anticipation and some frustration. All the men sensed that they would be joining the war soon, but except for a few headquarters colonels, most had no precise idea just when that would be. Simenson, Truly, and Reeder visited the American headquarters in London, ciphering out plans for the Special Troops. As operations officer, Simenson was privy to the whole theater-wide plan for invasion, the conquest of France, and the final move on Germany.

A special liaison group of five officers inspected British dummy installa-tions at Ramsgate, near Canterbury, to compare equipment and tech-nique. It was not a very profitable excursion. The British were creating a phantom but static army on their home ground. The Americans would face a different challenge: mounting many-faceted shows on a fluid battle-field. The British equipment seemed clumsy and not as durable as the proto-types of the American equipment they had inspected, which was due to arrive any time now.

Lieutenant Colonel Olen J. Seaman Jr. of Reeder's staff was temporarily attached to Special Plans Branch at 12th Army Group to help direct the second part of the cover plan for the Normandy Invasion, called FORTI-TUDE SOUTH, which would portray the following story to the Germans: "We are now planning a very large scale assault in two phases. The first, and lesser, of these, mounted in southwest England, will be directed west of the Seine. When this assault has established itself, and drawn enemy re-serves from the Pas de Calais area, the main assault will be launched from southeast England against the Pas de Calais. First assault will be launched in July, the second as soon thereafter as practical."

The officers huddled, the troops waited.

Many of the troops took advantage of the lowbrow entertainments of Leamington Spa, a few miles beyond Wellesbourne—music halls, burlesque shows, movie theaters. Leamington was, coincidentally, the headquarters of Britain's Civil Defense Camouflage Establishment, an enterprise of artists, designers, and engineers who set up shop in a large hall known as the Rink, where a special viewing balcony allowed them to sight on model targets through a captured German bombsight against a revolving cycloramic background. The CDCE was responsible for the same kind of work the 603d had done back in the States: designing and building camouflage over coastal guns, airfields, factories, and other high-value targets.

Oddly, the *Official History of the 23d Special Troops*, written by Fred Fox with help from William Flemer III immediately after the war, does not indicate that any of the camoufleurs ever visited the Rink. It was a top-secret facility, perhaps even secret from the Americans.

Walter Arnett from headquarters company was dispatched to Swansea, Wales, to gather the dummy equipment for the camoufleurs. Three years earlier, during a three-night blitz, Luftwaffe bombers had unleashed more than 30,000 incendiaries and high-explosive bombs on the quiet seaport, whose most famous native son was the poet Dylan Thomas. The blitz killed hundreds of civilians, wiped out 41 acres of the town center and docks, and left more than 7,000 people homeless. But like so many cities in Britain, Swansea had cleared away the rubble and was back in business. Arnett's assignment would take him weeks, from mid-May until early June. The crates were off-loaded onto the Swansea docks bearing bogus labels, all carefully coded: "GLUE 6679" indicated an inflatable Sherman tank. Other code words indicated dummy artillery pieces, jeeps, antiaircraft guns, two-and-a-half-ton trucks, observation planes, all manufactured by the United States Rubber Company in Woonsocket, Rhode Island.

In order to track down all the equipment, Arnett carried orders authorizing him to board any ship and sail to any port. One incredulous MP to whom he presented his orders said, "Damn! If I had orders like that, I'd be on my way back to the States."

Arnett saw to it that each crate was addressed to "HONEYBOURNE" at Stratford, then loaded aboard a freight train. Each night via pay phone he reported in to Colonel Rapwatt—a name he was convinced was as fake as the labels on the crates of equipment—at United States Army headquarters in London. General Devers was no longer in command at ETOUSA. He had taken charge of the Mediterranean Theater—but the Cover and Deception staff he had created was still in place, and these were coordinating with Reeder, Simenson, and Truly in the Special Troops.

When Arnett had secured the last crates for transport aboard a freight train, he boarded the caboose and set off to rejoin his outfit at Walton Hall.

Before long, on the billiard-felt lawns of Walton Hall, engineers of the 603d inflated their first battalion of rubber tanks.

Now that the equipment had been delivered, the leisurely routine of baseball and sightseeing gave way to hard work. Morton wrote home, "We are all going all out now. We are working long hours and Sundays too."

They practiced inflating the dummies with compressor pumps and hand pumps, then setting them in position and constructing camouflage around them. The task was more complex than it sounds.

To exploit the enemy's sophistication in intelligence gathering required the deceiver to act with comparable sophistication. British pilots used to recount the story of the decoy airstrip that the Germans constructed to lure RAF bombers from a real airstrip some distance away. They lined out a farmer's field and built a squadron of wooden dummy airplanes, wooden gun emplacements, a sham fuel depot, and wooden hangars. But their camouflage was faulty and photoreconnaissance experts in Britain tracked the progress of construction with amusement. When it was at last completed, a single RAF bomber swooped in low over the airfield and dropped its load right on target: one large wooden bomb.

The Special Troops couldn't afford such amateurish mistakes. Their assignment was to practice *sophisticated* deception.

They had two basic means to fool the enemy: they could portray the false, or they could hide the real. Usually they did both together, using misdirection. As they hid the real, the Special Troops portrayed the false.

Their signature props were rubber tanks and guns—officially called "target equipment" or just "targets," unofficially called "items" or "balloons" or even "rubber ducks." In reports, they were often referred to as "dummies" or "decoys." The distinction is not merely academic. "A dummy is an imitation of something on the battlefield," explains the army field manual on battlefield deception. "A decoy is used to draw the enemy's attention away from a more important area. When a dummy is used to draw the enemy's attention away from some other area, it is also termed a decoy."

Most often, the camoufleurs used dummies as decoys. They themselves became living decoys. Sooner or later it dawned on most of them: their primary mission was to be sitting ducks.

The pneumatic rubber dummies were not made of rubber at all but of neoprene, a synthetic rubber highly resistant to oil, heat, light, and oxidation. Sheets of neoprene fabric were stretched over air-filled neoprene tubes, which gave the dummy shape and rigidity. They were painted either olive drab or in disruptive patterns of camouflage. To prevent them from being blown over in high winds, they were designed with tabs at the bottom through which the camoufleurs staked them to the ground, like tents.

Two types of pneumatic dummies were available: high- and low-pressure. High-pressure items required an air compressor or bicycle-style hand pump, while low-pressure items could be inflated with a blower—the army favored an off-the-shelf portable Home-Lite—or even a mouth tube.

The Special Troops used mostly high-pressure dummies. Their "Catalog of Targets" listed twenty items: trucks, scout cars, half-tracks, artillery of all calibers, light and medium tanks, observation airplanes. None of them weighed more than a hundred pounds; all of them could be inflated or deflated in a matter of minutes. A single "deuce-and-a-half" truck could carry fifteen or more deflated targets. One of the most important functions of the decoys would be to fool enemy photoreconnaissance planes, which employed twin offset cameras. After the plane made its passes over a designated area and returned to base, photointerpreters on the ground viewed the images through stereoscopes to produce a three-dimensional effect that betrayed telltale shadows, or their lack. Every dummy tank and howitzer was crafted with hard edges at distinctive points to create a realistic shadow "signature." In ordinary usage, camouflage netting was never hung at right angles to the ground but sloped outward to blend in with the terrain. Osnaburg strips thinned out from the center in irregular patterns, so that from the air a flattop would never appear as a rectangle but rather as a random blotch of foliage—and never leave a straight-line shadow. The Special Troops became masters of making "mistakes" in garlanding the flattops.

Because so much reconnaissance was done by air, shadows were what World War II camouflage was all about: creating realistic shadows that concealed the shadows of the real object, and realistic shadows that drew attention to fake objects. In addition to familiarizing themselves with the rubber decoys, the camoufleurs also practiced simulating artillery blasts with flash devices.

Most of the Special Troops would remain in England only a matter of weeks. The invasion of Normandy was imminent, the great campaign for which they'd been designed, or they wouldn't be here. Along every lane, artillery shells and boxes of supplies lay stockpiled in camouflaged depots under the trees. An airstrip had been efficiently bulldozed through two farms, a cricket field, and a stand of prized ancient oak trees. From it, Wellington bombers flew sorties across the Channel to destroy bridges, railway yards, and tunnels preparatory to the landings.

As the date of the cross-Channel invasion neared, convoys of heavily loaded trucks, troop carriers, and Sherman tanks clogged the narrow roads on their way to embarkation points in the south. The villagers lined the roads and watched them pass with a mixture of exhilaration and dread.

England had been bleeding for four years—in fallen Singapore and Hong Kong and along the Burmese Railway of Death; in the desert of North Africa, on Malta, in Sicily and Italy; at Dunkirk and in the U-boat lanes of the Atlantic and the Western Approaches; in the lethal skies above Britain and in the rubble of Swansea, Coventry, Bristol, Southampton, London, and scores of other cities and villages. The invasion would be the beginning of the end, but it would come at a cost, and the English would bleed more on the road to Germany—their remaining sons, fathers, brothers, husbands.

At the end of May, the camoufleurs trucked their equipment more than a hundred miles east to Thetford Forest to mount an exercise called Operation CABBAGE, in which they impersonated an armored division, a rehearsal for a real operation planned later for France. Aptly enough, in the summer of 1916, Thetford had been the site where British camoufleurs prepared the first tanks, developed in great secrecy, for action in France. The artists painted a disruptive pattern of browns and greens to break up the distinctive rhomboidal silhouettes of the ungainly machines. Though the name stuck, even the term "tank" was a deceptive code name to hide the real nature of the weapon.

Since the sonic company hadn't arrived yet, CABBAGE was a one-dimensional portrayal, and the camoufleurs didn't learn much in the way of new technique.

Vic Dowd found a local kid who was willing to sell him his bicycle and spent his leisure time pedaling along the country lanes of Warwickshire. In the course of his travels, he met a young woman in the Royal Air Force auxiliary, and the two spent many hours exploring the countryside, often in the evening, taking advantage of the lingering daylight.

Then word came of the invasion—Allied troops were at last landing on beachheads in France. "And I thought to myself, here some poor guys are sloshing around on Normandy beach and I'm riding a bicycle with a beautiful English girl," Dowd recalls. "We're sitting in the woods hugging each other and these poor guys are getting shot at."

He kissed her good night and returned to Walton Hall, where a conference was under way inside a lighted tent. "Who's that?" came a voice from inside the tent.

"Dowd."

"Get in here."

"Wait till I park this bike."

A sergeant stuck his head out of the tent. "You're not going to need your bike."

By next day, 14 June 1944, Dowd was in Normandy.

After an uneventful crossing, the SS *Exceller*, loaded with the sonic troops and their gear, sailed up the Firth of Clyde on June 10.

"We had a great night going up the River Clyde," John Walker remembers. He sat on deck with one of the platoon leaders and a couple of supply sergeants. "We were all singers, and we just sang all the way up the river." With a capella harmony in the pitch-blackness of the river, under a clear sky studded with stars, they sang "Carry Me Back to Old Virginny" and "Carolina Moon" and "There's a Long, Long Trail A-Winding"—hours of traditional folk standards and country songs with a sweet flavor of home, enjoying the camaraderie as the other guys gathered on deck listened from out in the darkness.

By first light, the *Exceller* lay moored to a Glasgow wharf. The sonic troops and their half-tracks boarded a train for their journey of nearly three hundred miles south to Walton Hall. Walker traveled by road in charge of a convoy of two deuce-and-a-half trucks loaded with crates of spare parts. "It was unique equipment," he says. "If something breaks down, you can't go down to the signal depot to get one, because there's none there. We had to have duplicates of everything we needed."

Soon a convoy of eighteen sonic cars—their equipment stowed under tarpaulins—and numerous jeeps, trucks, and half-tracks rolled up Jubilee Drive and into the pastures of Walton Hall. For a few weeks, the sonic troops, too, enjoyed the diversions of Wellesbourne, Leamington Spa, and Stratford, in between more practice sessions with their equipment. Walker even got to see a performance of *A Midsummer Night's Dream*, just as Fred Fox had.

But by the time Walker was stepping onto the dock in Glasgow, Fred Fox was manning a radio for the 82d Airborne as it attacked across the Douve River in Normandy, Dowd and his platoon had already survived their first artillery barrage, and the Special Troops had already taken their first casualties.

Act II
Onstage

GEORGE VANDER SLUIS

SEVEN

SEEING THE ELEPHANT

June–July 1944

The adjustment from man-of-action to man-of-wile was most difficult. Few realized at first that one could spend just as much energy pretending to fight as actually fighting.
—Capt. Frederic E. Fox

As a privileged member of headquarters staff, Fred Fox didn't have to rely on bicycle, army truck, or taxi to get around; he had his own jeep. "Like every other soldier, I've named my jeep after my lady," he wrote to Hannah, who was now working for the U.S. Army Signal Intelligence Agency in Arlington Hall, Virginia, from where she would be able to track his whereabouts throughout the war. "There is now a little neat ¼ ton dashing about England with HANNAH painted in two inch letters on its side."

As both a writer and actor, he couldn't wait to see Shakespeare performed in the Bard's hometown. So on a Saturday night soon after arriving, he had driven to the Memorial Theater in Stratford for a performance of *A Midsummer Night's Dream* by a London company. He was not disappointed. "It was the best Shakespeare I have ever seen. There is no stilted reverence. It is played joyously for the laughs and moving for the sighs."

But hardly had Fox returned from the theater when he was given secret orders to report to Eisenhower's London headquarters, where he was "bigoted." An individual who was bigoted enjoyed clearence beyond "top secret" and had access to the invasion plans. Two days later he was quarantined in a concentration area in Cardiff, waterproofing his jeep, Hannah, for D-Day. "The concentration area was on a hill of cinders in Wales," he wrote. "We stayed there for another week. We couldn't get out. The only things you could do were:

(a) put that sticky gum in the engines and
(b) study maps of the Cherbourg Peninsula."

His lighthearted, offhand tone belies the anxiety he and the others felt. They were all tired of waiting, overtrained in one sense and undertrained in another, fearful of what was to come and yet eager to prove themselves in action. Those maps of Cherbourg Peninsula—actually the Cotentin Peninsula, with Cherbourg at the tip—were not just topographical diversions. They were marked with the rectangular numbered symbols indicating four infantry divisions and one Panzer division of German Seventh Army—some 65,000 troops. These made up but a fraction of the fifty-eight divisions, 754,000 soldiers, that occupied France, all potential reinforcements against the initial Allied assult of about 175,000 troops.

Along with only a handful of officers, Fox knew the enormous scale of the Allied gamble. As waves of B-17 Flying Fortresses and B-24 Liberator bombers turned the sky over Walton Hall into a solid sheet of glittering aluminum, a single platoon of Special Troops, led by Fox, joined the invasion flotilla aboard the *John S. Mosby.*

Fox was not among the first of the Special Troops, a squad of four sergeants, who came ashore on D-Day, each aboard a different landing ship tank (LST). Their original mission was to set up dummy "Q lighting" on specified areas of the beaches to draw German fire away from the areas where troops were assembling. But as darkness fell, so many lights blazed across the sixty-mile-long beachhead that a few more wouldn't distract anybody, so this plan was quickly abandoned. Instead, the four camoufleurs organized the camouflage of supply dumps and command posts. Almost immediately, two of the four were wounded by incoming fire—Chester Piasecki and Tracy Slack. Piasecki was the ranking sergeant in 4th Platoon of D Company—Vic Dowd's platoon.

Dowd didn't know it yet, but he was already promoted to platoon sergeant.

Meanwhile, after a restless night aboard the *John S. Mosby,* under constant bombardment from shore batteries, Fox and his undersized platoon of twenty-four radiomen and three officers in eight radio trucks landed on Utah Beach the morning after D day, June 7. Fox drove in through the surf in his waterproof Jeep, Hannah, feeling a naïve sense of adventure and excitement.

Their code name was TROUTFLY—in his words, "a delicate lure."

At Eisenhower's headquarters in London, Fox had been "bigoted" for D-Day—briefed on the plan for the invasion, OVERLORD, and assigned his role: Proceed inland with an armored convoy to join up with the 82d Airborne, which would have dropped in ahead of the invasion to hold key inland positions against Germans trying to reinforce their beach defenses. "My mission was to pretend that I was three Regiments of the 9th Infantry Division assembling in the middle of the Cherbourg peninsula," he wrote. "My 24 men and I were supposed to represent the radio traffic of a division of 15,000 men and thereby dissuade the Nazis from counterattacking the paratroopers."

Fox prepared for the assignment like an actor for a character role: "To get in the mood, I sewed on the shoulder patch of the 9th Division, a circle of red and blue popularly known as 'the flying asshole.' "

The deception would all be done with spoof radio traffic. The idea was to "strengthen" the airborne unit of six hundred or so lightly armed soldiers with the muscle of a fully equipped, phony ground division until the beaches were secure and they could be reinforced with real infantry.

At least, that was the original plan. Then the planners received new intelligence. "At the last moment," Fox wrote, "Eisenhower's G-2 found evidence of a Nazi division squatting squarely in the middle of the peninsula." So the paratroopers dropped in much nearer to Utah Beach, and the deception became both unnecessary and impractical. On a beachhead crowded with waves of landing infantry, there would be no place to spread out a false radio net without giving away the positions of real troops. Fox's radio platoon was simply attached to the 82d Airborne, which had lost most of its radios when the gliders carrying them crashed into the Normandy countryside in the predawn darkness of D-Day.

The Allies controlled the air most of the time, but at night Luftwaffe fighters and bombers still flew missions to harass and demoralize troops on the ground. They weren't very effective, but the Allies threw up such a weight of antiaircraft fire against even a solitary bomber that razor-edged shards of exploded shells rained down almost every night all along the line.

Ground troops quickly learned to dig deep foxholes, then tunnel into the sides for protection from the fallout. Whenever possible, they also covered their holes with fence posts or sheets of plywood or steel salvaged from damaged equipment. It was hard, physical labor. "The ground is either rooty, clayey, or otherwise unpleasant," Fox wrote. "It takes a full hour with pick, ax, and shovel." During that first night ashore, as they dug in against German artillery and aerial attack, two of the radiomen were wounded by fragments from American antiaircraft shells. Friendly antiaircraft fire became one of the most lethal hazards to the soldiers massed onto the narrow beachheads. Fox wrote that it "filled the skies with the most extravagant and deadly designs."

For the first time in his army career, Fox knew stomach-clenching fear.

"It is very noisy here. My foxhole is three feet to my right," he wrote. "During an air raid try dissolving a peppermint Life Saver until it is paper thin. I chew mine almost immediately."

The 82d was assigned to break out west across the Douve River, not far from Ste. Mère Église, ten miles inland from Utah Beach, the southernmost of the beachheads. The paratroopers had drifted down onto Ste. Mère Église at dawn on D-Day, their parachutes hanging up on rooftops and church steeples, exposing many of them as helpless targets for the Germans. They had been in the thick of the fighting ever since.

Fox was a little overwhelmed by the tough, battle-hardened ways of the paratroopers, who didn't enjoy the luxury of making war with their imaginations only. They were the guys at the pointy end of the fight, always the first in and the last out, and they fought ferociously with guns, grenades, knives, even bare hands. They patched up their wounded, buried their dead, and kept on fighting. "The company was too rough for me," he wrote. "I did get some more strong antiwar material—especially from boys who had just killed Germans or were just going out to kill some more."

At dawn on June 10, the paratroopers moved out, their faces blacked by grease. They attacked eastward over the bridge at Chef-du-Pont while American fighter-bombers swarmed in and raked the town. "There was an unpleasant burnt smell all around," Fox recalled. After they had secured the bridgehead, Fox settled back in his jeep reading his book, *The Robe,* a story about a man obsessed with finding the garment Christ wore to the cross, which he believes holds magical powers. He was nearing the end, "the part where the Roman Centurion transformed an ugly little town with the story of Christ." Then his reading was interrupted by the aroma of coffee—two paratroopers were boiling coffee over a blue flame. He sidled over to borrow a cup, then all at once realized they were cooking with plastic explosive.

Then he noticed something else: a gang of men working over a fire-blackened German staff car. Inside were two badly burned officers. But the paratroopers weren't trying to extricate them from the wreck—they were already dead. When he got closer, Fox saw that, using their commando knives, they were picking gold fillings out of the dead men's teeth.

Later, writing of himself in a curiously detached third person, he recalled, "He decided to return to his jeep and begin reading *The Robe* all over again. That was also the moment he decided to be a Christian minister."

The tableau stayed with him for the rest of his life, a moment that defined him and confirmed him in his spiritual convictions. He summed it up this way: "Looking back on that Normandy road, it sometimes appears like Fred's road to Damascus. He saw no blinding light and heard no heavenly voice, only a wild blue flame and the coarse talk of the paratroopers, but he thought he saw a meaning in it for him. *The Robe* could be the Bible and the people reading it could be the Church. The paratroopers cooking with dynamite are trying to blow up the world. The corpse pickers are callous men who do not give a damn. The Church is between them.

"There is hope for the world if Churchmen would leave their storybooks and climb out of their jeeps. Fires have to be put out and men— even enemies—treated as human beings."

Fox remained with the paratroopers almost till the end of June, his initial sense of adventure now tempered somewhat by the reality of what he was seeing: bombed-out houses and barns, ruined villages, bodies scattered about in fields, burned-out tanks on the sides of roads, their crews hanging out of hatches charred and mangled. The stench of dead livestock and human bodies choked the air along with the odor of smoke and char.

Yet it was beautiful country, full of apple orchards, grain fields, and thick stands of old-growth forest in full summer leaf. "This country is a very unreal combination of desolation and rich pastorals," he wrote. "I still think I am seeing everything at a newsreel theatre. I cannot accept this as an actual way of life."

More heartbreaking than the ruined countryside were the people, caught in the middle of the battle. Later on, as the Allies moved on to Paris and the Rhineland, there would be plenty of room behind their lines for refugees. But for now, the Allies controlled only a shallow area near the beaches, and there was no room for refugees. The French remained in their homes and villages, getting pounded by both sides. "The people continue to act stunned," Fox wrote. "One little child gave us the Nazi salute not knowing whether we were German or American—and not caring very much. All she knew was that we were soldiers and destroyed things."

Sergeant Vic Dowd arrived by airplane at the landing strip near Ste. Mère Église on June 14. On the big C-47 crossing the Channel, he struck up a conversation with two young women, army nurses. "What in the world are you doing here?" he asked.

"As soon as the plane lands, they're going to put severely wounded soldiers on the plane who can't be treated over there," they answered, "and we're taking them to hospitals in England." The big army hospitals in

England had already been cleared of any patient who could walk out, in order to prepare for the expected influx of mangled soldiers from the beachheads. And just as they had explained, as soon as the plane landed its load of fresh troops, medics began loading the worst casualties aboard: young soldiers who had lost arms and legs, who had been ripped apart by artillery fire and were held together by bandages and deft stitching, men who had been blinded, shot in the face, crushed under the treads of their own advancing tanks.

Twenty-four litters full of wounded were checked aboard by the nurses and a surgical technician, the litters fastened three-high into racks, and within twelve minutes of landing, the plane was on its way, and a seemingly endless queue of other planes was repeating the same routine.

Dowd's platoon of fifteen men under Lt. Bernard Mason carried with them a trailer full of dummy artillery. Their job was both to set up the fake batteries of 155mm rifles—to lure the Germans to attack them instead of the few big guns that had been landed—and to camouflage the real guns emplaced in other positions. A week after the initial landings, wrecked and shattered vehicles were strewn about everywhere, and the countryside was still littered with German corpses. The Allies had efficiently collected their own dead. Cows, disemboweled by artillery blasts, hung upside down in trees. The whole scene was surreal, nightmarish.

Dowd had been on the move for all of one night and most of the following day, and he was exhausted. He settled into his foxhole to wait out his first night ashore. Almost at once, he fell fast asleep. In the morning, the guys in his platoon were buzzing. "Christ, that was some bombardment last night!" one of them told him. During the night, they had been hit hard from the air, but luckily no one in his platoon was hurt. "I slept through it!" Dowd recalls, still incredulous. "Now if the cat sneezes, I wake up! But I'm telling you the God's honest truth, I sat there with my mouth closed sort of half wishing I had known what was going on."

His first night under fire, and he had slept right through it. He displayed the sort of reaction you couldn't predict—nobody knew how he would react to real war until he was right up against it. Training was fine, but ultimately it couldn't prepare a man for the actual stress of shelling, aerial bombardment, shooting and being shot at. Cliff Simenson says, "The first time a man is under fire, you see immediately what he is made of. Does he do what he has been trained to do, or does he freeze?"

Dowd's reaction, a product of physical exhaustion, was remarkable but not unheard of. As the war went on, there were plenty of stories of exhausted men falling asleep right in the middle of battle.

Other moments were equally strange, though not as dangerous. "Here we are, it's the first week of the invasion," Dowd says. "This is a war-torn part of the world: St. Lô was demolished. Carentan was demolished." A jeep pulled up and a one-star general hopped out of the jeep. He wasn't Patton, but he looked like him—bald head, imperious manner. "Now, you're just not used to seeing generals—you're just not."

"Who's in charge here?" the general demanded.

"I am, sir," Dowd answered.

The general pointed out a guy in Dowd's platoon. "This man needs a haircut—report him to your commanding officer!"

"The jerk was probably from the rear echelon, wanted to drive up to the front, throw his weight around," Dowd recalls, still shaking his head at the chickenshit—the enlisted man's term for petty harassment by moronic or sadistic officers. Veteran and historian Paul Fussell writes, "Chickenshit is so called—instead of horse- or bull- or elephant shit—because it is small minded and ignoble and takes the trivial seriously. Chickenshit can be recognized instantly because it never has anything to do with winning the war."

Dowd had seen his share of chickenshit in training, but somehow he had never expected it here, with lives on the line. "I thought to myself, *Christ, this is crazy.*" He never reported the long-haired soldier.

For his service under fire in Normandy, Dowd earned the Bronze Star. As he would for all decorations for individual service in the Special Troops, Fox wrote the recommendation.

The bulk of the camoufleurs, designated the ELEPHANT task force, started out from Walton Hall under Reeder on June 16, but they got lost in transit and wound up at Exeter for two nights until they finally reached Southampton. There they boarded two LSTs, No. 284 and No. 335, and headed for Normandy in a convoy of ships carrying fresh troops and supplies to the beachheads.

But they got lost again. Inexplicably, LST No. 284 dropped out of the convoy and anchored off the Isle of Wight—Fairbanks's old amphibious base—for a whole week. At least the men languished in comfort. They enjoyed nightly movies in the tank deck; hot bread, fresh butter, and coffee after the show; and an extensive ship's library of classical records. Occasionally they sighted "buzz bombs"—the recently unleashed V-1 rockets—headed for England, reminding them of what lay ahead.

The first LST carrying the ELEPHANT task force made it to Utah Beach on June 24, the "lost" LST three days later. The remainder of the

Special Troops, except for the sonic company, arrived later still on the same cramped Liberty ship that had brought Fox and his platoon to France, the *John S. Mosby*. Under command of Lt. Col. Hector Truly, the last headquarters officer to make the crossing, the troops scrambled down the side of the hull on cargo nets and rode in through the surf in "rhinos," small amphibious landing craft.

Probably no other unit in the army was sent to the continent in such a deliberately scattered fashion. As Fox reported, "It took two months, two planes, and nine ships to get all of the 23d from England to France."

Bill Blass, who had recovered from pneumonia in time to join his outfit and cross to Normandy, observes, "You got a bit wet. I just remember that you thanked your ass that you were out of England and off that boat. We didn't think of it so much as a challenge as a *destination*, that maybe this was the beginning of the end."

The little, curious details stick in the veterans' memories. Jim Laubheimer wrote, "Just before we drove the trucks up the ramp of the imposing LST, somebody came around to collect the gas masks that we had carried everywhere for nearly two years." Why they no longer needed gas masks was never explained. Each camoufleur, however, was allowed to keep his own carrying case, which made a handy safe for pens, ink, paints, brushes, pencils, and paper.

Laubheimer, very much aware of his lack of experience, used to study the other artists at work and try to learn from them. "I absorbed what they were doing. I'd watch them—not watch what they're doing but the *kinds* of things they did. What I thought of as *art* was really picture making. And what I learned from these guys is that art is the manipulation of form and space." Among the many fine artists in the outfit, Shilstone in particular impressed him with his eye and technique. "He was young, but he was a very good watercolorist," Laubheimer says. "He could paint fields—a plowed field—stuff like that. But they were *paintings*, not *pictures*."

Shilstone remembers standing at the rail of the ship, queued up for landing. "I looked around and saw all the ships and landing craft and barrage balloons, and it was really an amazing sight," he says. "I thought, this is really *history*. I really did think that." So he did what came so naturally by now—got out his Esquire spiral sketch pad and fountain pen and drew the whole scene, which he titled, "Landing in Normandy." Sketching was how he would get through the war. "You did it to keep from going crazy," he says. "It was just so automatic, like writing or talking."

Once they got on the beach, they were alert to the strange new world around them. "It was late afternoon, *very* quiet, and the beach was fairly

Arthur Shilstone's D-Day sketch (ARTHUR SHILSTONE)

clear," Laubheimer wrote. "If one did not look too closely, it was like coming in from a swim in the ocean and heading for the sand dunes that often rim the beach." Except for the silhouettes of soldiers and gun emplacements on the dunes.

And the small knots of soldiers pulling bodies out of the surf—men who had washed out to sea with the tide and were only now floating back in.

George Martin, who used to design sheet-music covers, was now the battalion photographer. He was astonished and shocked to see nurses and officers having sex on the beach. For him, it remained one of the strangest sights of the war: Waves of fresh GIs plodding out of the surf toward the dune line while naked young lieutenants and nurses cavorted in broad daylight on a beach where so many had died so recently, so violently.

The Special Troops were among 600,000 men and 104,000 vehicles landed on the Normandy beaches from D-Day through 18 February 1945. One million tons of supplies poured ashore through the surf. Forty-three thousand wounded were taken off, along with 24,000 German prisoners.

Laubheimer motored in through the surf in a convoy of a jeep and four trucks carrying the secret dummy equipment. With him were eight other enlisted men under the command of a lieutenant. They drove over the dunes and across the swamps behind them on a newly laid road. An MP halted them at a crossroads on the other side and told them that the area where they were headed hadn't been secured yet. They should stay put until nightfall. "Finally a colonel who had misplaced his own unit agreed to take us to his idea of a safe place, so we fell in behind his jeep and slowly set out," Laubheimer wrote.

They drove using only "cat's eye" taillights—two slivers of red. If they merged into one, the vehicle ahead was too close. Tracers arced into the sky—beautiful, lethal trails of automatic guns—and shellbursts illuminated the horizon. "Surprisingly, we were not frightened—probably because we were too excited," he wrote. They kept driving. After a while, they came upon a sign knocked down on the side of the road: St Lô. Now they could hear the rattle of machine guns, the *pop-pop* of small arms fire. The little convoy drove straight down the rubble-strewn main street into St. Lô, which was still held by the Germans.

At the other end of town, they halted at a sign that read: ACHTUNG MINEN! They had driven straight into a minefield.

"We were right smack dab in the middle of the goddamned thing!" Laubheimer recalls. "So we made that colonel turn around and we followed his tracks exactly with our trucks—turned around and went right back the hell out."

They found a haven for the night in a pasture surrounded by hedgerows and were awakened by an irate colonel berating them for having parked in full sight of German observers. They quickly moved into new positions under cover of the hedgerows and camouflaged their vehicles to wait for the rest of the Special Troops to catch up with them a few days later.

The Special Troops practiced their rudimentary French, learned from army phrase books. A few, like the Wood-Thomas twins, Alan and Gilles, who were born in Paris were fluent. They bartered American cigarettes and soap for fresh eggs, tomatoes, and apples from local farmers and filled their canteens with cider for five francs, about a dime. Beer came with the enlisted man's rations, Scotch and gin for officers. Wine and liquor were ubiquitous. "In the states I used to drink rye, beer, and highballs," Hal Laynor observed in a letter home. "In England, I drank bitters, half & half, ale, & scotch, here in France I'm drinking only champagne, cognac, cidre & a French version of panther fire called calvados. It will reline your tonsils at one gulp. We use champagne as a chaser."

Cognac was so plentiful, they fueled their cigarette lighters with it and slapped it on as after-shave.

Like so many of his pals, Laynor had grown a rakish mustache—his was redder even than his hair, now cut close—and smoked a pipe he had bought in London for four dollars. Like all the artists, he was simultaneously dazzled by the French countryside and appalled at the destruction in every field and village. This was the land he had dreamed about coming to as an artist, but he had never imagined he would see it amid the ugliness of war.

And like the others, he got his first taste of war, and of fear. "The anti-aircraft open up once or twice during the night and sounded like rapid-fire thunder, only a damn sight louder," he wrote home to his new wife, Gloria. The fear was not always rational: "Once an apple fell off a tree and landed on my head & I thought it was flak; it was only a sour apple."

Some of them felt an irresistible curiosity to see the Germans close up. Laubheimer crawled through a hedgerow and came face to face with a German soldier—and both retreated. Shilstone and one of his pals, Norman Sakowitz, decided they would get as close as they could to the front line and take a shot at the enemy. He says now, "When you think of how young you were and how stupid!" With his submachine gun primed to fire, he climbed up the ridge of a hedgerow and jumped down the other side. As he landed, the butt of his submachine gun smacked the ground hard and the weapon went off, zipping a burst of bullets right past his own head.

He says, "Then we decided it was a little ridiculous, and we went back."

Ellsworth Kelly found his first Germans by accident, during a recon mission with an officer and three other enlisted men. Their jeep driver got them lost behind enemy lines, and they blundered into a rest area full of troops. "We came into a clearing and there are Germans in their underwear washing clothes," Kelly recalls. "The Germans looked up, startled, but before they could do anything, we made a fast U-turn and drove out of there."

Not even an artistic sensibility could soften the devastation of war. As they followed close on the heels of the Allied advance, the Special Troops witnessed time and again the awful carnage of armies fighting at close quarters with automatic weapons and tanks.

Normandy was country boxed in by hedgerows—six-foot-high ridges of root-packed earth overgrown with thickets of oak, beech, and chestnut trees tangled in brush, flanked by ditches and often sheltering sunken roads—perfect hideouts for Panzer troops waiting in ambush. Every pasture was thus enclosed by a natural defensive line and entered by a swinging wooden gate. They called it *bocage* country.

Soon after landing, Shilstone's platoon entered such a pasture, filled with the shattered remnants of an American armored column. The Germans had been waiting in ambush inside the hedgerows and, as the column filed into the field, opened up with antitank guns, *panzerfausts*—literally, "tank fists"—and machine guns. They wiped out the entire column. It was the sort of mistake that was happening all over Normandy, as green troops struggled to survive their first battles. Shilstone spotted a German helmet lying in the grass and reached down to pick it up for a souvenir. Too late, he discovered that it held half a man's bloody head.

The camoufleurs often set up their own displays inside such "boxes" to fool aerial reconnaissance. They'd drive in through the gate and deposit four to six bags holding decoys—jeeps, trucks, tanks—around the pasture, then inflate them to mimic a small encampment. With a compressor, a gang of camoufleurs could set the stage in half an hour. Then the platoon would take turns standing guard, four hours on, four off, to keep out civilians and unauthorized "friendlies."

Ellsworth Kelly happened to be guarding such a pasture display one afternoon when an officious general and his three-man staff pulled up at the gate. The general sprang out of his jeep and demanded, "Who are you?"

Kelly lied—just as he had been ordered to. He gave the name of the unit they were impersonating, the one signified by his fake shoulder patch and the fake bumper markings on their real vehicles. The only true information he volunteered was his serial number. The general moved toward the gate, but Kelly refused to let him enter the pasture.

The general was livid. "You can't tell a general he can't come in!" he said. "Who are you and what are you doing here?" He pushed past Kelly and got as far as the first dummy jeep. He leaned against the "jeep" and it collapsed under his weight. "What the hell?" he exclaimed, looked around, realized he was invading some higher-echelon secret, and without another word climbed into his jeep and roared off.

It was clear the Special Troops were learning their job—and learning confidence. They could say no to generals.

Soon after landing in France, Colonel Simenson himself was forced to say no to a general—albeit with heartbreaking reluctance. An old comrade from Infantry School, now a lieutenant general in charge of a division, sought him out. "Can you get loose from your assignment and come with us?" the general wanted to know. He needed reliable commanders.

At last, here was the career opportunity Simenson had longed for: command of a combat infantry battalion. This was the job he had trained for as a company commander with the Philippine Scouts, the leadership position he had been groomed for at Infantry School and in the headquarters of Army Ground Forces in Washington. He knew the fighting army inside out—hell, he'd even made one jump with the airborne. He could almost taste the satisfaction it would bring.

Besides, for senior officers, the Special Troops was a dead zone for promotion. If he stayed with the unit, he'd never rise above lieutenant colonel—the table of organization called for only one full colonel, Reeder. If he transferred to a line outfit, he'd surely make colonel, probably even brigadier general before the fighting was over. Combat action was the path to promotion—and to glory.

"Boy, I thought, this was my chance," Simenson says. "But from West Point you have a code of Duty, Honor, Country." Simenson had been briefed on the theater plans—Eisenhower's overall strategy in Europe—as well as the more local plans of armies, divisions, corps, regiments. He even knew the details of the deception plan that would keep the Germans braced for a landing at the Pas de Calais for precious weeks after D-Day, their Panzer reserves waiting for an attack that would never come instead of repulsing the real invasion in Normandy.

"I was loaded with information," Simenson says. "It would have been terrible if I'd been captured—and they had ways of making you talk."

Duty prevailed. Simenson told the general, "I'm so loaded, I can't go with you right now."

He couldn't even tell the general what he knew, why he must turn down the best offer of his career. "I look back on that moment, and it was the crisis of my life," Simenson says. "I turned him down, but I think I did the right thing. The only reason I did it was Duty, Honor, Country."

He didn't have time to brood. As the Allies massed their forces to break out of their beachheads, attacking through a picturesque town called St. Lô, the camoufleurs would mount their first large-scale operation of the war, ELEPHANT.

The two Frenchmen wheeled their bicycles around a curve in the road and stopped short: A tall American soldier in full battle dress, brandishing a submachine gun, stood blocking their way. "Halt!" he demanded.

They dismounted and froze.

Around them loomed the thick woods of the *Forêt de Cerisy*, dense thicket and tall spreading trees, their top branches interwoven into a canopy that filtered the late summer light, refracted it across the narrow road and clearing in fluttering dapples. A dozen miles to the rear lay Omaha Beach, still littered with wreckage from the gale that had smashed its artificial "MULBERRY" docks little more than a week earlier. Less than ten miles down the road to the southwest lay the crucial crossroads of St. Lô, one of several German strongholds blocking the Allied breakout from the Normandy beachhead.

On D-Day and on every clear day since, Allied B-17 Flying Fortresses had pounded the city. Yet the Germans still held out. The Americans were massing for another push, shunting armies around to get ready, and the Special Troops were part of the plan.

Cpl. Arthur Shilstone was standing sentry duty in an area that was supposed to be secure from both German infiltrators and errant civilians. Yet here were two guys on bicycles casually wandering past. He checked their papers. They stood there in front of him gaping, and he realized all at once they weren't paying any attention to him.

"They were looking at something over my shoulder, their eyes getting larger and larger, their mouths dropping open," he recalls. Shilstone yanked his head around to see what they were staring at. "As I turn around to look, I see these four GIs picking up a forty-ton tank and turning it around so the gun faced a different direction."

Their cover was blown. Shilstone did the only thing he could think of: He crooked his arm into a Popeye muscle and declared, *"Les Américains—ils sont très forts!"* Very strong GIs, indeed! The Frenchmen mounted their bikes and pedaled away in a hurry, casting suspicious looks over their shoulders until they were out of sight.

Shilstone was part of Operation ELEPHANT, the first chance for the main body of the camoufleurs to show their stuff. Forty officers and 351 enlisted men took part. Staged from 1–4 July 1944, it coincided exactly with the eighty-first anniversary of the Battle of Gettysburg—won by Gen. George Meade, namesake of the army base where the camoufleurs had trained.

The 2d Armored Division had been held here in the forest in reserve. Now it was moving up to plug a dangerous gap in the line between First U.S. Army and Second British Army. The Special Troops were taking their place.

They would continue playing their show until the Third Armored Division moved into these woods, then they would, in Fox's showbiz lingo, "fade out."

The Special Troops moved on to their next operation through St. Lô, which had been leveled by heavy bombers and artillery and suffered the worst devastation of any inhabited place in France. When the Special Troops finally entered the town, all that remained standing was a single church steeple.

Laynor sketched the awful destruction and later painted the scene: *St. Lo, Omaha Beach Head,* Oil/Masonite, 25" × 13"—one of fifty canvases he would paint of wartime scenes he had witnessed.

In the painting, there is no horizon. The sky is a smear of olive-drab and black, with slashes of white limned by burnt orange. The sky melds with the wreckage of broken buildings, burned-out frames, a chimney of blackened white bricks thrusting into the gloom with no house left to warm. On the far right stands a charred white remnant of the facade of a house—door blackened, shutters hanging crazily. Nothing is whole.

You don't see them at first, camouflaged into the rubble: two soldiers, carbines at the ready, patrolling the wreckage of what was once a street—now clogged with debris. The soldiers have taken on the ultimate camouflage: the colors and texture of the war.

They are hiding in plain sight.

The D-Day invasion that opened the Battle of Normandy was a historical coup.

It was also a tragedy of errors, a scene of confusion, screw-ups, and lethal mistakes, saved only through the overwhelming surprise achieved by the FORTITUDE deception plan and the amazing courage and resourcefulness of the enlisted men and junior officers who made it past the beach.

The paratroopers were scattered far from their intended drop zones. Thousands of American troops were landed on the wrong beaches, and heavy weapons were lost in the high surf. Scores of men weighted down with heavy field packs and ammo drowned in deep water far from the beach. Twenty-seven of the thirty-two "dual-drive" tanks, equipped with flotation skirts and propellers, sank like stones, one after another, taking their full crews to the bottom. Aside from the loss of good men, each tank was a critical loss—there were so few in the first waves.

And off the beaches, the mistakes compounded. Despite months of training, infantry had not been taught how to secure a fortified house, of which there were thousands in Normandy, and had to discover through bloody trial and error which tactics worked. Infantry squad leaders couldn't communicate with the tankers who were supposed to support them, buttoned up inside their armor—sometimes they simply had to stand up directly in front of the tank and point toward a pillbox they wanted destroyed. And somehow Intelligence had missed the most glaringly obvious feature of the Normandy landscape: the dense hedgerows with their sunken lanes, impenetrable even to tanks until a special serrated plow was improvised and welded onto their fronts.

Small wonder—only a handful of the hundreds of thousands of men involved had any experience at all in combat. The Special Troops were no exception. In Operation ELEPHANT, they did just about everything wrong.

To begin with, the orders to simulate the 2d Armored Division came down on the same day that the division pulled out—leaving almost no time to reconnoiter the area, to plan, or to organize an effective deception. There was little coordination either with First Army headquarters or with the local commanders of the companies moving out. Sometimes tanks left the area long before the camoufleurs arrived to set up their shams.

The vehicles of the 23d were not painted with the bumper markings of the 2d Armored, nor did the Special Troops wear appropriate shoulder insignia to misidentify themselves to local collaborators, as those two French bicyclists might easily have been. No Special Troops were costumed to impersonate key officers in the 2d Armored.

"Lieutenant Fox came to me, said we need a major general," Simenson recalls. "I said, you know, it's a court-martial offense to impersonate a general officer. He just looked at me—I could tell he was thinking, *This old so-and-so.*"

No one was detailed to spread misinformation either to other friendly troops or to civilians.

Radio traffic moved off with the real units—only one spoof radio went on the air. In theory, the tankers would maintain radio silence. But in fact they rarely did, a breach of discipline that the Germans had already learned to exploit. Even if the dummy tanks were spotted from the air, any German operators listening would probably confirm in short order that they were fakes.

The real tankers rumbled away in full daylight and made no attempt to black out their unit markings or command post (CP) signs. The terrain was scored with their treads moving in obvious heavy concentrations toward a new location. It would have been easy for anybody to track their progress into their new positions.

In evaluating the effectiveness of ELEPHANT, one lieutenant colonel, James W. Snee, criticized the camoufleurs for not making enough "mistakes" in their camouflage—they were too good at it. "Teach platoon leaders to make mistakes instead of waiting for CC Commanders to spot them," he recommended. "As a general rule, make ⅓ mistakes very bad, ⅓ medium, and ⅓ barely discernible." He further admonished: "Everyone works, no one eats or sleeps until the job's done."

Snee's colleague at headquarters, Lt. Col. Edgar Schroeder, was not impressed either. "Signal Telephone Procedure is disgustingly inferior," he wrote. "Applies to officers and men." And then he hit a nerve: "Men feel doubtful as to the value of their work. Recommend that a thorough critique be held for all officers and men who participated in the operation."

After the operation, Fox lamented, "As in most of the 23d deceptive work, it was impossible to discover exactly how successful Operation ELE-PHANT was. There is every reason to suspect, however, that little good was done."

Fox and the others may have been a bit too pessimistic and premature in their initial assessment. A month later, headquarters staff reached a different evaluation. "The results of this operation are uncertain. . . . However, no movement of forces to counter the move of the Armored division was made by the enemy and captured documents indicated that the unit which was simulated was still considered to be the actual Armored division in its original location several days after the conclusion of the operation."

So they had gotten lucky.

But it was clear—at least to Fox—that the Special Troops had done an amateur job. There were big lessons to learn.

Never shy about voicing a strong opinion even as a lowly lieutenant, a week after ELEPHANT concluded, Fox fired off a three-page, single-spaced secret memo to Reeder and his colonels: "The attitude of the 23d Hqs towards their mission is lopsided. There is too much MILITARY . . . and not enough <u>SHOWMANSHIP</u>. The 603d Engr, on the other hand, contains too much <u>ARTISTRY</u> and not enough <u>G.I. TACTICS</u>. The successful practice of military deception by the 23d Hqs requires the proper amount of <u>SHOWMANSHIP</u> and <u>ARMY PROCEDURE</u>."

Fox's brash self-confidence and razor wit show through in the style of his writing—not the typical dry, bureaucratic prose of the regular army. He went on to recite chapter and verse of each mistake. "May we recount some past examples of the 23d's failure to play its role thoroughly—due either to its servile obedience to AR's [Army Regulations] or its lack of appreciation of the Fine Art of the theatre."

He quoted one colonel giving orders to a band of camoufleurs: "Get the installation in, then lie down and take it easy. All you got to do is blow up the tanks and then you can go to sleep."

Even his mimicry of bad usage—"All you got to do"—was a taunt to his superiors.

"This is very bad 'theatre,' " he wrote. "The Colonel forgot that we were in the show business and thought he was actually dealing with real tanks and tankers." But for Fox, the dummy tanks were merely "scenery": "—the <u>PLAY</u> must go on until the 23d is released to return to its base camp. They must repair 'Tanks,' hang out washing, go looking for cider and generally mill around in typical GI style."

Some of the dummy tanks were not tended very carefully—as the atmosphere chilled and reduced air pressure inside the tubular frames, they sagged noticeably. Barrels wilted. Fox wrote, "There is nothing so unawesome as a limp gun."

There must be radio traffic, he went on, especially constant demands for gas—the signature gripe of an armored unit.

"Some Frenchmen were amazed and delighted with our rubber tanks in the Forest de Cerisy," he wrote. "They have certainly spread this delicious gossip far by now." Security must be tightened. No civilians must be allowed to view the dummy equipment up close.

The man in charge of executing all deception was the Plans and Operations officer—Simenson. Still regretting the lost opportunity of a lifetime, he could easily have taken Fox's blistering memo as a personal attack on his performance and abilities, yet Simenson did just the opposite. He was more concerned with accomplishing the mission of the Special Troops than with salving his own ego. In plain testament to his flexible leadership style and personal character, he listened and incorporated Fox's ideas into every future action of the Special Troops, always giving credit to Fox.

Fox became more integral than ever to headquarters planning and would finish the war a captain with a Bronze Star for meritorious service. The two became friends and colleagues who respected and relied on one another for the rest of the war. Simenson still remembers him with admiration and fondness. "Here is this young officer coming in, a fine man with a good imagination," Simenson says. "He's the kind of guy who made it go—not the guys on top."

Together, acting on Fox's suggestions, full of common sense and stagecraft, they forged the core of doctrine for army deception:

From now on, Special Troops wore the distinctive shoulder patches and other insignia of the units they were ordered to impersonate. Sometimes they were borrowed from the real unit; other times the artists simply created their own. Everybody learned to sew. In seven minutes, they could take on the appearance of any outfit in the army. Even though this tactic violated the letter of Army Regulations, as Fox pointed out, it was a necessary deception.

"Since the enemy was known to be employing a large number of low-grade agents for the express purpose of ascertaining U.S. shoulder patches, bumper markings, and CP signs," he wrote after the war, "—and since it was quite apparent that a very accurate U.S. Order of Battle could be reconstructed by the enemy from these easy visual evidences—it was obvious that the 23d had a new 'spoof' weapon to play with. This weapon was called SPECIAL EFFECTS."

Under an umbrella of Allied air superiority, the Special Troops could not count on daily observation by Luftwaffe photoreconnaissance planes. They would direct much more of their show to ground agents: local collaborators, infiltrated spies, recon patrols.

Special effects included not just bogus shoulder patches and bumper markings, but a whole new bag of tricks:

Advance detachments now reconnoitered the unit to be "covered" just as if it were the enemy, learning how to imitate its style of encampment and movement, the peculiarities of its commanding officers, even the regional accents or distinctive Morse key-touches of its radio operators. They learned a nutshell history of the covered unit, to be rehearsed with other Special Troops, so that if captured and interrogated—by either the enemy or friendly forces—they could lie, credibly, about who they were, where they had been, what they had done.

Other guys were assigned to sham drunkenness at local cafés and brothels, to shoot off their mouths, deliberately spreading misinformation about their false unit's plans and capabilities.

Special Troops not in the field servicing the equipment or putting on sonic deceptions would drive around in convoys in order to be seen and recognized as belonging to a particular outfit that was actually someplace far away.

And men who resembled certain generals would be costumed accordingly, driven conspicuously around in jeeps with scarlet license tags bearing the appropriate number of silver stars to indicate rank. Fox complained that this idea had been dismissed prior to ELEPHANT because it violated Army Regulations.

In a parenthetical aside, Fox asked, "Is not the whole idea of 'impersonation' contrary to ARs? Remember we are in the theatre business. Impersonation is our racket. If we can't do a complete job we might as well give up. You can't portray a woman if bosoms are forbidden."

"Fred was always going to write a story called 'Generals I Have Known or Been,' " Hannah Fox remembers. "I don't think he ever actually played a general, but often when somebody was pretending to be a general, he was his aide."

Colonels, too, were impersonated. George Rebh, then a captain in charge of the Combat Engineers company, recalls, "On two separate occasions, two officers, a major and a lieutenant colonel, came to see me at headquarters, and I was wearing eagles." The distinctive insignia of a full or "bird" colonel, outranking them.

They said, "How the hell did Rebh get promoted so fast?"

Rebh answered obliquely, "Fortunes of war." He says, "Not only did we fool the enemy—we fooled our own people."

Fox recommended the use of fake road signs directing traffic to bogus command posts, fake sentry posts manned by MP impersonators, even double agents who would infiltrate across the lines and spread misinformation among civilian collaborators on the other side, to be picked up by the Germans.

Another important drawback had to be reckoned with. "His groups were certainly not welcomed by the units they were pretending to be when they came on the line," Hannah Fox says. "Because it always meant that there was a weakness." Just as at El Alamein two years before, if the Allies had sufficient tanks and soldiers in place, they'd have a lot less use for dummies. The number of landing craft available in England had limited the number of tanks and troops they could land on D-Day, and many were lost in the landings and subsequent fighting. Until the Allies captured a working port, all reinforcements would have to come in over the MULBERRY docks or through the surf.

From ELEPHANT's termination on, the headquarters colonels would not only have to work more closely with higher headquarters on their plans; they would also have to become traveling salesmen, selling the worth of their shows to skeptical commanders in other units—regular army officers as wary of their tactics as Simenson had been on first coming to the Special Troops. Fox noted, "It was not easy to convince a commander to buy a division of rubber dummies when he much preferred a battalion of real armored guns."

Putting on a convincing show required more than merely blowing up battalions of dummies, portraying the false. First, the officer directing the display must be thoroughly familiar with the way an actual unit of tanks or artillery would deploy and set up. Say they were setting up tanks, as they had in ELEPHANT. Days before any dummies were unloaded, the airwaves would crackle with radio messages, alerting Allied units that a column of tanks was coming into the line and tracking its progress: Fictional tankers— actually Signal Corps spoof radio operators using Fox's scripts—would ask for directions, request a tow for a damaged vehicle, call in routine reports to their forward command post.

Just before the camoufleurs prepared to deploy, a real tank or bulldozer would arrive to score tracks into predetermined positions—so that when a dummy tank was set up, on the ground leading to its position would be two lines of obvious tread marks, presumably the ones it made driving in there. The sonic cars would begin projecting the noise of tanks arriving and harboring, the shouts of guides directing them into position, then their motors shutting down.

Then the hard work for the camoufleurs began. In pitch dark, often in rain or snow, they would inflate each dummy as close to the desired position as they could, use muscle power to finish the setup, stake it down against wind, and then camouflage it. There was an art to making a fake tank appear to be a real, hidden tank—especially in the dark, when it was impossible to stand back and eyeball the setup to determine if it looked real and also remained just visible enough to be spotted by an alert enemy.

If they camouflaged it too well, as they'd been accused of doing during ELEPHANT, the enemy would never know it was there. They would have fooled nobody but themselves. Too conspicuous, and the enemy would suspect it was a sham. So they had to mimic the mistakes real tankers made when pulling into a "harbor" for the night: Leave a length of the barrel sticking out of the net. Leave a gas can exposed to catch the morning light and flash a telltale glint to an enemy spotter. Drape the net too loosely, so that the shape of the tank stood out. Leave a gap in the foliage.

Portraying an artillery battery was even more involved. Not only did they need to erect the gun behind a sandbagged position, but depending on the caliber of the gun, there would be certain other necessary props and stage dressing. The hardest part of a real artillery battery to camouflage was always the blast marks on the ground in front of the gun. Every time it fired, it left a new and definite mark. It blackened earth, seared vegetation, melted snow in a fan pattern easily recognizable from the air. So the camoufleurs had to reproduced that pattern—"paint" it on the ground.

Some calibers of guns required a separate fire direction post, connected by field telephone, so they had to construct that. Then there was the ammunition pit to dig and camouflage, the used shell casings to discard nearby, the slit trenches to dig for the fictional gunners, and of course sets of tracks to make—the tractor or truck that hauled the gun into position, the jeep used by the company commander making his rounds, the footpaths of men moving in and out of the position to the latrines, the field kitchen, their bivouacs. The Special Troops were essentially creating lifesized dioramas.

Setting up a display required many hours of physical labor guided by an instinctive sense of perception—how the display would look to the enemy.

In a strange way, their displays were realistic art installations—three-dimensional statements on the nature of reality. But in the darkness and cold and sleet of the front, during a long frightening night frequently punctuated by artillery barrages, there was little time to meditate on art theory. It was just hard and dangerous work.

The Special Troops hid the real through "blacking out" an actual unit—sending it to a new location under cover of darkness, in radio silence, all its identifying marks removed, under strict security against spies and collaborators. A team of advisors from the Special Troops would travel with the unit to ensure that the blackout was performed with thorough discipline.

And once in its new location, the Special Troops would supervise the concealment of troops and vehicles under garlanded nets, or their dispersal under the natural cover of shrubs, woods, orchards, vineyards.

When Joint Security Control authorized the activation of the 23d Headquarters Special Troops, it built the unit around the camouflage battalion, and for good reason: The British had demonstrated camouflage was the key to battlefield deception. And for the British, camouflage already meant not just hiding the real but showing the fake in such a way that its "fakeness" was concealed. The Special Troops took camouflage to a new level—they actually created faulty camouflage, camouflage designed to draw attention to fake objects. They were hiding the fake by making it seem real enough to hide. The whole mission took on a postmodern flavor. They were engaged in persuading an enemy to make a decision by altering his perception: things were not as they appeared.

The French Surrealists, many of whom had served as camoufleurs in the First World War, would have been delighted at the turnabout. Their signature technique was placing a physical object in an alien context, thereby creating an absurdity—a technique so familiar by now in art, movies, and advertising as to seem clichéd. But it is a technique that challenges not only our assumptions—whether an object is in the context where it "belongs"—but also our perceptions: What are we really seeing, and why is it there? What could be more absurd than an inflated rubber object on a battlefield? The camoufleurs called them "balloons" or even "rubber ducks," recognizing the joke. The inflated tanks were toys, more suitable for a child's playground than a killing zone.

If one can imagine the whole of the European battlefield as a giant "picture," a German High Command wall map that graphically illustrated the progress of the war, the Special Troops were painting on a huge canvas. By creating nonexistent armies and concealing the whereabouts of real ones, they were fragmenting the coherent picture, disrupting the overall pattern, altering perception on a grand scale.

In effect, they were camouflaging the Allied order of battle—a military term that means exactly what it sounds like: which armies are where, and what objectives they will attack and when.

In the phrase of the old practical joke, *camouflet*, this was blowing smoke up the enemy's nose in a big way. It was the ultimate hiding of the real—secret soldiers moving armies around like pieces on a game board. The hand was quicker than the eye: some of the armies were real, others merely imaginary, and only a chosen few knew the difference.

This was the new mission of the Special Troops—camouflage used in a highly sophisticated way. It required a new level of creativity, and with that came a new level of risk. "It was thinking on the spot," Rebh says. "Training on the spot."

"We didn't know how to teach them," Simenson says. "We didn't know all the techniques. We had to learn them on the battlefield."

They would get their next tutorial at Brest—a costly lesson that would haunt Simenson for the rest of his life.

EIGHT

BAD SHOW AT BREST
August 1944

The valuable lesson learned was that the deception plan must be based on what you want the enemy to do, never on what you want him to think.

— David Mure, in *Master of Deception*

In August, when Eisenhower moved his headquarters from England to Granville, on the far coast of the Cotentin Peninsula from Omaha Beach, platoons of the Special Troops erected flattops and hung fishnets across an entire field between hedgerows and camouflaged several acres beneath it. They felt proud to do it. Granville was strategically located near the crux of the Cotentin Peninsula and the Brittany Peninsula to the south. At the western tip of each was a deep-water port: Cherbourg and Brest.

On D-Day, the Americans had attacked from Omaha and Utah south across the Cotentin Peninsula, then turned east, toward Carentan, St. Lô, Coutances, Granville, and Avranches, cutting off the peninsula. By June 27, Cherbourg was in Allied hands. But Allied planners didn't believe that one port alone could supply the growing army on the continent.

Once the sonic company landed after Operation ELEPHANT, the Special Troops were again divided and sent on four long, interesting, and dangerous convoys to aid in the capture of Brest, at the far western tip of the Brittany Peninsula.

Simenson, still trying to get a handle on their mission in those early days, says, "With our first operation, we didn't do any good. On our next operation, we sent four columns out just to create confusion with no idea of what we were doing. . . . It was the breakout of Normandy, and we just wanted the picture that Americans were all over the place."

Their journeys toward Brest were organized into an operation called BRITTANY. "It wasn't a good time to use deception because everyone, friend and foe, was confused enough as it was," Fred Fox admitted. "Nevertheless, our special angel at army headquarters thought we could be useful."

Actually, the plan made some sense, despite the reservations of Fox and Simenson. The Special Troops would provide some cover for Patton's newly activated Third Army. Patton's very presence in Normandy had been a secret up till that point.

The "special angel" was "a crazy Yale man," Maj. Ralph McAllister Ingersoll, former editor of *The New Yorker, Time,* and most recently the New York newspaper *PM.* Ingersoll had made a reputation as a left-leaning New Deal disciple. Like FDR he was hawkish on going to war against Germany. But when he was drafted in 1942, Marshall Field, the Chicago department-store owner who bankrolled *PM,* intervened with the draft board on Ingersoll's behalf, and got him a new hearing. But Ingersoll was drafted anyway. The public furor caused reached Congress. "He lets other men do the fighting for him," Rep. John E. Rankin, a Democrat from Mississippi, told his colleagues. "So far as I know, he is as patriotic as any man who ever clamored for war and then dodged the draft by proxy."

Not quite fair: Ingersoll was a World War I veteran and purposefully traveled to London to experience the Blitz and write about it. He had considered his profession, newspaper publisher, essential to the war effort. But once in the army, he learned his trade well, first in combat in North Africa and later as a staff advisor who made frequent forays to the front lines. Ingersoll was one of six senior officers comprising the staff of Special Plans Branch of General Bradley's 12th Army Group. Special Plans Branch, working with two liaison officers from the Special Troops, formulated deception scenarios for the whole ETO and used the Special Troops to carry them out—exactly the setup that Douglas Fairbanks Jr. had urged two years earlier.

In addition, Special Plans Branch coordinated closely with the British deception staff at Field Marshal Montgomery's 21st Army Group, a fact that would become extremely significant in the campaign for the Rhineland.

Fox picked up his orders at "Lucky Forward," Patton's advance headquarters near Avranches, on the Golfe de St. Malo, like Eisenhower's headquarters at the crux where the Cherbourg and Brittany peninsulas joined. "I remember the smell very well," Fox wrote. "There was a bloated Nazi corpse on the ground outside the tent. Patton seemed to want to keep it there as a lesson of some sort. Or a hunter's trophy."

The Special Troops impersonated four combat teams of divisions from Patton's Third Army: the 35th, 80th, and 90th Infantry, and the 2d Armored. Each column assembled in the area of the actual division it was impersonating, then as that division moved out to the east as part of Third Army's envelopment of German Seventh Army, the Special Troops swung south and west into Brittany, eventually to converge at the end of the peninsula at Brest.

The BRITTANY feint worked in one unexpected way—what deception planners called the "monkey's paw" effect, minor unforeseen consequences resulting from a ruse: stragglers from the real divisions joined their columns.

"When they saw trucks plainly marked with their regimental insignia, it was hard for them to keep from jumping on board," Fox noted. But once aboard, the soldiers were confused: They didn't recognize any of their pals. Some were merely nonplussed; others broke down and wept because they assumed their buddies had all been killed, and these were their replacements. "One boy from the Eightieth went clean off his rocker," Fox reported. "He thought we were kidnapping him."

The Special Troops were still fighting the skepticism of combat commanders. Originally, they were code-designated "ARIZONA." But now assigned to 12th Army Group, they got a new code name: "BLARNEY." The mocking name stuck. Ever alert for irony, Fox adopted the term for future operations, referring to the "Blarney" signal plan for this or that campaign.

Already the Special Troops were settling into their new role, adopting a veteran mode of dress and behavior. Sculptor Harold Dahl, now sporting a blond mustache, wrote, "One amusing practice over here is that of wearing a scarf of parachute silk under our wool shirt—some of them are mottled green—mine is Dutch blue."

Jim Laubheimer's column rolled southwest down the coast of Normandy toward Brittany. The roads were lined with infantry, trudging along under the weight of rifle and pack. Everywhere they saw signs of recent battle—wrecked tanks, dead horses still hitched to German supply wagons, shell craters, bombed-out buildings. The Germans weren't very far away.

At Coutances, near the opposite coast of the Cotentin Peninsula from Omaha Beach and close to Eisenhower's headquarters, as Laubheimer's jeep motored past a building whose front facade had been blasted away, he spied something. "Look!" he yelled, pointing. "There's a whole store full of 'em!" Suddenly the convoy of trucks lurched to a halt and drivers tumbled out, hugging the ground. The infantrymen threw themselves into ditches and aimed their weapons, ready for a firefight. Laubheimer sat in his jeep, marveling at the sight in the bombed-out store: a whole showroom full of grand pianos, completely undamaged. After a few seconds of anxious silence, the other guys caught on. One by one, the infantrymen picked themselves up out of the mud and started to laugh. The drivers climbed back into their trucks. The tension was broken, and everybody relaxed.

They'd almost attacked a bunch of pianos.

Laubheimer played jazz piano and couldn't resist staring; he felt a nearly irresistible urge to jump out and go play some tunes. All through the war, in the most unlikely circumstances, he had the knack for finding a piano. Later some guy from his platoon wrote up the incident and sent it to *The New York Times*, which published it in a series about "Weird Stories from the Western Front."

They traveled on, one scene of destruction melding into another. The French were friendly, if shell-shocked, but there was something strange about the population. Richard Morton put his finger on it. "Of the French, we see only the old, the weak, and the children present. None of the young or of the strong are to be found left."

He formed the habit of illustrating his letters home with miniature sketches, some in color, of the sights along the way, especially the people: farmers standing in a dooryard, a family seated at a table with GIs, men and women riding bicycles, leaning across fences, often smiling and waving. One ink sketch pictured a little girl on her way to Sunday mass wearing a dress and bonnet, slogging along a muddy lane in wooden shoes, carrying a second pair of shoes in her hands. "The little girls are dressed up especially colorful and can be seen trudging along narrow muddy hedgerow lanes on Sunday wearing wooden shoes," he wrote, "but carrying a dress pair to put on just before going into church."

As company mail clerk, he was always the first to know when a new batch of letters caught up with the outfit. One of them came from Penguin Books in New York. Several of his army sketches depicting barracks life had been chosen to appear in a pocket-sized paperback to be published that same month, called *G.I. Sketch Book*, and the publicity department needed a bio and photo—and could he please supply a current address? Two other 603d camoufleurs contributed sketches to the same volume: George Vander Sluis and Olin Dows.

As they turned the corner west into Brittany, where hatred of the occupying Nazi army had been virulent and resistance heroic, they were even more shocked by the condition of the people: gaunt, homeless, shell-shocked, many deprived of everything they had owned in the world. But the Bretons welcomed the Americans with wild enthusiasm. "It is quite a thing to see the refugees on their way back to their homes," Harold Dahl wrote, "some of which are in a sorry state—not only because of battle but it seems the Germans had a way of smashing glassware & furniture & whatnot on their way out."

Dahl was an outgoing guy of medium build who could swing a hammer with either hand. His hair was dark brown and his face ruddy. Even before the army, he spent lots of time outdoors in the Adirondacks. An actor and singer as well as a sculptor and painter, he'd won a scholarship to Cooper Union in New York, but his folks couldn't afford the room and board, so to feed his appetite for learning, he devoured literary magazines, books, and plays.

In England, like the other guys, he had written home asking for candy and gum, small amenities to make his own life a little more comfortable. Now he wrote asking for food and toys for the bedraggled, malnourished French children he met, child-sized dresses for little village girls, Red Cross parcels to be sent directly to this or that family. Many others did the same—first sharing what they had and what they could cadge from the army—rations, spare clothes, shoes, blankets—then turning to their relatives back home to send more.

"Please send me also some cheap costume jewelry for the little girls. All 10¢ store things would please them no end," Dahl wrote. "When we take them 'bon-bon' they look at us like we were God Almighty."

For himself, Dahl collected a German compass and wooden shell box to store rations. Morton mailed his parents a French wine bottle—empty—and a handmade *tricoleur* French flag that had hung from the window of a mayor's house, a gift to him from the mayor's daughter. Others mailed back German helmets, French perfume and francs, strips of parachute silk. And always art: sketches of the countryside, paintings of farms, portraits of their buddies, the old men stationed in cafés, the kids. Laynor decorated his letters with cartoons. Art Singer drew exquisite miniatures of birds and animals in the margins of the letters he sent to his daughter.

For a young artist, the journey through Normandy and across wartime Brittany, despite its dangers and the ever-present destruction of war, was an adventure, the chance of a lifetime.

Between villages, the woods were still full of Germans. The columns took sniper fire, detoured around strongholds, collected prisoners from roving bands of *maquisards*, officially known as Free French Forces of the Interior (FFI). One column covered more than six hundred miles, to Lorient on the south shore of the Brittany Peninsula.

August 1944 was a chaotic time. In the early hours of August 7, in fog and darkness, four German divisions counterattacked Patton's newly activated Third Army at Mortain, near Avranches, Patton's headquarters. Under Lt. Gen. Hans von Funk, 116th Panzer, 2d Panzer, 1st SS Panzer, and 2d SS Panzer swept in from the east. But Patton had received an early warning of the attack from decoded ULTRA intercepts and blocked it with three divisions: the 80th, the 35th, and the French 2d Armored.

When dawn broke and the fog lifted, waves of British Hurricane and Typhoon fighter-bombers roared down on the advancing German columns. Then American artillery, directed by observers placed on strategic hills, opened up and stopped the attack cold. One of the objectives of BRITTANY was to keep those stopped German units from retreating long enough to surround them from the north and south.

The sonic platoons wouldn't be projecting their "music" along the march, merely playing the role of armored infantry. They were held up at Avranches until the German counterattack had been repulsed, then ordered on their way. Bill Brown, as usual, was in the half-track just behind Major Williams's jeep. Not far along the road, the commander stopped at an MP roadblock. "Now watch yourself," he heard the MP warn the major, "because everybody uses this road. The Americans use it, and the Germans use it."

They kept their eyes peeled and didn't spot any Germans. But really, at night, it was hard to tell whose army anybody belonged to.

The objective of Operation BRITTANY was to make the Germans believe that the Americans were weakening their forces on the main battle line and diverting them into Brittany on a large scale. This would embolden them to remain in the Normandy pocket. Once the Allies were on the move out of their beachheads, the longer German forces lingered near the coast, the greater the chance that Patton's forces in the south could link up with the British-Canadian forces to the north and surround the enemy. The Germans were confused about Patton's intentions, at least partly, and, for a combination of reasons, including the Brittany ruse, began their retreat too late to save a large portion of their army.

When they finally disengaged and began their retreat on August 16, the Germans were under constant fire from field howitzers, large-bore artillery, fighter-bombers, tanks, bazookas, and machine guns. By mid-August, as the Special Troops headed west deeper into Brittany, the Panzer divisions and the other remnants of German Seventh Army were in full retreat east, trying to escape the closing encirclement of the British Second and Canadian First Armies, led by the Polish 1st Armored Division, to the north and

Patton's Third Army, with the 90th Division leading, coming from the south.

All told, about a hundred thousand Germans attempted to escape through a narrow gap in the lines between the American and British armies that became notorious as the Falaise Gap, after the crossroads town in the center of the pocket. By August 19, the gap closed to a five-mile stretch between the villages of Chambois and Trun on the Dives River. About ten thousand Germans were killed outright, and fifty thousand more were captured. The remaining forty thousand got away, but left behind most of their vehicles, tanks, and guns. Their tortured path was strewn with the dismembered bodies of horses and men, many of them grotesquely flattened by tanks. Men wore gas masks to keep out the stench of death.

It was a stunning slaughter and a great victory for the Allies, but historians have argued ever since about who was to blame for not closing the Falaise Gap completely in time to capture German Seventh Army entire. As usual, on one side of the debate are partisans of Patton; on the other of his rival and nemesis, Montgomery, knighted after El Alamein and soon to be promoted to field marshal.

But other Germans units were fighting to the end. And the "German" units weren't always German. They were manned by every nationality from Nazi-conquered Europe and Japanese Asia, including Poles, Russians, Cossacks, Mongolians, Koreans, even Chinese. So even negotiating a surrender wasn't always simple. Many of the troops who were captured didn't even speak German, let alone English. Small bands of rogue or escaping troops roamed the countryside, firing on anybody who passed.

The Allied armies at first stalled and then after Falaise raced ahead of their supplies so rapidly that their order of battle was a mess. The operation was a success beyond what even Eisenhower had dared hope, but it was a success that needed to be brought under control, consolidated, and exploited.

Fred Fox often described the war in terms of football. In his analogy, the Battle of Normandy had begun as a slugging match between linemen for incremental small gains in yardage, but now the running back had broken out and was heading for the enemy's goal line—Germany. All the carefully planned blocking maneuvers were suddenly out the window. Everybody just raced ahead to keep up with the play.

But not the Special Troops. They were heading toward the wrong end zone.

While the four columns headed for Brest, one sonic platoon was detoured to St. Malo, on the north coast of Brittany, where the offshore fortress Ile de

Cézembre stubbornly held out. There it cranked up its heaters not to fool the enemy but to demand surrender. The Germans replied with shellfire, but missed. What the engineers at the Army Experimental Station had discovered was true: you couldn't hit a sonic projector unless you could also see it.

Company C of the camouflage battalion had an even closer call. Going into bivouac in an open field bordered by hedgerows, they had barely dug their foxholes when a barrage rained down on them. Holt remembers the harrowing moment. "We had our holes pretty well dug, and all of a sudden these shells started coming in—*shee-putt!* All around us." The men could do nothing but hug the earth and listen to the big projectiles slam down in the mud all around them.

Mysteriously, none of the shells exploded—just buried themselves in the mud. "We found out two weeks later that the shells had been made by slave labor and they had left the detonator caps out," Holt says. "We would have been *gone!* Company C, *gone.*"

The Special Troops' remarkable luck was holding.

Meanwhile, two liaison officers from the Special Troops traveled ahead directly to Brest to prepare for the show there: Capt. Edward M. Cowardin and Lt. Col. Frederick E. Day. Among other duties, they established radio contact with the four "notional" columns heading toward Brest, thus enhancing the deception. Day managed to earn a little unexpected glory. While reconnoitering with troops from the 6th Armored Division, which had unsuccessfully attacked and was now heading away from Brest, he helped capture three hundred enemy troops—and a cache of excellent German chocolate.

Far to the south, another Allied invasion of France was under way, Operation ANVIL. The landings on the Mediterranean coast were screened by daring seaborne deceptions, and Lt. Comdr. Douglas Fairbanks Jr. was right smack in the middle of them. He'd been given a choice: Sail with the Normandy invasion fleet as an observer, or stay in the Med and actively participate in the secondary invasion. Fairbanks was not by nature a spectator—he was an actor.

"The principal and ultimate strategic aim of ANVIL was to relieve enemy pressure on our forces in Normandy," Fairbanks wrote, "to attempt, after a great amphibious assault, to swing inland to the north and envelop the Nazis in a huge pincer movement."

Since shipping out to the Mediterranean Theater, Fairbanks had been on the inner loop of all deception planning. "In my case, I was the only American who had had practical experience in all this hocus-pocus," he wrote. "Hence I had to prepare, with help, the special operation plans for future tactical deceptions."

In addition to his diversionary missions during the landings at Sicily the previous July, he had performed further heroics in the campaign against Italy. Fairbanks and a group of four other officers, including Henry Ringling North, heir to the circus fortune, had captured an entire island— Ventotene, a prison island with a radar installation and a garrison of several hundred troops. They landed at night, mistakenly motored their whaleboat into the wrong cove, and eventually, after much cruising around in the dark, found the little harbor. The German defenders heard the boat noise in several places, assumed large landings were taking place that would surround them, and retreated into the hills, leaving their Italian counterparts to surrender first. Fairbanks and his contingent expected a horde of paratroopers to follow them onto the beach.

John Steinbeck, then a war correspondent, wrote wryly about the incident. "*December 8, 1943*—The five men from the destroyer moved restlessly about the quay on the island of Ventotene which they had accidentally, and with five kinds of luck, captured. The paratroopers did not arrive."

Eventually the Germans, too, were coaxed into surrendering—on a bluff that six hundred troops were already ashore, and two cruisers waiting offshore to shell them if they resisted.

By the time of ANVIL, Fairbanks had already won a combat Silver Star for his "conspicuous gallantry and intrepidity in action while attached to a special task group during the amphibious assault on Italy in September 1943." The Italians would later award him their War Cross for Military Valor. But he still didn't always get respect. When a plane was requested to fly him to Corsica to plan the diversions for ANVIL, a snide radio operator wired back, "Is Air Command carting Fairbanks over to look for his Corsican brother?"

The invasion target was the Marseilles-Toulon area—once again, the Allies were after a deep-water port. Fairbanks commanded a task unit of eighteen PT boats, one of several flotillas of small, fast boats armed with light weapons and heavy heaters, into the Baie de La Ciotat. On August 15, they were in position. "After darkness the first night we were to pull out all the stops—with some help from the air forces—in our efforts to suggest another major landing right there."

On August 17, the destroyer-corvette U-Jäger *Capriolo* and an armed converted yacht, *Kemid Allah*, appeared out of the morning mist and their big guns started hammering one of the other Beach Jumpers' units. Fairbanks didn't hesitate. He ordered his own boats to attack. For his quick, decisive action, he was awarded the Legion of Merit. The citation read in part, "On the morning of August 17, when two hostile vessels attacked a group of smaller craft, he courageously led the ships of his unit into action and, aggressively directing the combat operations with expert seamanship against heavy odds, greatly aided in the ultimate sinking of the two vessels."

In addition, he was cited for "immobilizing enemy reinforcements attempting to resist the landings." For those with any doubts about the scale and substance of his wartime service, the citation concluded, "By his brilliant leadership and steadfast devotion to duty throughout this vital period, Lieutenant Commander Fairbanks contributed materially to the successful invasion of a highly strategic area."

He was out of his father's shadow at last.

It seems appropriate that Fairbanks, the rakish, flamboyant Hollywood actor, reluctant hero of adventure films who worked always in the shadow of his swashbuckling father, should turn out to be a real hero, daring real dangers. That as movie star and friend of royalty and the very rich, he should fight this part of his war on the French Riviera. No place less suited for war has ever been invented. The climate there is sunny and dry, like southern California, the land of movies, which copied its Mediterranean architecture and lifestyle. As part of Vichy France, the south had not been ravaged by great battles. Its people were largely provincial, living a rural life of hard work tempered by a certain grace that comes with taking one's time. Except in resort areas along the coast, they lived scattered in small villages built on high ground, a legacy of the days when they had banded together to ward off Moorish marauders.

Now they had long since formed fierce cells of resistance to the Nazi occupation, and they jubilantly welcomed the Americans and British. Their tough native shrub lent its nickname to the French Resistance: the Maquis.

In the flurry of activity following the Normandy landings, German troops had moved from Brittany to reinforce positions in Normandy. But intelligence was fairly vague on exactly how many and which troops were left behind to defend Brest. Major General Leonard Gerow estimated that it was defended by only three thousand to six thousand Germans of mixed, ineffectual garrison units. Three weeks earlier, during the first week of August, he had sent the 6th Armored Division to capture the city. The tankers had raced a hundred miles in six brutal days of fighting across the Brittany Peninsula, isolating them farther each day from the main army. But at Brest, the heavy guns and fortifications stopped them cold.

Long before D-Day, Eisenhower and his planners had determined that capturing the ports of Cherbourg and Brest was crucial if they were to support an Allied army in France. Otherwise, they'd be forced to land tens of thousands of badly needed reinforcements and millions of tons of matériel on the beaches, through heavy surf and in chancy weather that would deteriorate into shipwrecking gales as summer turned into autumn.

Nobody had ever supplied four entire field armies across an open beach—unloading crates of ammunition by hand, rolling one truck at a time ashore through the surf, ferrying soldiers in by the dozens instead of the thousands. What they needed were deep-water concrete wharves, giant cargo cranes, fleets of sturdy forklifts, a line of big Liberty ships unloading at the docks twenty-four hours a day and more waiting behind them, all the materiel flowing in one smooth conveyor belt onto connecting highways and railroads.

This had evolved into an industrial war, and the Allies couldn't win it without massive superiority in tanks, motor transport, heavy guns, ammo, and fuel. Already they were running out of artillery shells, rationing gas, dragging shattered tanks off the battlefield with big tractors and patching them up as best they could while they waited for new ones to arrive from the factories in America. Without immense quantities of supplies and fresh troops delivered in a hurry, the whole invasion might falter, then disintegrate into another Dunkirk. It might turn out worse than if they had never invaded at all—so Eisenhower had feared. Even now, more than two months after D day, the Allies could still find themselves stalled in France while the Germans regrouped.

And Brest still held out. As long as it did, Patton's—and Eisenhower's—army was divided, with part of it fighting its way east toward Paris and part of it attacking in the exact opposite direction. This division was not only inconvenient but dangerous. It contravened the basic principle of waging war, laid down by Clausewitz, the great Prussian theoretician of warfare, during the last century: "There is no higher and simpler law of strategy than that of *keeping one's forces concentrated*." The big risk was that there wouldn't be enough troops on either front to win decisively. But Patton had little choice: Eisenhower had ordered him to take Brest, a paramount objective, while still breaking through toward Paris in the opposite direction. The imperative to capture Brest was a vestige of the original OVERLORD invasion plan, and as events developed it proved unnecessary. Once they broke out of Normandy, the Allied armies moved too quickly to be efficiently supplied by a port so far to the west. Cherbourg, too, played only a minor role, as the navy and quartermasters performed logistical miracles with landing craft of every size.

But following plans forged in England far from the scene of battle, Patton diverted precious men and tanks away from the main battle line in order to take the port. Since taking Brest was no use if the port were destroyed in the attack, he couldn't resort to the kind of massive aerial bombardment that had leveled St. Lô. Three infantry divisions from Third Army—the 8th, 2d, and 29th—would try to accomplish the hard way what the tankers of 6th Armored had failed to do: take Brest.

On August 20, with Operation BRITTANY successfully completed and the Special Troops more or less assembled at Le Fremondre in Brittany, they once again divided into three task forces for Operation BREST: X, Y, and Z. Cliff Simenson took command of Task Force Z and headed for Milizac, a wooded crossroad northwest of Brest. In two days his troops were in position, reconnoitering the most effective sites to mount their displays of decoys. Ten miles east, Capt. Oscar Seale in command of Task Force X was doing the same thing. And three miles beyond Seale's force, Lt. Col. John W. Mayo commanded Task Force Y, a team of camoufleurs who would impersonate a field artillery battalion. The mission was simple and rather brazen: to simulate overwhelming armored force and thereby induce the German garrison at Brest to surrender.

If the Germans could be coaxed into surrender, the 2d, 8th, and 29th American Infantry Divisions, already worn out from months of hard fighting and constant movement, could be spared an attack in which it was certain many of them would die. The rout at the Falaise Gap had broken the back of the Wehrmacht in Normandy, and in that sector, the Allies could hardly corral all their prisoners. Fox wrote, "It was reasoned that since the Germans had been giving up fairly readily, they might capitulate again if faced by a sizable corps."

But this was Brittany, not Normandy, and Brest was a fortified position held by an indeterminate number of troops. The estimate had increased from six thousand to sixteen thousand, and it was anybody's guess which units they were.

Both Task Forces set up dummy tanks among small detachments of real tanks from the 709th Tank Battalion, an independent unit attached to infantry to support attacks. If the effort to scare the Germans into surrender failed, the real tanks would go in with the infantry.

Simenson's Task Force Z emplaced its pneumatic dummies on the south side of a gentle slope about eight hundred yards below a ridgeline, facing south toward the city. This was typical deployment strategy for an armored force: avoid giving a silhouette to enemy gunners, but leave the tanks in a position to fire from camouflaged positions. A real tank drove around the area at dusk, scoring the ground with tread marks leading into the dummy positions.

After full dark, starting about 10:30 P.M., the camoufleurs began inflating their "balloons." "Work was extremely difficult due to complete darkness and constant rain," Simenson reported. The wet camouflage nets proved too heavy for the inflated tanks to support and collapsed them, so the nets had to be propped up with poles or left off altogether. Valves leaked, as did some of the tubular frames that formed the structure of the hollow tanks. Just before daylight, in C Company's area, only two tanks out of twelve were left standing. The camoufleurs worked on them in the blackness and pouring rain and managed to fix nine of them, but three remained useless.

All told, forty dummies mysteriously appeared in position overnight—a phony 69th Battalion of the 6th Armored Division—which at that moment was more than a hundred miles east, closing on the Vilaine River and anchoring the southernmost point of Patton's battle line.

The hard, all-night work paid off.

In the morning twilight, Capt. Thomas C. Perry, commander of A Company, 709th Tank Battalion, and Simenson walked the ridgeline to inspect the dummy positions through field glasses, then climbed into a church steeple in Milizac for a better view. Both were delighted at how realistic the dummies looked. Perry remarked that he couldn't spot the sham tanks among his real ones, which were strategically placed in fields along roads so troops and civilians could see them up close. Simenson reported, "He was enthusiastic about the display."

But Simenson realized something was missing from the show—there was little activity around the tanks. He ordered more movement: Rig up extra pup tents, light cookfires for breakfast, haul gas cans, hang out laundry, and generally act the role of tankers getting ready for a fight. By now, he, too, was getting the "theatre attitude."

Meanwhile, their unloaded trucks, now marked with the insignia of the 6th Armored Division, toured through villages in the area. Two men sat up front and two more in the rear looking out the tailgate, so that any spy seeing the truck pass would assume the whole truck was full of troops.

Meanwhile, thirteen miles east of Simenson's force, the camoufleurs of Task Force Y were having trouble with the igniters. Task Force Y's mission was to simulate artillery fire. They'd set up their pyrotechnics more than a thousand yards in front of the real 37th Field Artillery batteries, well within range of the enemy's big guns.

The night was pitch black, damp and chilly, again threatening rain. They had been ordered to dig in—and deep. At least five feet, Colonel Mayo told them: narrow, deep slit trenches. It didn't take a genius to figure out why: If all went well, they'd get a pounding.

If all went *well*. What in the world would happen if it went badly?

The platoons were broken down into six batteries of one "executive" and four loaders, commanded by two lieutenants under the company commander and connected to headquarters by a field telephone. One battery set up its sham artillery devices on the ridge of a hedgerow and took shelter in the sunken road behind it. Jim Laubheimer was squad leader, "executive," in second platoon of B Company.

Each loader slid a flash bomb containing half a pint of black powder into a tube fashioned from a used 90mm antiaircraft artillery shell casing, and ducked into his trench. Then on a signal from the officer, the "executive" switched on the juice by sparking two live leads together with a telegraph key. The current flowed from a battery into a wire resembling the heating element in a toaster. The igniter would glow hot and set off the flash. It was supposed to ignite the powder instantaneously.

From where the German observers were watching five hundred yards across the rough Brittany countryside, each shooting flash would look exactly like the blast of a 155mm gun. Laubheimer often wondered what the enemy thought when he saw the flash but heard no incoming missile, but that was for the higher-ups to worry about. They crouched in their slit trenches and waited—three seconds, five, ten—too long. Suddenly the flash shot out of the tube in a brilliant flare of sparks with blinding surprise.

But sometimes the flash bomb didn't fire at all. The powder was too damp or the battery too weak, and they'd have to gingerly unload the charge, set it up, and try again. In training at Fort Meade, they'd seen some guys get badly burned by not being careful enough. Basically, each time they lit the powder, they were setting off a small explosion, using the tube to blast the fire upward. Their instructors had warned them: You can get hurt playing with firecrackers.

Four igniters burned out on the second volley, and the spares simply dissolved in the dampness. They had to find a better way. This was Wednesday night. On Saturday morning, three battle-weary American divisions—forty-five thousand men—would launch themselves against the citadel of Brest, and Task Force Y was helping prepare the way.

Obviously, merely pretending to fire artillery shells at the enemy would do little to capture the city. The second and riskier part of Task Force Y's mission: *To draw enemy fire.* First, the enemy would spot the periodic flashes and zero in on their position. If all went as planned, the Germans would misidentify them as a real artillery battalion, calculate their position by targeting the flashes, and fire on them. It was known as "counterbattery fire" or simply "CB"—one artillery battery trying to pulverize the other. On the face of it, the mission was absurd, potentially suicidal. Here were a handful of guys starting an artillery duel against real guns and trained gunners, while they themselves were armed only with fireworks. Practically every other soldier in the army, from Patton on down to the lowliest private, was doing his best to avoid becoming a target. The idea was to shoot at the enemy, not to let him get a clean shot at you.

At some level, all the Special Troops were aware of this dangerous role, one they were to play many times. Today when they talk about it, they shake their heads and laugh a little nervously, admitting that in those days they did their best not to think about it. Dwelling on their vulnerability would have just increased their fear, made it harder to carry out the mission. Even so, they worked in constant fear, especially of artillery, which literally fell out of the sky on them without warning. To distract themselves from being afraid, they cracked jokes, shared stories, or just concentrated on the task at hand.

Laubheimer sums it up for all of them when he shakes his head in wonder and says, "How we came through it, I'll never know—I really don't. Sometimes we did stuff that was absolutely stupid." They were young, they obeyed orders, they trusted each other, and they trusted their luck.

It was all topsy-turvy. On this mission, the camoufleurs would "win" their battle only if the enemy shot the hell out of them. They didn't let themselves think too hard about it—just put their heads down, dug their trenches, manned their tubes, tried to get the damned igniters to fire.

But there was method behind the madness, the reason for the risk: Since the Germans would target the wrong map coordinates, real American guns wouldn't get knocked out. When the attack jumped off, the German gunners would keep firing at the false position, and the ruse would allow the 37th Field Artillery to pound the German positions with impunity. What's more, forward observers would note the angle of fire from the German batteries as they attacked the flash-bomb position, and from that they could calculate exactly where they were—and knock them out.

While Mrs. Fairbanks looks on, Lt. (jg) Douglas Fairbanks Jr. receives the Silver Star for conspicuous gallantry and intrepidity while attached to a Special Task Group during the assault on Italy in September 1943. (THE NATIONAL ARCHIVES, COLLEGE PARK, MD)

Col. Hilton Howell Railey. In being awarded the Legion of Merit, Railey demonstrated exceptional foresight and outstanding leadership in the development of a project entirely new to the United States Army. (THE NATIONAL ARCHIVES, COLLEGE PARK, MD)

Frederic E. Fox, who introduced theatrical special effects into deception operations. (REV. DONALD H. FOX)

Illustration detailing the magazine of the wire recorder-producer from the secret Bell Telephone Labs Division 17 report. (DARREL D. RIPPETEAU)

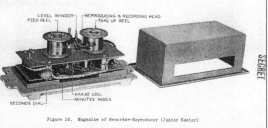

Figure 18. Magazine of Recorder-Reproducer (Junior Heater)

Walton Hall, aka Mouldy Manor, headquarters of the Special Troops near Stratford-upon-Avon, England—a mansion with a history of deception. (ED BIOW)

Darrel D. Rippeteau aboard Battle at Fort Snelling, Minnesota, in 1937. (DARREL D. RIPPETEAU)

Bill Blass, Robert Tompkins, Roy Thompson, George Vander Sluis, and Paul Seckel.

Maj. Charles R. Williams, commanding officer of the sonic deception company, nicknamed Heater—1 December 1944. (THE FAMILY OF GORDON WELLS)

Bill Blass in New York City, 1943.
(BILL BLASS)

Ed Biow and Dave Wynshaw somewhere in France in 1944. (ED BIOW)

Harold J. Dahl, a sculptor's apprentice from New Jersey, who joined the camouflem and wrote eloquently about the suffering of French civilians during the battle of Normandy. (ROBERT DAHL)

Lt. Dick Syracuse, head of the recon and security "haba-haba" platoon, with his first sergeant, Hartley, in Luxembourg in October 1944—a hell of a long way from the Bronx. (RICHARD M. SYRACUSE)

Inflatable tanks deployed in the field—light enough to be carried by two strong men. (THE NATIONAL ARCHIVES, COLLEGE PARK, MD)

Copy of the original master map overlay used by the Special Troops for Operation BREST, 20–27 August 1944. (THE NATIONAL ARCHIVES, COLLEGE PARK, MD)

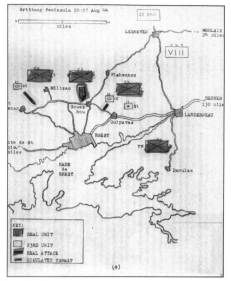

Ellsworth Kelly at work on a silk-screen board. (DARREL D. RIPPETEAU)

Alan Wood-Thomas, French-born camoufleur, who with his friend William Flemer III sneaked into German-occupied Paris wearing civilian clothes to rendezvous with *marquisards*. Wood-Thomas won the Bronze Star. (WILLIAM FLEMER III)

Dummy tank deployed—the edges cast realistic shadows to fool aerial reconnaissance. (THE NATIONAL ARCHIVES, COLLEGE PARK, MD)

Chameleon insignia of the 603d Engineer Camouflage Battalion: *We Conceal Our Might.* (ROBERT DAHL)

Lt. Col. Merrick Hector Truly, 1945. Truly masterminded the Rhine River deception for the U.S. Ninth Army. (JEANNE TRULY DAVIS)

Harold Laynor, somewhere in France in 1944. (GLORIA LAYNOR/THE LAYNOR FOUNDATION)

A sonic half-track with a tarp covering the secret gear. (THE FAMILY OF GORDON WELLS)

Lt. Col. Clifford G. Simenson, Department of Army War Plans, the Pentagon, 1952. Simenson was in charge of training at Camp Forrest and developed much of the doctrine of battlefield deception. (CLIFFORD G. SIMENSON)

Team A—1st half-track, 1st Platoon, 3132d sonic company, November 1944: Claude Zachary, driver; Donald Davey, sonic operator and commander; Bill Brown, radioman and gunner; and Royal the dog. (HAROLD FLINN)

Headquarters officers of the 23d Headquarters Special Troops (*left to right*): Lt. Adolphus C. Simpson, Maj. David Haviland, Maj. Charles H. Yocum, Maj. Frederick D. Vincent Jr., Lt. Col. Edgar W. Schroeder, Lt. Col. John W. Mayo, Lt. Boyd F. Reeder, Maj. Joseph P. Kelly, Lt. Col. James W. Snee, Maj. David H. Bridges, Col. Harry L. Reeder (Cmdg. Officer), Capt. James Dick Jr., Capt. Oscar M. Seale Jr., Lt. Col. Merrick Hector Truly (Exec. Officer), Maj. Thomas L. Raggio, Lt. Col. John W. Watson, Capt. Neil D. Elzey, Capt. Joseph H. Sidwell, Capt. Thomas G. Wells (KIA in Picard, Germany), Capt. Gerald N. Wagner, Capt. Nelson H. Hotchkiss. Absent are Lt. Col. Clifford G. Simenson, Lt. Col. Frederick E. Day, Lt. Col. Olen J. Seaman, Capt. Edward M. Cowardin, Capt. Murphy P. Martin, Capt. Imon M. Richardson, Capt. Frederic E. Fox, and Warrant Officer Aldrich V. Cousins. (THE FAMILY OF GORDON WELLS)

A Company, 603d Engineer Combat Battalion, V-E Day, May 1945: 1) Vladimir Bobovich, 2) Harold Skinner, 3) Jack Campbell, 4) Louis Phinney, 5) Arthur Abrams, 6) Robert Ross, 7) Ed Milburn, 8) Charles Ott, 9) Robert Nisley, 10) Douglas Jones, 11) Robert Petrucci, 12) Al Gorczyka, 13) Obscured, 14) Ed Sandler, 15) Jack Gell, 16) Ted Katz, 17) Robert Carden, 18) George Wilson, 19) Richard Faurot, 20) Frenchy Durand, 21) Baldassare, 22) Joseph LaCroix, 23) Ed Biow, 24) Frank Paynton, 25) Fred V. Lee, 26) Brown, 27) Angelo Borelli, 28) Stanley Wright, 29) David Wynshaw, 30) Walter Kadi, 31) Scotty Allen, 32) Thomas Fisher, 33) Philip Risberg, 34) Richard Schaar, 35) Peter Piscitello, 36) Jerry Gluckin, 37) William Allshouse, 38) Thomas M. Scabilia, 39) Randolph Smith, 40) William J. Shields, 41) Howard J. "Hop" Breisch, 42) Mike Crowley, 43) Leo Corcoran, 44) John Morgan, 45) John Wrysh, 46) Chris Lawless, 47) Thomas Ley, 48) Elmer Mellebrand, 49) Arthur Kane, 50) Jules Bakst, 51) Harold Rice, 52) Bernard Cullen, 53) Ellsworth Kelly. (ELLSWORTH KELLY)

Christmas card designed by Harold J. Dahl in 1944 demonstrating the principles of camouflage. (ROBERT DAHL)

Inside of the 1944 Christmas card designed by Harold J. Dahl. The silhouette on the left is a cut-out—when the card is opened, the camouflage disappears and the soldier is completely visible. (ROBERT DAHL)

I CAN'T CONCEAL MY WISH FOR A...
Merry Christmas

ARTHUR SHILSTONE   FRANCE, NEAR METZ

Portrait of camoufleur Richard Gardner near Metz, France, by Arthur Shilstone. (ARTHUR SHILSTONE)

Village, near Metz. 1945. Ink. 5 1/4 x 8 inches (13.3 x 20.3 cm) © Ellsworth Kelly. Photo by: Jerry Thompson.

Real American gunners wouldn't get killed, and real infantry could attack under an umbrella of artillery fire keeping the enemy's heads down. Fewer American soldiers would get hit by the enemy's artillery crossing the deadly ground between the line of departure—the starting line of the attack—and the enemy's defenses.

And the bottom line was the same as always: The Americans would have a better chance of winning.

The first two nights of the charade, the real guns to the rear remained silent, hiding from the German spotters. On the second night, one of the camoufleurs tested yet another solution to fix the igniter problem: he substituted a thin copper wire for the heavier igniter, and it worked beautifully. The wire glowed instantly from the electrical current and the black powder exploded every time, showering the wet ground with sparks. They set off flashes all night long, as an intermittent cold rain poured down and drenched them. The Germans had not fired on them yet. If they behaved according to their usual pattern, they would wait until they were sure that the attack was imminent, when a barrage would do the most harm.

The signal corps radiomen got busy, filling the airwaves with the fake traffic of the notional units. Whenever they were employed, the "blarney" radio crews were the least visible and in certain ways the most effective, since it could always be assumed that the enemy was monitoring radio traffic— even if no airplanes flew over to photograph the dummies, no collaborators were on hand to gather and report false information, no listening posts picked up the sonic activity.

Each task force also included a mobile sonic platoon. This would be their first operation of the war, and they were eager to show what they could do. In Task Force Z, the sonic operators under Simenson were all set to roll into position on schedule, to begin playing their music between 10:45 and 11:45 P.M. But their inaugural sonic operation almost ended it in disaster practically before it began.

It turned out that a real attack was to jump off from the same position exactly fifteen minutes later—at 11:00 P.M., 2300 hours army time.

Simenson and the other officers of Task Force Z knew nothing about the timing of the real attack, and clearly the commander planning the attack had no idea any deception operation was under way. Lieutenant Colonel Snee, the overall liaison officer from the Special Troops, found out completely by accident when he wandered into the area where the troops were forming up for the attack. He notified Simenson, who sought out the commander, and in the nick of time the sonic operation was canceled.

Simenson controlled his anger and frustration in the wording of his final report—but the underlining gives them away: "<u>Thus, had the sonic equipment been started at 2245 it might have served to arouse the Germans 15 min. prior to the infantry jump-off</u>. After the timely discovery the sonic employment was delayed."

So the attack went off as scheduled at 11:00 P.M., and the sonic cars didn't roll into position until 1:00 A.M. They deployed and cranked up their noise—a program produced by Walter Manser—like seasoned experts, despite the fact that this was their first operation: the grinding engines and squeaking treads of a whole battalion of seventy-two Sherman tanks moving up to the line and "harboring"—digging in ready to attack.

As the first program concluded, the "blarney" radio operator sent out a prearranged message on his call sign, "FJM": "First company of the battalion has closed into its assembly area 0140." No more messages would be sent until all the imaginary tanks were in place, when that would be confirmed by radio, along with the following to enhance authenticity: "Vehicle casualties one medium tank, three light tanks. Personnel casualties two men, no officers."

An observer for the 2d Infantry Division reported enthusiastically just how realistic the program sounded. "Careful consideration was given to details such as normal intervals between tanks for night driving, normal rate of speed, intervals between companies, etc. Sounds such as shifting of gears, tread noises, crackling of brush and voices of guides leading tanks into final positions could be clearly distinguished."

Twenty-four hours later, the camoufleurs deflated their "battalion," washed off the fake white bumper markings, and cut the fake shoulder patches of the 6th Armored Division off their sleeves. Meanwhile, in the darkness, the sonic cars played the sounds of a tank battalion moving out.

Simenson didn't see the point of simulating the removal of the tanks. If the German garrison didn't surrender by morning, the big attack would go off as scheduled. Why not let the Germans stew all night thinking that a tank battalion was still poised to swarm in on them? Wouldn't that be more likely to make them surrender, even at the last minute?

But he was overruled.

"It was mutually agreed desirable (by Lt. Col. SNEE, SIMENSON, and Capt. HILLER) not to use the sonic equipment to simulate vacating the area. Sonic activity was ordered from higher authority," he wrote. In other words, he and the ranking sonic officer on the scene didn't want to use the sonic cars, but a "higher authority"—probably Special Plans Branch—overruled their tactical judgment. Simenson concluded tersely, "Orders for employment of deception without coordination of plans of real units has possibilities of doing more harm than good."

The latter remark would prove to be fatally true.

His own Task Force Z had come within a few minutes of warning the enemy of a surprise infantry attack. Instead of being caught off guard in the dark, they would have been ready and waiting. Ten miles down the line, the same kind of breakdown in communications plagued Task Force X, and this time chance would not intervene to ward off fatal consequences.

Bob Tompkins, Bill Blass, and Arthur Shilstone were part of Task Force X, under Capt. Oscar Seale.

They arrived at the line on Wednesday afternoon in time to see German antiaircraft guns open up on an unarmed Piper Cub observation plane, used by the Americans for directing artillery fire.

The sonic soldiers moved up to the line as well, anxiously awaiting their first action. Bill Brown, in the lead half-track, soon got his first taste of action. "There was an artillery observation plane above us, and all of a sudden the ack-ack let loose on that plane," Brown recalls. "In the second track was a guy named Bob Finkelstein, of Lebanon, Pennsylvania. Well, we were sure they were shooting at us. He and I both dove off our tracks into the same slit trench. We both hit it at the same time and got wedged in—we couldn't get out! So that was my baptism by fire—I wasn't even shot at."

His was a common first reaction to battlefield fire, and with experience, he honed his instincts for survival.

At nightfall, D Company of the 709th Tank Battalion, with fourteen light tanks, moved into the area. An hour before midnight, the camoufleurs went to work. Before long, four platoons of camoufleurs had erected fifty-three dummies. They wrestled with the same problems as Task Force Z—leaky valves and nets so heavy they collapsed the rubber tanks. Two leaky tanks were replaced and one discarded. And they, too, worked long hours in the drenching rain and had only leaky pup tents with muddy floors to go back to for a few hours' rest before daylight.

The sonic cars moved in and played their music for thirty-minute periods, shutting down between each program first for five minutes and then for ten. Each of the three programs was meant to mimic a company of fifteen to twenty medium tanks lurching into position. They finished just after midnight. At first light, the camoufleurs could see that they were under observation from a church bell tower a thousand yards away. Perfect.

Tompkins had already started keeping a clandestine diary of the war in a two-by-three-inch address book. Strictly forbidden—if he were captured, the book would give the enemy chapter and verse about what he'd been up to. Though he was careful to write obliquely, it wouldn't take much to read between the lines. Of his second night at Brest, he wrote: "Maintained items—took them down at 9 P.M. Moved up 500 yards to new area and set up 10 tanks. Willy and I set up our tent with our feet sticking out in the pouring down rain and passed out about 3:00 A.M." "Willy" of course was Bill Blass. After the war, Blass's mother, Ethel, typed a copy of the diary from the little stained pages full of cramped handwriting.

As dawn turned to morning, the confusion started.

First, one of the sonic platoons was dispatched ten miles west to Task Force Z without anybody checking with Captain Seale, in command of Task Force X. Just before noon, Simenson arrived for a tour of inspection, along with Maj. William Hooper. Hooper had started the war as a first lieutenant and now was the popular new executive officer of the 603d Camouflage Engineers, soon to replace Fitz as commander. Their presence in itself wasn't a problem. In fact, it was proper for them to be inspecting the installations. But they did outrank Seale—one as his battalion CO and the other as overall commander of any mission under way.

Simenson's Task Force Z had also been responsible for taking one of Seale's sonic platoons without his knowledge, though it's not clear who gave the order. Major Williams, the CO of the sonic company, was himself leading the sonic platoons, and he may have exercised his own discretion or received orders directly from Special Plans Branch. About three hours later, Ingersoll, the "special angel," arrived with a contingent from Special Plans Branch—including Col. William A. "Billy" Harris, its head, who outranked everybody on the scene but, as a staff officer, was in command of no one. Ingersoll began photographing the dummy installations—without asking permission from Seale—but with Harris's approval. Seale ordered all his officers to allow no one into Task Force X's area without Seale's written permission, including Ingersoll and his camera.

But one of Harris's Special Plans Branch officers then immediately ordered Seale to give written permission for Ingersoll to continue his photography, which he reluctantly did.

At this point, it's not clear if Simenson and Hooper were still on the scene, but by early evening, Lieutenant Colonel Snee arrived. He had been in charge of the combined group before it dispersed into three separate task forces, and had already saved the day for the infantry attacking in Simenson's area. He went over Seale's plans and approved them.

At dusk, Lieutenant Colonel Truly, the executive officer of the 23d, arrived with Maj. Charles Yokum, in charge of signals—radio—for the 23d. About the only ranking officer not on the scene was Colonel Reeder. He had already moved west with his headquarters staff out of Brittany altogether.

The foregoing account comes from reports written in cold, truncated language after the operation and hardly begins to capture the emotion on the scene. Or the confusion. Who, exactly, was in charge? Was it Harris and Ingersoll, who controlled the strategic picture for 12th Army Group headquarters, but were staff officers? Was it Simenson, who as operations officer was responsible for the execution of all plans—and who had his own task force to worry about, making him both a staff and a line officer? Or Snee, who had been the commander on the ground when the combined group first arrived at Brest and remained to coordinate the three task forces? Or Williams, commanding both a sonic platoon and the entire sonic company in both task forces? Or Hooper, ranking officer in charge of the camoufleurs?

Or was it Seale, the officer actually designated commander of Task Force X?

The chain of command was all muddled. It should have been simple. Twelfth Army Group, acting under advice of Special Plans (Harris and Ingersoll) works out a plan with Special Troops Headquarters (Reeder, in consultation with his staff). Reeder then appoints a task force commander (Seale), who is charged with carrying out the plan. Only the task force commander then gives orders to the commanders of the camouflage, sonic, signal, and combat engineer companies assigned to his task force. Those commanders, usually majors or captains, then issue orders only to the platoon leaders under their command, usually lieutenants, who direct their sergeants, who direct their squads of enlisted men.

Instead, in this operation, staff colonels (advisors) were giving orders to captains and even corporals. The task force commander, Seale, had little control.

It's confusing just to read the blur of names, ranks, and units on the page. How much more bewildering it must have been for men already feeling the anxiety of impending action, men with difficult jobs to do in darkness and driving rain, listening to the arguments between their superior officers, the strident orders and countermands, trying to make sense of new written orders that contradicted the careful plans on which they had been briefed.

Orders seemed to be coming in from all over the place: 23d Special Troops Headquarters, company and battalion command, Special Plans

Branch, even the 2d Infantry Division, to whom the task force was attached. During the course of the operation, three captains, seven majors, five lieutenant colonels, and a full colonel were busy giving orders to about two hundred men—usually under the command of a single captain. Seale concluded his after-action report with barely contained anger. "The duplication and conflicting orders cause the officers and enlisted men to believe that the Task Force CO doesn't know what to do or when to do it."

Simenson concurred, in his own report: "<u>RECOMMENDATION:</u> that the principle of unity of command be employed in deception operations; that the Task Force commander be given sole responsibility and the necessary tools to accomplish his mission; and all staff officers, both of higher and lower staffs, serve to aid and abet the commander."

At 8:30 P.M., Seale visited the forward command post for the sonic units and found it in the wrong place: Harris, head of Special Plans Branch, had ordered it as far forward as possible, countermanding Seale's plan, approved by Snee. Williams, the sonic CO, seems to have at least acquiesced in pushing them way out in front, and perhaps he was making a point about the readiness of his men for hazardous duty. His after-action report, which echoed that of one of his platoon leaders, recommended in no uncertain terms "that sonic unit be located as close to friendly front lines as possible in missions of the above nature and not be considered nonexpendable in any operation." He closed the report by reiterating, "A sister unit is absolutely necessary, since this company is considered 100% expendable by its unit commander in any operation in this theatre."

That they were considered a hundred percent expendable was no secret to the sonic troops. Colonel Railey had drilled it into their heads back at Pine Camp. The explosives packed beneath the floorboards of their half-tracks were a constant reminder that their necks were stuck way out. If attacked in force, with their escape route blocked, they would blow the equipment to kingdom come and get out as best they could. But they had remarkable faith in Dick Syracuse's security platoon and Rebh's combat engineers to get them out of trouble. With these well-armed guys around, they felt they were in good hands, even if officially they were expendable.

The sonic troops moved into position as far forward as possible.

The commander of the 9th Infantry Regiment, part of the 2d Infantry Division, was not happy. He had other plans for that area. But after some hot discussion via field telephone with yet another lieutenant colonel, the five sonic cars were ordered to stay put—six hundred yards apart, less than two hundred yards from known enemy positions. To guard them, they had part of Syracuse's security platoon and a detachment of combat engineers under Rebh.

For three hours in the middle of the night, they played their music: three companies of tanks, eighteen to a company, rumbling into the front lines, poised to attack.

Bill Brown recalls what it was like during his first operation. "First platoon turned the sound on—Davey was operating. It was pitch black—I never saw a thing. We were there all night and played, then they came and got us."

The next morning, the confusion of conflicting orders continued: Snee arrived with orders to close out the operation, for the sonic troops to leave the area. Seale passed on the orders. Then orders from higher up the chain of command—presumably from Special Plans Branch—came down to hold the sonic cars right where they were. Shortly thereafter, Yokum, the signal officer, arrived with new orders for the sonic cars: " 'Play' the battalion out of the area after darkness." At 12:45, Harris and his Special Plans contingent came back to explain the new plan for withdrawal. Fifteen minutes later, the real attack started. In all the confusion and conflicting orders, light tanks of Company D, 709th Tank Battalion, jumped off on the line from the same place the sonic cars had been during the night. So much for misdirection.

In their inaugural show, the sonic troops were more successful than they ever realized: Hearing the realistic noises of fifty-four new tanks forming up for battle only a few hundred yards away, during the night the Germans had rushed in reinforcements to counter the threat. So by the time the 709th attacked with fourteen tanks, the Germans were waiting with more than twenty—and possibly as many as fifty—new antitank guns and bazookas.

For Simenson, that first "success" was a bitter pill: "During that time, the sonic company made a sonic 'attack' down a natural corridor for an armored attack into Brest. I do not know who authorized it, but we all thought it was a good idea—do *something*. We didn't know what the sonic company could do. But in the long run, company D of the 709th Tank Battalion made an actual attack down the same corridor, and the Germans had moved all their antitank guns against the phony attack. So when the real attack came, they shot the hell out of it and we lost men and tanks."

Snee, whose approved plan for the sonic cars had been countermanded by Special Plans Branch, was outraged. "Co 'D,' 709th Tank battalion was placed opposite the best ridge line for a tank attack into BREST. By our build up, more opposition was drawn in front of this company," he re-ported tersely. "It is believed that

1. Either this company should not have attacked, or
2. Deception should have been employed elsewhere to draw antitank defenses away from this ridge line."

The cost was high: four tanks destroyed before they even crossed the line of departure, one more out of commission, two tank commanders killed, two crewmen severely wounded. When they continued the attack the following day, Company D lost four more tanks destroyed, three more men dead.

But the numbers don't tell the whole story.

Saying a tank is "knocked out" or "destroyed" doesn't capture the terri-fying moment of truth for the men trapped inside its claustrophobic steel spaces. An 88mm shell has a high muzzle velocity—that means it shoots in faster than the speed of sound on a flat trajectory. It's not very big, about the circumference of a cocktail shaker, but longer and heavier, weighing twenty-two pounds, with a sharp-pointed nose. When it hits the outer ar-mor of a tank—in this case very light armor—it does not explode. Instead, it punches through, then explodes inside the tank. Searing, razor-sharp fragments of the shell and pieces of the tank spray around inside the hol-low hull, causing horrendous spall wounds in human flesh.

It all happens in a deafening instant. The Sherman tanks ran not on diesel but on gasoline, which was easily ignited by antitank shells. In that case, a secondary explosion would rip the rear off the tank in a bloom of fire and smoke. Ellsworth Kelly has a distinct recollection of an incident that happened in Brittany—one that could only have been the attack of the light tanks at Brest. His platoon had set up their dummy tanks on a hillside overlooking a valley and camouflaged them realistically, though im-perfectly enough that they could still be seen. "But real forces attacked right through us down in to the valley and met the German force head-on," he recalls. The brief battle ended in a violent collision of armor against antitank weapons, and the remaining American tanks retreated through the field of dummies. Clearly, the attack had been a big mistake. "The real tanks retreated through us," Kelly says, "and their crews were screaming at us that we should have joined them—'If you had been with us, we wouldn't have to retreat! You let us down!' "

The tankers thought the camouflaged rubber dummies were the real McCoy.

After the sonic operation and the tank attack, which was stopped almost before it got started, Colonel Harris and the "special angel," Ingersoll, belatedly noted the tactical error. "Deception involves the manipulation of the enemy's forces. If they are moved from the path of one junior commander, they are placed in the path of another. Only the senior commander's authority is sufficient to back up the Cover planner when he finds himself faced with the unpleasant necessity of drawing the enemy in front of any particular sector. Deception, like any other military operation, involves casualties—and the casualties which follow the intentional baiting of the enemy are among the least popular."

It was an old lesson, and it would find its way into U.S. Army doctrine long after the events of August 1944 were forgotten: "There should be no such thing as a deception planned separately from the true operation."

While the tank sonic reception failed, other elements of the operation were more successful—particularly the efforts of Task Force Y's camoufleurs. With that success came a frightening and dangerous draw of fire on their own position. Shells arced in from a high angle from very large guns with a grinding, rushing sound—caused by the friction of each huge projectile forcing its way through the air. When it slammed down around the camoufleurs of Task Force Y, the roar was end-of-the-world deafening, the explosion blinding.

On Friday, the day before the main attack, the incoming shells blasted craters six feet deep and ten feet across.

On Saturday, the Germans fired with a different kind of quick-fuse— punching out craters that were only four feet deep and six feet across, because the shells were bursting at ground level, before they buried their noses. This was called "good fragmentation": the thousands of steel fragments from a shell burst at ground level or slightly above would spread out farther, kill and maim more troops.

During both barrages, the Germans fired with patient, steady efficiency. The "fall of shot" was nearly perfect; the German gunners had calculated Task Force Y's exact position. The shells slammed in one at a time, three to five minutes apart—an excruciating timeless time of waiting and fear, time to burrow deeper into the mud and listen for the rushing, grinding, freight-train sound. Weeks into their war, the camoufleurs already knew the old soldier's wisdom: If you can hear it, it won't get you.

More than a thousand yards to their rear, the real guns of the 37th Field Artillery opened up against the Germans on Friday night, and not a single German shell burst among them.

Lt. Col. John Mayo, in command of Task Force Y, reported with typical army understatement the outcome of the ruse. "Apparently we were successful, as we received our first CB fire at 251330 Aug (Friday), 30 minutes after H-hour, and then again at 260900 Aug (Saturday). The 37th FA did not receive CB fire. . . . Flash devices do have a military value."

Miraculously, hunkered down in their deep slit trenches and hugging the sodden earth in the sunken road behind the hedgerows, the camoufleurs suffered no casualties.

But that was part of the theory—only thirty-five Special Troops had caused all the fireworks of a force more than ten times their size. Spread out a few men to mimic many, and the mathematical odds were that fewer men would be hit than in a sector crowded with real troops.

To the thirty-five camoufleurs hunkered in the slit trenches, it was a hell of a theory.

On Saturday, with the attack under way and his own job done, Tompkins and his crew of Task Force X—completely exhausted from three sleepless nights of heavy labor interrupted by bombardment—secured their equipment and prepared to move out of Brittany the following day for Torcé en Charnie, halfway between Le Mans and Laval. He wrote, "Just beginning to realize how vulnerable we were the last three days as stories came in from various sources." They'd have a few days' rest, and the reality of what they were doing would catch up with them, and with it, often, a kind of delayed fear. Busy on the line, they had no time for fear or second thoughts. In that way, they were just like any other soldiers.

When he arrived in Torcé, Tompkins wrote, "Got drunk for first time since England night of 28th."

Torcé en Charnie was largely untouched by the war. The Germans had retreated headlong eastward and fought no pitched battles nearby. So there was respite from wreckage and ruin, and morale ran high.

While the task forces had been working at Brest, Colonel Reeder and his headquarters troops had formally liberated Torcé—the only town in France for which they could claim that honor. The Signal Company provided a color guard, and schoolchildren dressed in white carried flowers. Reeder gave a speech—written by Fox and translated into French for him by Alan Wood-Thomas—and finished with a rousing "*Vive la France!*" The local fireman's band then played "La Marseillaise" for the first time in four years, followed by tears, handshakes, hugs, and kisses.

It's a stock scene, familiar from movies, TV, novels. A bit corny and romantic, a sentimentalized version of liberation. But in the world of 1944

France, the emotion was genuine, the liberation from fascist occupation authentic. There was little ambiguity. The Nazis were the bad guys, and the Americans, British, and Canadians were the good guys, putting their blood and treasure on the line for a country most had never even visited before now. Smiling, they gave candy to kids, handed out K rations and chocolate.

"We were always in trucks, always rumbling through little villages, and the people came out cheering on both sides along the road, throwing flowers— women, men, kids," Jack Masey, then a corporal, recalls. "It gave you a phenomenal sense of euphoria. You were liberating these people, and it went to your head, you know? My God—we're doing this! We in America came over here and we're saving this goddamned world!"

Masey's father had been gassed in the trenches of World War I, and he grew up a poor kid in Brooklyn. Before the war, he'd made it as far from home as Manhattan, to the High School of Music and Art—an extraordinary experience that widened his horizons and changed him forever. The second milestone of his young life was joining the camoufleurs. Here he was an ocean away from his boyhood, among talented artists, doing his part in an epic war against fascism.

"It was a good feeling—I remember that, feeling good about the United States. It's very moving to me, how this country showed itself, how it behaved generally overseas." That proud glow of patriotism would remain with Masey after the war, and he would join the foreign service—creating shows about America for international exhibitions, still merging artistry with love of country.

Though the Special Troops performed admirably at Brest—regardless of command error—the August attacks failed. Brest held for almost another whole month, until September 19. Victory cost the Americans ten thousand casualties.

At the surrender, they learned that the fortified port was held not by six thousand troops, nor even the sixteen thousand later estimated by Maj. Gen. Troy H. Middleton, whose divisions stormed the German line time and again to no avail. It turned out that thirty thousand German troops were dug in at Brest, organized around the 2d Parachute Division, a crack outfit of elite troops led by Lt. Gen. Herman Ramcke, a determined and cool commander who had no intention of surrendering.

He fell for the ruse, all right: Two new tank battalions of the 6th Armored had joined the three infantry divisions already besieging the city. He believed exactly what the deception planners wanted him to believe. Long

before the surrender of Ramcke, this was confirmed with the capture of
Colonel Feurst, commander of the St. Mathieu–Le Conquet area, stretch-
ing west of the city to the ocean. The chief of staff of VIII Corps attacking
Brest reported, "He said he was certain that we had the 6th Armored Division here because he had heard tanks in his area."

So he had thought what they wanted him to *think*. But they hadn't
worked the problem through to the next step: What would he then *do*?
Confident that he was now tying up an extraordinary number of American
tanks and troops, steeled in his determination to do his duty honorably,
what he did was hold out for glory.

The Special Troops had done their job. Every evaluation all way up the
line confirmed that the dummy installations were realistic, the radio traffic
authentic, the special effects good enough to fool even American troops,
and the sonic projection all too effective.

The deception show worked, and it had consequences. And next time,
the higher-ups handing down orders would have to do a far better job making sure they understood those consequences.

Even as the Special Troops were staging their ruse at Brest, the Allies
were rolling into Paris. By the time Brest fell in late September, the American and British armies were already beyond the Seine, too far away to be
supplied efficiently through Brittany. And they had advanced victoriously
while hundreds of thousands of soldiers streamed into France across the repaired MULBERRY docks and the open beaches, driving their vehicles in
through the surf in patient, inexorable lines, hauling supplies by muscle
power and truck to the front, as the front receded to Paris and then beyond, across Belgium and Luxembourg toward the Rhine River.

And in the deuce-and-a-half trucks hauling trailers of rubber dummies,
their sonic half-tracks, and in jeeps painted with the names of their sweet-
hearts, the Special Troops followed the front.

Simenson, who was not at fault for the debacle of Task Force X, nevertheless took it hard, and it never left his conscience. "There was no coordination,
and it was a military blunder, and sometimes I wonder if our secret classifica-
tion wasn't to cover it up," he says. "We never made such a mistake again."

NINE

HOLD THAT GHOST LINE
September–October 1944

Deception is common sense soldiering.
—Gen. Carl E. Vuono

The first camoufleurs arrived in Paris before the liberation.

Sergeant Alan Wood-Thomas and his buddy, Bill Flemer, the Princeton nurseryman, slipped in by themselves. Flemer recalls that they left from Verdun, but that seems unlikely. Verdun is far to the west of Paris and was still far beyond Allied lines when the Americans rolled into Paris on August 25. They must have gone in from Torcé en Charnie, Special Troops headquarters, while the main detachment was still out on the Brittany Peninsula at Brest.

Wood-Thomas was more French than American. If you were told to pick out the Frenchman in a photo of the 603d, your eye would immediately be drawn to the slight, fair-haired young man with the loose European posture—in civilian life a brilliant painter. Alan's twin brother, Gilles, was a corporal in the 603d. After the war, he would go to work as a draftsman in Darrel Rippeteau's architecture firm in Watertown, New York, a place he would first see when he mustered out at Pine Camp.

Alan had made himself indispensable at staff headquarters because of his fluency with the French language. There he formed a lifelong friendship with Fred Fox. When he fell on hard times after the war, Fox lent him a sum of money, which Alan repaid with a series of stunning oils painted from a veterans hospital bed. In one, two figures are framed in Mediterranean light inside an airy house whose open window and door look out upon the sea. The colors and forms arrest the eye and soothe at the same time.

Flemer and Fox also became friends during the war and rekindled that friendship when they collaborated on the *Official History*, with Fox writing and Flemer filling in details about the camoufleurs. "He was a fascinating guy," Flemer recalls of Fox. "Slender, a very handsome guy. Completely honest, and he had a great spiritual depth." Alan wasn't the only one with a twin: Flemer had his own "twin" in a French army outfit billeted near the camoufleurs, who also wore American uniforms. "I was always catching hell from French officers for being where I wasn't supposed to be, and he was always catching hell from my officers, who said he shouldn't be there. I met him—it was like looking in a mirror. We looked exactly alike—same build, same face, same everything."

Alan Wood-Thomas still had grandparents and friends in Paris, and he had close ties to the Maquis, the French Resistance. He and Flemer, who also spoke French, changed into civilian clothes. They rendezvoused with friends of Wood-Thomas, who picked them up in a *gazogène* car that had been converted to burn charcoal instead of gasoline, an ingenious French contraption necessitated by the gas shortage.

"It was a dangerous thing to do," Flemer remembers, laughing at his own youthful daring, "because he got me some civilian clothes, and if I had been caught, if he had been caught, why, we would have been shot summarily. But it was a great adventure. It was at a time when Paris was beginning to fall, and there was shooting all around."

They drove into the city though the northern gate at Montmartre and met secretly with Maquisards, spent a day furtively looking up old comrades and family of Wood-Thomas, then rejoined their unit. Flemer recalls the clandestine visit as purely unofficial. "We were in effect AWOL for a while, but we didn't care."

At any rate, Wood-Thomas would have been perfectly placed to deliver messages from the Maquis to Special Plans Branch, which would have had a keen interest in the state of the German defense inside the city, and it is tantalizing to speculate whether he was taking such grave risks for more than a social call.

After their mixed success at Brest, Special Plans Branch came up with a bold plan to use the Special Troops: send them south around Paris to hook up with U.S. Seventh Army charging up the Rhône Valley from the Mediterranean and block the retreat of German Nineteenth Army. They called it Operation SIDECAR, after a drink enjoying a faddish popularity among 23d Headquarters staff: one part Cointreau, one part lemon juice, and two parts Cognac.

"It was a charming and ghastly plan," Fox wrote. "We would pretend to close the Belfort Gap—stretch a rubber band of decoys from Sens to Dijon—and thereby snag the whole Wehrmacht kit and caboodle."

The Germans were surrendering so readily and in such numbers, the thinking was that placing an "instant army" in the path of the retreating Germans would induce them to throw down their arms wholesale. Reeder and his staff raced by jeep more than two hundred miles east to Patton's command post at Troyes to discuss the plan. German Nineteenth Army consisted of five depleted divisions, one of them Panzer—a minimum of twenty thousand troops. They were not fleeing headlong but rather retreating in an organized fashion, still under control of their officers, still able to fight.

On September 1, with the Special Troops already in position, Third Army vetoed the plan, much to Fox's relief: It would likely result in a bloodbath, with the Special Troops on the receiving end. So as the American armies rolled across France, liberated Paris, and crossed the Seine, the Special Troops found themselves briefly out of work, drawn up in some fields near Sens, some sixty miles south of Paris, without a show to perform.

While they waited for orders, some enterprising officers reconnoitered the surrounding countryside, scrounging for amenities such as fresh food and wine. At Les Granges, twenty-five miles away, they hit the mother lode: a German liquor cache containing 620 cases—6,240 bottles—of Cognac and 50 cases of Cointreau. The officers happily shared it with their men. "Instead of throwing our feeble selves against the retreating horde, we parked on a sunny hillside south of Paris, out of gas and full of liquor," Fox reported happily. "We already had plenty of lemonade powder in our K-rations. So we made sidecars and had a party. The Colonel lost control of the whole regiment. For three days, he had a drunken mutiny on his hands, but he didn't care either."

A couple of the sonic cars had thrown their treads, and Maj. Charles Williams told his men, "We're going to stay here until we fix 'em." At mess call, a two-and-a-half-ton truck full of Cognac appeared. Williams climbed up on the tailgate. As the mess sergeants dished up supper, he handed each man a bottle of Cognac. "Now this woods is yours, and I don't want anybody to leave it," he ordered. "If you do, you're in trouble. When you've drunk that bottle, just come back and get another bottle."

"They'd drink and fall down," sonic gunner Bill Brown recalls. "Couple of guys left the woods—looking for girls, I imagine. They got caught. He took them right by the mess tent and made them dig a hole. When they'd get done, they'd fill it up and dig another one. 'Now, these guys left the woods,' he told us. 'If you leave, you'll join 'em.' "

It must have been a prodigious spree. The Blarney Outdoor Theater showed an Abbott and Costello film, *Hold That Ghost!* four nights in a row—"but each night it looked different," according to Fox. Bud Abbott and Lou Costello played bumbling gas station attendants who inherit a roadhouse with a hidden fortune from a mobster who "had his lights dimmed" by the cops. The roadhouse turns out to be haunted by "ghosts"—other gangsters greedy to find the loot—and the picture is one long comic adventure of disguise and trickery as the bed-sheeted "ghosts" try to scare them away. At the finale, the boys turn the roadhouse into a nightclub, featuring the Andrews Sisters and Ted Lewis's Orchestra. Lewis croons his signature line: "Is evvv-rybody happy?"

The men drank and relaxed on what came to be called "Cognac Hill," watching Abbott and Costello while the war moved past them toward Germany. All these years later, the hard-drinking interlude is just a blur in the minds of most of those who were there, and nobody seems to remember the movie at all.

Apparently, the cache liberated by the Special Troops was not unusual. The Germans had been hoarding liquor all over France, and as they fled to the east, the invaders seized their stockpiles. Fox told the story of a Princeton classmate whose division captured its own cache of Cognac— thousands of cases. "My friend's division gave a few thousand cases away and hid the rest in an abandoned pillbox, which they locked by welding," he wrote. "Everytime they wanted another bottle they had to get a blowtorch."

Not everybody got roaring drunk. Many took the opportunity to sleep, mend their clothes, repair their gear, sketch, and write letters. And of course the unlucky ones pulled guard duty.

Hal Laynor wrote to his wife, "I'm on guard today and it's sort of relaxingly lonely. An old man and his granddaughter came up to speak to me & we did conversationally well. He told me of his consumptive sons, prisoners of *le Boche*."

And he confided: "I usually burn your letters after I read them for two reasons. I have to travel as light as I can. Can usually only take what I can carry on my back. Secondly, I can't carry any information on me that might be of use to the enemy if I was to be captured. And you'd be surprised at what letters from home contain."

Burning letters from home was common practice among the Special Troops, one that made them await the next mail call even more anxiously.

Late on the afternoon of September 7, the Special Troops arrived by motor convoy at a village just ten miles west of Paris, St. Germain-en-Laye, childhood home of the composer Claude Debussy and site of a magnificent fortified royal château. There the staff and the combat engineers took over the luxurious Maison d'Education de la Légion d'Honneur, a palace the emperor Napoleon reputedly had built for his wife, Josephine. Not far from the parklike grounds of the Maison, the camoufleurs and sonic companies went into billets at a French army base, Camp des Loges.

For the first time since leaving the States, the enlisted men slept indoors, not in soggy pup tents or foxholes. They enjoyed hot showers, hot food, even tennis courts and a swimming pool. Morale soared. Laynor wrote home, "Optimism runs higher now than it ever did before & speculation has it that the war will be over in a month or so. I only pray to God there is some ground, some foundation in this speculation."

Harold Dahl shared the general ebullience, as *The Stars and Stripes* enthusiastically reported on the lightning advance of the Americans and British across France. "The news makes everyone talk about prospects of getting home for Christmas,"

There were rumors that the Germans would surrender any day now, that the Special Troops would be sent home in November.

And just down the road lay Paris.

Fox lost no time getting into the city. "The main change—not noticed by me but by a good friend called Wood-Thomas whose grandparents still live here and who studied at the Sorbonne—the main change is a 'cheapening' of the mind and material," he wrote. "He says he is ashamed at the tawdry, blowsy appearance of the men and women. And he says they think the same way. There is a great deal of hasty hatred, shallow cynicism and petty bickering. Maybe it is because they are hungry, tired and irritable. They also have an inferiority complex which makes them quite touchy."

He roamed the city, taking in the sights, buying gifts and souvenirs. In a shop window, a display of handcrafted lead soldiers caught his eye. He stopped and admired them—they were exquisite, realistic, flawlessly formed and painted. He inquired who had made them. A dentist named André Hugo, he was told. Fox sought out the man, told him how much he admired his model soldiers, and the two struck up a friendship. The amateur craftsman showed Fox his whole collection and even gave him some as gifts. André Hugo turned out to be the nephew of Victor Hugo, the celebrated novelist.

It may seem strange that Fox should be fascinated by toy soldiers. He was morally repulsed by war and violence, tolerated the army with a kind of detached bemusement. He was by no stretch a career soldier—just the opposite: He felt deeply that, to oppose war and the forces that created war, he must witness it firsthand. And as a patriot, he felt obligated to do his part.

Shortly after leaving St. Germain and Paris, he wrote, "Today, I can wear a stripe-like thing on my sleeve indicating that I have been overseas for six months. I feel no special elation over this—I am merely stating a fact. I would just as soon not 'win' (if hanging around can be called 'winning') another. However, if at the end of Germany, we are still fighting Japan, I will expect myself to want to go to the Pacific."

Fox was a man of contradictions: an aspiring actor who felt the calling to the ministry, a writer who had taken a fling at Hollywood and network radio—popular, transient entertainment media—whose enduring works would be published sermons and an unpublished secret military history. So maybe his delight in the lead soldiers was perfectly in keeping with his character. He admired craft, admired artistic attention to detail, and enjoyed "playing" war—that's what the Special Troops did, after all. Their style of battle carried a certain dignity and was ultimately truly humane: they placed themselves in danger on behalf of their fellow soldiers, but they did not kill. And among those they saved were certainly lots of enemy soldiers.

Toy soldiers captured the art without the gore.

As for the others, whether a man got to Paris—and how often—depended on his rank and his willingness to bend the rules. For a time, it was off-limits, then it was on, then off again. But St. Germain was so close to the city, it was hard to resist.

"Two or three of us got to Paris every night," Arthur Shilstone says. "I remember getting so drunk on Champagne! I remember just sitting under the Arc de Triomphe at about three o'clock in the morning with my head in my hands, so miserable, trying to get back to camp." Luckily he hitched a ride with a passing army truck and made it back to St. Germain.

Richard Morton, like most of his comrades, had never been out of the States before. Unlike Fox and Wood-Thomas, he was blind to any flaws in the City of Light. For a young artist to visit Paris was to make a pilgrimage to the center of the world of art and culture. Scarcely two weeks after the 2d French Armored Division had officially liberated the city, Paris was in the grip of the biggest party in its history. To arrive as part of an army liberating it from four years of Philistine repression must have produced even greater euphoria than that which Jack Masey felt passing among throngs of welcoming French civilians in Normandy and Brittany. "Today has been one of the most memorable days in my life, comparable with few other experiences, and yet different from all the rest. I have seen some of the most beautiful sights I have ever laid eyes on," Morton wrote exultantly to his parents. "I am glad to pass on that scarcely out from under the heels of the oppressor the sophistication and gaiety of France known throughout the world lives again."

To celebrate his arrival, he bought his mother silk scarves and Parisian perfume.

He toured the city with a pretty, seventeen-year-old guide named Nicole, marveling at the elegance and style of the Parisians. "The Germans could never understand why the Parisians always dressed and looked so well and were very much put out by this display at times," he wrote. "They would ration everything more strictly and corner the market, but some way, somehow, the Parisians always managed to put something stunning together out of nothing; so it was not their abundance but their art and ingenuity which caused this."

Paris had escaped heavy bombardment and battle and remained largely unscathed by the war, at least physically. In a long day of sightseeing, Morton and Nicole visited the Arc de Triomphe, the Eiffel Tower, the Musée de l'Art Moderne, the Louvre. He saw the Grand Palais and the Petit Palais, still bearing the scars of German tank shells, fired against them when they were strongholds for the Maquisards. But though awed again and again by the beauty of the people and their city, he was not blind to their privation. At dinner with Nicole's family, he was shocked that all they had to share among them was a thin soup and a meager loaf of bread. He noted carefully, "I did not eat with them, of course, as we have our own rations. I have never seen a family table however so nicely arranged with so little to eat!"

In Paris, American cigarettes were fetching 250 francs, $5 per pack. Butter cost 700 to 1,000 francs, $14–$20. Three thousand francs—$30—could buy you two small bars of chocolate. Now that an occupying army was no longer confiscating the yearly harvest and commandeering storehouses full of goods, life was bound to improve. But it would take many months, perhaps years.

Dahl continued to be struck by the ordeal the French had suffered—occupation, then invasion, pitched battles on their own soil. Back in Brittany, he wrote, "Funny how things go—we were in one little village yesterday

that was untouched and had to go around another town, recently prominent in the news, because it is rubble. Poor people! Imagine how you
would feel if you suddenly found yourself with nothing in the World but a
few blankets on a wheelbarrow and all your neighbors in the same boat—
with no one to turn to but 'authorities' and the kindness American soldiers
show wherever they go. We will be well-remembered here."

At last in Paris, he counted his blessings yet again."We always consider
ourselves lucky to be in the ETO where moments of freedom can be spent
in civilization—so many people have longed to see the things we have
seen—it cannot but be a fine education for us all."

He was a few years older than most of his comrades and had been sorely
disappointed when his family couldn't afford to send him to college. As a
WPA sculptor's apprentice, he had done his best to fill the gaps in his education about art. He read voraciously, deeply, and broadly. Paris was a milestone on the road to the cultured life he envisioned for himself after the
war—a life of the mind, alert to aesthetic value.

Vic Dowd met an Englishman on a motorcycle who had served in
France in World War I, then after the Armistice in 1918 married a French-
woman and stayed on. The Englishman complained constantly and bitterly about the French, yet he had never returned to England, not even to
visit. Dowd shared some C rations and candy bars with him, and the
Englishman invited him to lunch. Over their meal, he asked, "Do you want
to go to Paris?"

"I'll never forget driving down the Champs-Elysées and seeing the Arc
de Triomphe," Dowd says. "That was my entrance into Paris, driven by
an Englishman from World War I, sitting in this bathtub sidecar of his
motorcycle."

Dowd, too, wandered the city, sketching old men and young women in
cafés. Like many of his comrades, he discovered that the sketchbook was a
magnet for attention. People loved to have their portraits drawn. Often he
would make a sketch for the subject and another for himself. "Now that
I'm older," he says, studying the many volumes of sketchbooks that he
filled with the faces of soldiers, prostitutes, children, refugees, "I can see
that there was probably more art in the drawing I did in the service than a
lot of the colder commercial work I later did, which afforded me a living."

Sketching in public places also assured a guy that he'd never be
lonely—Dowd always had a girl on his arm, eager for him to draw her
picture.

Laynor had dreamed of coming to Paris since he traded away his stamp
collection for paints at the age of twelve. His scholarship had been nullified

by the war, but he was finally here. "I've traveled a lot now & I've found no place to match or equal New York, unless perhaps it is Paris," he wrote home. "Still, Paris has an altogether different aura about it. The people are more aristocratic yet more humble than we. It is a city of age & history verging on the ultra-modern."

He went hunting for Parsons École des Arts, the place where he would have studied had not the war intervened. "It is in the Place des Vosges near the most well known bawdy house (whore house) in Paris," he reported. "In fact it's next door. I can now see where they get all their life study models from."

He longed to meet Picasso and see his studio, but his initial visit was too brief. Later he would return under more dramatic circumstances.

Ellsworth Kelly's friend Bill Griswold was dawdling on the Pont Neuf when a stranger touched his arm and said, "I do art, too," then signed his name—"Picasso." He invited Griswold back to his studio, where he used him as a model for a series of drawings. Griswold didn't know who Picasso was and asked Kelly, who informed him, but Griswold didn't invite Kelly to the regular evening salons hosted by the famous artist.

Bob Tompkins and Bill Blass rode into Paris on Sunday, September 10, aboard an army truck full of Special Troops. They parked in front of Notre Dame cathedral and at once were surrounded by happy mobs of Parisians. Carbines in hand and on the lookout for snipers, they warily toured the city for just eight hours, had time enough to drink beer at a café on the Champs-Elysées near the Arc de Triomphe, before they were ferried back to St. Germain.

"The black market had flourished and you could see there was an attempt at fashion even then," Blass recalls. "The women were all on bicycles, so they wore culottes. They wore turbans that were nothing but scarves tied around their heads. It had a certain look." In a couple of months, he would return to Paris on leave and remark on a striking change in the manner of the people. "The contrast with how nice Paris was on the day they were liberated—and then to go see them months later when they were so nasty! The Parisians themselves, they were sick of the GIs by then. They had more coal and black market stuff under the Germans than under the American regime."

But nothing could dampen the thrill of seeing Paris for the first time at such an exuberant moment in its history. "Visiting Paris had been a dream—in my particular case probably more than almost anybody else," Blass says. "It was still dangerous, so we were restricted. We didn't do anything—nobody got laid and nobody got drunk. It was just a matter of being there."

As they returned to Notre Dame, a sixteen-year-old Parisienne presented them with her personal key to the city. But they wouldn't have time to make themselves at home in Paris. Two days later, they were piled into those same trucks for a 250-mile journey east into Luxembourg, to stage Operation BETTEMBOURG from September 12 to 22.

Midday, a village in Luxembourg just across the French border, not far south of Bettembourg. Kids were spilling out the front door of the grammar school just as the motorcade squealed to a halt—at its center, a command jeep bearing the red, two-starred license tag of an American major general. It was an unusual vehicle—the hard GI seats had been replaced by luxurious leather ones cannibalized from a captured German staff car. On the front fenders were bolted four wooden ammunition boxes stenciled in German. A pair of escort jeeps bracketed the command jeep fore and aft, each full of troops and mounting a .30-caliber machine gun. The stenciled white insignia on all the front bumpers read "6Δ"—6th Armored Division.

The kids milled and stared. The general, a fortyish man with an impressive military mustache, stepped out of his jeep while the guards in the escort jeeps swiveled their machine guns and scouted the high windows of nearby buildings where snipers usually hid. The general's aide-de-camp—a tall, smiling, dark-haired man wearing glasses—climbed down from the backseat of the command jeep and opened one of the boxes on the fenders. As he lifted the lid and his hand disappeared inside, the kids watched, quiet, captivated.

He pulled out packets of candy and chewing gum and handed them to the general, who passed them out to the kids. Everybody relaxed. The Americans talked in English and a smattering of French and the kids chattered animatedly in French and German. They milled around the jeep eagerly grabbing for handouts until they had emptied the box, then the general waved magnanimously to the smiling kids, he and his aide mounted their jeep, and the little convoy barreled off through the village.

In another village, the motorcade stopped in front of a bar, and this time the mission wasn't to hand out candy to schoolchildren. The general and his aide strode into the tavern, accompanied by guards. The owner greeted them sullenly. He was notorious in the area for being an ardent Nazi sympathizer, the kind of citizen collaborator who passed along useful information to the Germans. The general spoke some curt orders and the guards ducked into the storeroom, emerging a couple of minutes later with six cases of Moselle wine—not the cheap stuff but the best in the house. The proprietor knew better than to protest. The soldiers carried the wine outside to their vehicles, and the general and his aide climbed aboard their jeep for the short ride back to their command post.

Stenciled on the driver's side of the jeep, was a woman's name: HANNAH.

The "aide-de-camp" was Fred Fox, and the "general" was another Princeton alum, a staff major who also enjoyed a little playacting. They didn't really need the wine. Fox himself despised looters in any army. But stealing it so brazenly, right in front of the proprietor, guaranteed that he would remember them. It would anger him enough to report them to the Germans: A major general of the 6th Armored Division—in Luxembourg! That division was still supposed to be way back in Brittany, near Lorient. The Germans would have to drastically revise their estimate of the American order of battle.

Likewise, by now Fox and his comrades were all weary of handing out chocolate to kids. "I know I'm sick and tired of throwing things out of a car to the crowd," he wrote to his fiancée. "These Europeans have been spoiled by so many generous boys in long, boring convoys that they line every roadway—cheering wildly and insincerely. The children's faces are so strained and ugly as they shout 'chocolate!' And they become mad, petulant little dwarfs as we pass without handing out any candy."

But this was Luxembourg, not France, and the kids would tell their parents—at least some of whom would likely be German sympathizers. They, too, would talk to the enemy about what their children had seen. Fox felt pretty good about their excursion—a fine day's work—and they'd play their act again tomorrow to a different audience. He loved this part of the war—playacting in minor farces and dramas. You weren't just slamming your tanks into the enemy's. You were putting him on, tricking him into mistakes, seeking a small share of glory without the blood. It lent a certain irony to the war, an artistic gloss. They were like advance men for a traveling show, drumming up business in town while the main troupe was setting up out at the fairground.

Operation BETTEMBOURG was just as brazen a ruse as confiscating wine by the case in broad daylight.

To the south, after a breakneck race across northern France, the Americans were trying unsuccessfully to slice a path into Germany. "The First U.S. Army was impaled on the Siegfried Line," Fox reported—the formidable border defense of pillboxes, minefields, and fortified villages that guarded the German frontier—"and the Third U.S. Army halted on the Moselle." Patton, stalled on the north-south line of the river, waited while his 90th Infantry attacked Metz, perhaps the most fortified city in Europe, across a single bridgehead.

After a frustrating and bloody two and a half months slogging through Normandy hedgerow by hedgerow, at a cost of nearly forty thousand dead, the Allied armies had streamed across France, hardly pausing to liberate Paris—two American divisions ceremoniously marched down the Champs-Elysées and straight out of the city to continue the battle. Since early August, the Germans had been retreating and surrendering so fast that Eisenhower abandoned his original plan to stop at the River Seine to regroup. Instead his armies pushed on to the German border, hard on the heels of tens of thousands of Wehrmacht soldiers desperately trying to get home.

This was Eisenhower's historic opportunity, and he recognized it and seized the initiative: Attack, attack, attack.

As a result, supply lines were stretched taut, gasoline for tanks was constantly shut off from one army to fuel another, replacements couldn't keep pace, vehicles broke down, weapons wore out, and hardly any division in any army was fighting at full strength. But they kept up the chase. Then, in early September 1944, just about the time when it seemed that ultimate victory was within their grasp, the Allies struck hard on the rock of the Siegfried Line. The Germans were turning and fighting. Their own supply lines were short, and they were defending home ground, with nowhere left to retreat to.

From Luxembourg to Metz on the Moselle River, the stalled American advance and the need to reinforce divisions already engaged in heavy fighting left a dangerous gap in the line—an undefended hole nearly seventy miles long patrolled by a lone reconnaissance squadron of the 3d Cavalry, the 43d. If the Germans realized the sector was virtually undefended, they could strike into Luxembourg and threaten Patton's left flank.

The Special Troops' story: The 6th Armored Division was galloping to the rescue, plugging the gap with tanks, massing to assault Remich, a dozen miles away, cross the Moselle into Germany, and break the deadlock.

Their objective: to keep the Germans from counterattacking on Patton's flank at Metz and turning Third Army's advance. If all went well, the Germans would instead fall back on the defensive, and the Americans would win precious time to bring up reinforcements.

It was a new mission for the Special Troops—completely defensive—and the riskiest ploy they had yet dared. If the Germans twigged to their trick and counterattacked anyway, they would roll right over the thin "line" of camoufleurs, sound-effects men, and radio platoons guarded by a smattering of combat engineers and sonic security troops. One cavalry squadron with a handful of light tanks would hardly stop a Panzer division. There would be no reserves to come to their rescue, and no escape.

To mimic the operations of the real division, the Special Troops divided into two teams, designated Combat Command A—assault—and Combat Command R—reserve—each consisting of specific battalions of the 6th Armored. Officers distributed a brief history of the 6th Armored to each enlisted man to memorize. They went to work sewing on shoulder patches, stenciling "6Δ" bumper markings, inflating two sets of decoys, setting up a spoof radio net, and driving their vehicles around in loops through nearby villages—Esch Alzette, Pont Pierre, Kayl—to create "atmosphere."

The Signal Company laid down sixty miles of field telephone wire between the two combat commands, the 43d Cavalry Squad, and the XX Corps Headquarters, so they could keep in close touch without using radios, which of course would be broadcasting bogus messages—and in the process captured two German infiltrators. Phony MPs, played by Rebh's combat engineers, set up fake checkpoints to guide the incoming fictional armored columns. Other platoons set up a water point in plain view of Bettembourg, and three times a day, gangs of men in trucks would arrive to fill enough jerry cans to slake the thirst of eight thousand imaginary troops. Truckloads of men showed up at local public bathhouses, cafés, even church services to make a show of overwhelming force—so many soldiers that they could be rotated out of the line in groups for R & R.

All of it created an effect they called "atmosphere"—the observable, convincing evidence of a buildup.

And of course, there was Fox and his "command jeep." "We also had a splendid Major General," he wrote. "You can't have a Division without one. Nothing gives a sense of Importance better than High Ranking Brass."

For BETTEMBOURG, the password sign was "Rocking," the countersign, "Chair." Probably Merrick Truly's joke—"Always rock with the grain, never across it." They would change it twice—to "Rippling" and "Rhythm," to "Wireless" and "Radio."

As a gamble to buy time for the American advance, Operation BETTEMBOURG was supposed to last just forty-eight hours. But it worked so well, and the Americans were so desperate to keep the gap in the line plugged, that the Special Troops stayed in the line for more than a week, from September 12 to 22.

Four nights running, the sonic cars "cooked" the problem—projected the sounds of armor, tank after tank grinding into Luxembourg, menacing the German border. "It's nighttime and the record players are blaring away," recalls Vic Dowd. "And you hear the recorded voice of a sergeant: 'Put out that goddamned cigarette! Now!' And you hear the rumble of tanks, and it sounds like a whole division is racing through the woods. And I'm told that the Germans are jumping on anything they can find to get the hell out of Luxembourg."

In the forest near Bettembourg, the weather suddenly turned sharply chilly with constant rain. Like the division they were portraying, the men were not allowed to have fires in bivouac and joined their shelter halves to make larger tarpaulins for shared dryness and warmth.

"By this time, we had also learned to wear all of our extra clothing, so it was not unusual to have two sets of long underwear covered by two pairs of O.D. trousers and two wool shirts," Jim Laubheimer wrote home. "In addition, if one had a sweater, this was worn under the shirts since they could not be worn on the outside. Add a field jacket, raincoat, a wool hat under a helmet, and gloves to this ensemble, and one can see that we looked like fat teddy bears waddling about the woods!!"

Hal Laynor also was getting used to the rain. "Lately the weather hasn't been so kind to us," he wrote his wife. "It's pouring raining consistently. Our little pup tents are our only abodes of protection. I've got about three feet of space that is bone dry—outside of that, all is sopping wet."

Like many of the guys, he was concerned that loved ones back home were hearing all sorts of unfounded rumors about where he was and what he was doing, and he sought to downplay the danger. "Don't believe anything anybody tells you . . . all a lot of malarkey," he wrote home. "I can see where they get so much to write now—they make up fictitious stories of phoney glory and gory. I will tell you everything there is to tell & if I don't tell it to you, it's because I can't, and if I can't neither can anyone else— remember that—incidentally—I love you—from plus to minus infinity."

Dave Wynshaw remembers how spooky it was out on the line. "I was put into an area that I was to cover the size of a football field and I was told, 'There is no one in front of us except the German line,' " Wynshaw recalls. Across the field was a thick forest.

One of the constant irritations was the poor quality of the GI clothing and the lack of crucial items, such as galoshes. Wynshaw managed to get a pair of size twelves from a supply sergeant he ran into by accident, an old friend from New York in another outfit. But he wore thirteens, so he had to bend down the backs and walking was clumsy, until he traded for a pair of thirteens with a lone GI from 4th Infantry he met on patrol who had also been wearing the wrong size. They met, traded galoshes in the rain, then resumed their separate patrols, part of a line stretched as thin as it could be stretched.

That thin line made Colonel Reeder more nervous every hour.

By now, Reeder—tutored by Fox and Simenson and other officers who were getting the hang of the deception game—understood that *timing* was crucial to a successful ruse. They could stage a hoax for only so long before the target caught on. He and his staff believed that two to three days was the maximum time such a large operation could be kept secret from enemy patrols, civilian collaborators, even friendly troops who might talk too loosely over a drink in a café. Thus every hour that passed increased the danger that the Special Troops would be found out. It was nerve wracking, expecting any minute to receive a panicked field telephone message that the Germans were overrunning the line, to get the hell out of there. And knowing there was nowhere to run. The nearest American troops were thirty or forty miles away. Paris was 250 miles behind them.

And unlike on previous operations, they could tell right from the start that this one was working beautifully—good news, but it ratcheted up the anxiety level. The Germans were watching and listening hard, and soon they might react.

"Civilians in nearby villages were quite interested in all movements of the command, and were seen copying bumper markings from vehicles," reported Capt. Oscar Seale, again in charge of one of the deception teams. "Numerous civilians questioned both officers and enlisted men regarding movement of the command into and out of the operational area."

Two civilians were spied surreptitiously photographing vehicles— from the front, to record the bumper markings. Another was detained and questioned—he had photos of GIs and knew the names of certain officers in the real 6th Armored.

France had been friendly territory, the people almost embarrassingly grateful to the American liberators. But here, so close to Germany, the countryside was alive with enemies. Only two days into the operation, a breach of security threatened the whole enterprise: "Capt. Rebh's corporal saw four (4) EM [enlisted men] carry a dummy tank through the area commanded by Lt Col Schroeder," noted the operational journal for 10:00 A.M. on September 16 with typical shorthand understatement. "A civilian riding by in a buggy saw the men carry this tank. He seemed very much impressed."

There was a brief investigation, but the civilian was long gone—luckily he must have been a "friendly," since nothing came of the gaffe. Meanwhile, on three nights—the eighteenth, nineteenth, and twenty-first—German observation aircraft, which had been nearly absent from the skies for a month—overflew their positions. It had begun to dawn on them how exposed they were—and, except for a small contingent of cavalry with a handful of light tanks, how alone.

"We're the only outfit on this part of front except for 1 cavalry Squadron spread very thinly," Tompkins wrote on September 16. "No one knows where front is."

The Special Troops stayed put, played their music, manned their spoof radios, stared nervously into the misty darkness, most of them armed with only carbines and pistols. Every night German patrols probed their lines. Just before midnight on September 15, some cavalry pickets got in a firefight with a German recon patrol. Three hours later, as fog shrouded the woods, another German patrol penetrated to within two thousand yards of the sonic cars. Late on September 17, the Special Troops received orders to prepare to withdraw—Intelligence expected a German breakthrough.

The troops strung tripwires attached to tin cans around their bivouac areas, to alert them to infiltrators.

"We should have moved out a couple of days ago, but attack seems imminent so I guess we have orders to remain until it begins," Bob Tompkins wrote in his war diary on September 21. They were all nervous, expecting the worst. Even the privates could see how far out front they were. Today when they talk about the operation, the veterans usually make a joke out of it, then some of them mention the fear that still overtakes them like a sudden chill when they think back on those days. The whole enterprise seemed almost unreal even back then. Training and esprit de corps seem to have steadied them. During the whole war, not one man in the Special Troops dodged a mission, refused a patrol, ducked out on his buddies. At Bettembourg, they settled into their deception routine and braced themselves for an attack. But the breakthrough never came. What came instead was more patrols—some attacking only a few hundred yards from their command post—probing their lines, testing for weakness, trying to gather intelligence on the armored division they were convinced was facing them.

Finally, German patrols became so frequent and aggressive that division headquarters had no choice but to beef up the 43d Cavalry Recon Squadron with reinforcements—enough to turn back the increasing patrols, but not enough to stop a real attack in force. Special Plans Branch ascertained that two full German infantry divisions—the 48th and the 19th—along with elements of the 36th moved into position to counter the phantom threat from the Special Troops. They were drawing the enemy away from Third Army's battle at Metz and onto their position, all right—but would the enemy be convinced of their overwhelming power, or would he attack?

As the hours and days ticked by, the incredible luck of the Special Troops held.

Then came the crowning piece of intelligence. On the night of September 21–22, the Germans blew their own bridge at Remich—meaning they had retreated behind the Moselle and could no longer attack with armor.

Intelligence also reported another German compliment to the wiles of the Special Troops: "After Bettembourg, the Army G-2 told us the Nazis nicknamed the 6th Armored Division, 'Phantom Division.' That made us feel good."

Now you see it, now you don't. Facing a handful of artists of razzle-dazzle, three German divisions not only didn't attack Patton's open flank, they retreated without a fight and blew their bridge behind them.

Tompkins recorded, "It seems the 603d had been given credit for pushing Nazis completely out of Luxembourg. Reports say we are a terrific success."

Patton still hadn't taken Metz, but he had gained valuable time to bring up reinforcements and stave off a German counterattack. As the Special Troops faded out, the 83d Infantry moved into the line. And soon the Americans would cross the Moselle in force and chase the Germans into their homeland.

≡ TEN ≡

CAN YOU HEAR ME, LUXEMBOURG?
October–November 1944

We were Cecil B. DeMille warriors.

—Dick Syracuse

Col. Reeder assembled the men in the Schobermesse Square in Luxembourg City—he had an important announcement to make. No one seems to recall exactly when Reeder made his speech, except that it was soon after the Special Troops occupied Luxembourg City after Operation BETTEMBOURG at the end of September 1944.

Reeder was a paunchy man in his fifties. His jowly face with its dark brush-cut mustache and graying hair was familiar to every enlisted man from the caricatures drawn by Richard Morton and Walter Arnett. For men and officers alike, he was mostly a distant and unapproachable figure, brusque and autocratic. "He was always kind of *harrumph*!" Jim Laubheimer explains. "He was apart from everybody."

Reeder made a similar impression on sonic platoon leader John Walker. "What bothered me was that he didn't come over as a buddy-buddy and say, 'Hi, John—How are things going?' " Walker recalls. "He would stand aside and look at you like, 'Oh, you're some of the troops, huh?' That to me did not show true leadership. He'd stand aside and scrutinize you instead of feeling like he belonged to you or you belonged to him."

Reeder probably was still chafing at his assignment. Simenson recalls being told by Hector Truly that back in August, during the Brittany and Brest operations, Reeder wrote a letter to 12th Army Group—Gen. Bradley—complaining that the whole concept of the Special Troops was a waste of time. In any case, Reeder tended to come down hard on junior officers, especially the popular ones, for minor infractions and was constantly bothered by the lack of military bearing of his troops.

"He wanted something a little more sparkling," George Martin recalls. "He thought he was another General Patton."

Before one of the earlier operations, Reeder had called a staff meeting and harangued his officers angrily. The troops were too sloppy, and when they moved out in convoy, they looked just like a caravan of gypsies, wearing bandannas and strumming guitars. He ordered his staff officers to station themselves at key points along the line of march to check up on them, then report back to him.

Fred Fox dutifully lay in wait for the convoy, then reported back to Reeder. "A very strange group came by, and I'm sure you would not approve of them. There were things hanging out everywhere and they were very sloppy and unmilitary. I went up to them and said, 'You look just like gypsies!' And they said, 'We *are* gypsies!' "

During another operation, Reeder strutted through the area, swagger stick under his arm, trailed by a coterie of staff, as the camoufleurs were setting up their bivouac on the side of a hill. Many of the men were making their beds on the soft white fabric liners that came in the original packing for the neoprene dummies. Reeder stopped the men and imperiously demanded, in his stilted accent, "Wheah did you get this plunduh?"

"He'd be perfect in the movies," camoufleur Howard Holt recalls. "From then on, we were always saying, 'Wheah did you get this plunduh?' You know how guys are, never stop."

In the spacious square in Luxembourg City, Reeder stood before a microphone, his voice amplified into a loudspeaker so that all the assembled troops could hear. They were engaging in too much fraternizing with the locals, he said, and that had to stop. They were here to practice deception, and that meant being very careful not be found out by local collaborators. Too many men were talking too freely about their work. "Now this is a very top-secret outfit, and you're not to talk about it!" he said, his voice resounding through the loudspeaker, echoing off the surrounding walls.

The men heard his every word—and so too did dozens of local citizens, going about their daily business—including, obviously, any collaborators in the neighborhood. "They couldn't help it! They were all around us!" Laubheimer remembers. From that day on, whenever someone was talking confidentially to his comrade, some other guy would pipe up, "Can you hear me, Luxembourg?"

"That was our main joke," Laubheimer says.

Announcing your secret business through a microphone and loud-speaker in the city square was a hell of a way to go undercover.

On September 25, just after closing down BETTEMBOURG, the Special Troops settled into Luxembourg City just to the north for what they figured would be the final weeks of the war. En route, they met a contingent of German soldiers mounted on bicycles, eager to surrender. The Special Troops, feeling cocky now that the war was winding down so fast, simply waved them down the road toward an infantry company bivouac. The rats were leaving the sinking ship, and spirits ran high. "At that time, even the worst pessimist did not predict that the headquarters would remain there for nearly seven months," Fox wrote.

Luxembourg City became their base of operations, from where they sortied into Belgium, France, Holland, and Germany, like fliers going out on missions, then returning each time to prep for a new one.

The camoufleurs, combat engineers, and signal operators occupied rooms in the Catholic seminary—the Priesterseminar Limpertsberg—at the north end of the city, once home to three hundred priests. The seminary had been commandeered by the Germans for an officers' barracks. Amid the statuary and religious ornaments, the Germans had disfigured the place with cartoonish propaganda scenes and slogans about the invincibility of the Nazi *Übermenschen* of Hitler's thousand-year Reich.

"The Germans have painted murals in many of the buildings we have taken over," Fox wrote. "Usually, they are either glorified, sentimentalized or cute pictures of soldiers at war. One barracks which used to house part of the Afrika Korps had a playful Nazi hanging his laundry on a line strung between the horns of two smiling giraffes. Every mural has a fraulein with thick cupid lips and plump arms." He concluded, disdainfully: " The Nazis have such a tendency toward bad taste."

Fox himself was billeted with the rest of headquarters staff in the much tonier Italian Legation two miles southeast, not far from the sonic company billet at the Hollerich School on the Verdun road. Not far from the Italian Legation, General Bradley set up his 12th Army Group headquarters—on the Boulevard de la Liberté, the main street of the city, which arced over the Petrusse River on a high bridge and had been renamed after Adolf Hitler when Luxembourg was "reincorporated" into Germany. Morton captured the scene on moving day in a cartoon illustrating a letter home: Three puzzled GIs stand before the wall of their new billet trying to decipher a German slogan. On the wall opposite he reproduced a cartoon mural of a heroic German soldier advancing under shell bursts across barbed wire.

Over the main entrance to the seminary stood a life-sized figure of Christ, hand raised in a blessing for all who entered—a strange counterpoint to the murals of armed conquest.

The men climbed upstairs, where they would bunk one squad to a room—except there were no bunks. The retreating Germans had also torn out all the light fixtures. Some of the men saw out the window another company unloading mattresses and stoves from a deuce-and-a-half parked in the courtyard. One guy stood in the truck pushing the gear out the tailgate, while other guys lined up to grab a mattress or stove and carry it off to their billets. Laubheimer and his buddies went out into the courtyard and joined the line, just as if they belonged there. "It wasn't long before we were brewing coffee on a nice little potbellied stove and had enough mattresses to keep most of our weary bones off the cold, hard floor."

The mattresses, though, were infested with bedbugs. Morton and Arnett, the cartooning team, doused theirs with gasoline and set them on fire—then smothered the fire quickly, before the mattresses could burn up. Only later did they learn that the cavernous basement had been used by the Germans as an ammunition depot and was still chockful of hand grenades and high explosive shells.

Such resourcefulness was the hallmark of the GI experience in Europe. Whatever the danger, however crucial the mission, the men were constantly obsessed with three things: food, warmth, and sleep. A hot supper of real meat and fresh vegetables could be more alluring than sex, and men fantasized about it just as often. Their GI battledress couldn't keep out the damp chill of the constant rain, snow, and sleet that would plague them from Brest to the end of the war. They wrote home asking for sweaters, mittens, long johns, heavy socks, scarves. They scrounged or built stoves for every billet, even dugouts in the field. Fox carried a stove in his jeep.

Patton recognized the critical role weather would play in the outcome of the war. In an October letter to General Bradley, he contended that the Allies were fighting three enemies: "One was the German, the second was the weather, and the third was time. Of these three I conceived the weather to be the most important, because, at that moment, our sick rate for the first time equaled our battle casualty rate, and the weather was not improving."

Sleep was precious. In a leaky pup tent on sodden ground, especially in an area vulnerable to artillery barrage, rest was fitful. Often it was interrupted by guard duty. In a foxhole, it was out of the question. And on a mission, the troops tended to work all night on their dummies or sonic projection, then work all day on special effects, catnapping when they could. An actual mattress was a rare treat.

Laynor wrote to his wife, "I had to laugh when you ask me what time we work, we can work from six in the morning until six the next morning or on the other hand we can do nothing from six in the morning till six in the morning."

Just a block east of the seminary, in a school off the Boulevard de la Liberté, Patton set up his Third Army Headquarters, a few more blocks down from where Gen. William Simpson set up Ninth Army Headquarters; across the boulevard from Third Army, the camoufleurs' Headquarters & Service Company took over an exhibition hall, which they called "the factory," where they repaired the dummy equipment.

Thus there were two clusters of units in Luxembourg City: on the north side, the main force of the Special Troops, their factory section, Patton's Third Army Headquarters, and Ninth Army Headquarters; farther south, the sonic company, Bradley's headquarters, and the headquarters staff of the Special Troops.

The Headquarters & Service Company's factory section fashioned a variety of unauthorized items, especially inflatable neoprene mattresses, some of the first to be used anywhere, made from the fabric of dummies that had been damaged beyond repair. H & S company included talented machinists who could tool gun parts and just about anything else the Special Troops needed.

They also made "trench art"—so called because it originated in the trenches of the First World War: fancy engraved belt buckles cut and welded from shrapnel, cigarette lighters fabricated from bullets, ashtrays cut out of artillery shells. Martin, the battalion photographer, took home a souvenir ashtray made from a cut-down high-velocity 76mm Sherman tank shell, still imprinted with the manufacturer's specs. And the firearms enthusiasts in the outfit, Dahl among them, collected all sorts of guns. A particular favorite was the Mauser used by the German infantry, which made a fine hunting rifle. The men would dismantle the rifles or saw off the stocks for shipment home, intending to reassemble them when they returned from the war. And they shipped or eventually carried home more lethal souvenirs: daggers, bayonets, and swords; whole boxes of German machine-gun ammo folded into belts; even live mortar rounds.

About a week after they'd settled in, Patton arrived in Luxembourg City on an inspection tour. "We wore white ascots in our shirts instead of buttoning up with a tie—it looked a little more relaxing and casual, but it was certainly not standard GI!" Bill Blass recalls. "I can remember when we appeared for Patton, and we all came out in our white ascots. You can imagine that the general did not take kindly to that."

The general also inspected their equipment. As they moved across France and into Luxembourg, many of the camoufleurs had been antiquing—dickering with locals for charming clocks, paintings, lamps, knickknacks, even furniture. They did not loot but bargained shrewdly, using French "invasion money," cigarettes, and anything else they could barter. Blass says, "Not only had we modified our uniforms—in the back of the trucks were Louis Quinze chairs and things like that, that we'd picked up along the way. And, boy, did Patton stop that in a hurry!"

In Luxembourg, Nazi flags turned up everywhere. Until the Americans arrived, they'd hung from the windows of homes and public buildings all over the city. Now children exchanged the swastika-emblazoned flags, buttons from SS uniforms, and other souvenirs of occupation for chewing gum, chocolate, and cigarettes. Richard Morton was one of many who sent home souvenir flags and listened to story after story of Nazi atrocities—hearing constant reminders of why he and other GIs were fighting so far from home. Along with the souvenirs, he sent home this message: "Something which I would like to pass on in writing is that I have heard enough accounts first hand, of those who lived under Nazi domination and were eye-witnesses to their deeds and methods, to back up the accounts of the atrocities and rule of terror with which they have been credited."

In time, the Special Troops would be overwhelmed with affection for the people of Luxembourg, who opened their homes to them and struck up friendships that lasted for decades. At a dinner given to celebrate the occasion of liberation by the Americans, the hostess gave a short speech, later reprinted in *The Stars and Stripes*. "Four years of bitter sorrow and restless daily fight have vanished in that one moment we saw the first of you smiling boys," she said in English. "Why can't we tell you our gratitude as we feel it? Why is the human tongue such a wretched helpless thing to a heart drunken with happiness?"

Many Luxembourgers had resisted the Germans, especially when they took away their sons to fight in the Wehrmacht. Others had simply endured the occupation with resentment for the way their neutral country had been invaded. But there were plenty of collaborators skulking about. On his first day in the city, Ellsworth Kelly and a couple of buddies wandered down the street into a café, where the surly owner and his wife served them beer. They seemed not at all happy to see the GIs, and it soon became clear why.

"Like a good soldier, one of the guys went in the back to see if there was a back door," Kelly recalls. "Suddenly there was a crash at the front door—a firebomb had been thrown into the café." The bomb didn't go off. It was a type of incendiary made from two bottles, one inside the other, each containing a chemical. When both bottles broke and the chemicals mixed, they would explode. But this time only the outer bottle broke.

Lucky. But the unnerved proprietor ordered them to leave anyway.

In October, the Special Troops engaged in only one operation—WILTZ, a spoof radio and special-effects deception meant to screen the advance of the 5th Armored Division north along the German border to an area near Malmedy, Belgium. Originally, the plan was to make it appear as if the division hadn't moved at all. But its clanking columns of tanks moved out in full daylight—under radio silence and with bumper markings blacked out, but still obvious to any alert observer.

So the Special Troops simulated movements by two notional combat commands from the 5th Armored Division to different locations south of Malmedy, near Malscheid and Wiltz.

Laynor was among those who provided special effects. "We're pretty close to the front now, as close as we've ever been," he wrote. "Last night for over a half hour planes kept roaring over us in the darkness. Even at this late stage of the game, it was awe-inspiring."

Like all ground soldiers, he worried most about artillery fire—their job was, after all, to convince the Germans that they were juicy targets. "Artillery is bursting a couple of miles away right now, & by the sound of it, it isn't too far away," he wrote. "We can see the bursting of the shells from the crest of a hill near us, & the fire is wicked!"

The signal operators spread out seventeen radios across an area of a thousand square miles and went to work. They were well prepped for their roles. "Since the 5th Armored radios had been active in the old area, our spoof radios began infiltrating into their real nets two days before the move began," Fox wrote. The spoof operators got a chance to study the habits of the real operators, who thoroughly briefed them in their procedure—call signs, frequencies, cryptographic systems, and other distinguishing traits—so that they sounded completely authentic. Fox complimented the success of such a theatrically rehearsed approach: "The transition from real to spoof was extraordinarily smooth and the enemy intelligence might have had some trouble detecting it," he wrote.

To confuse the Americans, English-speaking German radio operators often would go on the air and try to confuse the flow of orders and reports with false traffic of their own—one reason why, in action, the Special Troops communicated with each other by wired field telephones. If the German operators broke into a false net, it meant they were accepting it as real.

"One measure of success could be heard in the efforts of the Nazi operators to break into our spoof nets. This was as satisfying to the Signal Company as the shelling of rubber dummies was to the Camouflage Engineers. And not as scary."

A second operation, VASELINE, was planned for the sonic company. They would simulate a buildup by the same 5th Armored Division just south of Monschau, Germany—north of its real position—preparatory to an assault. And the 5th Armored would, of course, jump off the following morning from a totally different concealed position in yet another attempt to penetrate the Siegfried Line. But the area was too hot, the artillery fire too heavy and accurate.

After several postponements, the VASELINE operation was scrubbed and the sonic cars returned to Luxembourg City.

Though not assigned a new mission for several weeks, the Special Troops were far from idle. For one thing, there was constant need for reconnaissance patrols to gather intelligence, scout out country for future operations, and maintain communications with other outfits. Jeep drivers like Tompkins were always on the go. His war diary entry for October 11 is typical: "Left 8:30 south to Mars-Letours and then down to Pont-à-Mousson. Crossed Moselle came up East bank about 12 k from Metz, then took bridge shielded by smokescreen and returned by way of Belgium. Three Countries in one day."

By war's end, he would rack up just shy of ten thousand miles on his jeep.

And ever since landing in Normandy, whenever they weren't on a mission, their trucks and drivers had been employed to haul supplies, gasoline, and replacement troops to frontline units. And of course they had to supply themselves—with rations, mail, even payroll. Ellsworth Kelly logged many hours driving a truck across France and Luxemburg, ferrying troops and hauling loads of rations, ammo, and gas, first from the beachheads, then from inland depots. On ten-minute roadside breaks, he sketched flash portraits of GIs, drew the enchanting countryside and the ruined villages. With more leisure, he also produced full watercolors, finished ink sketches, multiple figure studies, and barracks portraits—along with portraits of children and café patrons in France, Belgium, and Luxembourg. His best work may be the series of revealing self-portraits done by candlelight in his tent that show him at various stages of his experience. In their deep shadows and hooded eyes, they capture the fear that followed him and his comrades everywhere on the front, the sober and somber feel of the war, the dread, loneliness, and discomfort of living from moment to moment, waiting for orders, with no end in sight.

The other artists all found time for sketching and painting. Having an indoors home, however lacking in amenities, made all the difference in the world: They could leave work-in-progress behind, go on a mission, then return to it. In the city, it was possible to buy or barter for art supplies—good heavy paper stock, new pens, tubes of paint. They could work out of the rain and biting cold, hang their finished work, even stage group exhibitions. They had been doing this all along—tacking up sketches in barns, even hanging them on a clothesline in an open field—but the seminary gave them at least the illusion of permanence in a life that was otherwise a gypsy existence controlled by mysterious unseen officers at Special Plans Branch.

Laynor wrote to his wife, "I told you I was art conscious again & I've painted three paintings that are almost up to my old standard in watercolour. One was done here in Belgium & two in Luxembourg. . . . I'm trying to make at least two or three paintings a week now."

George Vander Sluis painted a view looking out across Luxembourg City toward a bridge being crossed by army trucks. Harold Dahl was so entranced by the painting that he bought it and shipped it home. The war was turning out to be quite an adventure, as well as a graduate education in art. He wrote, "I'm fast growing international—this letter is in Claire's ink, the pen is French, I have English, American, French & German money in my pocket and later on will get paid in Belgian. Our dinner today consisted in part of beef captured from the Germans. Last night I drank some Luxembourg beer, and I just wrote to Mary in the Pacific."

The others roamed the city, sketch pads at the ready, drawing street portraits, recording the sights, drawing studies for future paintings.

And of course, Morton and Arnett kept their pencils sharp by caricaturing their buddies and their officers—including Reeder—and posting them on the barracks bulletin board. After Reeder tore down an unflattering caricature of himself, they posted a new cartoon of Reeder tearing down a caricature of himself. That got Morton in the soup, as Louis Porter recalls. "He got in trouble because his cartoons were a little bit too accurate," Porter says in his Louisiana drawl.

On October 17, instead of a new cartoon, a memorandum from Lieutenant Colonel Fitz appeared on the bulletin board:

1. No <u>Cartoons, pictures, memorandums</u> or similar matter will be posted on any wall, bulletin board or other surface exposing said material to public view without the approval of the unit commander.
2. Violation of the above will be deemed to be a violation of the 96th Article of War (Failing to obey a standing order) and is punishable by confinement at hard labor for a period of six months and forfeiture of ²/₃ of six months' pay.

So the cartooning came to an end—it wasn't worth a stint on the rockpile.

Early in November, just about the time they were feeling at home in Luxembourg City, the Special Troops drew orders for three simultaneous missions: DALLAS, ELSENBORN, and CASANOVA.

ELSENBORN (November 3–12) was a piece of cake for the Special Troops—another spoof radio and special-effects show. The object was to convince the enemy that the 4th Infantry Division was staying put at Elsenborn Barracks, a Belgian army rest camp just behind the front lines between Eupen and Malmedy. Meanwhile, the real 4th Infantry headed into the Hürtgen Forest to reinforce the 28th Division, the Pennsylvania National Guard, whose red keystone insignia was now called the "bloody bucket" because of the staggering casualties suffered in the Hürtgen. The Hürtgen Forest covered fifty square miles in a triangle between Aachen, Duren, and Monschau, on the Belgian border near its confluence with the border of Holland. Thirty miles east was Remagen, Germany, and forty miles south was Bastogne, Belgium. Both would become famous names associated with American victories.

But the Hürtgen itself was a deathtrap, a wilderness of heavily wooded ridges rising up to a thousand feet high accessible by narrow dirt tracks. The German West Wall ran through it, so it was defended by a chain of interlinked bunkers and pillboxes. The Battle for the Hürtgen Forest remains one of the most controversial of World War II. The enduring mystery is why the Americans didn't simply go around it. It was justified as an attack to capture the vital Urft and Schwammenauel Dams, which ran through it and controlled the Roer Plain, the staging ground for an attack across the Rhine. But by the time the dams were taken, the Germans had had ample time to sabotage them, flooding the watershed for weeks and stalling both British and American attempts to cross the Rhine.

From start to finish, it was an entirely American assault through rugged, heavily fortified country where tanks were confined to narrow, tree-tunneled tracks, vulnerable to *panzerfausts*, antitank mines, and 88s. Thunderbolts and P-51 fighters were no help to troops on the ground, because the dense woods made it impossible to recognize targets. The Germans wiped out whole units of American soldiers with tree bursts, artillery shells fused to explode in the treetops and shower thousands of lethal splinters into troops caught in the open.

The battle began in September and would last for six terrible months, as General Courtney Hodges, commander of First Army, ordered wave after wave of infantry into what became known as "the Death Factory."

But the Special Troops had no intelligence on the fiasco that was brewing, the battle that would go down in history as the greatest American defeat in the European War. For a full week before the operation, while the 4th Infantry was still holding a sector of the front, the Blarney radiomen handled all its actual communications. So when the division moved out, the Special Troops operators simply continued the charade, now using fake messages indicating that the 4th was slated for R & R at Elsenborn.

Also, they had coordinated with the signal operators of the 9th Infantry, which was actually at Elsenborn the week before the operation. Coached by liaison officers from the Special Troops, those operators had staged a three-day radio exercise, something normally not done at a rest camp, setting a useful precedent. So when the Special Troops arrived, they could continue broadcasting as part of a phony exercise—an excuse to stay on the air with misinformation when normally they would have been silent. A fake within a fake.

"We began to get a little more sophisticated as the War went on," Fox wrote. "Although our Colonel was an old soldier who much preferred 'short arm' inspections and bayonet drills, we were gradually able to persuade him to give us more freedom to practice razzle-dazzle."

The Special Troops painted the bumpers of their vehicles with "4 X," the signature of 4th Infantry. "4 X" MPs directed traffic past "4 X" command posts in the first heavy snowfall of the season.

A captured German map overlay incorrectly sited the 4th Infantry at Elsenborn, not in the Hürtgen Forest. And other evidence of the success of the charade came more immediately. "Even officers of the real division were lured to the phoney headquarters where they stared blankly around at unfamiliar faces," Fox reported. "One officer who had been wounded, and was returning to his regiment from a hospital in England, broke down and wept. He thought all of his old friends had been wiped out." They quickly reassured him and sent him on his way. But the officer was eerily prescient. The 4th Infantry would suffer more than seven thousand battle casualties in the Hürtgen.

The other two Special Troops operations were part of Patton's drive to get more divisions across the Moselle, farther south, and into Germany. As Patton was fond of telling his commanders, throughout history, wars had been lost by not crossing rivers.

Using sonic deception, spoof radio, and special effects, the Special Troops would simulate a buildup by the 90th Infantry Division preparatory to an assault across the Moselle at Ukange. Meanwhile, of course, the 90th would slip across the river miles away.

DALLAS (November 2–10) would cover the movement of XX Corps artillery to the location of the actual river assault, where it would lay down a barrage to cover the surprise crossing. Fewer than 200 camoufleurs with an arsenal of thirty-six dummy artillery guns and scores of flash devices would portray 2,230 artillerymen and forty-eight big guns. For extra realism, twelve real artillery pieces were salted into the mix, so each fake battery of flash bombs was formed around a real 155mm gun.

The Special Troops set up near Jarny, ten miles west of the Moselle, supported by five hundred "extras" loaned to them for the operation, while the main force of artillery moved out under cover of darkness, by all accounts undetected by the Germans.

"Squads alternate firing and guard every day," Tompkins recorded in his war diary. "Rain, wind and mud make for a horrible existence. Our hut is leaking like a sieve. Everything is soaked. Don't see how an attack can start in this weather."

But the following day, after a miserable night on guard duty, he felt the hut shudder from a thousand massed American big guns firing into Germany. The XX Corps artillery had moved into position as planned, and the 90th was attacking on schedule—through rain, fog, and flood. Third Army was now in position to drive to the Rhine.

CASANOVA, also covering the attack by the 90th Division and staged from November 4 to 9, turned out to be a bit trickier.

At Ukange, a dozen miles upriver from the actual bridgehead, the Special Troops set up their show—or they started to. The idea was to create all the clatter and commotion of a major bridging assault while the 90th Infantry, supported by the 10th Armored, crossed downstream. A detachment of the 95th Infantry was even scheduled to make a diversionary attack at Ukange to add to the realism and draw reserves away from the real bridgehead just north of Thionville.

The radiomen spread their net, the sonic cars drew wire reels dubbed with a bridge-building program, the special effects squads infiltrated the countryside wearing the insignia of the 90th Infantry.

In many ways, CASANOVA was shaping up to be a textbook operation. It was coordinated with the actual unit making the assault, as well as with a supporting deception operation, DALLAS, to cover the moving up of supporting artillery; it employed an integrated show using all the tricks in the Special Troops inventory except the dummies, which were being used in DALLAS; and its objective was specific and measurable: to get the 90th across the Moselle with minimal casualties.

It was such a showpiece that a number of Dutch and French officers were invited to observe. They showed up just after Dick Syracuse had positioned his security platoon about three hundred yards from the front—digging in their .30- and .50-caliber machine guns, laying out their lines of communications, sighting their fields of fire.

Syracuse reported back to Major Williams that his men were all in position, then returned to check on the emplacements, as he would periodically through the night as the sonic program played and the danger of infiltration or attack increased. When he got back to the line, he discovered one of his emplacements was missing—Sergeant Birmingham and a machine-gun team. "And I panicked," Syracuse recalls. "Where the hell is he?" He found his platoon sergeant, Dick Dawson. "What the hell happened to Birmingham?" he asked.

"The colonel moved him—he's providing security for some dignitaries," Dawson told him.

Syracuse was livid—no staff officer was supposed to be giving orders to his men. That violated the whole chain of command. He sought out Birmingham, who was shepherding the French and Dutch officers. "Birmingham, get your team together, get back to where the hell I had you set up," he told him.

Birmingham objected. "Colonel Snee is really adamant—"

"I'll take care of him," Syracuse said.

During the course of the night, Snee returned and discovered his dignitaries were wandering around unguarded, with Birmingham and his team nowhere in sight. He found them back at their original position and placed Birmingham under arrest for violating a direct order.

Syracuse says, "And then when Dawson tells me that Birmingham's been placed under arrest, he's going to be court-martialed for disobeying an order, I blow my cork."

"Well, this prick has had it!" Syracuse said, drew his .45 pistol and went hunting Snee. "I'm going to blow his fucking brains out!"

Dawson tried to head him off. "Lieutenant, Lieutenant!" But Syracuse shoved his way past him.

Just at that moment, somehow sensing trouble or perhaps only lucky in his timing, Major Williams appeared. "What the hell's going on?" he wanted to know.

"I'm gonna kill the bastard!" Syracuse said, waving the gun.

"Wait a minute, Dick," Williams said, and grabbed the pistol out of his hand. "Christ Almighty—use your head!" He spent several minutes talking to Syracuse, calming him down. Syracuse holstered his .45, Lieutenant Colonel Snee returned to headquarters, and the visiting French and Dutch officers presumably made themselves scarce.

And most remarkably, nothing ever came of the incident—Syracuse never received so much as a reprimand. "However Williams handled it, nothing happened," Syracuse recalls.

Even more serious trouble was developing elsewhere on the line that would threaten the whole elegant deception plan.

Major General H. L. Twaddle, commander of the 95th Infantry, belatedly decided to cross his troops at the deception site. Simenson was on the scene, in charge of CASANOVA. Twaddle told him, "Go ahead with your plans, but don't interfere with my plans."

So Simenson had no choice: He pulled the plug. He shut down the sonic cars, silenced the radios, and the 95th Infantry massed along the Moselle at Ukange.

Meanwhile, on November 8, the 90th crossed north of Thionville, taking the Germans completely by surprise and rolling up the enemy flank so thoroughly that, when the 95th crossed at Ukange right through the deception operation a few days later, they, too, encountered almost no opposition. The 90th laid down the longest Bailey bridge in the world—a prefabricated span that assembled in sections—and then pushed across in one piece.

Patton visited the 90th Infantry not long after. "The crossing of the 90th Division over the Moselle was an epic river crossing done under terrific difficulties," he reported later. "After they got two battalions over, the bridge went out and everything else had to come across in assault boats." He walked the battlefield where twenty-seven battalions had descended on the Germans unawares and recorded with amazement that he had never seen so many dead German soldiers in his life. The graves registration companies had policed the fields and lined up the dead along the road: "They extended for a distance of about a mile, practically shoulder to shoulder."

Despite the one snafu, based on after-action evaluations by Special

Plans Branch, CASANOVA went down in the books as a resounding success.

"We lucked out on that," Simenson says. "That was pure luck, that we got the ninety-fifth to cross without any casualties. What we did for the 90th Division also helped the ninety-fifth."

There were more rivers to cross—the Saar, the Erft, the Ruhr, and finally the Rhine—and Simenson knew better than to count on luck. Luck could run out.

The Special Troops convoyed back to Luxembourg City in a howling blizzard. They were cold and somewhat dispirited, despite their recent success. And the city was taking on an edge. "Luxembourg becoming a living hell at night," Tompkins recorded. "Last week 5 G.I.'s were found dead, in the Gulch. Shooting every night. Boys arriving from Front for rest. Get drunk and spray street with machine guns. Five civilians killed the other night. Still many collaborators working under cover of darkness."

Meanwhile air raids grew more frequent, and German "buzz bombs" rocketed over the seminary all night long. Clearly, the war wasn't going to end anytime soon. Dahl echoed the frustration and disappointment of his fellows in a letter home. "What keeps those Germans going is beyond us—they've lost almost everything in the way of sources of supply, army after army, and still they prolong what must inevitably end in their complete surrender. All they are doing is causing more men to die, more women & children, German this time, to go homeless for a dead cause."

Fox got his first glimpse of Germany, now a battlefield, in Aachen, a fortified stronghold of the West Wall on the northern border of the Hürtgen Forest. Aachen was the birthplace of Charlemagne, the seat of the Holy Roman Empire, which Hitler regarded as the First Reich, and the Germans had defended it tenaciously. The GIs battled house to house for more than a week. Sherman tanks knocked holes in walls so they could fight inside the buildings instead of being exposed to German crossfire out in the street. Even a self-propelled 155mm gun—a heavy artillery piece usually employed far behind the lines—was maneuvered into the narrow streets to fire point-blank at strongpoints. In this manner, Aachen was reduced to rubble at a cost of five thousand American casualties and many more Germans dead, wounded, or captured.

"It hadn't been reduced to the rubble of St. Lô, but it seemed more terrible because it still looked more like a city—like a corpse with only a head and arm missing is more terrible than a body which has been blown into little pieces," Fox wrote. "I think the worst part was the utter desertion. I saw no one in a city which used to contain 150,000 people—except a few army engineers who were filling a shellhole and they don't count. . . . The children cringed like dogs as we drove by. Certainly Germany is learning what war is."

On November 15, the troops were again drawn up in Schobermesse Square, the scene of Reeder's speech about secrecy, this time to witness the awarding of Bronze Stars to three sergeants and a lieutenant. "I wrote all of the citations—and apparently my adjectives were too glorious because the men got more than we asked for and it was quite embarrassing," Fox wrote. "This bronze star, silver star, DSC [Distinguished Service Cross] business—like everything else in this war (and every war)—is 90% farce and 10% courage. The real heroes are either dead or lost in the shuffle. I wrote three more citations today but I was much more reserved." He himself would later be awarded a Bronze Star for his service in Normandy.

Dahl was pleased by the ceremony of recognition. "One other nice thing," he wrote, "was to see how automatically the town citizens removed their hats to the American flag. One person said to me afterwards that the Americans even *sounded* nicer than the Germans as we marched by."

They had all hoped to be home by Christmas—yet here it was almost Thanksgiving, they'd been overseas more than six months, and the war looked like it would go on forever. "The damn war at this point seems to have made itself a permanent installation in world history," Laynor wrote.

When they weren't repairing gear, driving out on recon missions, hauling supplies, or guarding the post, the men were forced to attend basic courses in first aid, sanitation, interior guard, even military courtesy. The "Blarney Theater" stayed in business, projecting 16mm feature films starring Bob Hope, Bing Crosby, Douglas Fairbanks Jr., and a parade of leading ladies. Throughout the campaign, it showed 679 hours of movies, enough to fill almost an entire month, day and night, but its appeal was wearing thin.

Dahl bought a violin complete with bow and case for about fifty dollars. "It has a lovely tone—was made in 1779 and is marked on the inside 'Antonius Stradivarius Cremonentis—Faciebat Anno 1779,'" he wrote jubilantly. "It looks to me like an inferior Strad that has been somewhat abused, but it is still a pretty good fiddle and worth considerably more than $50."

Men got bored with waiting. Then Marlene Dietrich showed up at the seminary—bringing the only live USO show ever to visit the Special Troops. She performed in the sanctuary of the chapel, which had been converted to a mess hall by the previous German occupants. Hal Laynor acted as emcee and performed a stand-up comedy routine, then introduced the sultry movie icon that Ernest Hemingway affectionately called "the Kraut."

"It was freezing-ass cold, so it was impossible for her to be in any way flirtatious or seductive about what she wore," Blass recalls. "Anyway, she wore a cumbersome hostess outfit—It was warm."

Dietrich sang "See What the Boys in the Back Room Will Have" and "Lili Marlene," her signature piece, still banned in the U.S. because of its sentimental German nostalgia but wildly popular among GIs in Europe. For an hour she performed and filled the spaces between numbers with warm and friendly banter.

Blass recalls, "She sang, but then she played the saw—which is not the most seductive instrument for a woman. It would have been—with those legs—if she'd had stockings or something, but she did not."

Laubheimer remembers only how anxious he was for the show to be safely over. "It was a dangerous place, because if we had an air raid, we couldn't get out. There was no egress from this place—just one set of doors out the back."

It must have been a bizarre and charming performance—the exotic Dietrich, who had once conducted a secret, passionate affair with Douglas Fairbanks Jr. in the luxurious privacy of Claridge's Hotel in London, now bundled up in a shapeless wool suit in the sanctuary of a seminary chapel in Luxembourg, playing the saw for homesick troops.

After the show, Laynor sketched a haunting portrait of Dietrich so he could paint her later. In the painting, she lounges as if waiting to go on, languorous but brooding, staring distantly off the canvas. There is a darkness to his vision of her, maybe the aura of a woman who is risking her life with every show. As a German native providing aid and comfort to American soldiers, she would have been executed if the Germans ever captured her.

The night before Thanksgiving, Shilstone and his buddy Bernard Parke ventured out on the town to find a drink. "Parke was a feisty, angry little guy," Shilstone says. He had gotten into trouble before while drinking. "Luxembourg City was still not safe, so we were supposed to carry weapons, but we didn't want to carry our carbines," Shilstone recalls. So each of them took a pistol. Parke's was a Walther PPK—a German weapon he had somehow acquired. The locals often traded or sold them to GIs for souvenirs.

Unlike the American .45, the PPK was a double-action pistol: instead of having to cock the hammer before firing it, all you had to do was squeeze the trigger, which would push back the hammer and fire off a round. Plenty of GIs got hurt when they played with the trigger, thinking it safe, and the unfamiliar gun went off.

"We came back over the wall of the motor pool," Shilstone remembers. "I guess we were feeling pretty good, singing and staggering. We tripped and fell down in a mud puddle, and when I got up I realized I had lost my .45. I went back to town looking for it everywhere but I couldn't find it. Then I heard a shot, but I didn't think much of it. We were always hearing shots."

But this time the shot was nearly fatal. While showing off his gun to some buddies, Parke had shot a fellow camoufleur, Bernard "Bud" Bier, in the stomach. Shilstone says, "The bullet went in his stomach, nicked the kidney, and came out the back, just missing his spine."

"I'd just left the room at the time, and when the gun went off, I actually fell down on the floor from the report of the gun 'cause it made quite a loud noise," says George Martin, who appeared as a witness at the subsequent court-martial. "The two of them hated each other, the two Bernards! One couldn't tolerate the other. But it wasn't intentional, it was just accidental."

Parke was confined to quarters. Severely injured, Bier went to the hospital. Shilstone says, "They told me, if he dies, then you'll be court-martialed, too, for carrying an unauthorized weapon." Luckily, Bier eventually recovered.

Bier would be the only gunshot casualty of the Special Troops during the entire war, wounded by one of their own.

As the commotion over the shooting subsided on Thanksgiving day, many of the guys went to the soccer stadium to play touch football in honor of the day. The front page headline of the *Luxemburger Wort* (Word) newspaper carried the English headline: "Thanksgiving Day—American and Luxembourg united in God." The editors wrote, "Today the celebration has for us, the citizens of the old world, the same significance and importance that it has for our allies across the sea, where the custom of Thanksgiving originated."

The troops were treated to a traditional turkey dinner with all the trimmings, and many ate a second time as honored guests at the home of local citizens, but like most holidays its most emphatic impact was to make them homesick for loved ones and familiar places. Fox wrote, "The battle zones are now swept clean of civilians and we always manage to requisition a little home or two. It's a strange feeling sitting in foreign parlors with some unknown ancestors staring down from the wall."

Across the Atlantic, Douglas Fairbanks Jr. was home from the war for good. In November, he visited Pine Camp to witness one of Hilton Howell

Railey's theatrical demonstrations with a new sonic company, the 3133d, which used tank destroyers instead of half-tracks to mount its equipment, and was training to join the campaign in Italy in the spring.

A week prior to Thanksgiving, on the same day they were handing out medals, the restless staff of the 23d Special Troops began scouting its next operation. As Fox records, "On 15 November the command started planning what turned out to be the most embarrassing operation of the war."

But the blame lay not with the 23d Headquarters staff. The fault lay entirely with German Field Marshal Gerd von Runstedt, who was making secret deception plans of his own.

ELEVEN

THE LONG, CRUEL WINTER
December 1944–January 1945

How we came through it, I'll never know—I really don't.
Sometimes we did stuff that was absolutely stupid.
                                        —Jim Laubheimer

Just about the time the shelling started, a jeep pulled up outside the farmhouse where Jim Laubheimer, now a sergeant, and two companions had settled in for the night. They'd spent the day policing the area after the first stage of Operation KOBLENZ, a week-long deception portraying an American buildup in a quiet sector of the Luxembourg line for an attack down the Moselle River valley toward Koblenz, Germany. The idea was to hold the German units in place across the line, tie them up so they would be unavailable to defend against a real thrust farther north. With luck, they'd also move in fresh reinforcements, who also would effectively be put out of action in the battle for Metz to the south.

While the main body of Special Troops retired to Luxembourg City to prepare for the second phase of the operation, to begin in a week, the three camoufleurs drove around the area collecting fake 75th Infantry Division road markers and making sure the Special Troops had left behind no telltale trace of their presence. At dusk they found a farmhouse where they could get in out of the bone-chilling weather for the night. Now they were warming themselves in front of a fire, drinking GI coffee that they always carried, and heating up K rations over the flames.

The artillery fire startled Laubheimer—he couldn't tell for sure, but it sounded like German stuff, a heavy barrage. And since the 75th Division wasn't really here, those couldn't be their big guns. Still, it sounded rather far off and he wasn't too concerned.

After he heard the squeal of the jeep outside, the door opened and an American infantry lieutenant strode in, followed by two enlisted men. "Hiya, fellows—good to see you," the officer said, all smiles and good cheer. The enlisted men said nothing. Laubheimer's instinct told him something felt fishy. In his experience, an officer generally wasn't all that friendly with strange enlisted men—he'd remain somewhat aloof. But regular GIs usually struck up casual conversations with each other readily. "The officer did all the talking," he recalls. "I mean, he did ALL the talking." Laubheimer whispered to his buddies, "Don't tell 'em anything." They kept their weapons close at hand.

The lieutenant was outgoing, gregarious, asked all sorts of questions: What outfit were they with? What were they doing up here? Where were they going next? What other units were nearby? The enlisted men never spoke a word.

All Laubheimer told him: "We're leftovers from the seventy-fifth." They were wearing the bogus sleeve patches of the 75th Infantry, still in transit from England. Later in the evening, the garrulous lieutenant and his silent companions went back out into the snow and drove away.

Laubheimer and his team passed a rare warm night indoors and left after a leisurely breakfast in the morning. They hadn't gone far when they were halted at a roadblock, where they reported the strange encounter.

"You've just been dealing with some Germans," he was told. "That's what they're doing, impersonating American soldiers." All along the front, from Luxembourg north through the Ardennes in Belgium, special squads of English-speaking Germans in captured American jeeps, deuce-and-a-halfs, even Sherman tanks, were infiltrating the lines, gathering information, spreading rumors, changing road signs, sabotaging communications. Major Otto Skorzeny, the commander of the disguised commandos, had issued orders that they were not to fire their weapons while wearing American uniforms, but not all his scattered teams complied. Many were themselves captured and stood in front of firing squads.

If indeed the strange GIs at the farmhouse had been Skorzeny commandos, Laubheimer and his squad were lucky to get out—they were the last Americans to leave the sector.

The guns Laubheimer had heard were the opening salvos of Von Rundstedt's Operation GREIF—in English, "GRAB"—which came to be known as the Battle of the Bulge. The German counteroffensive "bulged" the line in a daring attempt to break through and "grab" the strategically crucial port of Antwerp. Now five entire German armies—two of them right across the Luxembourg frontier—were counterattacking behind massed Panther and Tiger tanks and the whole Allied line was falling apart.

KOBLENZ had started off beautifully—the Luxembourg sector was the perfect place to stage a deception. The Americans used it as a kind of rest area for troops worn out from hard fighting and an orientation or "school" zone for green divisions. Over a period of several weeks, one armored and six different infantry divisions had been rotated into the line, including the 28th "Bloody Bucket" Division, its ranks decimated and the survivors exhausted from a prolonged and futile battle in the Hürtgen Forest.

By pretending to be the 75th Division, the Special Troops could make the line seem too strong for the Germans to attack successfully, thus ensuring that the 28th Division to their north and the 4th Division to their south could recover somewhat from the beatings they had taken. The pretense would buy them time to bring up replacements and train them at least minimally. Time to rebuild morale, resupply weapons and ammo.

The operation offered the added advantage of drawing more German troops from more active sectors, who would have to position themselves to repel a possible attack from the 75th, which of course wasn't even there. For a time, the sector went quiet.

"On the other side of the line, the Enemy seemed to be doing the same thing," Fox noted. "They would apparently bring in a freshly conscripted Volksgrenadier Division and permit it to enjoy a short course of leisurely combat before moving it either north or south into the cauldrons of the Roer or the Saar."

KOBLENZ was designed to deny the enemy this privilege—to make him devote precious line outfits to defending against an attack that, of course, would never take place.

But the preparations seemed very real. Eighth Corps headquarters actually drew up plans for an attack through Trier to Koblenz, so that the Special Troops could imitate it authentically. And they had plenty of help this time. For five days beginning on December 9, the Air Corps launched bombing sorties down the attack corridor, as if softening it up for a major push. A few real artillery batteries moved in disguised with phony insignia as the camoufleurs erected their dummy 155s. Infantry reconnaissance patrols were stepped up, probing deeper across the lines, as if feeling out the enemy's weak spots prior to an assault.

The Special Troops—guys like Shilstone and Tompkins—also went out on constant missions of reconnaissance, usually in the middle of driving snowstorms, keeping an eye on the German lines through binoculars. They wanted no surprises.

U.S. Army intelligence at every level all the way up to Eisenhower's headquarters had determined that the Germans were incapable of launching a major offensive, that they lacked not only the troops and tanks but crucial fuel to run those tanks. And they had no air power, so that any attack under clear skies would be suicidal against squadrons of Allied fighter-bombers. Facing the Special Troops across the line were elements of German Seventh Army, which had taken such a mauling at the Falaise Gap. No one expected the Germans to expose themselves like that again, when they could fight the kind of relentless war they were still waging successfully in the Hürtgen.

What the recon patrols weren't seeing were the hundreds of thousands of fresh reinforcements brought up to the line and hidden under cover, along with hundreds of tanks, including many fresh from the factory. Allied intelligence analysts were confident that the relentless strategic bombing raid on factories in dozens of cities had destroyed Germany's ability to produce planes, but the High Command scrounged up fifteen hundred to support its last great counteroffensive of the war.

The Special Troops and the divisions holding the line on either side knew nothing of this buildup. For once, the Germans were staging a magnificent deception.

To keep the Germans off balance and convince them the threat of American attack was real, the 28th Division launched a small feint attack, while double agents were coached on the plan and let loose in Germany. Some real tanks moved into the line, as the sonic company projected a major armored buildup and preparations for crossing the Moselle below Grevenmacher. Special Troops vehicles, marked "75 X" at a secret staging area in Belgium, convoyed into the area following radio traffic controllers broadcasting in SLIDEX, an easy code for the Germans to break.

Reeder at last got be a general. He drove to the deception area in a two-star staff car. Meanwhile Fox and his "Princeton major general" requested an additional fifteen thousand billets east and northeast of Luxembourg City to house the influx of fictional troops. Civilians were evacuated from their homes—whole villages turned into eerie ghost towns—and a schoolhouse was commandeered for a divisional command post. Telephone lines were laid, phony fuel dumps established, bridging equipment trucked to the front. For most of the Special Troops, it was round-the-clock work in freezing weather. They augmented their K rations with venison—reconnaissance patrols routinely shot the abundant deer.

On December 21, the Special Troops were scheduled to move the whole deceptive show north and "play in" the 76th Division, but they never got the chance.

The Germans had completely fooled Allied intelligence, who maintained right up until the first Panzer tanks broke through the thin Luxembourg-Ardennes line in the snowy dawn of December 16 that the Germans were not capable of a major offensive, that even if they were, the Ardennes was the last place in the world they would try it. The country was too rough, the roads too few and narrow, the winter weather too harsh and unforgiving for a sustained attack.

The Germans had turned the tables. False radio traffic, stealthy movement of troops up to the line, aerial camouflage, and strict security had all resulted in one of their most successful deceptions of the war. Special Plans had forgotten its own doctrine: What the enemy thinks unlikely, he will view as impossible. The Germans had done the unlikely and proved it possible.

"It was just dumb luck that we packed up and pulled out," recalls Ed Biow, a truck driver in the camouflage engineers. "About midnight on the fifteenth of December they pulled us out, decided the exercise was over—and of course the Bulge started at five o'clock the same morning! So we missed it by five hours."

Some of the sonic cars had a similar close call. "Three or four tracks of us and Major Williams were in front of a Radio Luxembourg tower," Bill Brown remembers.

There was an inn near the tower. Williams told his men, "You can stay here tonight, or if you want to go back to Luxembourg, I'll let you have all day tomorrow off."

Brown and the other guys voted for the day off, and they made it back to their schoolhouse billet late that night. "And then the Bulge jumped off—we would have been asleep," Brown says. "The Bulge went right through there within an hour or two."

Walter Manser, the producer of the sonic programs, also narrowly avoided capture—on account of paperwork. Whenever the Americans billeted troops in private homes, they filled out billet slips, so that the hosts could be paid for the lodging. The main body of Special Troops had already pulled out for Luxembourg City. Manser had a stack of billet slips from the operation just concluded, and his job was to obtain the seal of the local *Bürgermeister*—equivalent to a notary's seal—to make them valid and ensure payment. Accompanied by a driver, an interpreter, and an engineer officer, he was running all over the countryside looking for a village big enough to have a *Bürgermeister*.

After trying several villages, he came to one where he was assured a *Bürgermeister* could be found—and was directed to his house. The interpreter asked, "Is this the *Bürgermeister*'s place?"

"Yes," the local man answered, but hastened to add that, of course, he himself wasn't the *Bürgermeister*.

"Where is the *Bürgermeister*?"

"He's gone." An unfortunate moment to be away, they all agreed.

It was getting late, and sundown came by five o'clock in the afternoon. It was cold and snowing and the roads were glazed with ice. The engineer officer said, "Aw, let's stay out here another night."

"No, I don't like this damned place," Manser said. They had been sleeping in a railroad station on cold, hard floors—their schoolhouse billet in Luxembourg City seemed luxurious by comparison. Manser said, "Ask him if the *Bürgermeister* has an assistant."

"Yes," the man said. Of course a man as important as the *Bürgermeister* must have an assistant. After some more coaxing, he admitted that in fact *he* was the *Bürgermeister*'s assistant.

"Do you have a seal?" the interpreter asked.

"Yes." At last—a straight answer. They went inside and got all the billeting forms stamped, then drove back in the dark over icy roads and turned in, exhausted. The next morning, Major Williams woke them with the news that the Germans had broken through. Had they stayed another night, they'd have been caught out there.

Manser was at first skeptical: "I don't think so—I was out there after dark last night."

"But sure enough, they had come through," Manser says.

Luxembourg City, where Bradley, Patton, and the Special Troops all had their headquarters, suddenly erupted in a melee of troops moving out, reinforcements moving in, couriers speeding back and forth, rumors flying, and panicked citizens hiding their American flags, pulling old rifles and pistols out of closets, and destroying any evidence that they had ever been friendly to the Americans. Many loaded their belongings into automobiles and wagons, ready to flee west.

At first, the Special Troops were assembled as infantry to help plug the line and waited to move out. Meanwhile, they manned machine-gun nests on the roofs of the seminary, the headquarters at the Italian legation, and the Hollerich School housing the sonic troops. Documents and records were loaded into vehicles under guard, ready to move out at a moment's notice. Trucks lined up at the factory section behind Third Army head-quarters to load the secret dummies aboard so they could be spirited out of town ahead of the advancing Germans, who were reported to be within five miles of Luxembourg City.

That night, the Luftwaffe swooped in over the city, as they did all along the new front, in its last great aerial attack of the war. Gunners from the Special Troops manned the rooftop emplacements all night long, shooting enthusiastically at the constant stream of fighters and bombers that had been hoarded for months in preparation for the surprise offensive.

For Bob Tompkins, the attack couldn't have come at a worse time. He was anxiously awaiting news from his wife, who was pregnant and nearly due. He spent the first night of the Bulge, a Sunday, on guard duty at the main gate of the seminary, watching the dive bombers attack the city.

Then on December 21, new orders came down to evacuate the Special Troops and their secret equipment westward toward Verdun. They left the following day.

Blass recalls the conflicting orders. "I think the thing that was most curious to us is that it seemingly made no sense," he says. "I mean, we're moving here and moving back, which might well have been part of a strategic plan. To us it seemed just another example of the officers fucking up."

Except for headquarters staff, the Special Troops packed their gear in a hurry and drove out of the city through a heavy snowstorm. "As we went through Luxembourg on our way out, the Luxembourgers prudently were hanging out white sheets again, just like they did when the Americans came in—surrendering to anybody they could surrender to," Biow says. "The one thing I sure as heck remember is, we got on the road and we're going west, and here comes Patton's Third Army and the armor going east—bumper to bumper tanks! Sherman tanks and all kinds of artillery going toward the Germans while we were scampering away."

Biow and the others were torn. They had a strong urge to stay and fight, but they were told they were too valuable to be thrown into the line as infantry. They were ordered away from the battle so they could fight other battles to come. There were too few of them to have made much difference against the weight of a massive German assault spearheaded by behemoth Tiger tanks.

Behind the American tanks streaming into Luxembourg, they saw also truckloads of green soldiers—replacements, kids who had just graduated high school a few months before, been rushed through rudimentary training in the States, and now were being hurried toward the front. As they passed, they could see their boyish, scared faces. The sight inspired mixed emotions. They knew they were damned lucky to be getting out, but here were these kids speeding toward the crucible of battle. For months now, they had transported enough replacements to the front to know what lay in store. Green troops tended to talk too loud, stick their heads up too often, and worst of all, bunch up under artillery fire—and so they often died quickly, in bunches.

The futility of the Ardennes counteroffensive angered Fred Fox. "No battle has ever seemed so personal or embittered me more," he wrote. "The Germans jumped us like a vicious, half-crazed brute who has slunk quietly into ambush. There is no denying that we were embarrassed. He tore into us with everything he had and slaughtered my associates at crossroads where I had stopped for apples."

Company C of the camoufleurs, including Jim Laubheimer and Howard Holt, wound up at Les Bulles, Belgium, holding a sector of the front after all. To their north, the Germans punched through the Allied line, in places pushing back the American lines forty miles, and separated Third Army in the south from U.S. First and Ninth and the British armies to the north. The Special Troops were on the south shoulder as the attack swung west and then north toward Antwerp. Their sector remained quiet, and after a week they joined the rest of their comrades at Doncourt.

As the battle raged, the signal company was pulled out of the column and sent on a new operation with scarcely any time to prepare—Operation KODAK. Ingersoll at Special Plans Branch named it: the twenty-four-hour-long deception aimed to fabricate a "double exposure" of the 4th Armored Division and the 80th Infantry Division, thus making them both appear to be in two places at once. Employing twenty-nine radios, the Special Troops created the impression that both divisions were being held in reserve northeast of Luxembourg to counter an attack against Echternacht, a key river crossing on the German border. The actual radio traffic of the 4th and 80th would, of course, show them charging toward the battle.

The German radio operators monitoring their stagey traffic—and the simultaneous real traffic—would unquestionably know that a deception was afoot. But could they guess which were the real 4th Armored and 80th Infantry and which the ghosts? The deception had the added flair of doing the exact opposite of the normal program. Instead of faking a strong buildup against the German attack, the spoof radio created an impression that two crucial divisions were too far from the battle to affect German plans. A chance existed that the Germans would take the real radio traffic for a bluff designed to scare them off Bastogne.

Usually, such spoof radio was indeed a bluff, an attempt to show strength where none existed. By now it was clear to Special Plans Branch that the Germans weren't going to be bluffed off so crucial a crossroads objective. So they double-bluffed, hiding the real movement and hoping to buy them the element of surprise.

There's no record of who concocted this interesting variation on their usual ploy. Since Ingersoll named it, it's a good bet that it was his idea, helped along no doubt by his buddy Fox, who was ever alert for new ways to use spoof radio. Ingersoll, a gifted and sardonic writer, left behind a vivid memoir of his tour of duty at Bradley's headquarters, *Top Secret*. Ironically, he could not write about the real top-secret stuff he did every day, since it remained classified till long after his death, and the book is mum on the genesis of this and other plans of the Special Troops.

The 4th Armored was in fact rolling toward Bastogne, in the heart of the Bulge, where the besieged 101st Airborne and elements of the 10th Armored were fighting off five German divisions. The 4th Armored punched through the German lines and linked up with the 101st Airborne the day after Christmas.

Meanwhile, the real 80th Infantry, which had made a 150-mile motorized march in just thirty-six hours to form a defensive line around Luxembourg City, now moved into battle alongside the 4th Armored. Its 2d Battalion, 318th Infantry, and the 1st Battalion, 319th Infantry, also drove on to Bastogne. The failure to take Bastogne with overwhelming armored might came as a stunning surprise to Field Marshal von Rundstedt. Equally surprising was the arrival of two divisions of reinforcements that should have been back in Luxembourg.

There was still hard fighting left to do, but the siege of Bastogne was effectively over.

Eisenhower greeted the news of a massive German counteroffensive, shocking as it was, with immediate enthusiasm. He rightly saw the attack as a foolish waste of Germany's limited fighting force, an attack bound to fail, a chance to destroy the enemy in the open. And once the weather cleared from the snow and overcast to sunny blue skies, that's exactly what happened.

Every veteran who was there remembers the morning before Christmas Eve when the overcast cleared and the snow quit and waves of Thunderbolts and heavy bombers crossed the bright sky in glittering formations to methodically destroy the long columns of Germans—first as they advanced, then as they retreated, abandoning their tanks for lack of gas, trudging home through the slushy mud. Two entire German Panzer armies, Fifth and Sixth, were virtually destroyed in the battle.

"The Germans kicked off the Bulge in miserable weather—it was heavy ground fog, rain, and the visibility was terrible, which was on their side, because the Americans couldn't fly against them," Biow recalls. "And I remember the day the sun came out, standing there watching these planes, I mean the sky was covered with bombers going east, and we knew things were getting the way they should be."

The violent clash going on all around him tested Fox's humane instincts to the limit. "Thank heavens we've had good weather these last days," he wrote when at last the battle had turned. "It's very cold but clear, clear, clear and that's what the airmen want. They have done wonders too. And when I say wonders, I mean they have obliterated Germans. For the first time since I joined the war, I like the idea of Germans being blown to hell."

The Special Troops made it as far as Doncourt, near Longuyon, France, twenty-five miles west of Luxembourg City. There they halted to wait for orders, occupying a filthy, cold "flophouse barracks" at the French army base, where most of them would spend Christmas, two platoons to a room, surrounded by the abandoned pillboxes of the Maginot Line. With rumors flying and the whole Allied situation in flux, they didn't take any chances with the pillboxes. Lieutenant Al Landry told one of his men from A Company, Dave Wynshaw, "Wynshaw—go in and check it out. See if anybody's in there."

"I don't know why he always picked on me," Wynshaw says, "because I was not a brave soul. So I took the front, there were three guys behind me, we went into the pillbox, and you can imagine how black it is in there. No lights and we have no searchlights. Took a couple of steps and I fell twenty feet." He landed on his lower back, which troubles him to this day. The other guys in the squad lowered a man on a rope, then managed to hoist Wynshaw out of the black hole and take him to a medic.

Not long after, a patrol from A Company captured two Germans masquerading as American GIs on the Doncourt road. "Drove out on that same road this afternoon in jeep," Tompkins noted. "Lucky I wasn't picked off."

Bad as it was, at Doncourt they counted their blessings. They knew all too well that many of those scared boys they'd seen speeding toward battle were spending their Christmas hunkered down in freezing foxholes out of doors, if they were even still alive.

The drive was typical—cold and uncomfortable for most. Dahl wrote, "About our most important possession these days is the stove that we load up and carry with us wherever we go. It works with either coal or wood and is a very good one. Looks funny to see a GI truck barreling along down a road with a couple of lengths of stovepipe sticking out the back end. But with a little persuasion it keeps us warm."

Once in their temporary barracks, the Special Troops decided to make the most of the season. Biow says, "Somebody cut a tree, a small tree, they made Christmas decorations out of everything, including blown-up condoms, stars cut out of the tops of tin cans, and it was so damn cold I smoked the first cigar I ever smoked in my life in some desperate attempt to get warm—and all I did was get miserable."

They'd also managed to acquire a package of "window"—aluminum-foil strips dropped in fluttering clouds by lead bombers to confuse enemy radar, a fittingly deceptive decoration—and added that to the tree, along with Christmas cards and garlands of wrapping paper from packages received from home. "Well," Dahl wrote on Christmas Eve, "we've made a bit of Christmas to start the tears in our eyes."

Some of the cards were their own. Back in November, some of the guys had designed cards and sold them. Third Army and 12th Army Group also issued their own cards. The most lighthearted featured four whimsical scenes of Paris, including two GIs driving a jeep—being chased by a leggy mademoiselle peddling a bicycle and waving an American flag—past Notre Dame cathedral. The most sentimental pictured a smiling GI holding two French children on his lap, a boy in a blue school suit and beret and a girl hugging a doll. The other two were more bellicose. In the first, Allied convoys streamed toward France, symbolized by the Arc de Triomphe, and in the second, a GI held the Union Flag and the Stars and Stripes in a V-for-Victory pose under the steady, beatific gaze of the Statue of Liberty, as the winged French Angel of Liberty, sword drawn, charged into battle.

Laubheimer wrote later, "Naturally, we sat around the tree singing carols (which was funny because half the guys were Jewish)."

In the village nearby, about a dozen families of "displaced persons" (DPs) had dug in for the winter in abandoned buildings. They were mainly Russians, Czechs, Hungarians, and Poles, escapees from slave labor camps or refugees liberated as the Allies swept across France and into the fringes of Germany. They were pale and gaunt, many were sickly. They lived on the barest scraps of food and huddled together at night for warmth. Most had no more possessions than the ragged clothes they were wearing.

At least in Luxembourg City the people, resentful as they were of the depredations of the Germans, lived in clean, warm houses in a community of friends and relatives. They slept in beds and still had their culture— their music, books, schools for their children. These DPs were the refuse of the war—the human wreckage of the Blitzkrieg and the slave camps, the most efficiently produced product of the Nazi regime. Many of their relatives were dead or missing, and their possessions, homes, and homelands had been stolen from them.

The idea seemed to occur to lots of guys at the same time—their own Christmas packages had found them in their temporary quarters, and they decided to share. They put together a Christmas package for each family—rations, candy, crackers, kids' clothes sent from home, socks, blankets, even lemon juice and sugar lumps for medicine against sore throats. On Christmas Eve, they hosted a party for all the kids—and every child got his or her own little package of Christmas treats, mainly candy, gum, ribbons, and small toys. The men sang Christmas carols in English and the kids sang in their own languages. A few of the guys could speak Russian or German or Czech enough to communicate, and while elsewhere American troops were turning back von Runstedt's Panzer corps, the Special Troops did their modest part in bringing humanity back to a world ruined by war—by making a bunch of kids happy on Christmas Eve.

After the party, teams of guys visited the temporary homes of the displaced families and gave them their gift packages. In one makeshift home, the family had put up a small Christmas tree and decorated it with a single package of LifeSavers from an American ration pack—each individual candy ring hung by its own string from an evergreen branch.

Morton recalls, "Enough was collected to make a Christmas for all of them. The men who took it to them said they were speechless. Absolutely speechless—as nothing had been done for them in so long. The children had never seen candy before."

In honor of the holiday, sergeants pulled KP duty and guard duty for two days and nights, letting the privates loaf in whatever comfort they could find.

Fox spent Christmas Eve in Luxembourg City with Reeder, Simenson, Truly, and the rest of headquarters staff. "The events of the past week have been anything but cheery. Tonight it is very cold and clear and the moon is nearly full. We can hear the rumble of big guns. As usual, the rumormongers are having a field day," he wrote on Christmas Eve. "Most of the church bells rang twelve. Way out in the valley we heard some lonely trumpeters blow 'O Holy Night.' How cold their lips must have been. On the road back, the air raid sirens went off."

That evening he found solace at church, praying for his family and loved ones, and for the soldiers caught up in the terrible winter battle. "I was in a little church and it was toward the end of the service," he wrote later. "As they were singing the benediction the door opened but I didn't turn around. As I went out I saw who had come in. He was staring straight down the aisle and up at the main window. His feet were wide apart and his white hair made him look like one of the frightening prophets. On his hips were two pearl-handled six-guns. They identify him. It was General Patton looking very fierce and dramatic—as if he had come to demand God's blessing for his sword."

Arriving in various detachments a day or two after Christmas, the Special Troops found themselves inhabiting abandoned French forts at Verdun, on the Maginot Line—drafty, damp bunkers which once had been wired for electricity and plumbed with running water but now were freezing relics crawling with enormous rats. Biow's memory of that miserable billet is clear: "They put us in the Maginot Line bunkers and it was cold! I mean it was cold! It was so cold that they had to take the lubrication off the .50-caliber machine guns because it was frozen and they worked better dry than with the normal lubrication on it."

"Verdun is a depressing city filled with a million ghosts of other unhappy soldiers," Fox wrote. "That makes it much too crowded." In World War I, the Germans had bled the French army white at Verdun. It was said that every family in France lost a male relative there.

Laubheimer wrote, "There it stood, stark white, partially destroyed walls serving as tombstones against the horizon."

The Christmas season didn't last long. Some two hundred of the Special Troops were detailed east again to the Moselle River near Metz, where they staged a two-day spoof-radio and special-effects show to cover the movement of the 87th Infantry, which had doubled back to Reims, France, to launch an attack into the Bulge. They set up a phony headquarters, filled the airwaves with the usual scripted chatter, made a show of troops moving about in trucks falsely marked "87 X," and generally played their role to the hilt.

They were getting good at deception. Gone were the amateur mistakes of the earlier days. Now when they went on a "problem," as the officers termed the deceptions, they fell immediately and completely into character. They used the neoprene dummies less often but more inventively, knowing exactly where to place the few to mimic the many. All the troops had become skillful at sewing on unit patches—and others were adept at silkscreening new ones at a moment's notice. The radio teams had their patter down, and they were also experienced technicians, flawlessly infiltrating radio nets with authentic procedure and plausible scripts. They would understudy the operators they were going to replace, then simply take over the traffic at an opportune moment.

The sonic troops not only deployed and played smoothly—they could also repair nearly anything on their vehicles but a busted track. Everybody was getting to be a fair actor—not only the ones impersonating generals, but the ones feigning drunkenness and talking "loosely" in taverns, the drivers touring villages with fake markings, the combat engineers playing MPs.

And their work had never been more important. Even before the German counteroffensive broke up Operation KOBLENZ, the Allies had virtually no reserves—every division was committed to combat. Thus the need to have a thin line of Special Troops hold a seventy-mile-long front back in September. If Eisenhower had had unlimited divisions, there would have been a lot less need for deception, which often covered weakness. Deception was a weapon that multiplied your forces in the enemy's eyes and bought precious time and room to maneuver.

But feedback was distressingly absent, as in so many deception operations. The most that could be said was that friendly troops were certainly fooled, as they usually were, and that the "covered" troops were ultimately successful.

On December 29, the day he arrived at Verdun, Tompkins finally got the news he had been waiting for: His wife had given birth to a healthy boy, which they named Robert William, the middle name in honor of Bill Blass, who became his godfather. Tompkins learned he was a father in *The Stars and Stripes*. He was just one of many men in the outfit who now had children back home whom they had never seen.

New Year's Eve was as bleak as Christmas. "It is hard to celebrate in dreary, cold, unlighted barracks," Fox noted, "especially when neither liquor, victory, home nor girls are available." Fox made no New Year's resolutions.

It was an edgy time. The Allies were about to kick off a major offensive against the Germans in the Bulge. Bastogne had held, but it would take a protracted battle to push the Germans back across their border. And while seemingly endless streams of green replacements arrived at the front daily, virtually every division had been fighting in the line without rest for months. The war that Eisenhower had bet Montgomery would be finished by Christmas had taken on a life of its own, and nobody in the Special Troops expected to be going home anytime soon.

And if they forgot the war for even a little while, reminders quickly found them. "I remember New Year's night we were on guard duty and a German Heinkel bomber came flying over and everybody went nuts," Biow says. "I mean, he was skipping the ground practically. He didn't drop anything—but he sure got our attention."

"Jerry just came in over town and a very heavy AA barrage opened on him," Tompkins recorded. "Looks like hot spot and these damn buildings are right next to railroad yard."

On the Feast of the Epiphany, five days after New Year's, they went into the line again—in the frozen mud at Metz. It was a familiar problem: Plug a gap in the line. Since September, except for the Battle of the Bulge, the war had hardened into a World War I–style standoff along the German border, with the Americans constantly probing forward, seeking a breakthrough.

In this instance, the 90th Infantry was holding the line south of Luxembourg and east of Thionville, France, on the Saar River. The 90th was a veteran outfit—it had landed the day after D day, many of its men rescued from their transport, the *Susan B. Anthony*, which struck a mine and burned and sank off the beach. They'd fought through Normandy and across the Moselle into Germany, and now they were needed to attack the Bulge—to be replaced in the Saar line by the 94th, which was still en route from Brittany.

Just south of their sector, in the Alsace region, American divisions were fighting off a fierce attack from Saarbrucken to Strasbourg—a smaller "bulge" in the line. Called by the Germans Operation NORTHWIND, the attack threw Panzers against the Maginot Line for the first time in the war. In 1940, the Germans had simply bypassed the old World War I–style fortresses. This time they had streamed across the border on New Year's Day and a week later were still hurling themselves at the American defenses with no sign of letting up.

As the 90th stole away to join the battle, the Special Troops took their place, holding the line until the 94th arrived, then "playing" the 90th into a reserve area near Metz, hiding the division from the Germans until it appeared magically in the Bulge on the attack.

To convincingly play the 90th Division, the Special Troops stayed out of doors from dawn to well after darkness in the freezing weather, driving on roads slick with packed snow, practicing their special effects, buying time for the 94th to come into the line. They used no dummies or sonic programs—just spoof radio and physical impersonation organized around a phony command post.

On January 7, after a long frozen day in the field, some of the sonic crews found refuge for the night in a caserne or barracks. Commander Harold Flinn and gunner Philip Dellisante pulled up in their half-track "Myrt," named for Myrtle, the wife of their driver, Chester "Chet" Pelliccioni.

Pelliccioni was a quiet, easygoing guy from Johnstown, Pennsylvania, well liked by his half-track team, a couple of years older than Flinn and Dellisante. The three of them were all Catholics—first thing after landing in Normandy, they had found a priest saying mass at a bombed-out church, and climbed over the rubble to take communion.

Pelliccioni was a careful and conscientious driver, always alert for mines and booby traps. And he kept their vehicle in tip-top condition. At every stop, he got busy cleaning it, clearing the fuel filter, greasing the bogeys on the rear tracks.

"He as well as Phil guarded me when I was in the back of the track running the recorders," Flinn remembers. "I couldn't hear anything, as the recordings were so loud, but felt safe as they were on guard—Phil at the .50 caliber and Chet walking around."

As the others went inside the caserne to check out the accommodations, Pelliccioni gathered wood and built a fire on top of the snow—and then the fire exploded. There was a grenade hidden under the snow.

"I was inside and heard the bang," Flinn recalls. He rushed out to the fire and saw the charred spot in the snow, the spray of shrapnel across the snow to where Pelliccioni lay, grievously wounded. "No one else was hit, so it was his time, I guess."

Chester "Chet" Pelliccioni, killed by
a German hand grenade
(HAROLD FLINN)

Pelliccioni never had a chance—he died of his wounds. After all the risks they'd taken manning ghost sectors and bluffing German Panzer divisions a few thousand yards away, enduring artillery barrages, fighting off Luftwaffe dive bombers from the rooftops of Luxembourg City, the first guy in the Special Troops to die on an operation was killed outside his own billet, where he thought he was safe, trying to start a fire so he and his buddies could at last get warm. On this cold night, the fabled luck of the Special Troops ran out.

The next day, Flinn and Dellisante's half-track broke down—the timing shaft on the engine snapped—and they waited for hours in the bitter cold for a recovery vehicle to come and tow them into camp.

The operation, at least, succeeded. "In spite of the fact that one 90th Regiment had pulled out without obliterating its identity, the 12th Army Group G-2 spotlighted the secret move as a model and called it a complete success," Fox recorded. On its first day in action in the Bulge, the 90th Division cut off an entire German parachute regiment.

The Special Troops scarcely had time to mourn their loss. The day after they closed METZ II, they speeded north to mount Operation L'ÉGLISE in Belgium. Again using special effects and spoof radio, the Special Troops covered the secret withdrawal of the 4th Armored Division from Bastogne and placed it in reserve twenty-five miles to the south at L'Église. In fact, the 4th Armored was swinging east to prepare for a new thrust against a different part of the German line—but that attack was postponed. Instead, the 4th Armored effectively went into hiding until March, when it would participate in the big push across the Rhine. "Until that time it remained under a security blackout and its location was not even carried on the 12th Army Group G-3 periodic," Fox noted.

After five days, the Special Troops closed their show and faded away to a new headquarters in Briey, France—leaving the Germans and Allies alike to wonder what had become of an entire armored division. After weeks of cold field billets, Briey was luxury itself. The Special Troops took over the Caserne Garde Mobile—which even had running water, though not reliably. "The Briey Water Commissioner demanded a 'pourbois' of two dozen bars of chocolate, a case of soap and 16 loaves of white bread," Fox reported. "This was not given him so the plumbing was very erratic."

A far cry from the grateful hordes who had swarmed the GI "liberators" only a few months before.

There were also delightful encounters with local people, as Vic Dowd recalls. "A woman—not a girlfriend, this was an older woman—saw me sketching and invited me to have dinner with her and her husband." The woman hoped he would sketch her little girl, Huguette—Dowd was happy to comply. He drew a charming likeness of Huguette wearing a beret. "I was going to see them the next day and put the finishing touches on the sketch and give it to them," he says. "Well, there was no next day—we moved out. And I felt bad about that."

After the war, Dowd's French mother returned to France for a visit and made a special excursion to Briey to find the family. She showed the sketch at the local post office, and it turned out that Huguette was the postmaster's granddaughter—whose mother at last got her sketch.

Two days after L'ÉGLISE, the sonic company sped north again to the banks of the Moselle to stage Operation FLAXWEILER, a one-night stand named for the village nearby. They were doing what they did best: simulating a river crossing twenty miles south of the real attack at Diekirch across the Our River, which joined the Moselle to make a continuous natural battle line.

This was likely the only operation ever joined by Hilton Howell Railey. He came to the front at some point late in the Battle of the Bulge, according to his own résumé, to see how his sonic troops were performing in action. Railey had corresponded with Jim Barrett, one of his original AES cadre, several times, asking for details about how the theoretical ideas were working out in action—but of course, due to censorship, Barrett couldn't tell him very much. Now Railey had come to see for himself.

He sought out Barrett, had a photo taken with him, and rode along on the operation. Oddly, for perhaps the only time in his career, he didn't leave much of an impression. Perhaps now that the men he had trained were seasoned veterans, they were now the experts. They had come a long way from Pine Camp—in miles traveled, hardships endured, and plain old experience gained in working their sonic magic. In the middle of a shooting war, Railey may not have seemed like such a big deal.

"We laughed because he wasn't gone very long," Ed Gilmore, back at the Army Experimental Station, remembers. "And we said well, there were so many colonels over there and all kinds of generals, so he wasn't showing up like he did in the United States—so he got his ass back in a hurry!"

The operation was unique in another way. The sonic cars broadcast on the move, driving along a small road that paralleled the Moselle River and the German lines just across it. The 2d Cavalry Group assisted them by throwing up smoke, moving up some real tanks, bringing up bridging material and boats, and sending patrols across the river.

In the morning, heavy artillery fire rained down on the road and the area of the "buildup"—but by then the sonic cars were long gone back to Briey.

At the end of January, the busiest month yet for the Special Troops, they mounted two simultaneous operations: STEINSEL and LANDONVILLE.

STEINSEL was a spoof radio deception to cover the movement of the reconstituted 4th Infantry Division north for a surprise thrust into Houffalize. Four officers and seventy-six signalmen infiltrated the 4th's radio nets two days before the move. Three other divisions were moving in blackout mode, and the resultant confusion, as much as the deliberate deception, probably contributed to the success of the 4th Infantry's surprise attack to win the same ground it had taken back in September—before the Battle of the Bulge.

Concurrently, in LANDONVILLE the Special Troops once again covered a dangerous transition, as the 95th Infantry came out of the line and were replaced within twenty-four hours by the 26th Infantry Division. Both divisions moved under blackout and pulled off the transition without being attacked at their most vulnerable.

The weather finally broke—the snow melted into slush, and the first day of February seemed almost balmy by comparison to the frozen months that had gone before. To celebrate, Fox and his cohorts in the Special Troops cracked a bottle of Southern Comfort and enjoyed their last night in the fake 95th command post, which Fox called "the gloomiest château in all of Lorraine."

The winter of 1944–45 was long and cruel, the coldest in half a century, with temperatures frequently dipping below zero for days on end. The Special Troops were cold indoors, cold outdoors, coldest of all on the move.

On the day the Germans launched the Battle of the Bulge, Fox wrote, "When I am riding in a jeep the wind has to go through seven layers in some places before it gets to my skin and that is just about as much as I can carry. However please continue to send me your love because at night that helps keep everything but my feet quite warm."

Bill Brown recalls nights in the open in his half-track. "We used to sleep in the half-tracks, and they're metal, you know, all steel. So a lot of nights we'd sleep on the ground underneath the track because that steel would be colder than the ground."

"Well I saw more snow here than I have ever seen before," Morton wrote. "When it arrived it arrived for the winter. That was about the middle of December. It began to melt about the 1st of Feb. The days were very short during this period and the nites very long. These factors combined produced a feeling of isolation over that period. It seems quite different now with the snow gone, the evenings longer."

Certain guys managed to enjoy an occasional lark. After the front-end suspension on his half-track gave out, Brown was ordered to find someplace to get it repaired. With a couple of buddies and a motor pool sergeant in a jeep, he went clear back to Verdun. "We weren't in a hurry to get back, so we found a place that would fix it but we said, don't rush it." Brown and his crew found an empty schoolhouse where they could billet, and then they came across some skis. "It was hilly around Verdun. We had one good rope and we skied behind the jeep and we'd go right through Verdun."

Despite an occasional spree, the Special Troops earned their army pay, and then some, always on the move or waiting to move. Fox described their

working hours eloquently. "Well, in war it seems that there are funny working hours. A little while ago I went forty hours without stopping but that
was perfectly alright because I'd just finished about a week of idleness. It
comes in spurts."

For a time, it had seemed the war would end in a glorious victory before
Christmas, but the Special Troops were still in the field, knowing they
would remain there for the foreseeable future of their young lives. On
January 20, the official 23d historical chronology recorded their one-year
anniversary as a unit, commenting tersely: "Passed without ceremony."

The winter of 1944–45 was a season of dashed optimism and a monumental setback recouped at a staggering cost in the blood of young men.
By February, when the Americans restored their lines to where they had
been before the Battle of the Bulge, they had lost 10,276 men killed in action, 47,493 wounded, and 23,218 missing in action—80,897 total casualties. The Germans lost between 80,000 and 104,00 men.

Now veterans of sixteen operations, the Special Troops performed with
a professionalism earned in their earlier engagements. They accepted artillery bombardment as a matter of course. They were old hands at keeping
warm, finding food, working all night, driving through snow and fog with
only blackout slits for headlights, handling their equipment for days on
end without sleep. They were doing their part, but some felt frustrated at
not being able to do more, even slightly guilty that their own casualties
were so few. The camoufleurs, combat engineers, and signalmen had been
in the army for more than two years, in action for more than six months;
the sonic troops only slightly less long. They had come of age in the army,
toured parts of five countries as liberators in a just cause. And almost none
of their brother soldiers even knew they existed.

"It will take me years & years to tell all about it," Dahl wrote home. "No
wonder the vets of the last war talked for so long after writing nothing."

TWELVE

THE DEADLIEST SHOW
February–March 1945

*I had horrible visions of a truckful of soldiers just being
decimated by one artillery round or machine gun.*
—Col. Clifford G. Simenson, USA (ret.)

In the biting cold of February, the Special Troops moved south, up to the
front on the Saar River, near Saarlautern, Germany. First Sergeant Jerry
Gluckin was calling for volunteers.

Dave Wynshaw had no love for Gluckin—for him, as for most of the
guys in A Company, 603d Camoufleurs, the short, burly sergeant was just a
vindictive, loudmouthed bully, an expert in chickenshit. Wynshaw had almost volunteered for the paratroops just to get away from him—quite a
desperate measure for a guy petrified of heights.

"Colonel Truly's putting together a reconnaissance patrol—do I have
any volunteers?" Gluckin asked.

Colonel Truly—now, that was different. Merrick Hector Truly had always impressed Wynshaw as an unusual officer, a West Pointer much at
ease with the enlisted men. From time to time he spoke to Truly, who did
not hold himself aloof from enlisted men, as did most of the other senior-
grade officers from headquarters. Wynshaw frankly admired him—after
the war, eager to be a civilian again, he would reluctantly turn down an offer to serve as Truly's aide.

And Truly stood out for another reason. Throughout the long winter
campaign, Wynshaw remembers that Truly never wore combat boots—he
always wore sneakers. Somehow that impressed Wynshaw. He figured if a
lieutenant colonel, the second-highest ranking officer in the outfit, could

get away with wearing sneakers around Reeder, he could pull off a recon patrol without getting his people into any trouble.

Though he had been thoroughly indoctrinated into the army habit of *never* volunteering, when he heard Truly's name, Wynshaw immediately raised his hand. Three other enlisted men joined him—including Warren Masters, with whom he'd shared a foxhole since Normandy. The two had become so close, Wynshaw would name his eldest son after him. At the supply tent, they picked up hand grenades and extra ammunition. As they drove off, Truly said, "Look, no shooting—we're only here to look over the place. So I'm just telling you up front: No shooting—unless we get into trouble."

At a roadblock, they were held up by a squad of regular infantry. Who were they and what were they doing up here? Truly briefed them. The guys manning the roadblock said, "Well, we want to warn you that we can't protect you further. Once you go past here, you're on your own."

They drove down the road and parked the jeep and Truly said, "Follow me," and they climbed an escarpment.

Wynshaw says, "He took out his binoculars—and I could see with my bare eyes, without binoculars—that German troops were down below the mountain where we were. And he was counting trucks and he was counting tanks, whatever he had to do, and I was looking around and I was amazed at the foliage because the bushes were all cut by machine-gun fire. And I'm looking at that, and I'm looking at him, and I'm looking down there, and I'm thinking, *Hope he doesn't stay too long!*"

After he had seen all he needed, Truly said, "Let's go!"

"We ran down the mountain—not walk—we *ran* down," Wynshaw says. Back at the roadblock, the infantrymen said, "You can't go any further. You can't go back now."

Truly said, "Why not?"

"Well, the Germans have us zeroed in," the infantryman explained. "If you go back where you came from, they can see you, and in about five seconds after you leave, you'll have a mortar shell on you."

A staff colonel trying to burnish a fearless John Wayne image might have ordered his men to ignore the prudent warning and brazen it out on the road. But Truly was listening, so the guy said, "You want me to prove it to you?"

"Go ahead."

"Okay. Get into your jeep, go ten feet, and stop." The idea was to trick the Germans into firing—they'd spot the jeep moving out of the cover of the hills and try to nail it—except the jeep wouldn't be there.

Truly ordered his driver to start out down the road, then stop and back up in a hurry. Almost at once, mortar shells rained out of the sky, blasting holes in the road where they had been headed. It was a familiar German tactic: zero in on a road intersection and wait for the right traffic—targets. Truly's recon patrol stayed put until after dark, then stole away, safely blacked out. Wynshaw had trusted the right man.

February opened with a double assignment for the Special Troops, combined under Operation WHIPSAW. The first part required only dummies, the second only sonic projection.

Near Saarlautern, in positions just vacated by real artillery, the camoufleurs erected four batteries of dummy guns. They were careful to replicate the tracks of artillery tractors and trucks in the snow.

Arthur Shilstone, like his comrades, lived in a dugout vacated by the gunners. It was a relatively easy setup, since the real batteries had left behind such essential props as spent shell casings and blast marks scorching off the snow in a telltale fan pattern. Shilstone climbed out of his bunker and started sketching the view. He was startled to see a GI, hunched over in the classic pose of advancing infantry, zigzagging across the muddy snow toward him.

"What the fuck are you doing?" the GI demanded.

"I'm just sketching."

The GI was exasperated. "Don't you realize the Germans are right over there by that last line of trees?"

Shilstone looked across at the tree line. "Nobody knows anybody's here," the soldier said. "It's been nice and quiet, and we want to keep it that way!"

"But that was the point of our outfit, to be seen," Shilstone says, all too accustomed to the strange role his outfit always played. This time the dummy display drew no enemy fire, and Shilstone completed several very good sketches.

Ellsworth Kelly also had been busily sketching throughout the war. In one sketch, a soldier sits on his helmet under a tree in the rain—a characteristic pose from the fall campaign. Now that the snow was melting, he completed a striking pen-and-ink landscape called "February Thaw" or "Zebra Country"—the countryside warped and woofed with striped fields, strips of snow between the dirt furrows, a seminal study for his later abstract pieces, which would be preoccupied with form.

In the army, Kelly worked in realistic forms, though the back of a gray-covered notebook displays what was probably his first abstract drawing—

irregular shapes inside a square frame: "It's almost a story," he says, explicating the figures inside the square form. Curving oblongs are a nude reclining in front of a pool; larger shapes are a farmhouse near a village; and in the upper left-hand corner, a bloom is the flower-burst of an exploding shell.

At Saarlautern, Ed Biow "liberated" his only illicit souvenir of the war: a bell hanging outside a barn. He explains why: "I took the bell and hung it on the sideview mirror bracket of my truck, and then I ran a string from the clapper into the truck through the side curtain, so that when I went through towns, I could go like a fire engine clanging my bell." The bell now hangs outside the front door of his house in Oregon.

The sonic troops played their operation thirty miles north on the Moselle River—in the same vicinity where they had staged FLAXWEILER less than a month earlier. Again, the objective was to draw and hold enemy troops in that sector of the front by a convincing fictitious buildup of Third Army infantry and armor.

On the night of February 1–2, the sonic cars simulated three tank battalions converging near Grevenmacher. The next night, they played the same program near Wormeldingen. On the third night, they projected the sounds of random tank movements in both areas.

Clearly the Germans were taken by the ruse—they overflew the area each night with reconnaissance aircraft and lit up the show with flares all three nights. John Walker recalls how exposed he felt after dispersing his sonic platoon that first eerie night. "We were up on that hillside, projecting in a vineyard again, and the thing that got us—the place lit up!" he says. "Tremendous! Because of flares. They were shooting flares to see what we were doing. And I had never been in such an intense flare attack before. I mean, you could read print. So it made you wonder whether you're really hidden or not."

The flares were just a prelude. Next came heavy shelling from mortars and 88s. The 88 was one of the deadliest German weapons of the war. It could be elevated to fire at aircraft, depressed to fire at tanks, or used as artillery. Because of its supersonic velocity, an 88 shell followed a flat trajectory, undistorted by the usual arc, making it lethally accurate. The heavy mortars were just as feared. A mortar shell was propelled skyward by a small charge. The shell reached its apogee, then dropped straight down without a sound. Taking cover behind fortifications offered no protection from a mortar round. And unlike big artillery pieces, a hundred yards away you couldn't hear a mortar being fired.

On an operation like WHIPSAW, there was always the prospect of instant death from the sky.

About a week later, the sonic troops were called out to perform a two-night stand just north of Saarlautern, fifteen miles southeast of Remich—Operation MERZIG. Intelligence placed the 11th Panzer Division at Remich, opposite the U.S. 94th Infantry. "In this position they were fairly harmless so 12th Army Group wanted them to stay there," Fox explained.

To hold the Panzers in place, the 3d Cavalry Group deployed some real tanks, laid down a smoke screen, and fired artillery from behind it. All through the night, once every hour, German planes illuminated the American positions with flares. In one sense, the headquarters staff had miscalculated: they had deployed no dummies to enhance the authenticity of the show, and Lt. Col. Edgar Schroeder, in charge of the operation, missed them. "The MERZIG commander was sorry he did not have rubber tanks to simulate a combat command in march column along the road," Fox noted.

But the inevitable pounding came anyway: twenty-eight artillery shells blasted the American position, mixed with 135 rounds from the dreaded 80mm heavy mortars—dropping straight down out of the sky with no warning sound. The Special Troops spent two harrowing nights under bombardment—the one experience that none of them ever forgot, a sense of fated helplessness, the world exploding first in front, then behind, then a hundred yards away. They could not shoot back.

They clung to their old luck—not one man was hit—but some felt they were pushing that luck pretty hard.

While the sonic cars were in the field, Fox received an unexpected present. Captain Irwin VanderHeide, the commander of the radio deception unit, returned from leave in Paris, bringing a parcel from Fox's old friend André Hugo: four handpainted Napoleonic model soldiers—including the emperor himself mounted on a horse. "He says Napoleon will help us get to Berlin because he's been there before," Fox wrote his fiancée. "By the time you receive this, maybe the Russians have too."

Back in their billets, the camoufleurs waited for their next mission, a few weeks away. As usual, they were playing music every chance they got—by now, they carried in their caravan an assortment of guitars, violins, harmonicas, and accordions. "We have a new addition to our music group—we found or rather the PX found an old piano, a few of us patched it up and now it goes like mad about every evening," Harold Dahl wrote. "There was snow on the ground when we got it so, since there were only 3 of us, we used a German bed spring for a sled and pulled it along behind the jeep."

As usual they scrounged for fresh food, which vied with pinup girls in their fantasies. Dahl, who kept a fan photo of movie star Deanna Durbin tacked to his wall, wrote, "In another room the guys have a page of pictures of things like ice cream, pie, strawberry short cake."

Weary from the muddy snow of the Saar and perpetually cold, Dahl nonetheless knew better than to complain. "Compared to some poor guys I live like a king."

They were far from idle. Often they were detailed for guard duty to supplement regular troops. And all through the winter, their white-painted trucks constantly ferried troops and supplies to the front. On one such trip, Wynshaw drove up to the line, then went around to the back of the truck to let down the tailgate—and recognized an elevator operator he had known while working in the garment center in New York. He said, "Carl! What are you doing here?"

"Same as you," Carl replied.

"He looked so bad and so discouraged," Wynshaw recalls. These guys were fresh from England, had never been in combat. He guided the platoon up to the line and gave some advice to the platoon leader. "Now, lieutenant, please—keep your head down, tell your men to keep their heads down, because the machine guns are going." The Germans had a favorite ploy of firing tracers high—then, when the men stuck their heads up, cutting them down with invisible fire.

Sitting in a Holiday Inn restaurant in Florida, in a soft voice he tells the rest of the story. "No sooner had I put them in there than I heard the machine guns going," he says. "I got out of there. I never saw this guy Carl, I don't know if he ever came out of it. But it was one of the scariest moments. I can still hear machine guns—I can still hear machine guns. I can still hear artillery at night. There are times when I'm sitting, like talking to you, and I hear it. I hear it. They're not shooting at me, but I hear it. It's indelible."

The war was changing in both obvious and subtle ways. Once they were on German soil, the Special Troops, like all GIs, were bound by Eisenhower's controversial "no fraternization" order. No soldier was allowed to talk to German prisoners or civilians except to conduct official army business, such as procuring billets or food. For months, in England, France, Belgium, and Luxembourg, they'd made friends with the local people— eating dinner in their homes, bringing them gifts of food and clothes, playing with their children. Somehow, those small interactions relieved some of the homesickness, reminded them of their common humanity.

Now they must behave like conquerors—like the enemy.

Dahl was struck by the strangeness of the arrangement. "I was guarding our truck in a fair-sized German town & spent the time watching civilians walk by," he wrote home. "It feels funny to see the people and know they must be ignored like they were so many chimpanzees. You can't help but wonder what is in their thoughts nowadays."

They were also seeing fresh results of "carpet bombing," from which the lightning chase to the German border had spared most villages in western France and Luxembourg. Paris had remained virtually unscathed by bombs. Dahl wrote, "It is remarkable to see on the spot what effective work the Air Corps has done—I passed thru one fair-sized city they had gone to work on and the result is appalling. I've seen small towns obliterated before, but not the entire heart of a modern city, some of which must at one time have looked like the 5th Avenue section of New York."

Fox just had time to get his inflamed appendix removed at a field hospital in Verdun—his collaborator on the *Official History*, William Flemer III, had already undergone his own appendectomy there shortly after Christmas—before the Special Troops launched a new radio deception on March 1: Operation LOCHINVAR.

"LOCHINVAR (March 1–11) is a hard operation to explain," wrote Fox. "It was a little like the old shell game with someone knocking over the table halfway in between." The veteran 94th Infantry was finally going to withdraw from the line, to be replaced by the 26th Infantry, which was holding the sector immediately to the right of the 94th.

Meanwhile, the 65th Infantry—in Fox's words, "Cosmolene-fresh from the States"—would take the place of the 26th in the line. In order to keep the Germans in that sector from realizing that they were now opposed only by green troops, the men of the 65th would wear the insignia of the 94th—a feared and respected outfit. If all went off as planned, to the Germans it would seem as if the 94th and the 26th had merely exchanged sectors. And the 94th could enjoy a well-earned rest.

The Special Troops had done this often enough before—covered for a division at the vulnerable moment when it was withdrawing.

But this time, all didn't go off as planned. In the middle of the deception, while the 94th was half in and half out of the line, the Germans attacked in force. The 94th then took up its old position in the line to repulse the attack. The resulting scramble of real and notional armies threw the plan into a tailspin. Two of the spoof radios were wrecked by shellfire, and two more radio teams were cut off for forty-eight hours before the line was restored. Fox concluded, "The effects of this double-dealing ruse were never revealed but if the enemy was half as confused as we were, LOCHINVAR was a glorious success."

Immediately, on March 11, the Special Troops went into action again near Saarlautern. Operation BOUZONVILLE lasted just thirty-three hours, but it turned out to be the deadliest show they ever staged.

"Leave Briey at 7:30 A.M. to Enney—extremely secret, will have to wait until problem is over to enter details," Tompkins wrote in his war diary a few days before the operation. "I'd be shot on the spot if I were caught with this in my pocket as it is."

The 80th Division, in concert with the 10th Armored, the 94th Infantry, and the 26th Infantry, was getting set to attack in force in the Saarburg-Trier sector and finally achieve a breakthrough. To draw attention away from the area of the attack, the Special Troops set up their show about thirty miles south near Saarlautern—a show to simulate that the 80th was in fact moving to Bouzonville, in the rear of the 65th Infantry holding Saarlautern, and that both were preparing a major attack there.

The Special Troops knew the script by heart. On March 11, the spoof radios went on the air, requesting periodic checks. A detachment of camoufleurs set up their dummy artillery batteries, then coordinated their flash-fire with the firing of the 65th Division artillery. Meanwhile, the rest split up into seven sections and played their special effects—appearing in the French towns of Bouzonville, Hestroff, Brettnach, and Filstroff and in the German villages of Ittersedorf, Dalem, and Picard with the insignia and bumper markings of the 80th. MPs monitored checkpoints; command posts and road signs announced the presence of the 80th Infantry.

Fox's old friend Tom Wells, the CO of Headquarters Company, was among those roaming the areas in jeeps to impersonate high-ranking officers. Fox recorded, "As we were trying to suggest a build-up in the Saarlautern sector, Tom Wells and others of us were 'making traffic,' building up vehicular movement for the phoney 80th. Part of this meant simply driving back and forth along the tree-lined roads on the west bank of the Moselle."

On the night of March 12–13, the sonic cars deployed two miles north of Saarlautern and projected a battalion of tanks rumbling into position for the attack. Throughout the operation, they stirred up a hornet's nest of artillery. Wynshaw recalls how bad it got for some of the guys doing special effects. "We were stuck on top of a hill, silhouetted against the sky. They couldn't miss us, but they did. Artillery was firing and we could not move. And I know it must have been four, six hours that we were stuck there." There was nothing to do but hunker down and take it. The ground heaved, the air itself was deadly with flying shell fragments, the concussions were deafening, and the flashes could be literally blinding. In the middle of an artillery attack, the men report that there was always the sense that it would never end, that to survive it would be a miracle. When the shelling stopped, men were afraid to move, afraid they had been grievously wounded and hadn't felt it. They touched their bodies gingerly—legs, arms, chests, feeling for blood, for missing parts.

Like Tompkins, Blass, and others in Companies A and B, Biow was busy setting off flash artillery and luckily drew no counterbattery fire before pulling out. But after the war, while riding the train from Indianapolis to Chicago on business, he struck up a conversation with a colonel in full uniform, wearing all his combat ribbons. It turned out that his outfit had been adjacent to the phony 155mm artillery batteries. The colonel said, "I'll tell you a story. Shortly after you pulled out of your position, the Germans opened up on that same space and blew the hell out of it. There was nobody there by then, but you guys were lucky."

On March 12, Tompkins recorded in his diary, "Artillery all around us living in town at road junction. Saarlautern several thousand yards in front of us. Went back to Ittersdorf after show this morning. Shells landed around last night by the way—hit the dirt a couple of times but they landed just over the rise about 200 yards in front of us."

Vic Dowd drew a dicey assignment from 1st Sgt. William German. "I want you to take a truck driver and take a truck and drive around this area, because we haven't the faintest idea of what's going on there. But we want the collaborators, and the Germans if there are any, to recognize this outfit."

"So I wasn't stupid," Dowd says. "I picked the guy who had the sense of an American Indian. I mean, you could put this kid in the middle of nowhere and he'd find his way out. He had an innate sense of direction that was wonderful. Spence was his name. And he was a skinny little guy from the hills of West Virginia or something. And he was great. He's driving, we've got a machine gun, and I'm sitting there and we're doing what we were told to do."

They made their reconnaissance and added to the "atmosphere," targets to be spotted. But what rankled Dowd was what Sergeant German said before they started out. "Sergeant Dowd, I can only say I wish I were going instead of you."

Dowd says, "And I thought, *Oh, bullshit! Please, don't do this to me. I'll go, but don't make it worse than it already is.*" As he had done dozens of times during the war, Dowd set out to become a moving target. He never got used to it. Like the sonic troops pumping out sound when every fiber of their being willed them to remain silent in the face of a hidden enemy, Dowd and the rest who went on such "patrols" had to fight against their human nature, the basic survival instinct that told them to stay hidden, move by stealth, not to drive around like fools in the open.

Saarlautern was a "hot" sector where anything might happen. Wynshaw recalls the lonely crawling fear he felt on nighttime guard duty. "I think I was more scared than anything else all these times. When you're out there alone— Every time they put you out there on guard, you're alone." In the blackness, he heard the muted tramping of feet, the chuffing of breath. "So I looked around and I got behind a tree," he says. "And I watched and I watched, and I'm waiting, and I've got my finger on the trigger. And the mist is rising—in the mist I couldn't see anything. Finally the mist lifts up and what is it? A bunch of pigs running by!"

It was a small incident, in retrospect almost comical, but it triggered a feeling he has never forgotten. "Fear. Fear. Everything you're doing is fear."

During a break in the action, Biow and his buddy, Howard "Hop" Breisch, decided to explore Saarlautern. They drove into town on the tree-lined cobblestoned main road in Biow's truck, took a few pictures, and on the way out stopped at a crossroads to take a photo of a bullet-riddled sign that read SAARLAUTERN. Biow was always leery of intersections. Near Metz, he had narrowly escape an artillery blast that pulverized an intersection where he and his truck had been only seconds before.

Biow recounts, "So I stopped the truck, got out, took my picture, got back in, took off, and again looked over our shoulder, and again there was the artillery hitting on the intersection we had just left!" He floored it and the GI truck strained to climb the hill out of town, slowly but surely putting distance between them and the artillery barrage.

Suddenly a jeep came speeding over the crest of the hill heading toward them. "You know in the wintertime you had side curtains on the truck— sort of a canvaslike gadget with isinglass—it all happened so fast I couldn't get the damned thing open. So I shoved my hand through the handhole on the side and tried to wave them down, and they thought I was waving at 'em, so they waved back." The jeep ran down into the intersection Biow had just left—and straight into the next barrage.

The jeep that passed Biow was carrying Tom Wells, who was coming out of Picard, less than a mile west. "On 12 March, Captain Tom Wells of Chicopee Falls, Massachusetts, was killed in action near Picard, Germany. He and I often shared quarters in the field. I knew all about his wife and infant child; his hopes for the rest of his life back home," Fox wrote of the man he had befriended all those months ago aboard the USS *Henry Gibbons*.

He had last seen him two days before, when Wells visited him at the hospital in Verdun. "We had a typical bedside conversation of little jokes and things. He laughed gaily and, as always, looked clean and handsome," Fox wrote Barbara Wells, Tom's widow, two months after his death. "I can think of no reason why the Lord would have wished to take him away from us except perhaps that He wanted us to feel the cruel price of this war and the absolute necessity for living peaceful, generous lives."

Writing many years after the incident, Fox was able to put some distance between himself and the emotions that must have gripped him upon learning of his close friend's death, riding in a jeep that Fox might well have shared, had he not been in the hospital. At the time, Fox could not even bring himself to write to his own fiancée about Wells's death. Later he could write, "As Tom was riding in the front seat of his jeep, a German shell burst in the tree directly overheard and ripped his throat in half." It's a frank, even brutal description, but Fox never glamorized or sanitized the war. He acted under a moral obligation to teach those who hadn't seen war except in censored reports and patriotic movies that, in a mechanized war, the human body was fearfully vulnerable and frail. Even all those decades later, the description carries a hardly disguised anger at the waste of a good man's life.

The artillery didn't let up. As Tompkins recorded on Tuesday, March 13, "Stood guard 12:00–1:45 last night. Heavy artillery. Finished firing at Midnight."

Worse was to come. Early on the morning of March 13, the 80th Division attacked near Saarburg and met only light resistance—so far, so good. With the operation complete, the various units of the 23d Special Troops packed their gear to move out. The trucks were loaded, the men waiting beside them, anxious to leave Saarlautern behind.

Dowd recalls their worst moment of the war. "I'm a platoon sergeant sitting next to my driver, and the back of the truck is full of soldiers. And we're here ready to go, but they won't give us the damn signal," Dowd says. "And I'm thinking to myself, *Let's get the hell out of here!* Because the big missiles are coming. And the truck behind us got hit, just as we were moving out. It's difficult to move many, many vehicles—and that's what happened."

In the first published account of the Special Troops right after the war—an article that caused a minor furor in the War Department because of the breach of security—Sgt. Sebastian Messina told a hometown reporter for the *Worcester* (Mass.) *Telegram*: "There was heavy fighting going on with the Germans trying to hold the city, and our column of trucks had to push right in to clinch the bluff." His account had the column driving right into the teeth of a German 88 registered on an intersection. "My best friend was in the first truck to stop one of the shells, a Pennsylvania boy."

"Frankly," Dowd maintains, "whoever was in charge was moving too slowly. The German guns zeroed in on us and before we could get the hell out of there we lost a couple of people."

Whatever the reason, the toll was high. George C. Peddle, a radio platoon sergeant, was killed. Fifteen more men were wounded, several of them horribly. One of them was Captain Howard Raynor, the kind and popular CO of D Company who had sent Dowd to New York to say good-bye to his family before shipping out, on pretext of retrieving an AWOL soldier from a Washington stockade.

Tompkins had pulled out earlier with B Company and didn't learn about the shelling until late that afternoon. "All happened on same road we were on this morning," he wrote. "It was under enemy observation from the opposite side of the valley. Saw Tom Weir's jeep had hole right thru front panel and steering post. This has really been a hell of a blow to us all. We just thank God that ours wasn't up today. We were darn glad to get out of that hole."

For a combat infantry outfit the casualties might have been considered minimal. But the Special Troops had been literally dodging the bullet for so long that the loss of Wells, Peddle, and fifteen wounded comrades came as a disheartening shock. Though they were playing roles, creating fictional armies, and faking out the enemy, the game had always been a potentially deadly one. Now that came home to them in a sobering way. The wonder was that they had soldiered so long virtually unharmed.

Hal Laynor painted the moment when the shell came crashing out of the sky with his name on it—a stricken GI illuminated by an orange flash over his right shoulder, titled *Not Me, Please*.

"I had already experienced seven months of combat and although I had felt myself a seasoned veteran, I still blanched and choked when I hit the

Not Me, Please: painting by Harold Laynor (GLORIA LAYNOR)

ground after a close shell burst," he wrote after the war in an unpublished story called "Pain (A true short story)" for Dr. Lou LaBrant's Advanced English Composition class at NYU.

"Before I would get up I would tense my muscles and feel myself praying that I'd find no blood. Finally the day in March it came. We were standing by our vehicles awaiting orders when we heard the whine of eighty-eights over our heads. We stiffened and nervously looked at each other, and then what we silently prayed against happened. It was a shattering, smashing, blinding series of explosions around us and on us. I didn't have to throw myself to the ground, I was hurled to the ground, then picked up by concussion, smacked against a truck, and rolled under it. As I had always done before I tensed and felt myself. I was black with mud, but no pain, no blood. None dead, eleven injured, four badly injured, amputees out of the war. This wasn't as bad as expected."

Actually signalman Peddle was dead, but he was not in Laynor's battalion. Laynor moved out with the remnants of his company, and a few days later woke to a searing pain in his lower back, which bulged with a baseball-sized lump. Hot and feverish, he reported to the medic. "By the time I was seen, my mind had become fogged, dull, and my whole body shook and throbbed with each heartbeat," he wrote.

The doctor found a hunk of shrapnel embedded in his back—and the wound had festered into acute gangrene. Laynor was rushed in an ambulance to a nearby airstrip. "There on the ground between other stretcher cases, I felt like a key on a huge piano," he continued. "It was hours, it was hot, the sun beat down, and we waited. This I swore was the worst moment I had ever lived. My ears throbbed with my heart and yet through that throbbing I heard the moans, groans, pleadings, screams, and shrieks of those around me, like the notes of the piano off key in a crazy macabre symphony. I heard men crying for morphine and saw the red grease 'M' on their brows warped in the furrows of pain. I put my hand to my head and felt the grease that told me I was also awarded an M. I didn't remember when it was given to me. I looked at the tag which was tied to my stretcher and noted the scribbled word *penicillin*. Both arms hurt, so I supposed that I had been given penicillin shots also."

Woozy from the morphine, Laynor could hear the medics talking. The C-54s were flying the worst cases to England, while the C-47s were taking the rest to Paris. Captain Raynor, his leg and thigh ripped by shrapnel, had gone to England. Laynor wondered which it would be for him—then, in a spasm of pain, he screamed once and passed out.

"I suddenly awoke feeling my stretcher being lifted and a voice saying, 'Take it easy, GI, you're in the Air Corps now,'" his story went on. "I heard the hum of whirling propellers, talking men, shouts, I quivered, bit my lip, and opened and shut my eyes. I was lifted into the body of the plane, my stretcher strapped above one stretcher and below another. The door was shut and the plane moved. I didn't remember when the plane left the ground, there were no windows, no bumps, no indication of movement, yet I knew we were flying. In the air my body felt like a nebulous jellylike mass waving around a nucleus of pain. I fell asleep but soon awoke with a pressure on my ears that told me we were landing."

The wounded were taken off the plane four at a time and immediately loaded into waiting ambulances. Laynor was strapped in first and he watched as the next stretcher slipped in beside him. "There was no need for speculation, a bandage over his eyes and powder burns still livid on his face told me enough. As I turned to look at him, the ambulance started with a lurch and my companion opened his mouth in a scream of silence. Finally it came, and I was glad, the voiced scream came from a twisted mouth."

To a wounded man, every small bump in the road was an agony.

"Both hands clutched his bandaged face as he screamed, 'Oh God, driver take it easy, please driver please, my foot, my foot,'" Laynor recounted. " I glanced quickly along the olive drab blanket and saw the bandaged stump of his left leg, staining fresh with new blood over the old brown of dried blood. I looked back over my shoulder at the driver and saw a thin red neck, quivering with drops of perspiration standing out like sun flecks. 'Sure kid, sure,' he said, 'I'll do the best I can for you, soldier.' Then my eye caught the rearview mirror and I saw the driver's face, he was crying. I could see it. He was biting his lips and his face was white though his neck was red. I reached out and grabbed the blind boy's hand. 'Take it easy, chum,' I choked, 'we'll be okay.' We rode for about ten minutes or so still holding hands. Finally we stopped and the doors were opened. I felt my hand squeezed, and the kid turned to me and said, 'Don't let it getcha, fella, don't let it getcha.' "

But of course, it got him. Not just the terror he had felt at the moment when the shells had started exploding all around him, but the haze of morphine and the unreal flight to medical help, the driver holding back tears, the stoic encouragement he got from a blind GI with a bloody stump for a leg.

Laynor had glimpsed a darkness that would find expression only in his paintings—a darkness not just of color but of severe slashing lines, uncompromising edges, paintings in which human beings shared the somber hues of the landscape and blended into it nearly invisible, as if hiding from the violence of the scene: soldiers on their knees and stomachs during a bombardment; soldiers creeping through an eerie bombed-out town; soldiers hurtling into combat; soldiers cowering under the airbursts of artillery shells.

Like most young men, he probably had never imagined his own death before. He'd spent three quarters of his adult life in the army—gone from being a careless kid with a snappy joke for every occasion to being a soldier, a wounded veteran. During these arduous months, he had grown up.

He felt a renewed sense of determination, a seriousness of purpose. If he ever got home, he would finish school, paint some great pictures, teach everything he was learning to some other kids coming up, find the beauty in all this wreckage and fear and death.

For now at least, he was out of the war. As he recovered from his wound in the Paris hospital, he met Pablo Picasso for the first time. Picasso was visiting the ward of wounded soldiers and the two talked briefly about art. Trust your instincts, Picasso told him. They talked for a while about art and light and color, and Picasso invited Laynor to drop by his studio if he got the chance.

More than a month after he was wounded, he sought out Picasso in his cluttered studio and was dazzled by the great man. "He is wonderful & it's not difficult to see why he's the top figure in the art world today," he wrote home. "Still, I was disappointed in the fact that he is not as honest in his work as I thought he might be. His interests are political & his paintings all try in their modernistic attempt to press a political viewpoint."

In the hospital, Laynor painted portraits for a hundred francs apiece and won eighty dollars at poker to supplement his army pay, reduced while he recovered. "I'm still hanging around the hospital with my ass literally in a sling," he wrote. "I've been doing quite a bit of painting here."

Supplied with paints, brushes, and paper by the Red Cross, he created posters, full-sized paintings, and even murals to while away the hours and get his artistic edge back. And as always, he found a stage. In a production called *Sweating It Out*, with an all-patient cast costumed in his original designs, he acted and sang.

When he was well enough, he explored Paris, catching up on some of the experience he had missed when the war canceled his scholarship. He relaxed one evening at a macabre theme-café: "We sat on tombstones & drank gruesomely colored drinks out of bone straws on top of coffins," he wrote. "They had a mystic seance & a spookier than hell show."

There was no question: the war had changed him. He had gone from chubby boy to lean and worldly man.

And despite the soft time he was having in Paris, the pull of camaraderie was still strong. "Although I am having a heck of a good time here, doing art work & seeing Paris occasionally, I do really want to get back to the outfit," he admitted.

Early in the war, while he was still laboring under stacks of paperwork at Army Ground Forces headquarters in Washington, Col. Cliff Simenson had argued persuasively that soldiers bunched together in trucks made too good a target for enemy artillery and machine guns. Thanks to him, the army had scrapped its plan to drive soldiers into battle. Instead, they would be transported to the front, then dismount and fight on foot. The Special Troops were playing infantry when they were caught bunched together in the backs of trucks—a grim example of Simenson's nightmare come true.

Now the Special Troops drove back to Briey to lick their wounds and prepare for their grand finale on the Rhine.

THIRTEEN

GRAND ILLUSION

March 1945

No one knows that there are two of us—that will be our sharpest weapon!
  —Lucien Franchi to his twin brother Mario, both played by
  Douglas Fairbanks Jr. in *The Corsican Brothers*.

The convoy of four trucks pulled into the courtyard of the Château de
Vivonne to wait until full dark. Ellsworth Kelly was one of the drivers ferrying fresh troops to the front—green replacements coming in from the
coast just in time to glimpse springtime in Germany and to be hurled into
the Battle of the Rhine.

He shut off the motor, went around to the back of his truck, and got a
good look at the young troops he was carrying. They were kids, their boyish
faces ashen with fear. Their officer ordered them to remain in the trucks
until they pulled out again, one sure way to curb desertion. Kelly pulled
out pen and paper and started drawing the anxious faces crowded together
in the covered box of the truck. As he formed their faces in ink, he was
struck by a chilling optical illusion: the rectangular mouth of the truck resembled a coffin, and the pale scared boys huddled silently in its shadows
looked already dead. Before he had finished drawing, the order came down
to move out. He climbed behind the wheel and drove to the Rhine, where
the artillery on both sides kept up a constant but sporadic duel—what was
called harassing fire or, if a specific target had been sighted, interdictory
fire. The night sky was always pink with shell flashes, always filled with a
far-off rumble like rolling thunder—unless you were unlucky enough to be
the target that night. Then it dropped on you with a roaring flash like the
end of the world.

The replacement troops disembarked from the truck in a nervous cluster and their officer led them into the line. Kelly watched them go.

Only later did he hear what happened next. The whole bunch of kids he had delivered got wiped out in their first barrage.

Like all the old hands, he was furious that they'd been sent to the front, untrained, to be slaughtered. His drawing would remain forever incomplete, its composition frozen in that brief pause in the action in 1945, the young replacements, haunted by fear, peering anxiously out the back of the truck, their lives, too, forever stopped in that moment just before their first and final battle: the conquest of Germany.

Young Soldiers Being Transported to the Front, Remagen, Château de Divonne,
France. 1945. Ink. 5 ¼ x 8 inches. © Ellsworth Kelly. Photo by Jerry Thompson.

It was time to pull out all the stops: to launch Operation PLUNDER.

Three Allied armies—U.S. Ninth, British Second, and Canadian First—under Field Marshal Montgomery would assault the Rhine in force in the vicinity of Wesel, Germany, on the night of March 23–24. They would be supported by massive artillery and aerial bombardment and two divisions of paratroopers who would land in daylight behind the German lines after the assault troops had crossed the river. This monumental crossing would be the largest amphibious operation since Normandy. It had been Eisenhower's strategy since D-Day—an unstoppable push onto the northwestern plains of Germany, perfect country for tanks and mobile maneuvers, designed to settle the war for good.

The Allies had battled past the concrete "dragon's teeth" of the Siegfried Line and into Germany and now were poised on the Rhine River—the last natural barrier keeping the Allies out of Hitler's stronghold. During the time of Christ, the Rhine was the boundary between the civilized world of the Romans and the warlord country of the Germanic tribes.

As the Allies advanced across the frontier from France, Luxembourg, and the Netherlands, they'd had to root out the Germans house by house in the villages, pillbox by pillbox in the countryside. Hordes of dispirited Germans surrendered easily, but not the stubborn Panzer units and Parachute Troops, and the suicidal Hitler Youth Brigades. Along the Siegfried Line, at the outer perimeter of Germany, advancing infantry fought their way across acres of minefields behind forty-ton British Churchill tanks specially outfitted with "flails"—long arms holding a rotating drum wrapped in chains that beat the ground ahead of the tank and detonated the mines in its path. Then, when the flails bogged down in the thawing spring mud, the infantry crawled forward on hands and knees and dug out the mines by hand. Sometimes a soldier would step on a land mine and be blown into the man next to him, who would fall onto another, detonating a whole string. The rear-area hospitals were full of men missing amputated hands, legs, and feet.

They burned out blockhouse after blockhouse using special tanks called "Crocodiles," which could shoot a jet of flame three hundred yards.

Sometimes, when the tanks ran out of gas or ammo or were knocked out of action, whole platoons charged with fixed bayonets, World War I–style, into the teeth of machine guns.

What would lie in wait across the Rhine?

The campaign long ago had turned into a war of tanks—and rivers: the Seine, the Moselle, the Saar, the Maas, the Erft, the Roer, the Ruhr, and now the Rhine. And tanks couldn't swim—they needed bridges. Either captured enemy bridges, or pontoon bridges slung across by combat engineers after infantry in boats had secured a bridgehead on the other side. As the result of luck and remarkable bravery, soldiers of First Army had already captured the Ludendorff Bridge at Remagen, some ninety miles south of the place chosen for PLUNDER, on March 7—an unexpected coup. Remagen was far from an ideal bridgehead. Just across the old World War I–era railroad span, the country rose into a sheer 550-foot-high fortified escarpment known as the Erpeler Ley. For ten days, First Army tried to hammer its way out of the bridgehead while the Germans shelled the bridge with artillery, bombed it from the air, even sent suicide squads of frogmen—under the command of Col. Otto Skorzeny, whose American-uniformed commandoes had fed the chaos on the Allied front during the Battle of the Bulge—floating down the river to blow it up from below. After ten days of such pounding, the old bridge finally collapsed, killing twenty-eight engineers and dumping as many as one hundred more into the river. But the Americans had already put across two pontoon bridges, and reinforcements continued to stream into the German Reich, slugging their way beyond the bridgehead in weeks of bitter fighting.

A special SS "Flying Tribunal West" rounded up the officers accused of letting the Ludendorff Bridge fall into American hands—court-martialed them and had them shot—then announced the executions on Radio Berlin. The message was clear: Retreat was punishable by death.

Even farther south of Remagen, Patton's Third Army—depleted by divisions assigned to Seventh Army—had also busted across the narrow upper Rhine, crossing on pontoon bridges on March 22. Patton had been feuding relentlessly with Montgomery throughout the campaign and had raced to get across before him. His Third Army had been starved of gas and ammunition to feed Montgomery's ponderous monolith in the north—as had First Army. Eisenhower didn't want a flying attack by individual columns punching through in various sectors, leaving behind large pockets of German troops. He wanted first to clear the Rhine plain of Germans, then strike a sledgehammer blow with combined armies.

Ralph Ingersoll, the Special Plans Branch man, likened the whole show to a three-ring circus. In one ring was Patton's daring bridgehead, a kind of swinging trapeze act, as his advancing columns grabbed for the next objective and gambled they could hold on; in the second was the daring tightrope-walk across the Remagen Bridge; and in the third—Eisenhower's center ring—Montgomery's three-army assault in the north was billed as the main attraction. And nobody wanted to be a sideshow.

Indeed, now that the end was in sight, the Anglo-American alliance was showing signs of serious strain. In private, Patton called Montgomery "that little fart." Montgomery confided to his staff that he thought Eisenhower was a pretty dull blade and blocked his orders every chance he got by going around him straight to Churchill. Eisenhower was at last coming to the conclusion that Montgomery was a psychotic. General Bradley had threatened to resign if he were ordered to serve under Montgomery. He believed Montgomery had been holding back U.S. Ninth Army, which already should have pushed across the Rhine. He also bridled that Americans were serving under a timid Brit, when the Americans had done so much of the hard, straight-ahead fighting. The Bulge had been entirely an American battle—and an American victory—though Montgomery ignited a firestorm of controversy when he took credit for it in the London papers.

The European Theater of Operations was hardly large enough to contain all the egos, and as the various armies neared the Rhine, the Allied generals were running out of strutting territory. The aperture of the war was closing down on Germany. The Americans, now the senior partner in the war, fielding two thirds of the combat troops in Europe, didn't want the British to grab all the glory. And neither the British nor the Americans wanted the Russians to be first into Berlin, though that was beginning to look inevitable. It was no accident that armies from three Allied nations would make the final major river assault together. Just as at D-Day, the strategy was as much political as it was military. Montgomery's combined armies had the force to deliver the knockout punch. Nearly eighty thousand troops would cross in the first waves of the assault, and there would be enough glory to go around.

But even this late in the war, nothing was a sure bet.

Since D-Day, the Germans had developed a deadly habit of counterattacking at the most unexpected moments—exactly when the Allies thought they were licked: in the rugged Hürtgen Forest, where some American units sustained more than one hundred percent battlefield casualties—the original units and waves of replacements decimated; in the Ardennes Forest at Christmastime, when they rolled back three months of Allied gains won at the cost of tens of thousands of lives, won back at the cost of tens of thousands more; at the Roer River dams, controlling the floodplain on which the impending combined Allied attack, Operation PLUNDER, was now being staged. It was a muddy stage—the retreating Germans blew a gap in the Schwammenauel Dam and slowly flooded the plain into a mudhole that three armies had to slog across just to be able to position themselves for an assault across the Rhine. The floods delayed PLUNDER for more than a month.

With the Russians sweeping in across their eastern border toward Berlin, revenging themselves for Stalingrad on prisoners and civilians alike, the Germans' own self-interest dictated that they surrender to the western Allies—who were known to treat prisoners of war decently, who severely punished any Allied soldiers convicted of rape and murder, and whose unofficial policy in the field was never to destroy a town unless it offered resistance. Though many of Hitler's generals appreciated the simple logic of surrendering to the Allies at the Rhine, sparing what was left of their army and their country from the preventable ravages of a war to the death, the American President had all but guaranteed that would never happen.

Without even consulting Churchill, Roosevelt announced that the Allies would accept no conditions to Germany's surrender. The German regular-army generals who otherwise might have called a halt to Hitler's insane strategy of defending to the death every foot of German soil had nothing to bargain with and were forced by a sense of duty to go on fighting for their homeland. To make matters worse, a high-level attempt at deception had backfired disastrously. The White House deliberately leaked a vindictive blueprint for postwar Germany, the so-called "Morganthau Plan" after Henry Morganthau Jr., Roosevelt's secretary of the treasury: to level German industry, flood all the mines in the Ruhr Valley, and corral the population inside an agrarian prison-state guarded at its borders by British, American, and Russian armies of occupation. American newspapers played the story, which was aimed at breaking the German spirit of resistance.

But the propaganda machine of Dr. Josef Goebbels—the so-called "Poison Dwarf"—exploited *both* pronouncements to stiffen resistance as the remains of the Nazi armies dug in to make their last stand for the Fatherland. Hitler had given one order, fanatically and relentlessly: No retreat! Fight to the death!

It would be crucial that the three Allied armies not have to fight their way across the Rhine, as they had been forced to do at the Roer River, almost exactly a month before. Then German 88s slammed into them as they crossed and wiped out the soldiers a boatload at a time. Each time they had finished a bridge, the German artillery blew it up. The attack was stopped cold at the river for twenty-four hours. The infantry who made it across faced Panzer counterattacks without antitank guns and almost lost the precarious bridgehead.

The Germans knew Montgomery was coming, but they didn't know exactly where or when. The Special Troops would capitalize on that crucial piece of missing information.

Operation PLUNDER depended on the readiness of three armies, one of them U.S. Ninth Army. The job of the Special Troops was to lull the Germans into believing that Ninth Army couldn't possibly mobilize before April 1, and then would cross not at Wesel but at Düsseldorf, more than thirty miles south. Montgomery was infamous as a cautious commander, one who would not move an inch until all his forces were fully in place and ready. Since his daring victory at El Alamein more than two years ago, he had been elevated to Field Marshal the Viscount Montgomery of Alamein, KG, GCB, DSO—the grandest military hero since Wellington to a nation that badly needed one. His vocal critics in the American army accused him time and again of being afraid to attack unless absolutely sure of victory—lest he tarnish his lofty reputation.

Now the Special Troops would use that knowledge—surely shared by the Germans—against the enemy: that if Ninth Army wasn't yet ready, Montgomery wouldn't launch his attack. Lieutenant Colonel Hector Truly masterminded the deception plan. PLUNDER relied on U.S. Ninth Army's assault plan, FLASHPOINT, and Ninth Army headquarters, at Truly's instigation, developed Operation EXPLOIT—a plan to deceive the enemy as to the whereabouts of two of its key divisions, the 30th Old Hickory and the 79th Cross of Lorraine. Both divisions were currently training for the Rhine assault on the Maas River, in a rear area just across the Dutch border. They were to move clandestinely into a staging area in XIII Corps sector across the Rhine from Wesel.

The orders from Ninth Army Headquarters to the advance parties were explicit. "Prior to the movement of the Division as a whole, all Commanders, Staff officers, and parties going forward on reconnaissance, and the 30th Rcn Troops which had been moved to the assault area for the purpose of establishing Divisional OP and a reconnaissance base, were carefully briefed to avoid disclosing their unit and intentions in any way, even to friendly troops, and all shoulder patches, vehicular identifications were removed."

The main bodies would also move under strict radio silence and blackout—having stripped all sleeve patches, bumper markings, and other insignia. They would travel by night, haul their artillery into position under camouflage nets, park their tanks under trees, and disperse their trucks, jeeps, and tractors into concealed positions with the help of camouflage engineers. German agents were known to be working among the civilian population, so security details would sweep the area clean of civilians.

"Finally," according to a directive from Ninth Army, "only thoroughly dependable men who could be trusted not to talk in the event of capture were selected for reconnaissance patrols to the far side of the river."

All troops would be denied furloughs and passes and be confined to camouflaged areas until the jump-off, so-called "H-hour." Just prior to H-hour, they would sew their sleeve patches back on—this, too, was part of the ruse: Phase II.

In the best of situations—good weather, safe home ground, with rested troops and vehicles in tip-top condition—moving an infantry division of ten to fifteen thousand men any distance required detailed planning and support: Maps must be printed and circulated, convoy guides briefed, road signs erected along the route, MPs placed at key intersections to check credentials and direct traffic, traffic regulating points chosen and manned by competent officers. Hundreds of trucks, jeeps, tanks, tank destroyers, half-tracks, artillery tractors, weapons carriers, heavy equipment transporters, and staff cars must be fueled and serviced, drivers and assistant drivers assigned, equipment loaded in such a manner that it would be ready for use in a hurry at the destination. Along the way, thousands of men had to be fed, watered, sheltered at long stops, and cared for medically, kept under organized discipline, and their personal gear had to be transported along with them.

Moving an infantry division in secret in hostile territory would be a remarkable accomplishment, but it had been done before. Civilians had to be cleared from all along the route of march, camouflage discipline maintained at every stop, the larger convoys broken up into smaller units that could travel less obtrusively. And of course radio silence must be maintained, so lost drivers could not call in for directions. Nor could divisional road signs be erected. And all travel must take place at night—increasing the chances of accident and of drivers getting lost on unfamiliar roads in captured territory where the inhabitants might still be hostile and in communication with the enemy, who was not far away.

Moving two divisions secretly into the same small sector to concentrate troops and heavy armor for a major attack would be an extraordinary feat of security, planning, and logistics.

On March 18, the leading elements of the 79th Division set out from the Maas, followed on each of three successive nights by more convoys, each motoring for about four hours. All told, 1,765 vehicles, including 485 artillery vehicles, traveled some sixty miles from Geilenkirchen, Holland, to their staging area on the Rhine.

The 30th Division faced an even greater logistical challenge. Traveling for a total of more than thirty hours from March 16 to 21, 3,321 vehicles stealthily advanced from Echt to the Rhine—including field artillery, combat engineers, camouflage engineers, tank destroyers, armor, antiaircraft artillery, treadway and ponton (pontoon) bridge companies, maintenance companies, and medical detachments.

By the night of March 23, more than twenty thousand soldiers, backed by tanks and artillery, were in position on the west bank of the Rhine—forming the southernmost anchor of Montgomery's northern push.

A further twist to the plan sent new divisions into river-assault training on the Maas, so there would be no telltale interruption of activity in that area to let the enemy know that training had stopped and the real thing had commenced. Embedded within EXPLOIT was VIERSEN, the part of the deception plan to be executed directly by the Special Troops: "Phase I: The enemy presumably knows that the 30th and 79th infantry Divisions are engaged in river-crossing training on the MAAS River. On or about 21 March these two divisions will be moved (notionally) into the rear of the XIII Corps area. These divisions are to be reequipped and rested in this area prior to moving into forward assembly for the attack."

That was the story for enemy consumption: the Special Troops would "play in" the divisions to a position far to the south of where the actual troops were—in the sector between Düsseldorf and Uerdinger, designated XIII Corps, instead of in XVI Corps at Wesel. Anything being done for real up north would be duplicated more obviously down south: emplacing tank destroyers to fire across the river, bringing up bridging equipment, sending out recon patrols, firing artillery.

The back end of the plan would commence once the real crossing had been accomplished, duplicating the scheme carried out so effectively after D-Day in France, when deception planners had kept the Germans convinced for weeks that the Normandy landings were only a diversionary attack to mask an impending main attack someplace else: "Phase II: The 30th and 79th Inf Divs have now been identified in an actual crossing of the Rhine (24 March) and two new divisions are in the rear area of XIII Corps. There is a decided build up for a crossing in XIII with elements of the two new divisions reconnoitering for crossings and moving to forward assembly areas." Thus it would seem to the enemy not that two divisions had been conjured out of thin air in the Düsseldorf sector—which of course they were—but that the Americans had merely switched divisions on them, and a new and larger attack was still imminent.

For the first time in the war, the Special Troops used every man and resource they had, and then some, in a single operation. Nearly 1,000 extra troops were attached to the unit for the operation, including infantry, antiaircraft artillery, and six bridging engineer companies. In addition, real equipment arrived to augment the dummies: 366 various assault craft and four Bailey bridge rafts, along with 1,000 feet of floating Bailey equipment used to prefabricate bridges robust enough to carry armor.

As for dummies, the camoufleurs brought up everything they had: Each "division" could emplace 5 aircraft, ten 105mm howitzers, 88 tanks, and 250 trucks and trailers. In fact, the two combined fake divisions dispersed 618 dummies, almost equally divided between them. To "dress" their stage, they hauled in 200 fifty-gallon drums, 1,000 camouflage nets, 100 reels of bridge cable, and truckloads of other miscellaneous materials. They constructed dummy airstrips, supply depots, and command posts. The work was broken up by company and platoon, spread out over a wide area.

Throughout the area of operation, in clearings along a muddy road deeply scored by bulldozers to mimic tank tracks, stood fake supply dumps and motor parks full of jeeps and two-and-a-half-ton trucks, mostly derelicts scrounged from other outfits and towed there. Hidden among the thick woods and the berms were more than 600 tanks, tank destroyers, and howitzers—harmless decoys. Inflatable rubber dummies. For the first two nights of the operation, each platoon spent the dark hours manhandling the rolled-up dummy tanks and howitzers off its two allotted trucks, hauling them to their positions, stripping off their canvas covers, setting each in a preselected place according to a meticulously detailed map, and inflating it with a mobile air compressor mounted on a jeep.

Half an hour per dummy, and they wound up with two divisions of deadly-looking Macy's parade balloons.

The physical demands of the work exhausted the men. During the day, the men were not allowed simply to sleep but had to play out their roles as tankers, engineers, armored infantry. So they might spend all night inflating dummies, then spend half the day riding in the lurching backs of trucks to nearby villages, in order that enemy agents there could report a new column of infantry arriving on the line.

When the decoys were all in place, there was guard duty. Always.

The men must stay close to the dummies—usually in foxholes covered with a piece of canvas, what the army called a "shelter half"—the two pieces together forming one pup tent. If the night were especially cold, the air would compress and the tank barrels wilted. In the morning, they'd have to reinflate the droopy ones, then later, as the sun warmed the rubber skins, start carefully deflating each dummy a little. Otherwise, as the sun heated the rubber skin and the air inside expanded, the dummy would pop. And there was always the threat of enemy artillery. Farther north, near Krefeld, the rubber artillery emplacements were getting hit by counterbattery fire. As fast as the shell fragments ripped into the rubber decoys, the camoufleurs darted out of their foxholes to repair them—they always carried chewing gum for quick fixes.

For realism, Ninth Army ordered them to patrol aggressively, while at the real staging areas, recon would be minimal. Each night at specified intervals, antiaircraft companies projected "artificial moonlight"—training mammoth truck-mounted searchlights onto the cloud cover to cast a reflected glow across the river and light the enemy's positions. Since Montgomery was using smoke screens up north along a seventy-mile front, they generated smoke screens down south.

And of course, all civilians were evacuated from the deception areas. Any who were caught wandering around were detained until after the operation. Likewise, if any "friendly" soldier of whatever rank or nationality could not produce satisfactory identification when challenged by a guard or fake MP, he would be arrested and sent to the provost marshal stockade at Anrath.

The Special Troops split into two task forces, one to mimic each division. Simenson took command of the notional 79th, simulating a buildup in the Anrath area, two miles northeast of Viersen on the Niers River. With Simenson masquerading as a general, seven others, including Reeder's son, 2d Lt. Boyd Reeder, played colonels and majors. From the 603d camoufleurs, Simenson's task force comprised Headquarters & Service Company, including Morton and Arnett; D Company, with Dowd and Dahl (Laynor was still recuperating in Paris); and C Company, including Holt and Laubheimer. Also part of Simenson's command were half the sonic, radio, and combat engineer companies.

The 30th Task Force under Lieutenant Colonel Schroeder fielded thirteen other fake senior officers, including two more bogus generals, and simulated a concentration in Dulken, six miles west of the 79th. It contained the rest of the signal, sonic, and combat engineer companies, the 23d Headquarters Company—with Fox—as well as two companies of camoufleurs: A Company, including Biow, Kelly, and Wynshaw; and B Company, including Blass, Shilstone, and Tompkins.

The operation was just as complex for the fake units as for the real ones.

The convoy route took the two real units through Sittard, Holland, where their "doubles" in the Special Troops—broken down to mimic each actual regiment, battalion, or company—began their journeys south while the real units, blacked out, eventually hooked north. The real radios fell silent as the blarney radios went on the air, following the false convoys south and east. Thus to anyone monitoring the radio traffic, the journey of the two divisions would seem continuous.

To direct such a complicated scheme, Ninth Army and 23d Headquarters issued top-secret written orders—called operational memos, letters of instruction, or simply plans. This was standard practice with every mission, but in this case, owing to the scope and scale of the operation, the paperwork was voluminous. For instance, the notional convoys—traveling with fake bumper markings and other insignia—received a directive to keep them from being strafed and bombed on the roads by Allied planes until after the crossing:

Cerise (red) panels will be displayed until 25 Mar as follows on vehicles larger than 1/2 ton only:

  1 per 5 vehicles in convoy of 10 or more
  1 per group of 5–9 vehicles.

Panels will be displayed on forward portion of truck immed in rear of cab.

A strict schedule for deploying the fake artillery was kept—Instructional Memo #2 from Reeder to Simenson and Schroeder directed that they set up one battalion during the hours of darkness each night from March 20–23.

Another directive detailed the plans for firing flash devices to simulate artillery fire.

A directive was issued on how to employ the coventional engineer companies attached to the Special Troops to "multiply" their numbers and equipment: "Equipment of 74th Engineer Light Pontoon Company and 982d Engineer Treadway Bridge Company to be removed during hours of darkness and returned to new bivouac locations during daylight hours as many times as possible before D-Day depending upon limitations of camouflage units."

Intelligence reports from Maj. Joseph Kelly, in Simenson's task force, issued security warnings: "Military personnel in civilian clothes are known to be operating in NUSA [Ninth United States Army] area, and, in addition, all German civilians, including women and children, must be considered as potential agents. Ground agents are used to obtain identification of units by noting bumper markings, shoulder patches, road signs, CP signs, etc. They are usually able to locate troops concentrations, CPs, supply points and note the types of equipment used. Their means of communication in NUSA area are believed to be excellent. Active telephone communication across the Rhine is known to exist. Tapping and cutting of military telephone lines has been reported by several units in the area."

An enemy agent could literally phone home—and give away the whole show.

Schroeder's task force occupied the area around a small lake, where amphibious training sounds were projected. As in all such secure areas, password protocol was rigid and written out in advance. In this case, the word *Authorized* was added to whatever word was selected for the day, as in Password FREE AUTHORIZED; countersign: RANSOM.

For atmosphere, Schroeder was directed to send one half-track from each company on the average of every two hours between 8:00 A.M. and 6:00 P.M. to Viersen, Willich, Suchteln, Vorst, Niehasen, and the northern edge of München-Gladbach.

Simenson ordered: "All possible use will be made of courtyards for dummies. Real vehicles should be parked outside of courtyards. *Do not park real vehicles side by side with dummies.*" The contrast might give them away.

Special effects were to be employed at Krefeld and St. Tonis, just to the north. Directives gave explicit instructions about where the field kitchens would travel and set up, how laundry and bathing would be handled, where aid stations would be established. They covered such minutiae as how many trucks would be dispatched in what sized convoys and to which depots to pick up real supplies and gas, which trucks would carry officers and which not, how many pounds of air to pump into a dummy tank or truck to properly inflate it per army specifications.

There was even a stern order about the handling of mail. Troops were forbidden to write their unit designation—their return address—on outgoing mail until just before dropping it into the mailbox, to prevent a mislaid letter from tipping off an enemy ground agent. Alternatively, an enlisted man was permitted to write the unit designation on the letter in the presence of an officer, then turn over the letter to him for mailing. All envelopes from incoming mail and portions of V-mail that showed the soldier's unit were to be burned at the place of distribution. Unphotographed V-mail was to be read and burned at the place of distribution.

The Signal Company Special had its own set of orders. It broke into three groups—one for each phony division and a third to manage the traffic control net. Among other duties, they laid seventy miles of telephone wire to connect command posts and headquarters—including six extra circuits to each divisional and regimental command post beyond what was necessary for communication. Seven radio teams handled the phony 30th Division and nine teams covered the fake 79th. The blarney operators got a thorough briefing from their counterparts in the actual divisions and went on the air after a period of radio silence on March 16—the silence intended to alert listening Germans that something was up. The radios then came alive with the normal chatter of divisions assembling at new locations in Dulken and Anrath—normal chatter that in this case was carefully scripted, ending in another period of radio silence after midnight on March 22, twenty-four hours before the real attack started.

Meanwhile the third group, operating the traffic control net, carried the key to the deception. Knowing that a good lie always begins as close to the truth as possible, the blarney operators first broadcast the *actual* movements of the 30th and 79th Divisions away from the Maas—the times when various units crossed their IPs—initial points—and met up with the Special Troops. From there on, the real units headed north to battle, and the Special Troops turned south and east toward the deception area, taking the traffic control net with them.

Whether it was Fox or Major Yokum or some other creative officer who came up with the idea, this time the signalmen added a new wrinkle, as Yokum reported: "Honesty and variety were injected into the traffic on the net by having each operator transmit during part of each day but without a prepared script. It is felt that no prepared scripts could have presented the variations in expression, voice, and phrase which the operators themselves achieved."

So the radio broadcasts at selected times turned into improvisational theater, augmenting the scripted plot and transmitting just as if monitoring real columns from the two divisions. The operators didn't just ad lib— they worked from five "cue cards":

1. A road map tracing the routes of the real convoys and their junctions with convoys of the Special Troops, then tracing the routes of the notional convoys, which contained a fraction as many vehicles, as they veered away east and the real divisions turned north—the 30th at Bruggen, the 79th at Dulken.
2. A crib sheet listing frequencies, callsigns, SLIDEX code keys, fake locations of various "TRPs" (Traffic Regulating Points), basic convoy procedure such as speed limits and time intervals between "serials" of one hundred vehicles and "march units" of twenty-five vehicles, real convoy code numbers chalked onto bumpers of the Special Troops' vehicles, and real "traffic personalities"—names of actual officers from Ninth Army—including those officers manning the TRPs under the assumed names of their real counterparts.
3. Ninth Army SLIDEX card for aid in encrypting transmissions via a simple substitution of letters into a code the Germans could easily decipher.
4. Ninth Army Traffic Movement Form No. II, the so-called "short form," completed with appropriate data for each convoy: number of

vehicles, serials and march units, time length in minutes to pass a TRP, height and weight of largest vehicle, and so on.

5. Ninth Army Traffic Movement Form No. 5, the so-called "long form," filled out each day by the officer in charge of each TRP and radioed in to headquarters. The TRPs were numbered from Echt and Geilenkirchen—the 30th and 79th Division starting points, respectively—to Viersen, TRP 9, closest to the enemy lines. The phony TRP officers made actual reconnaissances of their stretches of road and sent them in. Yokum explains, "The integrity of the information followed the same policy as the nightly convoy reports. TRPs Nos. 1 and 3 sent in straight road reports; TRPs Nos. 6 and 7 distorted theirs somewhat by emphasizing highways and traffic in the direction of the notional areas; TRP No. 9 was almost solely interested in phony traffic data within—and later leading eastward from—the notional concentration areas."

Typical traffic just a few minutes after midnight on March 20: "C131 POINT CONVOY ENTERED PUFFENDORF 192035." In plain language, Traffic Regulating Point No. 2, at Puffendorf, was reporting that a few hours earlier, at 8:35 P.M., the lead command car of a column of the 79th Division, consisting of 418 vehicles, passed through its checkpoint twenty-five miles or so south of Dulken, where it turned left onto highway N-57 to swing north.

Fifty-five minutes after midnight, when all the vehicles had passed, TRP No. 2 radioed, "C131 TAIL CONVOY CLEARED THIS LOCATION AT 200055." These were factual reports. Beyond Dulken, the reports would turn fictitious. Thus, shortly after 9:00 A.M., the TRP at Viersen reported, "TAIL OF C131 CLEARED AT 200253"—2:53 A.M. In fact, Convoy 131 had bypassed the turnoff for Viersen and was already miles to the north.

Fox, in charge of the traffic net, enjoyed his role to the hilt. "I wandered around in a jeep pretending to be several convoys of trucks and reporting any progress through powerful radios set up along the way." He often transmitted in the clear, to make sure the enemy heard him.

Thus, routine truth led inexorably to a big lie—two actual divisions disappeared from the Germans' map and their ghosts reappeared in an area where Ninth Army had no intention of attacking.

When not riding around in his jeep, Fox monitored the bogus radio traffic from inside a makeshift command post. It would all go silent just before the big push. For most of the war, he had enjoyed the comforts of a headquarters billet behind the lines, but not during operations. He wrote to his fiancée, Hannah, "I have been fairly busy but mostly, I've been living under difficult writing conditions. I don't like to make letters all crunched up in a dark corner."

Fox had written the program notes for the whole show back in July of '44: "The presentations must be done with the greatest accuracy and attention to detail. They will include the proper scenery, props, costumes, principals, extras, dialogue and sound effects. We must remember that we are playing to a very critical and attentive Radio, Ground, and Aerial audience. They must be convinced."

On the headset, he listened to the transmitting operator—one of more than a hundred on the air each night. He listened for accents, for the flavor of the routine. The operators were guys from Signal Company, Special, impersonating real operators from outfits that had moved north to attack. The deception lay in the true details. The calls had to sound ordinary, dull almost—the hundreds of minor communications between columns of tanks and trucks moving up to assume their places in the assault formations. The Americans were notorious for chattering on the radio too much, giving themselves away. This was one more chance to use what the enemy "knew" against him.

Over the past couple of nights, Fox had heard, "C 126 MOVING UP EAST BETWEEN HERE AND BOISHEM, MOVING SLOWLY, OVER." Tankers, coming down from the northwest and bogged down in mud and traffic—that's what the Germans would hear.

"THERE ARE GUIDES AT DULKEN TO DIRECT C 130 THROUGH VIERSEN, OVER." The map references were important. It was easy to picture the Germans sticking pushpins in their tactical maps, tracking the progress of a phantom enemy—and moving their troops to counter it.

"TELL ENGLISH HIS PROMOTION CAME THROUGH, OVER."

A nice touch, that. Mentioning a real name was just the kind of casual detail that would convince a German "sleeper" monitoring the traffic that it was the real McCoy. English was the name of a real officer in the 30th—not the guy who was pretending to be him at Traffic Regulating Point No. 7 at Bruggen.

"WATCH SECURITY, OVER."

The routine radio traffic went on day and night—listening posts reporting in to headquarters, company commanders sorting out orders of march, platoon leaders checking on supplies, tankers requisitioning gas. Fox always believed that radio deception was the key to the whole show, though many of the camoufleurs felt that sonic deception was the most convincing element of their charade—it sounded damned realistic to them.

Combat commanders on the ground tended to trust the dummy emplacements, the visual evidence that a beefed-up part of the front had suddenly turned dangerous for the enemy. They were more or less familiar with camouflage—all frontline troops used it to some extent. The dummy tanks and guns were in some respects the simplest, least sophisticated part of the whole deception show, concrete evidence for the eyes—and oddly reassuring for the other troops in the line, who often counted them as real. Line commanders tended, pragmatically, to trust the simple approach to work best. Sonic projection was intangible, and spoof radio was downright invisible. And both required a high degree of complexity as well as technical proficiency in planning and operation.

But if the Special Troops had learned one lesson in their ongoing tutorial across France, Luxembourg, Belgium, Holland, and Germany, it was this: The enemy commander would be fooled most effectively if his intelligence from one source were corroborated by others. If his ears—listening posts—told him to see tanks, and come daylight his eyes—patrols and spotters—actually saw them, and his radio operators reported that indeed tanks and troops had moved into the area, he would fall hard for the con.

Reprising Montgomery's tactic at El Alamein, the Special Troops were using the old magician's "pull"—the trick of getting the audience to look at the flourishing right hand while the canny left hand performed the trick. Or like a football game, Simenson, Fox, and Ingersoll's favorite metaphor: Fake and feint and deceive the linebackers, then rush around the other end for a touchdown.

In VIERSEN, the Special Troops were the right hand. The lethal left hand was the Ninth Army, who would magically appear miles to the north.

And there was another resonance with El Alamein: U.S. Ninth Army was originally to be designated U.S. Eighth Army—but the British requested that it be numbered differently to avoid confusion with the famous British Eighth Army, which had pulled off the trick under Montgomery against Rommel in Africa.

At Anrath, Simenson's area, first and third platoons of the sonic company, led by Major Williams and including Bill Brown's crew, played four nights running from 7:30 P.M. until just before midnight: "Sounds of truck columns and individual trucks were played to the surrounding villages," Simenson reported. And then at daylight they shifted programs: "In the daytime sounds of wood sawing, bulldozers, jackhammers, pounding, loading and unloading of gas cans, heavy duty engines, and air compressors were intermittently played in various areas."

• • •

Just after dusk, as he had done for five nights in a row, Lt. John Walker directed his lead half-track into position. Walker steadied himself with gloved hands on the cold armor. He preferred to ride in the turret, the gunner's position, from where he could peer into the darkness ahead and direct the driver. He had and still has excellent night vision. The roads in the Viersen sector were narrow, country lanes edged by ditches and woods—in daylight beautiful country, if you didn't count the cities leveled into rubble by Allied heavy bombers. Walker was raised in the Susquehanna Valley of Pennsylvania, just south of the hard-coal region of Wilkes-Barre. As a boy he loved to roam the hemlock woods with his collie, Queen, and he had drunk in the magnificent countryside from Verdun to Briey, from Luxembourg to the Saar Valley. Now the deep forests, wooded hills, and lovely fields and orchards of the western Rhineland reminded him of home.

The half-track rode solidly, the rear tracks gripping the muddy lanes—four fast tons of bulletproof chassis and armor. Bulletproof, but not tank proof. Not artillery proof. With blackout headlights—slits of light in a metal hood—it was hard to see anything, and they went slow.

Walker led the first platoon of six half-tracks or "sonic cars." Each carried three men: driver, gunner—who also operated the radio—and sonic operator. They wore tanker's coveralls and wool caps under their helmets. Behind Walker's lead half-track at intervals were strung out second and third platoons. His platoon deployed along a front of five thousand yards—nearly three miles. The three platoons together would be spread out along twenty-five—an absurdly thin line.

At twenty-five years of age, he had fought in every campaign since Normandy. He wanted to become a teacher after the war. Walker knew the Big Push was coming. He'd been briefed by Major Williams, but really he could already feel it in his bones. This long into the war, it was not hard to read the signs: Every platoon in the line at once. Extraordinary security, even by the standards of the Special Troops. And this river, the boundary of Germany's heartland. Before they saddled up, he had told all his guys, "Be at your best tonight. We need your best production." They were all good guys and he trusted them. They'd never let him down before.

They backed the half-track into the overhanging cover of a cherry orchard near the river, stripped off the tarp covering the sonic equipment, then the sonic operator cranked the "coffee grinder" and the enormous wooden case holding six forty-watt Jenson speakers rose on a rotating bracket like an upright coffin out of the armored box. They pointed rearward, toward the Rhine.

Within minutes, sonic troops from the headquarters platoon appeared and strung copper telephone wire between Walker's half-track and the rest of the half-tracks in his platoon, then connected each platoon to the company command post. They would keep radio silence and communicate only by land line.

The driver, Jimmy Barrett, got out and dug a foxhole next to the half-track—that's where he usually spent the night, keeping guard with his carbine. Walker manned the .50-caliber machine gun in the turret. The sonic operator flicked on his flashlight and loaded the two magazines with spools of specially recorded magnetic wire. Each sonic car had a different program to play.

It was full dark now. Silent. Walker got the word on the field phone, told the sonic operator: It's time.

This was always the heart-stopping moment. The sonic operator pushed the "start" button and the generator roared alive. It was not much bigger than a lawn-mower engine, but starting up in that tense silence, it sounded like the loudest motor in the world. It went against every instinct in a soldier's nature to deliberately make noise within earshot of the enemy—yet that was exactly what they were doing. Nobody in any of the sonic cars had ever gotten used to it. One minute they were invisible in the quiet cover of the orchard, the next they were giving themselves away—on purpose.

And they were about to make even more noise.

The sonic operator started the first magazine unspooling at five feet per second, gradually ramped up the volume, and suddenly a metallic racket reverberated through the orchard. Heavy-duty motors groaned, tailgates slammed, soldiers cursed, sergeants barked out orders, more trucks arrived, work gangs complained. Anybody listening heard the noise of a whole fleet of trucks and several hundred men unloading ammunition and supplies.

All make-believe, all the sounds of a massive buildup for an assault. All the sounds of a target.

Walker had been briefed by Major Williams on the importance of the operation, and he recalls urging his men to do their best, then waiting night after night and wondering if the ruse was working. "You had to just sit back and hope—like you're cooking something, it's on the stove cooking, you're not sure what it's done, but it's cooking," he says. "That's the feeling I got—boy, we're just producing sound, sound, sound."

The Germans were close—out there in the blackness of a moonless midnight, just across the Rhine, waiting for the Americans to make their move.

• • •

In the shotgun seat of his jeep between Walker's and the river, Lt. Dick Syracuse could not make out the Rhine through the thick screen of riverine forest along its banks. The river itself was visible only in shadowy patches through the haze. It was a clear night following a sunny spring day, but not a single man in his security platoon of thirty-five men could see the stars. There was supposed to be a moon tonight, but it, too, remained invisible.

From Krefeld down to Düsseldorf—across the river—the chemical companies had been laying down oily smoke to confuse the Germans.

Syracuse would stay put here awhile, then circle around on the dirt road to check on the other positions—dug into foxholes.

The night went gradually from silence to sound. All around them, the misty darkness filled with all the ruckus of two restless divisions preparing for battle. All eighteen sonic cars were playing their "music."

Syracuse's job, as always, was recon and security: lead the sonic cars to the right location, then keep them from falling into enemy hands. Laid across the bed of his jeep was a bazooka, with a dozen rockets scattered carelessly nearby—in case they got hit by tanks. Invisible in the hazy darkness, enemy patrols were likely crawling about, counting tanks, trying to recognize the bumper markings on the trucks and the shoulder patches on the arms of soldiers. Trying to spot a two-star general's jeep outside a command post in the darkness behind him, watching who saluted whom and how quickly. Except everything here was an illusion.

Between the security platoon and the river was deployed a thin screen of infantry dug into foxholes, also invisible—and not enough to stop a real attack. And somewhere out there were also the 406th Combat Engineers, a rough-and-ready bunch of fighters under Capt. George Rebh—but still fewer than 175 armed soldiers.

Syracuse's guys knew he would go to the wall for them when it counted. He was also smart, with good instincts for keeping his people safe. Whenever he scouted out positions for the sonic cars and his squads, he always left them a back door—a fast way out if all hell broke loose. Thanks to planning and luck, they'd suffered very few casualties. As many times as they'd pulled off the show, it was always a little spooky. In a real line outfit, you'd have nothing to the left and right of you but more of your own guys, armed to the teeth with heavy weapons. But his men were spaced in three-man squads a couple hundred yards apart and each team was isolated, couldn't see the others. Nine of the teams had jeeps and .30-caliber machine guns. Two of the teams were mounted in armored half-tracks with .50-caliber machine guns.

Through wool glove liners, Syracuse fingered the cold grips of his tommy gun. Syracuse knew the noise around him wasn't real—he'd listened to the show for more than a year now. But some part of him was still irrationally convinced there was an army of trucks, artillery, and tanks behind him in the woods. Amazing.

For a twenty-five-mile stretch along the Rhine River, the night came alive with an eight-track symphony of battlefield racket:

The clatter of hammers on steel, the trademark noise of engineers assembling pontoon bridges for an armored crossing—which meant to anyone listening that they were days, maybe weeks, from assaulting the river.

The groaning of Ford motors and the grinding of heavy gears as Sherman medium tanks lurched into ranks. The muted chatter of nervous infantry in their foxhole bivouacs laughing, swearing, snoring, talking on the radio, betting on cards. The rumble of two-and-a-half-ton trucks coming and going, the banging of tailgates as ammunition and supplies are unloaded and stacked under camouflage netting. The faraway insect buzz of outboard motors being tested on the amphibious barges on a lake a few hundred yards back from the riverbank. At the dummy landing strip, an observation plane was heard to take off, and a few hours later, it bounced in for a landing.

And over the sonic noise, the sporadic bark of real antiaircraft guns and artillery.

All the sounds of two armored divisions—twenty thousand men and tanks—preparing for an assault.

The sound rose gradually, slacked off, punctuated by small silences, then blared out again and seemed to swirl around, move away, come back. A hundred yards from the massive speakers, it was hard to tell exactly where the sound was coming from. The deceptive fidelity was uncanny—the sound had depth and timbre. *Presence.* It would be fifty years before the movies had sound this true.

Sergeant Jimmy Laubheimer was having fun—sort of.

When the 30th and 70th Divisions stole out of the area, they left behind a scattering of artillery pieces and antiaircraft guns among the rubber "balloons." Jimmy and his driver had been racing around all night in their jeep and firing off the guns—a few rounds from this one, then a few rounds from another one, and so on. They were not shooting at anything in particular, just shooting for the noise and flash—like nervous green troops brought up from the reserves to beef up an assaulting division. As he put it, "Blissfully firing into space."

Except for a few combat engineers, not much of anybody was guarding them tonight, he knew—just a bunch of battle-rattles, the dregs of the infantry that the generals couldn't count on to cross that river. He tried not to think about it.

Back in the fall, somewhere in France, he had been blinded by an artillery blast. As a result, he would always have one damaged eye. But he never put in for the Purple Heart, never even went to see the medic, because then they might have shipped him off to the hospital and away from his buddies. They'd been working all night and were pretty exhausted. They'd just banged off a few rounds and were skidding down a muddy lane toward another battery when the jeep bumped over something big and hard. He got out to investigate, hunted around with his flashlight, and found a German hand grenade right there in the tire track. He tossed it away and went back to firing the guns, too exhausted to do anything else. But when the operation was all over, he remembered that odd bump under the jeep's tire and felt a delayed rush of fear.

In another clearing not far from the river, Sgt. Vic Dowd and his men were loading empty 105mm shells with flash powder and setting them off with an electrical charge. The flash was brilliant, totally harmless, and from a few miles away looked exactly like the flash of a real gun. The idea usually was to draw fire from an opposing enemy battery, then the real hidden American battery could spot the enemy guns by *their* flashes and knock them out. Tonight the object was just to put on a fireworks show, let the enemy think there were all sorts of artillery units out here firing to harass them. Even as he set off the flashes, Dowd reflected that it was a crazy tactic. "Live guns are going off and live guns are coming this way, and I'm sending off these stupid simulated bursts!" he says now. "It just seemed ludicrous to me."

Too often when they put on a convincing show, the Germans started bombarding them with artillery. They never forgot the terrifying helplessness of waiting out a barrage, and all of them describe it in virtually the same way. The shells rushed in over their heads with a noise like a freight train, then the explosion shook the earth and deafened them, knocking the wind out of them, and they clawed as deep into the mud as they could. Often they didn't even remember how they got on the ground. The theory at headquarters was that, since there were so few men occupying the sector—a skeleton crew of illusionists—the chances of the Germans hitting anybody was small. But when it had happened at Saarlautern, the theory was no consolation.

Dowd and his crew kept firing off flashes, while the Germans were lobbing in shells of their own—and getting better at it. At first the firing was light to moderate and not particularly accurate—firing just to disrupt American activity. Such random fire had the effect of keeping everybody constantly keyed up, on alert, since there wasn't any rhyme or reason to it. You couldn't predict when or where it would fall. The odds were heavily in your favor, but the very randomness of it was unnerving—which was exactly the point.

Then the Germans began to pour it in, and to hit what they were aiming at. Joseph P. Kelly's intelligence staff noted: "Peak of activity reported on 18 March with 48 shellreps consisting of 549 rounds of various calibers received. Firing prior to 18 March was scattered and inaccurate but on 18 March accurate C/Btry fire was received, continuing to end of period. A considerable portion of this C/Btry fire was rptd as being in the vicinity of dummy artillery positions."

The Germans were indeed hitting their targets—but the targets were the deliberate shams the Special Troops had so artfully emplaced and helpfully registered for the enemy guns with their own flash bombs. As the German shells found their marks, the camoufleurs scrambled around in the dark to repair the dummies punctured by shrapnel. Again, their amazing luck held, and though plenty of dummies were knocked out of action as hundreds of shells a day for five successive nights exploded around them, not one man from the 603d was hit.

The show seemed to be playing. The enemy was even daring aerial reconnaissance—this at a time in the war when American and British fighters ruled the skies and almost every city in Germany had been pounded in daylight raids by waves of heavy bombers, which the dwindling Luftwaffe squadrons were powerless to stop.

Each night, single planes would fly over fast and high—dropping parachute flares to illuminate the ground for their cameras. Intelligence reported: "While some of the flights may be using visual reconnaissance, the almost exclusive use of fast fighters, including jet-propelled planes, for this purpose indicate [sic] that the main reliance is being placed on photographic reconnaissance. Most of the aerial reconnaissance flights are carried out in the early morning or late afternoon when long shadows facilitate interpretation of photos."

The design of the dummies, coupled with the camoufleurs' art of carefully, but not too carefully, camouflaging their emplacement, created an authentic, three-dimensional landscape of threatening shadows to be photographed and believed. These recon flights were good news to Simenson and Schroeder—their show was at least drawing an audience. In the fake 30th Division task force, Schroeder explained the use of his AA batteries: "The antiaircraft had emplacements throughout the area serving a double purpose:

1. To keep enemy reconnaissance planes at a high altitude above the dummies and
2. To give an additional impression that there was a large concentration of troops and material in the area that needed protection. Barrages were fired at night to enhance that impression."

Fox was captivated by the spectacle. "On some nights, the AAA would send up fierce demonstrations of firepower, deadly beautiful displays which reminded me of the early nights on the Normandy beaches," he wrote. "We hoped the firing would suggest that the protected area below was bristling with anticipation."

In fact, things were heating up. On March 17, recon planes overflew the deception area morning, noon, and night. Beginning the following day and continuing until the real crossing up north, fighters swooped in low for strafing runs, and at intervals dive bombers dropped their loads on the dummy emplacements. On the ground, intelligence reported considerable road and railroad movement, indicating the arrival of reserve forces in the sector. It was becoming clear to G-2—Intelligence—that the hostile audience across the Rhine was growing extremely interested in the Special Troops and their fake divisions: "Up to 19 March our patrols E [east] of the R [Rhine] were able to accomplish their missions without too much opposition, finding a majority of the enemy outpost positions unoccupied. Beginning on 20 March enemy outposts became extremely alert and aggressive and reacted strongly against our patrols." Small arms, mortar, and machine-gun fire increased in forward areas, under a sky lit up by flares every night.

The American patrols brought back interesting news. Units facing the two bogus American divisions now included the 183d VDG, elements of the 176th Volksgrenadier Division, and most significantly, Parachute Lehr Regiment 2 and elements of the 2d Parachute Division. Additional elements of the VDG were believed to be in the Duisburg area at the northern boundary of XIII Corps, and all the identified units were supplemented by Volkssturm troops—hastily formed militias of boys, old men, and refugees drafted for one last stand. But the parachute troops were key—seasoned, reliable troops who could counterattack a bridgehead. It was parachute troops who had held Brest until it was no longer of any use to the invasion forces. If the parachute troops could be held here, they would be neutralized as surely as if they were surrounded, unavailable to oppose the bridgehead north at Wesel until it was too late.

All the signs were favorable, yet the whole operation was a colossal gamble. If it failed, if Ninth Army found the German 2d Parachute Division waiting across the river to catch the assault boats in the open, the crossing could be thwarted. Lots of men could die.

"In the whole range of human activities," wrote the wily old Prussian general Karl von Clausewitz, whose wisdom Simenson had studied at West Point, " war most closely resembles a game of cards."

At this late date, nobody seriously believed the Germans could still win the war, but some worried that they could somehow force a stalemate in the West. If they stopped Montgomery at the river, it would be months before he could concentrate the forces for another assault. Meanwhile, despite constant bombing, German industrial war production had reached its peak, V-rockets were still accumulating in the German arsenal, and Luftwaffe jets were shooting down Allied bombers. After the Bulge, nobody took for granted an easy German surrender.

"Optimism is generally proportional to your distance from the front," Fox wrote. "The further away you are, the cockier you get. When somebody shoots at you, the sky suddenly turns black. The other day I went over to the Rhine's edge, was overcome by a wave of pessimism, and came right back. It was a foolish thing to do."

As the days and hours ticked down, Simenson waited at Anrath. Schroeder waited at his fake 30th Division command post at Dulken. Blass erected dummies and guarded them. Tompkins drove his lieutenant from one position to another, ran between the front line and the company command post. Laubheimer fired off artillery. Dowd set off flash-bombs that only looked like artillery. Walker, Brown, Flinn, Barrett, and the rest played Manser's sonic programs day and night.

Syracuse and his platoon guarded the precious sonic cars and their crews, and Rebh's veteran combat engineers patrolled the whole area.

Fox broadcast phony troop movements, then monitored the radio traffic until it went silent just before the jump-off

Simenson listened to the artillery open up—a two-thousand-gun "serenade," with each weapon trained on the same small area, firing more than sixty-five thousand rounds in all from 90s, 105s, 155s, mortars, tanks, and tank destroyers, anything that would shoot. Thirty miles away, the flashes pinked the horizon like dawn.

"I remember we worked steadily day and night," Blass recalls. "But we had no idea of the Big Picture, of course." Nor did most of the Special Troops—enlisted men like Dowd, Laubheimer, Dahl, Biow, Masey, Morton, Brown, and Flinn. Though it was the climactic moment of their war of illusion, today, they remember very little about it.

This is ironic, but hardly surprising. The army deliberately told them no more than they needed to know to do their jobs. There was always the risk of capture, and in that event, knowledge was dangerous. It could ruin plans, cause the deaths of good men. What you didn't know, you couldn't tell to the enemy. Each worked in his own small sector, unaware of the sheer scope of the operation.

And they had been poised to invade Germany before, way back in September, before the lightning race across France got stopped dead on the Siegfried Line, and before the Germans overran their lines during the Battle of the Bulge, prolonging the war by half a year. The staff colonels, Major Williams in the sonic company, the captains, and even lieutenants like Walker, understood this was a defining moment. But to the enlisted men of the Special Troops, VIERSEN was just one more operation in a war that seemed to have no end, though by any sane reckoning, it should have ended long ago. When the war in Europe was over, they knew they were already slated to go to the Pacific war, but they didn't want to even think about that. One war was enough. Only when it was finished did they understand they had been part of a momentous undertaking, and only then was the scale of the risk apparent.

They did as they were ordered, day after day and night after night, but when that serenade of big guns popped off in the north, they all knew that something unusual was up.

Simenson, Schroeder, and Fox knew that the first waves of Old Hickories of the 30th Division were crossing the river, with the 79th Cross of Lorraine Division poised right behind them. Though he had long been criticized as overcautious, egomaniacal, high handed, arrogant, timid, neurotic, intolerant of American officers, and disdainful of American troops, Montgomery was the perfect figure to command the show. It was Montgomery who had written the book on battlefield deception at El Alamein, and now things had come full circle. The American Special Troops had learned how to practice deception better than their British tutors.

While Montgomery slept at his headquarters back in Holland—battle or no, he hit the sack at precisely 10:00 P.M. every night of the war—

Eisenhower spent the night prowling the front, wide awake, watching the American troops wrestle their assault boats into the river and cross.

Were the Panzers waiting for them? At that moment, were hundreds of machine guns and mortars spraying the river with lethal fire, cutting down the exposed infantry in the open carriers?

If they made it, the Cross of Lorraine Division would be right behind, and then the rest. And before the sun came up, armored bulldozers would breach the dikes and the bridge-builder tanks would lay down pontoons for the armor to cross. And the final campaign of the war would begin. That was the plan.

From the time the 23d Headquarters Special Troops was formed, this was the moment they'd been training for, rehearsing for, under live fire on the night battlefields of Europe: deception as a way to attack the enemy on his home ground and win the war for keeps.

At 2:00 A.M., the artillery up north went still. That's how John Walker knew the attack had begun. "I guess the ease of noise in the distance is how I knew," he recalls. "Things moved away, they subsided." Somehow it seems fitting that such important news should reach him, a sonic soldier, by sound—or the absence of it.

The crossing at Wesel took the enemy completely by surprise. The 30th and 79th Divisions met only disorganized resistance and suffered only thirty-one killed—an astonishingly low number of casualties for such a large-scale attack. Within hours, they were driving armor across the Rhine. Farther north, the British and Canadian armies ran into somewhat heavier opposition, but still they crossed in force on schedule, and the war was all but won. After all the long preparations, the crossing was swift, finished in a few hours—though the silent passage across the river in the dead of night must have seemed a lifetime long to the troops hunkered in the first waves of assault boats.

Hector Truly, the genius behind the whole plan, spent the night at Ninth Army Headquarters, watching the fruits of his plan unfold. He left no record of his thoughts, but when the first reports came back from across the river, he must have felt an immense glow of pride and relief for all those American lives he had saved. Surely that mattered far more to him than the Bronze Star he earned for inventing and overseeing the deception plan.

During the night of the crossing, according to plan, the Special Troops washed off their fake bumper markings, stripped off their bogus sleeve patches, recovered all their traffic and command-post signs, deflated their dummies, and were already in the process of fading away.

By daylight on March 24, Schroeder and Simenson reported to their troops that the ruse had worked—Ninth Army was across the Rhine in force. Tompkins noted with satisfaction in his war diary, "Generals who viewed our stuff from air yesterday claimed a great deal of credit for this deceptive move goes to us. Jerry must have copped it all with his camera past couple of days. 13th Corps really think we're hot stuff."

Even as the Special Troops packed up their show, Phase II of the large deception, EXPLOIT, continued. For the next twenty-four hours, from noon to noon, Corps artillery kept up the charade that an attack was impending near Düsseldorf, lobbing 5,179 rounds across the river. And 103 tank destroyers fired an additional 1,367 rounds—setting ablaze an oil warehouse and shooting objects floating in the river that might be mines.

And as G-2 Kelly reported, the parachute troops continued to hold across the river from the deception troops, belatedly releasing only one regiment to reinforce the single depleted division opposing Ninth Army: "The continued presence of 2 Prcht Div in the N of the Corps zone after the crossings further north by XII Corps on 24 March appears to indicate enemy concern over a possible crossing in the MUNDELHEIM area. Road and rail activity in enemy rear areas from 18 to 20 March indicated a possible movement of reserves into the area opposite XIII Corps. Accurate and well coordinated enemy fires from 18 March on indicates that enemy intelligence agencies were functioning in a creditable manner and the considerable increase in air activity from 18 March to the close of the period is ample evidence of the increased enemy concern over this sector."

Though he had created an Anglo-American juggernaut and placed it in position to deliver the decisive blow to Germany, once across the river, Montgomery lost the center ring and with it, control over U.S. Ninth Army. Montgomery had yearned for the glory of capturing Berlin, but the Russians were already closing in on the ruined city, which lay within the sector allotted to their control by the Yalta Conference, at which the Allies had long ago planned the division of postwar Germany. So Eisenhower sent Montgomery's 21st Army Group northeast, to capture Hamburg and the Baltic ports—a sideshow to the real endgame.

Three weeks after crossing the Rhine, Ninth Army, once again reunited with Bradley's 12th Army Group—as it had not been since before Christmas, when the Battle of the Bulge split the American line—attacked south and linked up with First Army, which was charging north from its bridgehead at Remagen. Together on April 18, they forced the surrender of 325,000 Wehrmacht troops trapped in the Ruhr pocket, captured 30 generals, and virtually eliminated German resistance. Ninth Army pressed on and was halted only fifty miles from Berlin on Eisenhower's orders. Thus the Americans, displaying mobility and initiative, checkmated the Germans in the west.

Ralph Ingersoll glowingly chronicled the fruits of Ninth Army's unopposed crossing of the Rhine, as they cut off the entire industrial valley of the Ruhr. "It was in the bag for the British—only within a scant two weeks of crossing under Montgomery's command, the American Ninth Army was literally to run away from Montgomery's control and to justify its insubordination beyond criticism by forming the northern pincer of the most brilliant encirclement action won by either side during entire World War II—and probably in all military history."

The Special Troops had accomplished their most important mission—and, as it turned out, their last. VIERSEN proved to be their finest hour—and the beginning of the end of their usefulness to the Allied war effort. From now on, events moved so quickly, the Third Reich collapsed so swiftly, that deception was extraneous. Within six weeks, Hitler was dead, and the Russians were in Berlin, and, with the American armies, had broken the Wehrmacht into unconditional surrender.

Fox reported just how well things had gone—and why. "The beauty of the Operation lay in three facts:

1. the contribution of the 23d was only part of a giant spectacle involving practically all of the Ninth Army;

2. the 23d had reached its highest state of efficiency and all its deceptive strength was employed;

3. from all evidences, the operation was a success."

He wrote his bride-to-be, "With four armies across the Rhine, I don't see how this part of the war can last much longer."

For once, Reeder could report unequivocal results on a grand scale. "Unlike the majority of deception operations, the results in this case appear fairly obvious from the intelligence reports and from the low casualties suffered by the troops engaged in the real operation."

"Were the above elaborate, and sometimes annoying, measures successful?" the real 30th Division Headquarters asked, then answered its own question: "A German Order of Battle map captured by the 79th Division showed all the U.S. Divisions WEST of the RHINE, NORTH OF COLOGNE, in their locations except for the 79th Div which was shown considerably further SOUTH than it actually was, and the 30th Div, whose location was not shown anywhere. . . . So it is apparent that the extensive deception measures undertaken were highly successful and resulted in the attack of the XVI Corps being a complete surprise to the enemy with a consequent saving of many American lives."

The German map overlay was captured hours *before* the attack.

Way back at Pine Camp, unbeknownst to them at the time, the sonic company had been training to cover the crossing of the Rhine—the ultimate sonic deception. Just as in their training film, scripted while they were still fumbling to master their new equipment, they had come through brilliantly.

The camoufleurs too—trained for one mission and then forced to learn a more complex and demanding one in action—had shown their stuff. They had created shadows realistic enough to fool stereoscopic cameras. The radiomen, castigated after their first mission back in Normandy for their inept handling of traffic, had starred in a radio program worthy of rave reviews. The security platoons and combat engineers had enforced airtight secrecy around the mission.

"This operation was the most extensive and most satisfactory in which the 23d Hq Sp Trs has participated," Reeder wrote. "Because of the scope of the operation, its careful planning and execution by all concerned, and its evident success, many matters connected therewith are worthy of study as a basis for planning future deception operations."

For once, the Special Troops had been allowed to operate on a grand scale, using all their men and resources. Truly's plan had been inspired, the timing had been perfect, and the occasion suited their talents. They were at the peak of their effectiveness, and working with an army staff that understood their mission, they performed brilliantly.

Special Plans Branch agreed, first noting all the reasons that deception had not always worked as effectively as it might have in previous operations: "*Despite all these handicaps, it may be stated flatly that tactical cover and deception was effective whenever the minimum requirements essential to its success were fulfilled.* An excellent example of the successful employment of tactical deception was in the Rhine crossing operation, when the enemy was lead [sic] to misappreciate the intentions of the 9th Army. This action alone provides sufficient evidence on the practicability of tactical deception in battle."

A more personal kudos comes from Charles Kizina, a loader and driver for the 135th Anti-Aircraft Artillery (AAA) battalion, Ninth Army, attached to the 23d for the VIERSEN operation. Kizina was near Krefeld, firing real guns and also helping repair dummies nicked by shrapnel.

"We had ninety-millimeter guns, so we had ninety-millimeter bal-loons," he recalls. "We didn't know what was going on. The Germans threw some artillery on us, and the shrapnel would knock out the balloons, so I was going around repairing them and pumping them back up."

After the war, Kizina was assigned to Dachau, where thousands of Ger-man POWs were being held. He spoke German and, working in the prison-ers' compound, got to talking to one of the Germans POWs there, who told him his last action of the war had been at Krefeld.

Kizina said, "Well, I was there!"

"Well, when the smoke lifted, we knew we didn't have a chance," the POW said. "The Americans had so many guns, so many tanks and other equipment, we knew we didn't have a chance, so we had to give up."

Kizina told him the truth: "What you saw was rubber guns and rubber tanks, all balloons."

The POW was adamant. *"Nein! Nein! Es ist nicht wahr!"* He insisted: No! No! That's not true! "I saw them with my own eyes—it was the real thing."

All these decades later, Kizina gives the Special Troops their highest praise, perhaps the only recognition that truly matters. "These men are real heroes," he states with conviction. "Not heroes because they killed a lot of Germans—heroes because they saved thousands of American lives."

None of the Special Troops would ever call himself a hero—each was just doing a job that was part army, part show biz. Like most GIs, they rarely knew why they were doing what they were doing, but they played their parts conscientiously and with flair. They had learned their business well—their "Big Show" was a rousing success.

For the first time in the war, after completing twenty-one operations with four armies in five countries, the Special Troops received a unit com-mendation. General Simpson, commander of the Ninth Army, expressed his gratitude and appreciation for the Special Troops on March 29. His let-ter read in part, "The unit was engaged in a special project, which was an important part of the operation. The careful planning, minute attention to detail, and diligent execution of the tasks to be accomplished by the per-sonnel of the organization reflect great credit on this unit. . . . I desire to commend the officers and men of the 23d Headquarters Special Troops, 12th Army Group, for their fine work and to express my appreciation for a job well done."

At last, official recognition for their secret contribution to victory. It's hard to overstate the importance of Simpson's citation. Virtually every vet-eran interviewed mentioned it with pride, a signal confirmation of their contribution to winning the war. They had worked for more than nine months in utter secrecy, never recognized for the risks they took on behalf of other troops. Now, by a simple and sincere letter from a general they respected, they felt vindicated.

With that commendation from General Simpson, it began to dawn on the enlisted men of the Special Troops that they had been part of something significant, probably even historical. There was an enduring rumor that the Special Troops also would be awarded a presidential unit citation, but that honor never came. Still, the officers who knew the larger plan and witnessed the cunning deception understood just what it had made possible.

"A half a million men crossing the Rhine," Simenson reminisces, "and it was just beautiful."

Act III
Closing the Show

HAROLD LAYNOR

FOURTEEN

STRIKING THE SET
April–August 1945

. . . don't saddle your folks and your friends with inside stuff
that they'd rather not have the responsibility of knowing.
　　　　　　　　　　　—Army Separation Lecture, 1945

The American troops—in full battle dress and heavily armed—marched through Vohenstrauss, a small German village sixty miles east of Nuremberg on the Czechoslovakian border. Under their commander, Lt. Col. Cliff Simenson, the 2d battalion, 291st Regiment, 90th Infantry Division, were making a deliberate show of force. Other troops stationed themselves along the route, rifles at the ready, alert for any sign of resistance. The 90th had hit the beach the day after D-Day and fought on the front lines through three bloody seasons of combat, across the Seine, the Moselle, and the Rhine. They looked the part of battle-toughened veterans.

Along the streets, townspeople sullenly watched the troops tramp past. Nobody waved American flags or threw flowers as they had in France and Belgium and Luxembourg, and no smiling pretty girls darted into their ranks for a quick liberation kiss, but when the American colors paraded past, the men grudgingly removed their hats.

Things had gone suddenly quiet on this front. But the Germans occupied strongholds across the rugged Bohemian Forest in Czechoslovakia, and even this close to the end, Simenson wasn't trusting them to surrender easily.

Simenson, recently reassigned from the Special Troops, recalls, "The shooting stopped, and we were very, very jumpy. We said, where is it going to hit us? What are they up to? These were war veterans, they'd been shooting at the Germans actively on the Czech border, and as a battalion commander, I said we've got to do something—so that's when I became a chickenshit officer at the head, and I took action."

One elderly man failed to uncover his head for the flag—Simenson immediately ordered him arrested and thrown in jail for three days. He was out to make a point. "I said if that old sonofabitch is going to do something like that, what's he going to do when we're not looking? I wanted to paint a picture of a very tough guy at the head."

Then Simenson called a meeting of all the *Bürgermeisters* in the area—ninety-two answered his summons. "And my first thought was, for crap's sake, who am I to be telling these guys what to do? It puzzled me." But he covered up his own doubts and projected nothing but surety and confidence.

They waited, hats in hands, to hear what this tough American officer had to say. Simenson laid down the law. "I can't keep law and order," he told the *Bürgermeisters*, "but I know how to use force—and if I do, I will use too much force. You keep the law and order, or I'll eliminate you."

Then just to impress them that his authority was arbitrary and absolute, he threw the interpreter in jail alongside the man who had failed to show proper respect for the American flag—where he, too, enjoyed good army chow and a warm bunk.

It was all an act—a soft-spoken, thoughtful officer masquerading as a ruthless conquering tyrant. "I wanted them to get the position that I was one tough sonofabitch," Simenson says. "And this worked wonderfully well."

He had no problems with law and order—the *Bürgermeisters* kept their people under control and the area remained remarkably quiet. Outside of town, Simenson discovered hundreds of bodies of slave laborers killed by the Nazis as they fled the advancing Americans. He ordered the townspeople to dig up the main avenue in the middle of town. "We buried them there—put a monument up for them," he says. "Later, I went back there as an attaché, the road was paved over and the monument was gone. That's the Nazi for you."

He had deceived them, and in return, they had caused the evidence of their own civic atrocity to vanish.

About the time that D Company of the camoufleurs was getting plastered by 88s in Saarlautern back in mid-March, Colonel Reeder was agitating for a promotion to brigadier general. Specifically, he wanted Simenson to support a new Table of Organization and Equipment for the 23d that would call for a general to command it. Then he, Reeder, would at last get his star.

"I told him I didn't think I could support that," Simenson says. There were plenty of colonels running around, so nobody paid any attention to one more—maintaining a low profile for the Special Troops. "But you put a general in there, right away it draws a whole lot of interest. We shouldn't have a general at the top. He should be separate, in some other position, but not on the 23d. And I lasted two weeks after that."

Relieved as operations officer shortly after the Rhine crossing and replaced by a major—his reward for a job extraordinarily well done—Simenson languished as antiaircraft officer for two more weeks and then, with the war in Europe nearly finished, at last got his infantry battalion—first with the 75th Division, which almost immediately left for the States, and then with the 90th. His deception days were over.

He had trained these troops, developed their mission, invented their tactics, led them in the field for ten months, and now he disappeared from their ranks without ceremony.

Other officers, too, found themselves suddenly transferred out to units where they could be more useful. Hector Truly departed for England as quietly as Simenson. Captain Howard Raynor, who had been badly wounded in the leg and thigh during the artillery barrage at Saarlautern, briefly returned—to the delight of his men—but his wounds kept troubling him and before long, he, too, was gone for good.

Instead of ending the war as a cohesive unit, the Special Troops simply began to dissolve.

Suddenly, the show was over. Just like that—the war moved beyond them too fast for there to be a front line anymore. The Order of Battle became a five-army race across Germany, with the Russians closing in on the eastern suburbs of Berlin. They all knew the war was over days—even weeks—before the official coded announcement from Eisenhower's headquarters was "broken" by signalmen of the Special Troops temporarily attached to Bradley's 12th Army Group Headquarters.

The end came more like the circus leaving town than like the climax of a monumental cataclysm. All at once, the lot was empty, the trash scuttling past in the wind along the deserted grounds, which had been packed with troops only days before, and now it was time to collect all the equipment, fold the tents, and strike the set for good.

Ralph Ingersoll at Special Plans Branch couldn't even tell for sure whether the war ended on May 7 or May 8—there was an ongoing argument at Bradley's headquarters about exactly which day should be celebrated as V-E Day. He lifted his head from the map he had been studying the whole war and went outside into the spring sunlight like a man in a daze— suddenly the great unifying purpose was gone. The focus of millions of lives had simply vanished like a waterspout spinning into nothingness over the open sea.

Harold Dahl pulled guard duty on V-E Day and missed the wild celebra- tion: "As usual, those who could celebrate were not the ones who had the most to celebrate," he wrote. "Another thing for G.I.s over here, of course, is the knowledge that there isn't much point in celebrating half a job. What all of us want is some homelife—a chance to start building our families— and we all know we are still prisoners of the Army until after the Japs go down, too."

Hal Laynor was still in Paris recuperating when the end came. He wrote jubilantly, "I prayed and got drunk as a lord last night marching through the streets singing with the conglomeration of French & Americans in a victory parade."

The war was over, and it left behind a void of relief, elation, and a slight bewilderment. As much as all the guys yearned to be home, in truth the end also came as a letdown. One day there was a war, a great cause—the next day, there was not. In Europe, the Special Troops' reason for being vanished. And hovering over their imaginations like the indistinct loom of a distant storm lay the invasion of Japan. Weeks before the German surren- der, they'd been shown a film called *Two Down and One to Go*, explaining the redeployment of troops to the Pacific.

Halfway across the world, Julian Sollohub, the commanding officer who had formed the 603d Engineer Camouflage Battalion back in 1942, experi- enced a different kind of V-E Day. He, too, had finally gotten his wish: he was assigned as division combat engineer for the 32d Division, the Michigan- Wisconsin National Guard, in the Philippines, and was building an assault road under fire near Agno, Luzon, when his moment of heroism arrived.

A Japanese patrol had infiltrated the division area. Sollohub gathered a squad of engineers and personally led them into combat. His Silver Star ci- tation for gallantry in action reads in part, "The enemy were contacted and a vigorous fight ensued, during which a number of our men were wounded. In spite of these losses, Colonel Sollohub led the patrol in a direct assault through the thick underbrush. He came upon three Japanese soldiers, and in an exchange of fire killed all three of them."

Like the other officers, Fred Fox was asked to state his preference for a future with the army—the choices ranging from "get out as soon as possi- ble" to "want to stay in for thirty years as part of the regular army." He wrote Hannah, "I think you would have voted as I voted: 'Will stay in until end of emergency' (meaning V-J)."

Even with the war against Germany finished, the country remained a spooky place, a hostile country, a land where a GI could never quite let down his guard. "The nights in Europe have much more dread in them than those in the States," wrote Fox, who routinely pulled duty as officer of the guard. "Take last night for instance. It was balmy with a nice moon in a quaint village. If I had been home with you the darkness would have held all sorts of wonders and little lights. But here in Germany all the shades were drawn and your imagination runs to fearful, lurking things."

Dave Wynshaw remembers pulling guard duty at Düsseldorf, shortly after the Rhine crossing—a night when he almost killed one of his own men. The residents were all under strict curfew to stay indoors, and he had been ordered to shoot to kill any German who so much as stuck his head out a window. "I'm standing there all alone in Düsseldorf looking down the street. No one around, very quiet. All of the sudden, I heard a window open. I turned around, ejected a shell, made sure there was a shell in the chamber, and I took aim and I looked up there and who was it? Duran the cook—who was opening his window to get some air." Wynshaw was a crack shot—he wouldn't have missed. "I never said a word to him, how close he was to getting killed."

After the war, Wynshaw went on to become a top executive at Columbia Records, working routinely with Barbra Streisand, Tony Bennett, Jim Nabors, and other entertainers.

Not every moment was heavy with dread. "I remember this fellow Max David, our platoon sergeant. He was really a rough, tough character, but a very funny guy," Arthur Shilstone recalls. "Completely uneducated, but very intelligent, and I would consider him a leader of men." David always got a kick out of the way the artists in his platoon whipped out their sketch books and paintbrushes and oils—he called them "erls"—to capture every new scene throughout the war. "One day we were in Germany at the end of the war, we were bivouacked on the side of a hill," Shilstone says. "And I was writing a letter or doing a drawing or something, and I saw David up on this hill—it was evening—with another guy."

Max David yelled, "Shilstone! Shilstone! Get up here, quick!"

"And I thought, *Geez, the war's over, what could this be?*"

When Shilstone reached the top of the hill, David swept one hand toward the magnificent sunset and slapped the other to his breast as he melodramatically declared, "Oh, if I only had me fuckin' erls!"

Because he had shown himself to be a superb writer who paid attention to details, Fox was designated by Reeder as unit historian. Thus he began the enjoyable task of compiling maps, anecdotes, and statistics. A headquarters friend, former illustrator for *Cosmopolitan*, went to work designing and painting a cover. Stateside, he would finish the work with William Flemer III.

On 6 June 1945, Reeder threw a party for all his officers to commemorate D-Day. Cognac, gin, and Champagne flowed liberally, chilled by ice brought from Wiesbaden with the daily messenger. A troupe of ten displaced Russians danced acrobatically and sang to an accordion and piano, three guitars strummed lightning folk tunes, and, as Fox recorded, "For an evening, the black shadow of the Soviet burst into a thousand rainbows."

After the Rhine campaign, without a stage for any more shows, the Special Troops took on new duties—once again, operating in separate contingents. Fox noted, "The command was immediately split to the four winds and given some very strange assignments."

Part of Signal Company, Special went to First Army as a monitoring unit for Corps, handling communications with far-flung divisions. It reached Pollwitz on the Czechoslovakia border. The wire platoon worked for Third Army recovering costly "spiral-4" telephone wire. In five weeks they rolled up eight hundred miles of the stuff at five hundred dollars per mile—saving the taxpayers four hundred thousand dollars. Another part of the Signal Company served in the code room of 12th Army Group and on May 7 "broke" the surrender announcement received from Eisenhower's headquarters. Fifteenth Army took the remainder of the Special Troops and assigned them to XXIII Corps "to ride herd on a hundred thousand hungry, homeless, haunted Europeans." The displaced persons—"DPs"—included men, women, and children of twenty-six nationalities, including lots of Poles and Russians, freed from concentration camps.

The 23d Headquarters staff took over the Hotel Hermes in Idar-Oberstein, also headquarters of XXIII Corps. Now the troops wore snappy, clean Eisenhower jackets, and ties were mandatory. Life took on a strange normalcy—strange, because they were still occupying the territory of their enemies. "If you have any more trouble with maid service, I suggest that you hire a one-time Nazi," Fox wrote home. "We have two cleaning our present house and their ceiling wage is $5.50 per month. We are not allowed to talk to them or even smile. While I was shaving yesterday morning I tested them by whistling Martin Luther's A MIGHTY FORTRESS IS OUR GOD and they listened very respectfully."

Fox set up his office in a factory that made ersatz honey butter. "Our office has LONG LIVE THE FÜHRER! in white-wash every ten feet around the wall," he wrote. "Almost every available space (where we would put up 'Drink Coca-Cola—It's Refreshing') has been used for a party slogan: WHAT HAVE YOU DONE FOR THE FÜHRER TODAY? HAIL VICTORY! VICTORY OR DEATH! HEIL HITLER! etc., etc., etc. It is a complete snow job—black, bloody snow."

Even as the fighting swept inexorably across Germany, news began to come in from liberated slave-labor and concentration camps. Red Sonnenfeld, who had created the sports leagues at Fort Meade and then left the camoufleurs for demolition duty with the combat engineers, met up with his old unit in Germany. His assignment was to clean up the notorious concentration camps at Dachau and Buchenwald—including bulldozing the emaciated corpses of slaughtered Jews into mass graves. "Some of it was so evil that it just washed out of my mind—because at first, Christ, I had nightmares after I'd been to the concentration camps."

The Nazis, abetted by millions of ordinary Germans, had done their best to wipe out the Jews of Europe. In his letters, Fox meditated often on the dangerous complacency that had made possible such an abominable state policy. "I don't like the idea of being a reformer," he wrote. "They usually are such cold, hypocritical, abnormal people. But if the gentle people don't stir themselves, they will be carried every which way by the swirling tongues of dirty men like Goebbels. I'm afraid we're going to have to fight for the rest of our lives."

But though Fox found the Germans stubborn and irritating in their self-righteous fanaticism, he also admired the energetic way they immediately cleared up the rubble in their streets—though their houses lay in "ruins." "Don't run over this word quickly. A city in ruins is a very depressing sight. There are no roofs. Walls are jagged and bare. You can see through all the buildings and there is nothing inside."

And among the ruins labored only the very old and children—he and his comrades saw no young men. "If we do, they are on crutches or wear black leather gloves at the end of a limp arm." But women and children were everywhere. "It is hard to look sternly on these cute little blond pigtails. They are the prettiest and cleanest children we've seen yet," he wrote. "You can look at one of the tiny blond kids and wonder whether he'll be goose-stepping 20 years from now."

The whole show had been marinated in secrecy from the beginning. In Fox's case, from the moment he had been bigoted—given clearance beyond the designation "top secret"—for D-Day, he had moved from one masquerade to the next, never able to write home about even the most basic facets of his duty, and the constant habit of dissembling, covering up, even outright lying about his activities began to wear thin. "Someday we can tell each other *everything!*" he wrote Hannah exultantly. "I'm sick of burning papers, avoiding stereotyped phraseology, saying: 'Awfully sorry old man but that's TOP SECRET.' "

The habit of hush-hush persisted among enlisted men as well. On the one-year anniversary of D-Day, Dahl wrote his mother and sister, "By the way—anything I say is just between us & no information about me is to be told to any newspaper. O.K.?"

From April 11, the Special Troops headquarters company acted as a DP staff section for XXIII Corps—keeping track of a mountain of paperwork in several languages—while the rest of the troops took over management of five camps in a sixteen-hundred-square-mile area across the Luxembourg border in the Saar-Palatinat. The camoufleurs took charge of camps at Bitburg, Trier, and Wittlich; the sonic company at Lebach; and the combat engineers at Baumholder. Their shepherding and security duty was by turns boring, frustrating, difficult, and heartbreaking.

Facing a chronic food shortage, the sonic platoons hunted deer with their machine guns to feed the displaced persons at Lebach—who boiled up moonshine out of potato peels in the camp kitchen. The sonic troops looked the other way, since the alcohol seemed to improve morale and keep the troublemakers quiet.

"Our job was to keep them from taking revenge against the Germans," sonic radioman and gunner Bill Brown recalls. "We were supposed to shoot them if they left camp. But when they ran, you know, we would just fire over their heads. We'd been fighting the Germans for a year and a half—we didn't care what they did to the Germans."

At the DP camp, Ellsworth Kelly wandered among his charges, drawing portraits of their haunted faces, always requesting that the subject sign his or her likeness. "They never laughed, they never smiled," he says. His collection of portraits shows the refugees moving like shadowy ghosts among the drab, derelict buildings in which they lived.

The camp in the hills outside Trier was typical—cleared of vegetation, organized around a black-cinder drill field and blocks of apartments. Trier was the oldest city in Germany, founded in the sixteenth century B.C. under the Roman emperor Augustus as Augusta Treverorum, later the seat of the Roman Empire in the West. Now the great city was a colossal ruin. The battle had passed right through. In the Cathedral of Trier, the mausoleum for twenty-five archbishops and electors, was secreted the so-called Holy Coat of Christ. A gift of Saint Helena, it was the fabled robe Christ wore to the cross, which Fox had read about while fighting alongside the 82d Airborne in Normandy.

If Fox ever visited the relic, or even knew it was there, he made no mention of it in his letters. He did note the death of Roosevelt on April 12 with mixed emotions. "I never thought he was the Great President that many people considered him. I was shocked and sorry when he died. I feel that he has done much for us but has weakened us too. We became so dependent on him."

Headquarters Company was lined up and told that Roosevelt was dead. Somebody said, "I wonder who the vice-president is." Memorial music played on loudspeakers all day long in honor of FDR.

The Special Troops also found themselves now protectors of their former enemy—and it didn't go over well with many of the men who had lost buddies, who had witnessed the destruction in France, heard the horror stories of German atrocities in Luxembourg and Belgium, and seen with their own eyes the pitiful plight of the former slave laborers of the Nazi Reich.

"Incidentally," Laubheimer wrote, "when we were in Germany during those last days, we could find no Nazis. Everyone said they had been innocent victims of Hitler and the 'Black Shirts,' so we had to wonder where the hordes that had been shooting at us came from."

Ingersoll, who had lived through weeks of London's Blitz, campaigned in North Africa, and stayed with Bradley's advance headquarters throughout the European campaign, wrote, "The Germans were conspicuously healthy. You could see with your own eyes that they had sucked the blood of Europe and grown fat on it."

The Special Troops saw prosperous Germans living in fine homes with plenty to eat, relatively untouched by the privations of war, except in the cities like Trier that had been fought over.

"Here are all the things which all the other countries have had to do without," Richard Morton wrote home. "There are cars, tractors, bicycles. There are fine furnishings, and all well kept. There are large stores of coal, wood, all types of food, including meat, preserves, vegetables, etc. . . . In fact it stands in such contrast to all we've seen elsewhere and represents all that was pillaged and plundered and confiscated from all the other peoples to the point where I personally would like to see every home razed to the ground just as Sherman did on his famous march through Georgia to the sea. . . ."

Morton bunked on the floor of the study of a large house. "On the desk were several framed portraits of different ones of the family," he noted. "Of the ones who wore the Nazi uniform we politely took the photo out, tore it to bits, and put it back in the frame."

Dahl had similar impressions. "Everything here is pretty, except the ruined town," he wrote, "—the apple trees are in blossom, the hills flanking the river are just lovely. Way too good for the miserable characters the Germans are. They look pretty good now—poking around in the ruins & pushing wheelbarrows down the street just like we used to see the French doing. But, take it from me, plenty of them *still* persist in thinking of themselves as the master race."

Tompkins reacted with equal distaste for the Germans. "Rode in on German's milk wagon as guard against Russian bandits 7:00 this A.M.," he wrote in his diary on April 15. "Russians and Poles stealing everything they can get their hands on and I don't blame them. Resented having to guard a Goddam Heinie. Some Russians are hiding in hills with weapons and raid German homes at night. If we were smart we'd turn our backs."

A few days later, two Russian soldiers trying to buy food were murdered and others pitchforked by a mob of German villagers. Two platoons of camouflage engineers raided the town. Tompkins recorded the encounter: "Russians went first and when crowd came out with pitchforks, Jeeps with 50's closed in. Russians choked hell out of Heinies and Tony [Young] let loose with 50's to stop Heinies from running away. A Russian hopped a German who was coming at Beef [Charles Boullianne] with a pitchfork. Six of them were arrested."

The situation in Germany was chaos. Russian deserters from *both* armies, escaped DPs with vengeance on their mind, old-fashioned bandits and thieves—all roamed the Saar-Palatinate stealing, killing livestock and occasionally people, terrorizing the populace. And the locals weren't always the innocent victims—they, too, took out their frustrations on hapless refugees. And thousands of Russians, Poles, and other Slavs either didn't want to go home or had no home to which to return—the Nazis had seen to that. They lived off the land, feeling no sympathy for the Germans who had abetted their enslavement and the slaughter of their landsmen.

In an irony that would seem heavy-handed if concocted by a novelist, the Special Troops—most of whom had gotten through the whole European campaign without firing their weapons—now found themselves shooting to kill. And not Germans, as they had expected, but Russians, allies, the victims of some of the worst German atrocities. On April 26, Tompkins pulled guard duty, but he recorded the violent day's events in his diary: "Raid on Russians—Wehrmacht sympathizers who were raiding town. [William] Senat killed two and one was wounded. Messy business.

It's one hell of a problem. You don't know what to think. LeHive and I went out this evening to hunt a couple of Russians who were supposed to have kidnapped 8 children. No luck."

Jack Masey recalls seeing the two Russians shot by Senat. "And I saw these bodies—they were like sixteen- or seventeen-year-olds, lying in a field," he says, regret in this voice that such violence had to mark the end of their war. "And he was there with his gun. He said, 'Look, I had to do it—they were killing people. I had no choice.'"

The following day, Tompkins, Paul Seckel, George Vander Sluis, and Masey were detailed out to a country estate to guard a German family from Russian raiders. The family had lost two sons killed in the Luftwaffe. Remembering a high school friend who had been shot down and killed over Germany, Tompkins wrote, "It made me cringe to think we were actually protecting them."

There was pressure to keep the Russians corralled so they could be repatriated—the Russians were holding American POWs and threatened not to return them unless all their own people were handed back. Victor Dowd remembers patrolling for escaped Russians who had been raiding food from the countryside. "Now in my opinion, who gives a damn?" he says. "The Germans were our enemy and the Russians were our ally. And here I am with my .45 automatic going through the woods looking for Russians! And I captured one! Thank God I never had to pull my trigger, because I don't think I'd have been able to live with myself." Dowd heard some rustling in the woods, yelled for whoever it was to surrender, and a scared eighteen-year-old Russian gave himself up without a struggle. "And I breathed a sigh of relief," Dowd says.

Not all the search parties ended so happily, however. Another kind of pressure was coming down from above, the need to make examples out of some of the runaways and so discourage others.

"They were strange people who were outwardly friendly but totally disregarded any kind of authority," Laubheimer wrote of the Russians. "One day, we located a Russian who had climbed a tree to avoid detection. When he was ordered to come down, he pulled a pistol from his belt and aimed it at us. Not waiting to see whether or not he was serious, we shot him in the rear end."

Told that way, the incident sounds almost comical—but Laubheimer wasn't the only one who shot the Russian. Others in the patrol shot him at least thirteen more times. It was a complicated moment. Some were proud of having killed a marauding Russian. One even saved his empty shell casings as souvenirs of the encounter. Others felt ashamed or saddened by what they considered a needless death. Dowd—who was not on that patrol—recalls hearing a lieutenant bragging about the kill, and the officer's behavior revolted him. "What the hell's enjoyable about somebody dying? In an incident like this, which was trivial?" he says, still troubled by the death. "I have this vague memory of this person bleeding to death and this guy being happy about it. That's the story I heard. It's not a good story."

In retrospect, it became clear why the Russians were so unruly. "We were gathering up the displaced-person laborers from Germany and we were sending the Dutch back to Holland, and the Belgians to Belgium and the French to France and so on," William Flemer recalls. "And we also had a bunch of Russians, and we wanted to send them back to Russia, and they rioted—they didn't want to go back." They called in a detachment of Russian marines. "They came in and beat the tar out of them, loaded them up in trucks."

As the trucks rolled out of the camp, the displaced persons aboard kept crying out to their American keepers: "They're going kill us when we get back!"

And guys like Flemer kept reassuring them, "No, no, you're Russians—you'll be welcomed back."

Shortly after the war, a Russian delegation visited Flemer's nursery in Princeton as part of a cultural exchange program. Flemer asked if they knew what had been the fate of all those repatriated Russians. And they said, "Oh, yeah—they were all killed."

Even before the end was announced, new rumors made the rounds. Morton wrote home, "Well, as you are no doubt reading in your papers the past days, the news is very good, and appears to be more like the beginning of the end than anything so far, but we always guard against overoptimism."

The most persistent rumor held that they would be home for the Fourth of July, then train for redeployment against Japan—and for once, the rumor turned out to be true. On April 28, the Special Troops were relieved from camp duty by field artillery sections and left with almost nothing to do until late May, when they were ordered to prepare to go home. The top-secret sonic gear, which they'd lugged across Europe willing to kill or die to protect it, was now junk. They loaded their precious dummies onto trucks and shipped them off to be sold or destroyed.

The whole unit assembled on hills outside Idar-Oberstein, sleeping in tents for the first time in months. Inspections and rather pointless training filled their days—along with the standard Preparation for Overseas Movement (POM) lectures. Then for three days, they convoyed across 350 miles of France, on June 16 reaching a staging area near Rouen—Camp Twenty Grand, named like all the embarkation camps for a cigarette brand included in GI rations. It was almost exactly a year since they'd arrived in France. Fox recorded the trip as a pleasant idyll, far different from the rush into battle during the bitter cold of the previous winter. "The wheat was ripe and mixed with poppies and bluebells. To men dizzy with thoughts of home, every field could have been a rippling flag—or the neon lights of Broadway, a colorful county fair, a mardi-gras, or a whirling rodeo in Flagstaff, Arizona."

Camp Twenty Grand was rocky ground with a painter's view of the Seine. Showdown inspections were routine—every half hour, or so it seemed. Men collected their souvenirs—footlockers of Champagne, captured Nazi memorabilia, antiques and artwork. Trucks drove the men into Le Havre and out onto the concrete wharfs. *General O. H. Ernst* sailed for home from LeHavre on 23 June 1945 showing all lights. Fox reported: "The voyage was smooth, the quarters clean, the food good, the prospect glorious."

They staged shows featuring Red Cross girls and played music every night. Laubheimer got his piano. He played with Tom Cuffari on guitar, while Art Kane pounded the drums and other guys sang along. And the eternal poker games continued. One of Laubheimer's pals won twenty thousand dollars—and was petrified of being rolled for his money. Other lucky guys stashed money in every hiding place they could find to get it home.

The *Ernst* docked at Newport News, Virginia, on July 2—the one-year anniversary of their first operation, ELEPHANT, in the Forêt de Cerisy. At Camp Patrick Henry, they traded in their woollens for suntans in the sticky southern heat and entrained for reception centers and thirty-day furloughs— "temporary duty for recuperation, rehabilitation, and recovery."

On August 7, the Special Troops drifted back to Pine Camp in small groups, anxious and subdued about their impending redeployment to the Pacific. Howard Holt recalls the redeployment lecture. "They gathered us all together in a huge auditorium, and a general gets up there and tells us, 'Well, now that we've got Germany conquered and you had your rest, you're going to get ready to invade Japan.'"

Sitting next to Holt was George Diestel, a maverick who had served as a motorcycle courier and would go on to star in an episode of *Highway Patrol* with Broderick Crawford and become even better known in Hollywood as a set designer. "Oh, Diestel stood up and told the general off: 'Goddamn this and goddamn that, we did our job, blah-blah, what the hell are you doing this for?'"

Holt couldn't believe his ears: " I thought, *Jesus Christ, he's gonna get put in the brig,* you know? And I'm sitting next to him, the other guys are all crawling down, and he's up there telling the general off, 'Go to hell!' " While the other men sat in stunned silence, the general stammered something and left the stage, and Diestel was never punished.

Then almost immediately came news of the atomic bomb. Holt says, "We cheered—like three days we cheered. We don't have to go now!"

Reeder then issued his most popular edict of the war: he ordered all his men to leave the post for the weekend.

Soon the Special Troops were bound to disappear altogether. Fox wrote sardonically, "On 30 August, Army Ground Forces wrote SECOND ARMY that the 23d was to be deactivated by 15 September. Its ashes were to be placed in a small Ming urn and eventually tossed into the China Sea."

Gloria Laynor tells of the anxiety she and Hal shared during his reentry into the civilian world. "Since we were only married seven months before he went overseas and he was overseas for a year and a half, it was like getting to know him all over again," she says.

Like all the other GIs at Camp Patrick Henry, the first thing Hal Laynor did was get to a telephone booth to call his loved ones. "I was living with my parents in this little alcove with a desk, and I was sitting by the phone all night waiting for his call," she remembers. She ran upstairs and took a shower, put on her pajamas, then came back to sit by the phone and wait for it to ring. When Hal's call finally came and she heard his voice on the line after all those months of separation, instead of bursting with excitement and joy, she said in a very low-key way, "Yeah—hi, how are you?"

Hal thought, *Oh my God. It's the end—I'm going to get a "Dear John" letter*—so he confided to her later.

Some time before, she had been to a picnic and a Japanese beetle got stuck in her hair—she could hear it buzzing in her ear, unnerving her, as she tried to get rid of it. When she got the call, the emotions flooding her played tricks on her composure. Gloria says, "I had Japanese beetles all over me—that I imagined. Had to go in and take another shower, I was going nuts. But I didn't—I didn't show my emotions. I was so emotional, that I was, 'Hi. How are you.' You know, 'Did you have a nice trip?' kind of thing! Emotions play funny tricks. Here he's coming home after a year and a half overseas, and you don't know how your emotions are going to react."

But when he showed up at her door, things fell into place just like the old days, and they remained together, in the best sense of the word, for almost five decades, until his death of a heart attack in 1991.

Jim Laubheimer caught a train to Fort Meade, where his father ran the Post Exchange. Since no other transportation was available to take him home, his father asked a favor of one of his vendors—thus Laubheimer arrived at his front door in Baltimore in a Coca-Cola truck.

Tompkins reunited with his wife, Bunny, at Bill Blass's apartment in New York—and for the first time met his son, now seven months old.

Dick Syracuse had played poker all through the war—to kill time between missions. The stakes were reasonable, a few dollars a hand in the pot. "Well, for some reason or other, I was a lucky sonofabitch, because I used to win most of the time," he says. "I guess I came home with a couple of thousand dollars. Just enough to make a bum out of me for a couple of months."

As an officer, he didn't have any trouble converting his scrip to real dollars before leaving France. Not so for the enlisted men. "They were complaining that these guys were pocketing the dough—the scrip, the invasion money. And just limiting them to I think it was six hundred dollars—that was all they were allowed to take back with them. So I had a little shouting match with this first lieutenant at one of the tables. I said, 'It's chickenshit, the usual.' 'Oh, I got my orders, Lieutenant—' 'That's bullshit, you got your orders.' It didn't go beyond that. He eased up."

His men would go home with full pockets.

Syracuse had one last encounter with the officer he had threatened to shoot at the Moselle River. "On the train, after the war's over, after our redeployment leave, on the train back to Pine Camp, guess who I run across? Lieutenant Colonel Snee!" he recalls.

Snee told him, "You know, Syracuse, you're a good officer and you ought to think about staying in the service—we need guys like you."

Syracuse said, "I would, except I can't stand the chickenshit."

Snee considered that and asked him, "Is it true that you were going to blow my brains out?"

"You're fucking-A right!" Syracuse said.

"Holy Jesus!" Snee said. "No wonder your men think so highly of you."

After the army, Syracuse joined his family's construction company and became a successful builder and real estate developer in New York.

Hardly more than a week after he arrived home, Fred Fox married his sweetheart, Hannah Putnam, in Kentucky, and they flew to Arizona to honeymoon at his family's ranch near Sedona. And as soon as he was out of the service, he enrolled in Union Theological Seminary in New York City.

Freed from the army, Ellsworth Kelly went back to Paris for six years. Initially he worked as a night clean-up man for the administration of the Marshall Plan to rebuild Europe. Reporting for work each night at 8:00 P.M., he never saw any of the staff who worked there, but he made many drawings at night. Then he got a job designing for a silk manufacturer, but couldn't wait to get off work and make his own paintings and drawings. After six months, he gave up figurative painting to begin concentrating more abstractly on form and began his lifelong mission as an artist: to bring to the world joy and clarity. In Paris, he saw a Jacques Cousteau movie short about tropical fish. As the colorful forms flowed across the screen, the audience oohed and aahed. Kelly says, "I thought, *That's the reaction I want them to have to my painting.*" His recent work has taken him back to Germany on a commission to install large panels on the facade of the new Bundestag building in Berlin.

For him, the military experience was a mixed blessing. "The army was good in that it made me more self-reliant—it's good discipline," he says. But he remembers also the fear—and the knowledge of what even a humane person may be capable of in extreme circumstances. "A lot of times in our foxholes at night, we were terrified of German paratroopers coming at us," he recalls. "And if that had happened, I guess I would have killed. That's because we were young, twenty-two or twenty-three." Shooting another human being would be unthinkable to him now. Though a sharpshooter, he never fired his carbine except on the rifle range.

The survivors of the Special Troops have had decades now to sort out what the experience meant.

Dowd says, "It's trite, but it really wasn't—I don't remember the real negatives very well. I remember the goofy things that happened. I remember the stupid things. And I remember us thinking, *What we're doing— does it mean anything? I mean, does it really mean a rat's ass? Or are we just wasting our time?* Now that I'm older, I'm comfortable with thinking it probably did some good. It probably did lessen the loss of life in the crossing of the Rhine River. But we had a very narrow view of what we were doing, you know."

Luck played a big part. "We were just a small group and we were extremely close to what was going on," he says. "We were extremely lucky that either the feinting that we did worked, or we were just dumb lucky that nobody decided to charge more often than they did, because we didn't have any firepower to speak of."

"I've since wondered if we were allowed a certain leniency, they overlooked certain things, because they thought that this was something that was elite," Bill Blass says. "It was a daring concept, in a sense—because we would all have been killed had it not worked."

"You try to think about the lighter stuff, but the heavy—well, you forget about it," Holt says. He still can't get over the things they dared to do—and got away with. "It's exciting," he says. "But as you get older and then the guys start leaving the good earth and they're up there in the battalion in the sky, you start talking among each other, you become sort of closer—holy cripes—you realize what we did?"

After the war, Dowd realized his dream of becoming a commercial artist, first working on comic books for Stan Lee: Blackstone the Magician, Nellie the Nurse, Hettie Divine—always people, faces. Then he drew advertising, for GM, Pepsi-Cola, all the big accounts. For Dowd, the chance to travel to Europe was a priceless part of his education—as was the responsibility entrusted to him as a platoon sergeant. "It's not a big deal, being a platoon sergeant—but you're in charge of a group of guys, you know?" A lot of other guys shunned promotion, didn't want the responsibility, but Dowd feels it helped him grow.

"Yes, there was patriotism, but you didn't beat your chest about it," he says. "I kind of recoil when I see guys my age wearing their overseas caps and bragging about the good old days. They weren't good old days. It was a necessary thing to do, and it was done."

Most of them came of age in the army—the experience of war left an indelible imprint on their character. "I entered as a boy, and came out with confidence that I could face anything that might confront me as a man," Laubheimer wrote. "I entered as a dreamer and emerged with a purpose and a real sense of direction." He finished the art education he had started before reporting to Fort Meade and became a successful artist, teacher, and arts administrator.

Was there a memorable moment that crystallized the experience? "Surprisingly enough, it's when you realize these are not just people that you're with but they're your family," he says. "And I remember when that happened. We were still at Fort Meade. And we'd been together maybe six or seven months. And we were all in a formation by the barracks. And you looked around at these guys and you knew them very well—you knew them better than you knew your own family. You realize, *God, this is my family.* I wouldn't have wanted to be transferred for anything."

For lots of camoufleurs, the 603d was a combination club and college, tempered by hardship and danger. Flemer says, "It was a battalion without any serious friction of any kind. We all got on together and it was one of the nicest units in the whole army."

The experience caused other epiphanies. "I have already made up my mind that I do not want to go into a job or be an employee in someone else's business," Richard Morton wrote his parents. "I have seen all the routine of subjecting all personal interest to fit into someone else's design that I ever want to see by being in the army." He became an artist and teacher, opening his own art school and studio.

Sonic platoon leader John Walker went back to the university to pursue his dream of becoming a teacher—or at least he tried to. The army recalled him from graduate studies at the University of Iowa to serve in combat in Korea. He stayed in the service through the Vietnam War, before retirement chalking up ten campaigns—five in World War II, two in Korea, three in Vietnam—and winning a Legion of Merit and a Bronze Star. He finally did finish an MS in biochemistry at the University of Wisconsin and taught after all—going from theater to theater teaching generals about the effects of such agents as nerve gas.

Of his service in World War II, he says simply, "Being a soldier was an honorable thing."

Walter Manser, the guiding genius behind the sonic recordings, opened an appliance store near Chicago specializing in the latest electronic breakthrough—television. He stayed in the reserves for thirty years and retired a lieutenant colonel.

Arthur Shilstone, like so many of his camoufleur comrades, returned with a sheaf of priceless sketches. He made his mark as a painter and illustrator, publishing his work in thirty-two national magazines, including *Life, Sports Illustrated, National Geographic, Smithsonian,* and *The New York Times Magazine.*

"It was a good experience because we didn't get into any really heavy going," he says. "And it was a wonderful sort of coming of age for a young guy from a small town to see the world and have this experience and meet characters like Max David."

The sense of camaraderie stays with him yet. "The thing about the service was there was always somebody to go to town with. I mean to go and have drinks or go to a dance hall or whatever," he explains. "And strangely enough, when I got out of the army, suddenly it was all up to you—there was nobody telling you what to do, there was no one to go anyplace with. You were alone. And I really did feel that—not that I ever wanted to be back. The happiest day of my life—truly—was the day I got out of the army."

Jack Masey remembers his army days with fondness—though his was a decoy outfit designed to draw fire away from other units. "But we were always joking about it. I was always laughing—I laughed through two and a half years of Europe," he says. "We were forever joking about everything, because we couldn't take any of this nonsense seriously."

After the war Masey went back overseas for the U.S. Information Agency, designing shows about the American way of life to exhibit all over the world. Twice he worked with architectural legend Buckminster Fuller—the first time to create a geodesic dome for a fair in Kabul, Afghanistan; the second to create an even larger dome for the Montreal Expo. For the show in Montreal, Bill Blass designed and donated the uniforms for all the American guides.

Probably Masey's most famous show was a modular American house he exhibited in Moscow—which became the site of the "kitchen cabinet" debates between Richard Nixon and Nikita Khrushchev. More recently, his design firm created the immigrant-experience exhibit in the renovated halls of Ellis Island and the National D-Day Museum in New Orleans, in cooperation with historian Stephen E. Ambrose.

"It was kind of wonderful, the army—for a kid," Masey says. "To knock around Europe, see things that I had dreamt about and heard about—Paris, the Eiffel Tower, the Arc de Triomphe. I felt, how lucky can I be? It's a terrible thing to say."

Darrel Rippeteau left the Army Experimental Station to serve at the Pentagon in the Office of the chief signal officer with the express responsibility of declassifying or destroying all the documents related to the AES mission. He left the army but remained in the reserves to retire a colonel as he pursued a distinguished career in commercial and public architecture in New York State.

"It has to do with coming of age as a man for me—fulfillment of what I wanted to do," Bill Blass reflects. Blass left an indelible mark on the American fashion industry—in fact, many critics have called him the father of American fashion. He designed evening gowns for Jacqueline Kennedy and Nancy Reagan, among a long list of distinguished celebrity clients, and created a mass-marketed line of clothing for women notable for its simple, tailored elegance. Before he retired from his company, his trademark name was worth up to $700 million per year in gross sales. But for Blass, it was never about money—it was about the dream he had as a kid doodling sketches of chic women on balconies, an idea of creating beauty.

"I'm one of very few designers who also owned their own business. I could never have handled that without the security and the knowledge that the war had given me," he explains. "I had a surety about myself. I was willing to wait. It didn't happen when I was still very young—it took years to attain. But I do think that all of that goes back, more than anything else, to that three and a half years in the army. . . . It also taught me to wait. You criticized it all the time—'Hurry up and wait'—but on the other hand it does give you pause to plan what you're going to do with your life."

Like other GIs who survived the war, the men of the Special Troops had been tried in an extreme circumstance, one that demanded physical courage and stamina, good judgment, and emotional maturity—and in the process earned a confidence in themselves, in what they could endure and accomplish, that shaped their whole lives forever after. If there was any personal good to come out of the war, it was that. Young men had been tested and their worst doubts about themselves laid to rest for good.

"I've always felt that, somehow or other, men are intended to be at war at some point in every generation," Blass says. "The army was the best possible experience for me. It truly formed me more than anything else. Let's put it that way. I simply have the greatest respect for what I learned—how it gave me the ability to cope with Seventh Avenue, which was tougher than Hitler's Germany, for different reasons, I must add."

Toughened by the Tennessee maneuvers before going overseas, he never found the real thing to be worse. The army forced him to experience a different, rougher kind of life. "I'd never gone hungry or wet or cold or unhappy or anything of that sort to that degree. But it does strengthen one, prepare one for the rest of what comes later. It doesn't destroy one."

Like Kelly, Blass found a paradoxical freedom in the army that allowed him to pursue, not just a livelihood, but a purer dream. "Well, the other thing, of course, is that everything is out of your control. Out of your hands. There's a sense of freedom about that. You were not responsible for the rent being due. I made very little money before I went in the army, on Seventh Avenue. I had very inferior jobs. And it was a challenge you know, to keep your head above water. And all those things were taken out of your hands. So that in a way you had time to think, to concentrate."

And he ponders the lingering question that, one way or another, all the veterans of the Special Troops ask: "There never was a conclusive answer to our contribution, was there?"

How effective were the Special Troops? Did they really help win the war? A 1978 report prepared by the army's Tactical Operations Analysis Office had this to say: "Beginning with simple equipment and an age-old idea, the 23d Headquarters Special Troops grew from a group of amateurs resembling a traveling theater show into a highly skilled, efficient, and valuable military unit. . . . Although most of the operations of the 23d Headquarters give very little concrete evidence that the Germans were misled regarding our intentions, practically all combat maneuvers by real troops cooperating with the 23d Headquarters met with success . . . finally, even though there were instances where the 23d Headquarters failed to accomplish their mission, due to poor cooperation, poor intelligence, or incomplete security measures, there is not one occasion of such a failure leading to a military defeat for friendly forces."

The 23d was not planned from scratch as the ideal deception unit. The Informal Report to Joint Security Control by the experienced Special Plans Branch officers in the 12th Army Group, evaluating the 23d's war of deception, found many faults with its organization; for example, "The equipping of a field unit with a numerous and high ranking staff is simply a source of unhappiness for all concerned."

All those colonels. And too much equipment, too rigid an organizational structure, and so on. The 23d was created out of expediency—combining several units that were already in place awaiting missions with a newly developed, untried sonic deception unit, and it had all the flaws of any ad hoc organization.

The Special Plans Branch officers concluded: "It is the final appreciation of the undersigned that Cover and Deception is a weapon of very great value. It is doubtful if another can be named which can do the enemy more damage with the expenditure of less personnel and materiel resources."

The Special Troops had required a new kind of officer to handle a new kind of mission. In the event, the army chose commanders who were a mixed bag, whose ability to inspire and lead ranged from excellent to awful, whose attitude toward the mission ranged from passionate enthusiasm to embarrassment.

Colonel Harry L. Reeder, the armored infantry officer chosen to lead the combined Special Troops, was already old in rank. Reeder wanted more than anything to get a combat command and secure a promotion to general. But the Special Troops was from the outset a dead zone for advancement. A few junior officers might go from lieutenant to captain, but no senior officer advanced in grade. Reeder had no taste for the assignment—either didn't understand it very well or simply was not cut out for it. A Special Plans Branch evaluation of senior officers in the ETO with cover and deception experience found his record lacking: "It is felt that he is not suited for this type of work. This statement is primarily based on lack of flexibility and receptivity to new ideas in Colonel Reeder's planning."

Lack of flexibility and receptivity to new ideas—crucial flaws in the theater of deception.

Harold Dahl wrote of Reeder, ". . . the Colonel I complained of so bitterly & who made our lives so miserable was relieved of his command after an investigation of just such complaints as mine, made by everyone from a Lt. Col. on down." Reeder was retired in rank—an ignominious end to a career that could have been burnished bright by active service in the war that defined the twentieth century. He had never managed—or perhaps even tried—to make his men like him. Far worse for him, he had never inspired their trust in his judgment, ability, or commitment to their mission.

The same evaluation that slammed Colonel Reeder for lack of flexibility and receptivity to new ideas praised both Simenson and Truly each in the same words: "An excellent officer with the ability to plan and implement tactical deception with Corps and Armies." Not till he arrived home did Simenson learn he had been awarded a Legion of Merit for his deception work, thanks not to Reeder but to Colonel Harris at Special Plans Branch.

Probably the single most important factor in the success of the 23d Special Troops was the ingenuity and resourcefulness of the men themselves. They took a half-baked idea, imperfect tools, a flawed organization, and uneven leadership, and on the freezing, muddy nighttime battlefields of France, Luxembourg, Belgium, Holland, and Germany, they perfected that idea and made it work. There's no doubt they saved lives—thousands, tens of thousands, more, ours and theirs. No one can say exactly, since all speculation is based on things that didn't happen—battles avoided, catastrophic attacks diverted, enemy defenders fooled into being in the wrong place at the wrong time.

On at least three important occasions, the Special Troops succeeded brilliantly: the holding of the line at Bettembourg, Luxembourg, in September 1944; the crossing of the Moselle by the 90th and 95th Divisions in November 1944; and the crossing of the Rhine by the Ninth Army in March 1945.

The wonder is that, with almost nothing to go on, the Special Troops created sound doctrine and learned their craft on the front lines of the most titanic war in history. That it worked, and their plans mostly succeeded. And that all for all those years afterward, all those smart, articulate, gregarious individualists in the ranks kept its secrets.

Two kinds of American soldiers are seen in history books of the Second World War: the professional—the West Point officers like Eisenhower and Patton and Bradley, Simenson, and Truly, or the career first sergeants who formed the cadres of new units; and the citizen volunteer or draftee—serving only for the duration, learning basic military skills to do his part.

But a third kind of soldier sometimes made all the difference—the citizen-soldier who, through advanced training and experience coupled with native ability and civilian experience, became sophisticated in the art of war-making, contributed plans and innovations, often rose to high rank and, even if he did not, enjoyed the counsels of generals. He sometimes remained in the reserve officers corps, but more often walked away when the war was won. Fox was such a soldier nothing but a war that called for every man to do his duty would have induced him to enlist. So was Ingersoll, the reluctant draftee who became so crucial to Special Plans Branch. So were Railey, another journalist turned warrior, and Fairbanks, a moviemaker with a deep strain of patriotism and an irrepressibly creative spirit.

Indeed many of the Army Experimental Station men and Special Troops would never have chosen the military as a career, yet they excelled at a very unusual and complexly orchestrated brand of warfare, requiring them both to master new technical skills and to apply their native intelligence to a new and urgent challenge. Often as not, they invented their own jobs and the tools with which to perform them.

This brand of civilian soldier has been missing from our army since that great war. Korea was largely a war of veterans called back for one last hour of service, and new draftees. Vietnam was waged by a corps of professional soldiers, augmented by many thousands of mainly reluctant draftees. Now that we have an all-volunteer army, the military has become separate from mainstream society in a way that was not possible during World War II.

Who can imagine a *New York Times* journalist today being put in charge of a secret weapons board for the army? Or a movie actor taking the lead in developing amphibious landing techniques for the navy? Or a newspaper editor designing battle plans for an army group headquarters? Or a scriptwriter and aspiring minister creating battlefield scenarios to be executed by a top-secret unit composed of artists, designers, and electronics experts? Nowadays such an integration of civilians into the culture of the army would be unimaginable—and perhaps that represents an important loss to society and to the military itself.

Somehow the genius of the army in that hour of crisis was to not only utilize such men but to inspire them to help shape, transform, and manage the very military organization they found themselves a part of by an accident of history.

The closing page of the Tactical Operations Analysis Office report on the Special Troops states unequivocally, "Rarely, if ever, has there existed a group of such few men which had so great an influence on the outcome of a major military campaign."

The Army Experimental Station shut its doors forever on 1 November 1945.

Railey sent a telegram to the chief signal officer: "THE ARMY EXPERIMENTAL STATION HAS TODAY BEEN DEACTIVATED. IT WAS ONE OF THE PROUDEST AND MOST SPIRITED OF YOUR MANY COMMANDS. IT HURTS BUT MEMORY WILL SUSTAIN US. FOR YOUR SUPPORT AND FOR THE GREAT PRIVILEGE DELEGATED TO ME I SHALL ALWAYS BE GRATEFUL."

The secret equipment that was shipped to the Signal Corps Engineering Laboratory at Bradley Beach, New Jersey, included nine complete heaters units (loudspeakers, power units, amplifiers, magazines, and accessories); one rerecording or dubbing system for transferring sound from disks to wire recorders, including a field-recording studio; one set of the disk recordings supplied to the sonic companies; one library to include all material accumulated by the Army Experimental Station and master recordings used for the production of field programs; and one mobile weather station.

What became of the equipment after that is anybody's guess.

In a special ceremony at the Pentagon on 17 September 1945, Col. Hilton Howell Railey was awarded the Legion of Merit in front of an audience that included Robert Gaskins—his adjutant—Sgt. William D. Railey, and Douglas Fairbanks Jr. The citation must have delighted him. "Colonel Hilton H. Railey, as Commanding Officer of the Army Experimental Station at Pine Camp, N.Y., from January, 1944, to August, 1945, demonstrated exceptional foresight and outstanding leadership in the development of a project entirely new to the United States Army. In fulfilling this mission, he exhibited a courageous pioneering spirit in the technical development and operational application of ultra-specialized signal equipment and in the activation, training and equipping of special type signal units."

But soon, Railey faded from the scene. For a time he operated the Black River Inn, a bar and restaurant in Watertown. Later Dick Syracuse went to work for him briefly in New York City when Railey was head of the Greater New York Fund—a precursor to the United Way. Railey remained connected to the army as president of the Pine Camp Association, a civic group whose goal was to reactivate Pine Camp. There were reports in the early 1950s that he was to head a new War Department Agency, but if he did, he never regained the prominence he had once enjoyed in military circles.

Gaskins, his wartime adjutant, recalls his last—and curiously sad— encounter with Railey. "After the war was over, he had really no place to go, and he showed up at our house in Wichita, Kansas, stayed for a couple of days. I could tell he would have liked to have moved in with us—because he felt like we were linked in the past. But we were starting to raise a family. We had a comfortable house, but Colonel Railey sort of dominated any place that he occupied, and my wife and I just didn't feel we could raise our family properly with him there."

Douglas Fairbanks Jr. had already won a Silver Star and a Legion of Merit with a bronze V for Valor from the U.S. Navy. On 12 April 1945, he was awarded the French Legion d'Honneur in the degree of Chevalier and the Croix de Guerre with Palm for his service in the invasion of southern France. Eventually he would also be honored with the British Royal Navy's Distinguished Service Cross (awarded only for action under fire) and Brazil's Order of the Southern Cross, as well as the Italian War Cross for Valor and two campaign medals. He would at last earn the rank of captain in the U.S. Naval Reserve in 1954 and retire at that rank in 1969.

In April 1945, his wartime career played its third-act curtain. Fairbanks visited Washington and floated a plan to secure the surrender of Japan through a circle of prewar social relations. Using a network of mutual friends, he would persuade the Japanese dowager empress to urge Emperor Hirohito to issue a proclamation of surrender, to be swiftly followed by a planned coup d'état against the military regime. Though Roosevelt, then gravely ill, and his advisors rejected the plan, it was not as fanciful as it might seem. The cornerstone of the plot would be a guarantee that the emperor would remain on the throne—the key provision that secured the Japanese surrender after the atomic bombs. In hearings before the Senate Judiciary Committee in 1951, Gene Dooman told the committee chairman, ". . . I would like to put on the record here that the preamble to the Potsdam Declaration was taken from a document prepared by Douglas Fairbanks, who was then in the Navy Department in the Psychological Warfare Department."

As they prepared to be "separated" from the army, the Special Troops heard their last lectures on security. "If you had any connection with intelligence or counterintelligence, secret communications, radar, or radio equipment, or codes and ciphers—KEEP IT UNDER YOUR HAT . . . if you're not sure about whether or not you should talk about certain things, keep them to yourself. . . ."

They were warned that spies and fifth columnists didn't look like movie villains: "They don't go around with shifty expressions, coat collars turned up, and their hat brims pulled over their eyes. They are more likely to be that nice old guy who wants to buy you a beer—and wants you to tell him all about it because he has a 'couple of kids' overseas himself. Or that sweet young thing you just happen to meet—who will be just 'too thrilled' to hear all about your experiences—in detail."

Some of them heard the warning in fairly ominous terms. Though the War Department no longer had jurisdiction over them, the FBI did, and they should not jeopardize their futures in the community, since any investigation of them might "cause a temporary or permanent shadow upon your loyalty, character, and former service."

The lecturers made a final appeal to their honor and patriotism. "Those of you who were specifically connected with intelligence matters or who handled classified equipment and material, have been endowed with a 'trust' evidencing your government's confidence in your loyalty and integrity, not just for a period of service in the army but in some cases forever. . . ." That trust was considered a "decoration of honor."

There were no parades, no ceremonies. Singly and in small knots, scattered across army bases from New York to Alabama, the Special Troops slipped away from the army and vanished from history. Because the Special Troops ceased to exist as a unit, as did the 3132d Sonic Company and 603d Engineer Camouflage Battalion in August and September 1945, respectively, the men were scattered about in other units, such as the 103d Combat Engineers, the 110th Infantry, and the 28th Infantry, from which they left the army. This was probably not a deliberate tactic by the army to cover its tracks, just part of the routine of demobilizing seven million men according to a system of points awarded for combat, overseas service, etc. But the effect was to erase another part of their unit legacy.

Fox tried for years to publish their story, writing in 1970, "From 1944 to 1945, this unit won five battle stars in service with twenty-three divisions, six corps, four armies, and one army group. In all, it engaged in twenty-one deceptive plays from Normandy to the Rhine. I was its combat historian and for 25 years I have been waiting to tell its story openly. The [kindly] Pentagon has just given me permission to do so."

But he never published his book.

Ralph Ingersoll did publish an edgy memoir of his days at Bradley's headquarters in 1946—*Top Secret*—but not once did he mention the operations of the Special Troops, which had occupied so much of his effort. All that was still classified.

Art Kane made notes for a Broadway musical based on the exploits of the Special Troops—but no more came of that than of a rumored movie, purportedly to star Cary Grant as the commander.

Like Fox, George Martin wanted to leave something for history. He drew a large map illustrating all the campaigns of the camoufleurs from England through Germany and earned a week-long pass to New York to have five hundred copies printed by his old employer, Schirmer Music. Today only a handful of those original prints—creased and dog-eared—survive.

Dahl alerted his family to stay tuned for newspaper reports of the exploits of the "Ghost Army": "Look in newspapers on Thursday, Friday, Saturday for story (I.N.S.) on 'rubber divisions' furnished to the Army by U.S. Rubber Co. and cut them out for me," he wrote. "And watch the papers closely now for stories about the ways the Germans were deceived, either by American or British units, especially anything referring to any 'ghost' or 'phantom' army."

But news of their exploits was limited to a few hometown articles with oblique and generic references—and often garbled facts.

The camoufleurs did stage one last show—a charity exhibition to raise money for war orphans in Luxembourg. Ten artists, including Laynor and George Vander Sluis, donated twenty-five paintings and sketches and five photographs for a traveling exhibition that wound up at the Galerie Bradtke in Luxembourg City in 1948. In the catalog for the show, Dahl wrote: "We are thankful that we could see the full meaning of the war and be better men for it, thankful that we in Luxembourg acquired the feeling that is prized above all others: that of being at home, abroad."

After a stint in Mississippi, Laubheimer was ordered back to Pine Camp, where he was issued a new uniform and brand-new equipment—the day before he was scheduled for discharge. At his preseparation physical, the doctor noticed that one eye was still damaged from the blast of an artillery shell back in the autumn. The blast had temporarily blinded him, and he had his buddies lead him around by the hand for a couple of days until the sight gradually returned, first in one eye, then in both. Now the doctor wanted to keep him in the army awhile longer, get him some medical attention. But Laubheimer was itching to get out. When the doctor left the room, Laubheimer got the orderly to sign him out.

At the Watertown train station, he stuffed all his spare uniforms and gear into a locker and threw away the key. He headed south with just the clothes on his back. He'd been in the army three years and a day.

John Walker recalls: "When they broke us up in '45, they told us to go home and be quiet for fifty years. We didn't even tell our wives what we had done. It was all supposed to be top secret." Like good soldiers, that's exactly what they did.

To the very end, they remained secret soldiers.

 EPILOGUE

CURTAIN CALL

Fort Drum, N.Y.,
15 September 2000

On a rainy Autumn day, two busloads of veterans of the 23d Headquarters Special Troops, many accompanied by wives and sons or sons-in-law, return to the place where many of them trained for their strange brand of warfare: Pine Camp, New York. It was as well the place they came home to from Europe, to train for the Pacific War—except the atom bomb suddenly made civilians of them. Today the old camp has been folded into Fort Drum, the headquarters of the 10th Mountain Division, rangers who are always the first ones the President calls when American troops are needed abroad, who can deploy to anyplace in the world ready to fight within ninety-six hours from that phone call.

The fort is a vast country of forests and plains named for Lt. Gen. Hugh A. Drum, who commanded the East Coast defense zone during World War II.

The youngest in the bunch is Roy Tucker, a sonic soldier who stayed in the army and retired a colonel, and he's seventy-four. Colonel Simenson is the oldest, ninety-one. "I'll be ninety-two next month and I'm looking forward to ninety-three," he likes to say, chuckling.

John Walker is robust as ever, tall and still somehow in charge. It's remarkable how the habit of command never leaves a man, settles on him as part of his nature that he and others simply take for granted. They aren't the spry young soldiers they were in those days, back when Colonel Railey bought many of them their first beers on a twenty-four-hour pass into

Watertown. Their hair is gray, or thinned to baldness. Many wear hearing aids and eyeglasses. Their bellies are no longer the flat hard bellies of men in combat for months, living outdoors on C rations and Spam. They wear Perma Press slacks and nylon windbreakers, and a dozen or so wear bright yellow ballcaps emblazoned with the name and logo of the sonic company. Others wear ballcaps that announce, "World War II Veteran." Their wives are dressed in slacks and sweatshirts, running suits, sensible shoes.

Last night, they danced to a swing band at the hotel playing the old music—Glenn Miller's "In the Mood" and "Moonlight Serenade," the signature arrangements of Benny Goodman, Harry James, the Dorsey Brothers.

Today, in damp cold, the veterans walk stiffly.

The chill reminds them of the thing they hated worst about the war— the cold. The constant cold that wicked into bones and made joints ache, that turned the steel of the half-tracks to stinging cold, so that they slept under the half-tracks in the frozen slushy mud rather than face a night on the cold steel bed.

Syracuse remembers. "You ever have to take a shit and it's cold and raining and it's the middle of the night? You go out in the mud and squat and drive in your M-1 knife to steady yourself. That was the whole story of the war—rain and mud and shit."

One of the veterans has had two strokes, suffers from depression, experiences wild mood swings brought on by the medication, and is legally blind. Sometimes, for no apparent reason, he'll burst into tears. Another suffers from Alzheimer's, doesn't always know where he is, and his wife looks after him with a patient love that is half a century deep. Many lean on canes, nursing artificial knees and hips, climb the steps into the bus carefully.

When he walks from the daylight into the dim indoors, Colonel Simenson must pause and let his eyes adjust. For just a few seconds, he is shadow blind.

All of them complain about faulty memories, admit with a certain sheepishness that they remember far more clearly the events of 1944 and 1945 than the events of six weeks ago.

There are fewer of them than when they started gathering for a yearly meeting. At that first meeting, in 1996, forty veterans showed up from the sonic companies. By 1999, only twenty came. Even with the inclusion of the other units of the 23d Headquarters Special Troops—the Combat Engineers, the Camouflage Engineers, and the Radio Deception company— they're down to about thirty men, plus wives and relatives. The sons and sons-in-law and even one daughter come along to drive or do other younger folks' chores. They all know it's likely that by the next reunion they will lose a few more—to illness, age, death.

And many of the camoufleurs, the artists, are not present—some explain that they are not by nature joiners. But as they grow older, guys like Shilstone, Dowd, and Blass are drawn to revisit the camaraderie they felt during that difficult, exhilarating, frightening, golden moment in their lives when they were all young and had embarked on the adventure of their lives together.

On the two blue government buses, the ones who came tour the enormous camp. The old coal-heated barracks have mostly been demolished, replaced by brick buildings well insulated against the Canadian winds that blow down from Lake Ontario, only a few miles to the west. From a little farther north, where the St. Lawrence runs into the lake, Colonel Railey used to sneak in his truckloads of bootleg Scotch.

They do recognize one set of the old "temporary" barracks, still standing, though likely not for much longer. The old movie theater where the sonic soldiers got their first briefing is gone—there's a graded slab of ground the size of a football field on which the army is erecting a new multiplex cinema.

Two young, attractive women act as tour guides on our bus—part of the New Army. The first, Jennifer Vchulek, is a petite enlisted soldier dressed in camo fatigues, her blond hair tightly bunned under a camo fatigue cap. She's an E-4 Specialist, the equivalent of a corporal. The other, a brunette named Karin Martinez, is the daughter of a career army officer and is herself an army veteran, a sergeant, who now works as a civilian public relations employee of the army. "Just can't seem to get away from the army," she says, and laughs easily. "They say after you've been in the army long enough, you bleed green."

She's been on the job for only three days, but she's done her homework, and as the bus winds along the smooth curving roads, she points out all the old landmarks—and all the new ones.

What was, all those years ago, a nearly impenetrable pine forest now is crisscrossed with smooth macadam roads leading to cleared areas aproned with spacious asphalt parking lots: a state-of-the-art health club, a Commons that houses dining rooms and banquet rooms, training facilities, a furniture store, a Burger King, a fenced-in motor pool full of two-and-a-half-ton trucks, Humvees, trailers, tracks.

Karin banters with the men, working in facts and figures about Fort Drum: The fort now sprawls over 107,265 acres. Eighty thousand troops train here annually. Between 1986 and 1992, the army added 35 miles of new roads, 130 new buildings, and more than 4,000 family housing units at a total cost off $1.3 billion. Fort Drum offers such a high standard of living, it's one of the most requested postings in the U.S.

That's not how these veterans remember it. They remember drafty barracks, blizzards, and bivouacking out in the open, spending frigid nights on maneuvers in the snowy primeval woods.

With a fetching smile, Karin asks, "Any questions?"

"Yeah," comes a rough New York voice. It's Syracuse, the original haba-haba-jab boy, still cracking wise. "Where were you beautiful girls fifty-five years ago? I just might reenlist!"

Next stop is the cavernous hangar at the airfield where the sonic deception units once practiced their tradecraft indoors during the long northern winter. It now houses a fleet of Blackhawk helicopters, the medevac unit that serves the base, plucks injured rangers out of remote rugged terrain when the training gets too real.

Over lunch in one of the new banquet rooms at the Commons, Maj. Jeffrey Price, a clean-cut young adjutant in the 10th Mountain Division, delivers an engaging speech about his personal code of honor. He speaks with a quiet conviction, asserts without irony, "I want to be an honorable man," and heads nod. They've thought about this too. They know where he's coming from. It's not a personal ethic that's common in civilian life during these me-first times.

Price says he began his eighteen-year career with an ethos of "Duty, Honor, Country"—the old West Point code that affected Colonel Simenson so profoundly, that hectored him with doubts when he first learned he would have to lie, deceive, dissemble, pretend, misdirect, trick, and fool the enemy in order to serve his country.

"My ethos now is 'Honor, Friends, and Family,' " Price says. "If somebody says 'country,' what's the country to me? The country to me is my wife, my kids, my family, my friends. To me, that's the United States." He goes on to include the friends and families of his comrades in the profession of arms, of their comrades, and so on, until the circle is complete.

Price commanded a platoon of M1 Abrams tanks during the Gulf War, four tanks, each manned by four tankers. "We spent 166 days in the desert, of which only three days were actually shooting combat," he says. "I don't know if it matters how much combat one actually sees in order to have the mutual experience that binds you together." Like the World War II veterans, they were men who would probably never have met one another under any other circumstances but the army. Who would never have understood something very profound about themselves and each other except through war.

By the time they deployed to the desert, waiting nervously for what would happen next—as soldiers in every army in every war have sweated out the anxious hours and days before going into action—something changed. "We already had a brotherhood, a certain bond, that no matter what—we've all gone our separate ways—we share."

It's an emotional moment. The men, their wives and sons, nod silently, hanging on every word.

"There are all kinds of legacies, and one of them in the army that we hold up high is the unit legacy," Price says. "That is your legacy: that there are young soldiers out in this division that are all over the world, that are potentially anywhere in the world in ninety-six hours, and when they look at the patch on their sleeves, it has a history." Buildings and streets on Fort Drum are named for soldiers who have distinguished themselves in their duty. Geographical features are named for battles where their forebears fought and shed blood. The base itself is a physical embodiment of public memory: "Your history, your accomplishments."

They understand this thing he's talking about, this bond that goes on down the generations and one day will go on without them. They've been there.

It's a moving speech—too informal to be called a speech, really. Just remarks from the heart, a little talk about what's on his mind since he became a warrior and saw real combat, and he believes every word.

So do the veterans. They've just met him fifteen minutes ago, and in half an hour they'll leave and probably never lay eyes on him again, but they talk about him over and over later with pride, as if he's their son. All of theirs.

After Major Price's speech, the last stop—the highlight of the tour—is the base museum. The veterans are eager to see how they are remembered here, what artifacts have been saved from their experience making a war of fictions, of feints and cover operations, of notional units pretending to attack real enemy positions, of what Simenson calls their "traveling road show."

The sun has come out and the air carries a hint of the hard winter that will fall as snow for three, four months, and soon. The way it snowed in northern France and Belgium and Luxembourg during the winter of 1944–45. The time when the Germans made one more desperate lunge into their lines at the Battle of the Bulge and the Americans were caught, as Eisenhower's staff admitted, with their pants down, and the Special

Troops manned machine-gun posts on rooftops and then retreated before the onslaught of tanks.

The clouds sweep along the horizon, their bellies darkly purple with rain. But overhead the sky is clear, blue like bottle glass, and the light is apple-crisp, October light, weeks early.

Outside the long one-story museum, on concrete pads under the pine trees, the big motorized artifacts of war stand on display. There's a Sherman medium tank, the same kind these guys watched roll past with Patton's Third Army during the Battle of the Bulge, hell bent for the relief of Bastogne. The kind they mimicked with blow-up rubber dummies camouflaged with deliberate inexactness on the forested western bank of the Rhine in the days before Ninth Army's big push, their rubber snouts pointed toward real Panzer divisions. There are a few jeeps, assorted trailers, tracks, even a modern Cobra attack helicopter.

But there's no half-track—the signature vehicle of the sonic troops—in which they mounted the enormous Jensen speakers to play their deceptive "music" across the front line to the enemy. In which they raced down muddy country roads to get into position for the next cover operation. In which they ate and slept and ducked artillery barrages.

"There should be a half-track here," one of the men says with conviction, and the others nod and murmur agreement. "I bet they could find a half-track."

They discuss a half-track one of them knows about that is privately owned and for sale, and they agree to talk to the museum about buying it for the display.

And there's also no "slug"—the M10 motorized gun carriage that replaced the half-track in later sonic platoons that fought their war in Italy. They stripped it of its awesome tank-destroyer gun, instead mounting enormous speakers capable of being heard with clarity fifteen miles away. The story goes that Railey's boxing moniker was "Slug" and they named the vehicles after him. Another Railey legend.

Inside the museum, the men fan out and study the exhibits with the fascination of professionals examining the artifacts of their calling. On the walls hang maps, battle flags, training photographs of the 10th Mountain Troops, photographs of the rangers in action in various battles in half a dozen wars. There's a World War I doughboy helmet. Under it, in the same display case, a 1917 Infantry Training pamphlet is propped open to fourteen rules. Number thirteen reads: "Do not hesitate to sacrifice your command if the result is worth the cost."

There's a ceremonial dagger presented to the 10th Mountain Division by the government of Thailand, a standing mannequin fully dressed in vintage arctic gear: white thermal suit, goggles, canvas rucksack. Crossed wooden skis hang on the wall next to photographs and decorations.

One of the framed decorations is a Silver Star, awarded posthumously to a young Pfc. named Robert H. Lathrop, for action in Italy during World War II—he was shot in the chest carrying bandoliers of machine gun ammo up to his buddies on the line, who were in danger of being overrun by the Germans. This was in the Apennine Mountains, and the 3133d Sonic Deception Company was in the same battle. Lathrop carried on despite his grievous wound, stayed in the line fighting until a mortar round killed him.

There's a case full of bayonets—fitting all sorts of rifles from seven wars. There's a scale model of a Wehrmacht antitank emplacement, the terrifying "88s" that tore up that tank column at Brest, another of an advancing Panzer tank.

But there's not a single mention of the sonic companies or the Special Troops. Until these men showed up, the curator never even heard of them.

In the museum, there's no inflatable dummy tank, no collection of fake sleeve patches of the thirty-six different units impersonated by the Special Troops, no photos at the Rhine.

There are no model half-tracks mounted with the special Bell Laboratory–designed speakers, no 250-watt tube amplifiers that used to melt the cores of those speakers when they played their "music" at too high a volume. None of the heavy turntables that used to play the sixteen-inch disks, as they recorded the sounds of tanks and trucks and bridge-building and men swearing onto wire recorders in a field studio built into the back of a radar van. The curator guesses all that expensive top-secret equipment probably wound up as surplus junk after the war ended, buried in an unmarked landfill.

Somebody says, "The army probably stuck it all away in that gigantic warehouse next to the Ark of the Covenant, like in the Indiana Jones movie!" That gets a laugh.

There are none of the priceless disks that Walter Manser and his gang spent so many hours perfecting at Fort Knox, Kentucky, and later on the battlefields of Europe. Tucker remembers what happened to the ones in the 3133d, eight linear feet of records. When the hostilities ended, and his company was waiting in Italy for transport home, he drew trash duty. His CO ordered him to take all the records to the dump—just throw them on the trash heap.

Top secret one day, rubbish the next.

Even then, before he became a history aficionado—meticulous at labeling photographs, preserving dates, times, places, names—he was aghast at the order. He saved one of the disks for a souvenir and mailed it home—but it was glass. You can guess how it survived the U.S. Mail.

There are no photos of Fairbanks or Railey, or of any of them.

There's just a single uncaptioned photo of a "slug." Tucker recognizes it by its painted number—it was the one he served in. He recognizes all the crew. But the picture must have been taken just before he was assigned to the slug, because he's not in the photo. He makes a note for the curator—now at least it will have an accurate caption.

But it's not much of a legacy.

One of the men, sweeping a hand to indicate the whole museum collection, says, "We're not here."

Others agree, nod, more baffled than angry.

The only vestige of the Special Troops on the whole of Fort Drum, all 107,265 acres of it, is Railey Avenue, named for the man who pioneered sonic deception, who bought many of these guys their first drinks, whose remarkable and adventurous life before the army was "touch'd with madness," who used to warn them that if they shot off their mouths in town, they'd be liable to fall off the back of a truck some dark night and he'd have to file an accidental death report on them, who bragged about them shamelessly and treated all his men like his own sons, who believed fervently that deception warfare was a way to save countless American lives in the battlefield.

Railey Avenue survives. One of the men points out that, on the sign, it's misspelled.

At the Fort Meade Museum, they would find the same story—or absence of their story: no vestige of the camouflage troops. The museum houses World War I tanks, a Civil War field piece, and all sorts of other militaria from the special service units, the medical corps, the cavalry, the infantry, the armored, but it owns not a single photo or article of memorabilia of the 603d. Period maps of the post don't even show the 603d in any of the cantonments.

Camp Forrest, Tennessee, has been gone for decades—dismantled after the war like so many of those boomtown camps, auctioned off in pieces to the highest bidder. Whole buildings were carted away on trucks. Nothing remains but a Web site. The Special Troops are not included in the list of units that trained there for war.

The inflatable tanks and half-tracks and howitzers are all gone—vanished. The neoprene rotted away years ago. So did the canvas. Even the director of the Army Ordnance Museum at Aberdeen, Maryland, doesn't know where to find any.

Oddly enough, dummy tanks came back into vogue during the 1980s. The army again began using them with its M1 Abrams tanks—three-dimensional and two-dimensional decoys made from a life-sized photo of the tank that also contained a thermal signature to fool heat-seeking missiles. The decoy was stored in the tank and set up whenever the tank bivouacked for the night. They were manufactured not far from Fort Meade by a company called TVI. After the Cold War ended, TVI stopped making them.

There's no record of the Radio Deception or Sonic Companies at the Signal Corps Museum in Fort Gordon, Georgia, nor at the U.S. Army Communications Electronics Museum at Fort Monmouth, New Jersey.

The U.S. Army Training and Doctrine Command at Fort Huachuca, Arizona, which drafts doctrine for cover and deception on the contemporary battlefield, has no record of the exploits of the 23d.

In the desert at the Patton Memorial Museum at Chiriaco Summit, just east of Palm Springs, California, a handful of metal dummy tank skeletons stand—the prototypes for the pneumatic ones—beside actual Sherman tanks.

You can see them complete in a 1942 photo that hangs on the wall inside—taken during the days when Company D of the 709th Tank Battalion trained here at the Desert Training Center, which covered parts of California, Arizona, and Nevada. Company D of the 709th was the outfit of light tanks that ran into a hail of German 88mm fire on that ridge in Brest, the guns drawn there by the simulated sonic attack by the 3132d. In front of the Patton Museum, a giant statue of the general stands in an amphitheater made of bricks, each brick etched with the name of a veteran. Thus are memorialized Robert W. Carpenter and SSgt. Mario Garcia of the 709th Tank Battalion.

Walton Hall in Warwickshire, England, is now a golf, riding, and tennis resort. Nissen huts and pyramidal tents have been replaced by time-share condominiums. But the great lawns on which the men of the Special Troops pitched their tents remain, cropped by wandering sheep, shaded by the jubilee trees planted by old Lord Mordaunt, whose widow haunted the shuttered north wing of the old mansion dressed in black, while the lucky officers of the 23d Special Troops dined on precious American meat and vintage wine. In the maze of low tunneled cellars under the old house, now storage caves for wine and restaurant food and equipment, hangs a reminder of the old days: a flatpan British infantryman's helmet casually slung from a nail in one of the wall supports.

The Forêt de Cerisy, where the 603d first practiced its trade in combat, remains a storybook forest on the road to St. Lô, the thick trees shading the highway and muffling the racket of diesel engines passing through it at high speed on the picturesque straightaway. It's a forest right out of a fairy tale—tall broadleaf trees with thick trunks and spreading canopy that puts the forest floor deep in shadow even in the bright of noon. Oddly clear of underbrush, almost parklike, except that sometimes the trees themselves grow so close together that a man would have a hard time squeezing between. Then sudden clearings where the light comes streaming in, surrounded by a green wall of trees and foliage. You can imagine ogres and witches concealed in the gloom, storybook wolves ready to pounce from the shadows. It's a beautiful and gloomy place.

Route D 572 runs through the forest for about ten kilometers, a straight fast road even in 1944. From the air, the whole area is shaped like a Halloween ghost, with the head toward Bayeux, site of the famous tapestry depicting the invasion of England by the Normans in 1066, the arms flung like wings across the highway, the tail flaring toward St. Lô, the road running like a spine down the length of the figure from NE to SW.

St. Lô itself has been rebuilt, unimaginatively, in straight lines and square walls, and the modern city lacks the kind of architectural character that comes with centuries of endurance. Only the citadel on the hill and the patched-up church remain to remind the visitor of the charm it must have held before thousands of tons of Allied artillery shells and bombs reduced it to a ghostly memory of itself, while the men of the Special Troops watched the pyrotechnics show in awe and understood they were in the middle of a war of no quarter.

A blow-up of an aerial reconnaissance photograph taken in 1944 after the raids on the town hangs in the hôtel de ville—showing not a roof left standing, hardly any walls, just a pile of rubble under which were buried not only Germans but an untold number of French citizens.

In the center of the rebuilt city, beyond the Gothic cathedral whose broken parts were rebuilt with cement so that it resembles a maimed person wearing plaster casts and bandages, in Place Général de Gaulle, stand the remains of the bombed-out prison gate, tall iron bars set in the stone archway. It is now a memorial bearing an inscription that reminds the world why the Allies were fighting in the first place and honors the sacrifice of St Lô in that cause: "AUX VICTIMES DE LA REPRESSION NAZIE." It pays homage to the victims of racist persecution and crimes against humanity perpetrated by the Vichy government in collaboration with the Nazi regime, 1940–44, and concludes: "N'OUBLIONS JAMAIS": *Let us never forget.*

Far to the south, along the lovely half-moon Baie de La Ciotat, where the deep water is indigo offshore and the shallows nearer shore pale to aquamarine, outlining the depth contours of the bay, runs a beach crowded with tourists for much of the year.

On it stands a monument commemorating the Allied liberation of the town, though it includes no mention of the Beach Jumpers or Fairbanks. But he might appreciate the other memorials. A stone obelisk commemorates Henri Langlois, the founder of the Cinémathèque Française. Another monument honors the Lumière brothers, who did their pioneering work here, including, it is said, their famous film *"L'arrivé d'un train en gare"* ("The Arrival of a Train at the Station")—which featured a locomotive steaming head-on toward the camera. When it premiered in 1895 in the first public movie theater in Paris, the patrons panicked and fled screaming in terror as the train bore down on them from the flickering screen.

Appropriate that Fairbanks's band of illusionists would have done their tricks at La Ciotat, since cinema itself is based on an optical illusion called *persistence of vision*. When the human eye watches a movie, more than half the time it is seeing frames of darkness, but the brain is tricked into thinking it is seeing a continuous moving picture. *Nothing*—darkness—appears to be *something*. A deception in the service of art and entertainment.

Exactly the effect Fairbanks—and the Special Troops too—often wanted to achieve for a more serious purpose.

At the farewell banquet later, the men and their loved ones sit eight to a table. Bouquets of red, black, and yellow helium balloons float over the center of each table, anchored by miniature sandbags. The men trade more stories, some even their wives haven't ever heard. Some stories they didn't even remember till now, this minute, sitting across from a guy they haven't seen for more than half a century, but he said something, or gave a look, and that brought it all flooding back.

One reticent veteran confides, "I fired every kind of weapon the army had, and I made sure I was good at it. But I tell you, I left all trace of weapons in Europe. I'm a hot guy—if I had an M1, I'd have killed somebody right here in the States. I had the hair trigger. It's like an alcoholic—he has one drink, and he's good for a three-week bender."

Others reminisce about liberating a stockpile of Cognac, of their first glimpse of the Eiffel Tower in Paris, of the way the kids in Luxembourg followed after them for chocolate and shoes. Talk and more good talk.

The speech tonight is more formal, and it's also about legacy. Sergeant

Major Good of the army reserves speaks about the unbroken legacy of combat veterans everywhere, speaks with passion about the proposed World War II monument in Washington, D.C.

Every country in Europe, even remote islands in the Pacific, has a monument to World War II American soldiers, he says, and we're finally getting around to it almost too late for the men who deserve it to ever know they've been honored. "Every day," someone at the table adds sotto voce, "two thousand vets die." He's talking about his comrades, these men, himself.

Monuments of the war are built into the countryside of France, Belgium, Luxembourg, and Germany, in every village, on every plain, in every mountain pass, alongside every major autoroute. Yet none honors the 23d—soldiers in a pretend army who fought a very real war.

Heroism is most often counted in blood and death, and though a handful were killed in action, the men of the 23d mostly heeded General Patton's famous maxim—"Your job is not to die for your country"—and survived the war. Some of them were wounded, many of them were enlarged as men and artists, all of them were changed by the suffering and devastation they witnessed, by the cruelty and compassion, and most important by the intimate, prolonged association with a group of remarkable men who would never come together again united in such patriotic purpose.

Most of the World War II generation—even the veterans who fought in Europe—never knew the Special Troops were there. That was the point, after all.

How many scared young men in frontline foxholes took heart after hearing a division of tanks rumble into position on their wooded flank—never realizing that their reinforcements were a couple dozen guys in half-tracks playing "music"?

How many American and British fighting men didn't die because, instead of striking the Allied line at a vulnerable point, the Germans discovered a regiment of dummy tanks concealed—but not too well—in the Normandy woods and pulled back instead?

How many Old Hickories survived the push across the Rhine because the Germans were preparing to meet the attack thirty miles away, where the Special Troops were sending up their racket on heaters and radios and massing their decoys with the help of stagecraft and impersonation?

There were casualty lists aplenty in that war, but there were no lists of GIs who *didn't* die, who *weren't* wounded. There's no monument in the forests of Bettembourg where a German breakthrough *didn't* take place in

September 1944 because a few clever men were holding the thinnest of lines. No parks established on the sites where impending battles *didn't* occur at the last minute. No monuments to heroic action against attacks that never came.

So in the end it's impossible to measure exactly what the 23d Special Troops accomplished. Their achievement is measured in negatives: men who didn't die, battles that never took place, defeats that were avoided. And you can't count negatives.

As in the Gulf War—which seemed so effortless to the CNN watcher, but only because of strategies designed to minimize the need for pitched battles—avoiding heroic death in the service of victory does not usually inspire legends.

It is fitting to honor with mighty reverence those men who gave their last full measure of devotion to their country. The greatest heroes, these veterans all agree, are the ones who didn't come home.

But there is enough honor to go around.

In his luncheon speech, Major Price quoted his father: "Wherever my boot tread stomps is American soil—not just a little bit, but completely." He said, "The one thing a thirty-million-dollar airplane can't do is the one thing a nineteen-year-old infantryman with a rifle can do: control a piece of ground."

Again and again, the secret soldiers held their piece of ground.

All the veterans of the 23d Headquarters Special Troops are entitled to wear the good conduct medal, the ETO Ribbon with Five Campaign Stars; the Meritorious Unit Sleeve Insignia; the Free French decoration with one palm; the *Couronne de Chene* of Luxembourg; the Allied Colors Ribbon; and the Verdun Medal.

But they never received a Unit Citation.

And though they constantly served on the front lines, according to the U.S. Army they are not eligible to wear the Combat Infantry Badge (CIB).

Fred Fox and Douglas Fairbanks Jr. finally met each other at a special symposium on Deception in Warfare at the Pentagon during the 1960s. Though they treated him like a rock star—chauffeured limousine from the train, first-class hotel—Fox considered the session "a lot of sound and fury."

His calling to the ministry led him to Congregational churches in Arizona, Ohio, and Massachusetts. Then, in 1956, President Eisenhower invited him to join his administration as spiritual advisor—writing speeches, letters, reports, memos. After that, he taught at a missionary school in Africa, then wrote and published a memoir about the experience.

Fox finished his career at Princeton University, where he preached from the pulpit just once every two years. In his penultimate sermon, "Surprise," delivered in 1977, Fox talked about his time in the army. The occasion was the two hundredth anniversary of Washington's victory at the Battle of Princeton. Fox was still fascinated with deception, and for him, that battle, more even than El Alamein, provided the textbook template. He compared the operations of the Special Troops on the Moselle and Rhine Rivers to Washington's audacious nighttime maneuver, talked about rubber tanks, sonic projection, blarney radio. "It was a perfect assignment for me," he told his congregation. "I could say I had fought in battle but I never shot anyone. It was just pretend."

At the end of his sermon, he handed out pictures of General Washington seated on his white horse, the smoke of battle swirling around him. "Down at the lower right-hand side of the painting is Washington's friend, General Hugh Mercer," he pointed out. Mercer had hurled his small advance guard at an enemy that outnumbered him four to one, to win time for the rest of the army to come up. "He is lying under a blanket, mortally wounded, bleeding to death from seven thrusts of an enemy bayonet. Let him remind you of others who have bled for us—and continue to bleed for us, on farms and in factories, in homes and schools, and in a thousand battlefields around the world."

Fox succumbed to pneumonia just four years later. His family buried his ashes under the chapel at Princeton University, where a memorial stone is inscribed, "Our friend and pastor, a light to our lives, Frederic E. Fox, class of 1939."

Writing the official history—a secret history the army never intended to be read—was Fox's last official duty. "So now it's done," he concluded, "and tomorrow I will be a free man again."

Douglas Fairbanks Jr. died only a few months before the reunion—on May 7, V-E Day. He ended the second delightful volume of his memoirs, *A Hell of a War*, "To be continued."

Colonel Hilton Howell Railey, who pioneered the blueprint for sonic deception, died in 1975.

Merrick Hector Truly, the mastermind of the Rhine crossing deception, passed away in San Antonio in 1977. *The Assembly*, West Point's alumni magazine, declared, "It can be said that Hector was truly an officer and a gentleman—an officer by training and a gentleman by heritage and instinct." Any man who served with him would agree.

Harold Laynor the young art student who was wounded by artillery fire near the end of the Special Troops' long road tour, and who painted the haunting images of his wartime experience on fifty canvases, died of a massive heart attack in 1991.

George Diestel, the actor and set designer; Harold Dahl, the sculptor and art appraiser; Alan Wood-Thomas, the painter who sneaked into Paris before it was liberated to rendezvous with his *Maquisard* friends—all have passed away, keeping their secrets.

Others have simply gone missing—no one is sure whatever happened to them. And on and on—the roster of the absent comrades-in-arms.

Some of the missing have brought home wounds: Dave Wynshaw nurses a bad back, injured when he fell twenty feet into that pillbox on the Maginot Line. Jim Laubheimer's right eye, already damaged before the army, never recovered from that artillery blast in Normandy. Red Sonnenfeld, whose last duty was driving a bulldozer at Dachau, plowing bodies into mass graves, hasn't slept a night through since the war.

At the reunion, the liquor flows, the men wolf down their salmon or ham steaks not like senior citizens but with the relish of men who've been dining on cold Spam and C rations. Many of them chain-smoke, an old soldier's habit.

It's a dressy affair. The women are wearing evening gowns. The men wear suits or blazers and ties. Colonel Simenson looks dignified in a tailored charcoal wool suit with a white handkerchief folded into a peak in his breast pocket. The men still call him Colonel, still revere him. He takes it all in with grace and humility. He laughs easily and often, rarely raises his voice, appears sharp and lucid as ever.

In these late days, he laments how few firsthand records survive, especially the diaries and journals so common among other soldiers. "They kept saying it was top secret, so we didn't write anything down," he says, "and that was a mistake."

After dessert and coffee and more stories, after the group photos and the first of a seemingly endless series of emotional farewells, Syracuse saunters over. He cuts a dashing figure in a dark suit and immaculate white starched shirt and tie, red handkerchief spiking from his breast pocket, silver hair slicked back like a forties movie star, tall cocktail in one hand, long white cigarette in the other. He does everything with style, uses the cigarette the way the movie actor William Powell used to, like a casual stage prop, waving it expressively in his big graceful hands to make a point. He's been drinking liberally and is feeling good.

They've been talking about legacy—about how at Fort Drum there is no legacy, no sign that the men of the Special Troops were ever there.

For all the inspiring talk at lunch about army unit legacy, embodied in the uniform sleeve patch, it's on their minds that there are no sleeve patches that bear the legacy of the 23d Special Headquarters Troops. The Special Troops lived for only eighteen months, and there are no soldiers to carry on their story on the next battlefield.

The Special Troops always operated in disguise during the war, wearing the insignia of dozens of other combat units and never their own, and now, it seems, the disguise is permanent.

As usual, Syracuse has the last word: "This is the last big deception," he announces. "The ultimate deception." He waves the cigarette to include the room, winks. "None of this ever happened—there *was* no deception unit. No sonic company, no camouflage company, no 23d Special Troops. We staged this whole reunion. We never did any of it."

But of course, nobody believes him for a second.

Of all the soldiers in all the armies of the Second World War, these men know the difference between appearances and reality. And this thing here tonight, these last few days—this celebration of duty and shared hardship and memory, this deep indescribable feeling of men who came of age in a world at war, who huddled together in the biting cold of Belgium and Luxembourg and the Saar Valley and drove on without rest into the heartland of Germany, who protected each other's back on the night battlefield that was their stage, this cause for firm handshakes and slaps on the back and old ribald jokes and stories of mud and cold and liberated Cognac and absent friends, this comradeship of half a century—this is the real thing.

Final Note: Since the 2000 reunion, the curator at the Fort Drum Historical Collection is actively seeking records, photographs, and artifacts relating to the accomplishments of the Army Experimental Station and the 23d Headquarters Special Troops.

Anyone with information can contact him at:

Fort Drum Historical Collection
Fort Drum, NY 13602-5000
www.drum.army.mil

Afterword and Acknowledgments

Some veterans will undoubtedly be surprised by what they learn in these pages—almost none of them was let in on the Big Picture during the war, and any book must try to capture the scope of events outside any single individual's view—or memory. Some appear only briefly or not at all as individuals—though the information they provided is incorporated into the larger story. The writer's hardest task is always selecting what—and whom—to include in order to tell the story.

The writer hopes that through the stories of the few emerges the greater story of the many, that every veteran finds himself somewhere, somehow, in these pages.

Nearly two thousand men served in the Special Troops and the associated Army Experimental Station, 3133d Sonic Deception Company, and U.S. Navy Beach Jumpers. Their stories and truths vary as much as their personalities.

The Special Troops traveled widely and most often worked in small groups, frequently putting on "shows" simultaneously at several far-flung locations. Hardly any two men shared the same experience. Colonels sometimes billeted in posh mansions; privates often slept in the mud. Men got to know the fellows in their squad, platoon, and company, but rarely worked closely with other companies. Signal Corps men hardly saw camoufleurs, who heard but rarely saw the sonic platoons. And the headquartees staff were often in another country—literally—making their plans with the staffs of generals.

Also, it has been more than half a century since their exploits. Memories fail, letters have long ago been destroyed or mislaid, and many veterans years ago disappeared back into the civilian population or are no longer living to bear witness to their experience. So even eyewitness testimony is necessarily limited to those who are available and willing to give it.

And because their organization, mission, and achievements were all top secret for decades, many records were destroyed, misplaced, or forgotten— or never kept in the first place. Secrecy also limited the number of men who knew about any given operation or event. Consequently, the number who can now recall it is small.

I have resisted the ever-present temptation to make up scenes that never happened, though I have tried to paint scenes that did happen in a way that captures the drama of the moment—drawing on war diaries, thousands of pages of letters, photographs, maps, histories, reports, written orders, the testimony of men who were there, even weather reports. Recreating a scene decades after the fact is never as accurate as reporting a scene as it is happening—the best the writer can hope for is to approximate the living feel of the moment without doing damage to important facts.

You try to achieve both *truthfulness* about all the details and *truth* in the larger sense.

In a project of this scope, it is inevitable to make a mistake, to get something wrong, to misspell a name or misinterpret a piece of information. Any shortcomings in this book are entirely my own, and I hope they are trivial.

To get a living feel for the experience of these extraordinary veterans, I traveled more than forty thousand miles—to the Desert Training Center in California; Fort Meade, Maryland; Fort Drum, New York; Walton Hall, Warwickshire, England; Normandy, St.Lô, the Forêt de Cerisy, St.Germain-en-Laye, and Paris in France. And to interviews and archival sources in twenty-two cities and towns in nine states, and the District of Columbia.

I have tried my best—through a quarter of a million transcribed words gleaned from extensive interviews with more than sixty veterans and veterans' family members and dozens of other experts in military history; wide-ranging archival research yielding more than two thousand pages of previously classified documents; deep reading in reliable published histories and memoirs; and sound reporting—to bring their story to light, and life, with accuracy and respect for what they accomplished.

As I conducted my research, the veterans were without exception gracious and helpful, welcoming me to their reunions and inviting me into their homes, often providing a meal and a guest room for the night, sharing their memories, photographs, letters, and other memorabilia from the war period, and answering my questions patiently and with great eloquence.

The greatest pleasure of this project has come from meeting such a fine class of individuals. These are of the generation who still write— and answer—letters. Who always offer you refreshment when you show up at their door, invited or not. Who feel responsibility to their community and to history. I'm not sure their graciousness has survived down to my generation, but I hope so.

They have entrusted me with a significant part of their lives—their stories—and I have done my utmost to honor these men and their trust in me.

Without exception, they do not call themselves *heroes*; they have spoken with self-effacing modesty about their own contribution to the war. They tell me that the real heroes were the line infantry, the guys fighting inside Sherman tanks, the paratroops, the fighter pilots and bomber crews, the marines on Iwo Jima and Tarawa, the Coast Guardsmen who ran the landing craft at Omaha Beach, the sailors in all oceans. Especially the ones who never came home.

But the Special Troops risked more than they knew. And all of their missions can be seen as altruistic—they operated only for the purpose of aiding other units, never themselves, drawing fire away from their fellow troops.

They created an imaginary army—one that often turned the tide of battle.

So here's to a bunch of bright and talented guys, the ones who slipped in and out of the greatest war in history so deftly that even most of our own troops never suspected they were in the line. Though some of them were wounded and killed in action, they were never allowed to wear the Combat Infantry Badge. As far as the War Department was concerned, they were the men who weren't there—but as we've seen, they were very much there, manning the front lines when it mattered most.

My heartfelt thanks to the following veterans, who contributed stories, reminiscences, photographs, diaries, letters, hospitality, and moral support:

Albert R. Albrecht
James V. Barrett
Ed Biow
Bill Blass
William W. Brown
Leo J. Corcoran
Charles R. Cuppet
Q. C. DeAngelis
Philip B. Dellisante
Victor Dowd
William Flemer III
Robert B. Flickenger
Harold W. Flinn
Robert E. Gaskins
Jules Gilbert
Edward Gilmore
Lee J. Haug
Howard Holt

Ellsworth Kelly
Charles Kizina
Joseph A. LaCroix
James B. Laubheimer
Christopher L.
    Lawless
Walter P. Manser, Lt.
    Colonel, USAR (ret.)
George A. Martin
Jack Masey
Richard H. Morton
James Mulder
Louis Porter
General George A.
    Rebh, General,
    USA (ret.)
Darrel D. Rippeteau,
    Lt. Colonel, USAR
    (ret.)

Lt. George V.
    Rittenhouse
Donald Schubbe
Thomas M. Schwerin
Arthur Shilstone
Clifford G. Simenson,
    Colonel, USA (ret.)
Julian V. Sollohub,
    Colonel, USA (ret.)
Martin Sonnenfeld
Richard M. Syracuse
Robert R. Tompkins
Roy Tucker, Colonel,
    USA (ret.)
John W. Walker,
    Colonel, USA (ret.)
Robert E. Wendig
Thomas Winfield
David Wynshaw

A small army of other good people also helped to make this book a reality. I express my sincere gratitude to the following:

Joe and Susan Trento of Film &
    Ink, for assistance in research
    and for suggesting the idea for
    this book.
Mark Cox, Chair of the
    Department of Creative
    Writing, UNCW, for making it
    possible to take a partial leave
    from the university to complete
    this book.
Kathryn Herel, my sister, for
    lodging and hospitality.
Keith Newlin, for encouragement,
    technical support, and help with
    Internet research.
Gloria Laynor, for generously
    sharing the letters and writings

of her late husband, Harold
    Laynor.
Rev. Donald H. Fox, for sharing
    letters, manuscripts, and
    memories of his father.
Bob Dahl, for sharing memorabilia,
    letters, and memories of his
    father.
Roy Eichhorn of the U.S. Army
    Management Staff College, Fort
    Belvoir, Virginia, for advising on
    military history, usage, ordnance,
    practice, strategy, and tactics,
    and invaluable research
    assistance.
Craig Schneider, for a fine job of

copyediting a difficult manuscript.

Jeff Kleinman, my agent, for his vision and hard work, and for making the whole thing happen.

Gary Brozek, my editor, who has championed the project, shaped its final course, and provided steady guidance.

Kathleen Johnson, my wife, for her translation expertise in French and German, unstinting support, practical advice, critique, and encouragement.

The following individuals also provided invaluable assistance with this project:

Dr. John W. Arnett

Sgt. Chris Barton, Intelligence Doctrine Division, USA, Fort Huachuca, Arizona.

Maj. R. Bateman, Military Historian, U.S. Military Academy at West Point.

Allen Bender, President, TVI Corporation.

Mrs. J. Brace, Wellesbourne (Warwickshire, England) and Walton Local History Group.

Ann Brennan, curator of collections, St. John's Museum of Art, Wilmington, North Carolina.

Jason P. Buntoff, Audio Visual Services, University of North Carolina at Wilmington.

Sergeant First Class Frank A. Carrano, curator, Goffe Street Armory Museum, New Haven, Connecticut.

Sue Cody, Historian and Research Librarian at William Madison Randall Library, UNCW.

Nathaniel Dahl.

Ruth Wells Danckert.

Jeanne Truly Davis.

Gina DiNicolo, DUSA-IA/CPI.

Col. Jeffrey Douglass, USMC, Chief of Staff, Dept. of Defense 50th Anniversary of the Korean War Commemoration Committee.

Mark W. Dunn, historian/archivist, U.S. Army Signal Corps Museum, Fort Gordon, Georgia.

Hannah Fox.

Marvin Freeman.

Philip Furia, Chair, Film Studies Dept., UNCW.

Mrs. Jules Gilbert.

Lois Laynor Goldblatt.

Jerry Griffith, TVI Corporation.

Lady Elizabeth and Sir Richard Hamilton, Walton Hall, Warwickshire, England.

Peter Harrington, World War II Art Collection, Brown University Library.

Mark Henry, staff, Fort George G. Meade, Maryland, Museum.

Mrs. F. Iris Herwin, Wellesbourne (Warwickshire, England) and Walton Local History Group.

1st Sergeant Frederick G. Horn, Second Company, Governor's Foot Guard, Goffe Street Armory, New Haven, Connecticut.

Ken Johnson, archivist, Operational Archives, U.S. Naval Historical Center, Washington Navy Yard.

Peter Johnson, staff of Walton Hall.

Robert S. Johnson, Director, Fort George G. Meade, Maryland, Museum.

Wilbert Johnson, Custodian, Goffe Street Armory, New Haven, Connecticut.

Gary M. Kraak, Doctrine Division, USA, Fort Huachuca, Arizona.

Mike Ley, Senior Doctrine Writer, Intelligence Doctrine Division, USA, Fort Huachuca, Arizona.

James W. Leyerzapf, archivist, the Dwight D. Eisenhower Presidential Library, Abilene, Kansas.

Maj. David Linder, USA (ret.), intelligence specialist.

Wilbert B. Mahoney, archivist, National Archives, College Park, Maryland.

Karin Martinez, Public Affairs Office, Fort Drum, New York.

Al McGloin, assistant to Bill Blass.

Yvonne Miller, assistant to Bill Blass.

Tom Mikolyzk, research consultant.

Jim Neville, curator, Fort Drum Historical Collection.

Lou Nunez, consultant, Information Technology, Stevens Institute of Technology

Maj. Jeffrey Price, USA, Fort Drum, New York.

Hilton Howell Railey II.

Dr. Jon Roper, Dept. of American Studies, University of Wales, Swansea.

Laura Lynne Scharer, Historian for Jefferson County, New York.

Joyce Schiller, curator of art, Reynolda House, Winston-Salem, North Carolina.

Mrs. Jane Schubbe.

Barbara Taylor, staff, Fort George G. Meade, Maryland, Museum.

John E. Taylor, archivist, National Archives, College Park, Maryland.

Richard H. Truly, Vice Admiral, USN (ret.)

Katrina West, staff of Walton Hall.

Staff of the United States Army Communications Electronics Museum, Fort Monmouth, New Jersey.

Staff of Wellesbourne (England) Branch Library.

The following provided information and research assistance:

General Patton Memorial Museum, Chiriaco Summit, California.

Creative Writing Department, University of North Carolina at Wilmington.

Charles Cahill Research Award, University of North Carolina at Wilmington.

Dwight D. Eisenhower Presidential Museum, Abilene, Kansas.

Flowers Memorial Library, Watertown, New York.

Fort Drum, New York, Historical Collection.

Fort George G. Meade, Maryland, Museum.

Goffe Street National Guard Armory, New Haven, Connecticut.

The National Climactic Data Center.

Norfolk Public Library.

William Madison Randall Library, University of North Carolina at Wilmington.

Interlibrary Loan Service, University of North Carolina at Wilmington.

TVI Corporation, Glenn Dale, Maryland.

Wilson Library, University of North Carolina at Chapel Hill.

U.S. Army Ordnance Museum, Aberdeen, Maryland.

United States Army Communications Electronics Museum, Fort Monmouth, New Jersey.

United States Military Academy.

U.S. Military History Institute, Carlisle Barracks, Pennsylvania.

U.S. National Archives, College Park, Maryland.

U.S. Naval Historical Center, Washington, D.C.

Wellesbourne (England) Branch Library.

The Laynor Foundation is seeking a buyer for its World War II collection to exhibit the paintings on permanent public display, the net proceeds to fund scholarships for artists. Contact:

http://www.laynor.org

—Philip Gerard

Selected Published Sources

BOOKS

Allen, Peter. *One More River: The Rhine Crossings of 1945.* New York: Charles Scribner's Sons, 1980.

Ambrose, Stephen E. *Citizen Soldiers: The U.S. Army from the Normandy Beaches to the Bulge to the Surrender of Germany June 7, 1944–May 7, 1945.* New York: Simon and Schuster, 1997.

———. *The Supreme Commander: The War Years of General Dwight D. Eisenhower.* Garden City, New York: Doubleday & Company, Inc., 1970.

Behrens, Roy R. *Art and Camouflage: Concealment and Deception in Nature, Art, and War.* Iowa: North American Review, University of Northern Iowa, 1981.

Breckinridge, Robert P., with a foreword by U. S. Grant. *The New Science of Protective Concealment.* New York: Farrar & Rinehart, 1942.

Breuer, William B. *Storming Hitler's Rhine: The Allied Assault, February–March 1945.* New York: St. Martin's Press, 1985.

Clausewitz, Carl von. *On War,* ed. and trans. by Michael Howard and Peter Paret. New Jersey: Princeton University Press, 1976.

Cruikshank, Charles. *Deception in World War II.* New York: Oxford University Press, 1979.

Dwyer, John B. *Seaborne Deception: The History of U.S. Navy Beach Jumpers.* New York: Praeger, 1992.

Fagen, M. D., ed., and members of the technical staff, Bell Telephone Laboratories. *A History of Engineering and Science in the Bell System: National Service in War and Peace, 1925–1975*. New York: Bell Telephone Laboratories, Inc., 1978.

Fairbanks, Douglas, Jr. *The Salad Days*. New York: Doubleday, 1988.

———. *A Hell of a War*. New York: St. Martin's Press, 1993.

Fisher, David. *The War Magician*. New York: Berkley/Coward-McCann, 1983.

Fussell, Paul. *Wartime: Understanding and Behavior in the Second World War*. New York: Oxford University Press, 1989.

Hamilton, Elizabeth. *The Warwickshire Scandal: A Tale of Royal Dalliance, Aristocratic Intrigue, Adultery and Deception*. London: Pan MacMillan, 2000 (first published by Michael Russell Publishing, Ltd., Norwich, 1999).

Hartcup, Guy. *Camouflage: A History of Concealment and Deception in War*. New York: Charles Scribner's Sons, 1980.

Higginbotham, Don. *The War of American Independence: Military Attitudes, Policies, and Practice, 1763–1789*. Bloomington and London: Indiana University Press, Wars of the United States Series,1971.

Hughes, Dale Adams. *331 Days: The Story of the Men of the 709th Tank Battalion*. Arizona: D. A. Hughes, 1980.

Ingersoll, Ralph. *Top Secret*. New York: Harcourt, Brace and Company, 1946.

———. *The Battle Is the Pay-Off*. New York: Harcourt Brace and Company, 1943.

Kern, Stephen. *The Culture of Time and Space, 1880–1918*. London: Weidenfeld and Nicolson, 1983.

Knightley, Phillip. *The First Casualty: From the Crimea to Vietnam: The War Correspondent as Hero, Propagandist, and Myth Maker*. New York and London: Harcourt Brace Jovanovich, 1975.

Latimer, Jon. *Deception in War*. New York: Overlook, 2001.

Marshall, George C., H. H. Arnold, and Ernest J. King (with foreword by Walter Millis). *The War Reports of General of the Army George C. Marshall, Chief of Staff; General of the Army H. H. Arnold, Commanding General, Army Air Forces; Fleet Admiral Ernest J. King, Commander-in-Chief, United States Fleet and Chief of Naval Operations*. Philadelphia and New York: J. B. Lippincott Company, 1947.

Mendelsohn, John (editor). *Covert Warfare: Basic Deception and the Normandy Invasion*. New York: Garland Publishing, Inc., 1989.

——— (editor). *Covert Warfare: The German View of Cover and Deception*. New York: Garland Publishing, Inc., 1989.

——— (editor). *Covert Warfare: Cover and Deception by the Royal Air Force in World War II*. New York: Garland Publishing, Inc., 1989.

Miller, Robert A. *August 1944: The Campaign for France*. California: Presidio Press, 1988.

Montagu, Ewen. *The Man Who Never Was*. New York: J. B. Lippincott and Company, 1954.

Montgomery, Bernard Law, Field Marshal the Viscount Montgomery of Alamein, K.G., G.C.B., D.S.O. *El Alamein to the River Sangro*. London: Hutchinson & Co. Ltd., 1948.

———. *Normandy to the Baltic—Invasion*. London: Hutchinson & Co. Ltd., 1947.

———. *Normandy to the Baltic—Victory*. London: Hutchinson & Co. Ltd., 1947.

Patton, General George S. *War as I Knew It*. Boston: Houghton Mifflin, 1995.

Railey, Hilton Howell. *Touch'd With Madness*. New York: Carrick & Evans, Inc., 1938.

Reit, Seymour. *Masquerade: The Amazing Camouflage Deceptions of World War II*. New York: Hawthorn Books, Inc., 1978.

Sorel, Nancy Caldwell. *The Women Who Wrote the War*. New York: Arcade, 1999.

Stanley, Roy M., II. *To Fool a Glass Eye: Camouflage Versus Photoreconnaissance in World War II*. Washington, D.C.: Smithsonian Institution Press, 1998.

Steinbeck, John. *Once There Was a War*. New York: Viking, 1958 (first serialized in the *New York Herald Tribune* June–December 1943).

Sun Tzu. *The Art of War*, trans. and intro. by Samuel B. Griffith. London and New York: Oxford University, 1963.

Thayer, Gerald Handerson, and Abbott Handerson Thayer. *Concealing-Coloration in the Animal Kingdom; an Exposition of the Laws of Disguise Through Color and Pattern: Being a Summary of Abbot H. Thayer's Discoveries*. New York: The Macmillan Co., 1909.

Whiting, Charles. *The Battle of the Hürtgen Forest: The Untold Story of a Disastrous Campaign*. New York: Orion Books, 1989.

PAMPHLETS

Fox, Frederic E. *Seven Sermons and One Eulogy as Preached in the Chapel of Princeton University from 1965–1980*. Fox Head Press, 1982.

Hamilton, Elizabeth, ed. *Wellesbourne at War 1939–1945*. The Wellesbourne (England) Village Society (Stephen England, Elsie Grant, Alan Griffin, Elizabeth Hamilton, Rety Harrison, Robin Harrison, Dennis Heath, Eric Herwin, Nancy Little) n.d.

About Fort George G. Meade, Maryland. The Chesapeake and Potomac Telephone Company of Baltimore City, 1943.

ARTICLES

Austra, Kevin R. "The Battle of the Bulge: The Secret Offensive." *Military Intelligence Professional Bulletin*, January–March 1991, Vol. 17, Issue 1, 26, 8p, 2bw.

Baker, Bob. "He Fought a War Armed With an Air Compressor; Secret WWII Unit Misled the Germans With Inflatable Tanks." *Los Angeles Times*, 11 November 1986, Metro, Part 2, 1.

Boyanowski, Henry J. "Ghost Army Fools Foe in Neatest Trick of the War." *Worcester Daily Telegram*, 4 October, 1945.

Koenigsberg, Allen. "The Seventeen-Year Itch." Lecture delivered at the U.S. Patent Office Bicentennial in Washington, D.C., 9 May 1990.

Meryman, Richard. "A Painter of Angels Became the Father of *Camouflage*." *Smithsonian*, April 1999, 116–125.

Michel, Annie. "A Letter from Luxembourg." *Stars and Stripes*, 1 December 1944.

Park, Edwards. "A phantom division played a vital role in Germany's defeat." *Smithsonian*, April 1985, 138–147.

Riddle, Perry C. "Reflections: 'That's When We Really Knew That We Were Going to Be Decoys, Sitting Ducks.' *Los Angeles Times*, 10 June 1986, Metro, Part 2, 7.

Thayer, Gerald Handerson. "The concealing coloration of animals. New light on an old subject (an essay on the question of how, and to what extent,—not why,—animals are concealed by their colors) with pictures from photographs and paintings." *Century Magazine*, Vol. LXXVI, 249–261.

Westbrook, Stephen D., Major, USA. "The Railey Report and Army Morale, 1941: Anatomy of a Crisis." *Military Review*, June 1980, Volume LX, No. 6, 11–24.

[No byline.] "Ingersoll: Pen vs. Sword." *Newsweek*, 20 July 1942, 28.

[No byline.] "Fort Meade Soldier-Artist Carves Thirteen-Foot Bust of President." *Fort Meade Post Enterprise* (undated).

[No byline.] "Pin Sticky—23d Hq. GIs Rate Bowl of Fruit Salad." *Reveille*, newspaper of Second Army Special Troops, 18 October 1945, 2.

[No byline.] "Col. Railey Honored in D.C." *Pine Post*, Pine Camp, N.Y., 20 September 1945, 1.

[No byline.] "The War's Strangest Army." *New Haven Register*, 10 February 1946, 1.

[No byline.] "Railey to Head New War Agency." *Watertown Daily Times*, undated, circa 1950.

Notes

INTRODUCTION

Pages

1 **23 March 1945.** For details of the battle of the Rhine, I am indebted to Peter Allen, *One More River: The Rhine Crossings of 1945* (New York: Scribners, 1980); Stephen E. Ambrose, *Citizen Soldiers: The U.S. Army from the Normandy Beaches to the Bulge to the Surrender of Germany, June 7, 1944–May 7, 1945* (New York: Simon & Schuster, 1997); William B. Breuer, *Storming Hitler's Rhine: the Allied Assault, February–March 1945* (New York: St. Martin's Press, 1985); and Bernard Law Montgomery, Field Marshal the Viscount Montgomery of Alamein, K.G., G.C.B., D.S.O., *Montgomery of Alamein, Volume III: Normandy to the Baltic—Victory* (London: Hutchinson & Co. Ltd., 1947).

5 **All warfare is based** Sun Tzu, *The Art of War*, trans. and intro. by Samuel B. Griffith (London and New York: Oxford University, 1963), 66.

5 **In 1943, the *Flat-Top*** "When Camouflage Made History," *Flat-Top*, Vol. 1, No. 5, 8 July 1943, 6.

CHAPTER ONE
The Swashbuckler
1941–1942

11 **I have at times** Douglas Fairbanks Jr., *The Salad Days* (New York: Doubleday, 1988), 25.

11　**They knew little else** Phillip Knightley, *The First Casualty: From the Crimea to Vietnam: The War Correspondent as Hero, Propagandist, and Myth Maker* (New York and London: Harcourt Brace Jovanovich, 1975), 272–273.

12　**But tonight's gathering** Fairbanks, *A Hell of a War* (New York: St. Martin's, 1993), 88–89.

12　**This movie** Ibid., 84–85; All plot details and quoted dialogue from *The Corsican Brothers* (United Artists, 1941).

13　**Fairbanks explained** Fairbanks, *A Hell of a War*, 87.

13　**It wasn't easy** Biographical details here and elsewhere from Fairbanks, *The Salad Days* and *A Hell of a War.*

14　**Now Fairbanks** *Gunga Din* (RKO, 1939).

15　**From the end of April** Ibid., 63.

15　**When he was posted** Ibid., 71.

16　**Fairbanks never made it** Ibid., 41.

16　**From England,** Fairbanks, "Message from Malta," at sea aboard USS *Washington*, 29 April–15 May 1942, Command File World War II, Operational Archives, Naval Historical Center, Washington, D.C. Contains a gripping account of the heroic adventure of the USS *Wasp* task force delivering warplanes to Malta under heavy German and Italian attack.

17　**But Fairbanks senior** Commander Douglas Elton Fairbanks Jr., U.S. Naval Reserve, "Transcript Record Service of," Navy Department, Bureau of Naval Personnel, 20 February 1946, Command File World War II, Operational Archives, Naval Historical Center, Washington, D.C., 2.

17　**One of those men** Fairbanks, *Salad Days*, 248.

17　**The British had learned** "Cover & Deception Report, ETO (Top Secret, Copy 3 of 6): 'Cover & Deception Synopsis of History' (forwarded 11 December 1944 with critique by Col. John H. Bevan, London Controlling Section Offices of the War Cabinet, London)," RG 319, National Archives, College Park, MD, 1.

18　**Throughout 1942, Mountbatten borrowed ideas** David Fisher, *The War Magician* (New York: Berkley/Coward McCann, 1983). Details the remarkable career of Jasper Maskelyne as a pioneer of deception.

19　**Again like Baron Colonna** Quoted in Frederic E. Fox and William E. Flemer III, *Official History of the 23d Headquarters Special Troops,* 14 September 1945, RG 407, SPHQ-23-0.1, National Archives, College Park, MD, 1.

19　**Months before the victory** Fairbanks, *A Hell of a War*, 148.

20　**His face was too well known** Ibid., 159.

20　**Fairbanks was barely ashore** John B. Dwyer, *Seaborne Deception: The History of U.S. Navy Beach Jumpers* (New York: Praeger, 1992), 3. Unless otherwise noted, this excellent, clear, and authoritative history is the source for details about Douglas Fairbanks Jr.'s exploits with the Beach Jumpers.

20 First, he proposed Fairbanks, "Deceptive Warfare and Special Operations—Comments on," Memorandum for Colonel Newman Smith, U.S. Army, Command File World War II, Operational Archives, Naval Historical Center, Washington, D.C., 4.

21 Next, Fairbanks argued Col. John H. Bevan, London Controlling Section, cover letter to Copy 3 of "Cover & Deception Report ETO: 'Cover & Deception Synopsis of History,' " 2.

21 Once again, the impetus Dwyer, *Seaborne Deception*, 5.

22 And not just King Gen. George C. Marshall, Chief of Staff of the Army, "Memorandum (secret) for the Secretary, Joint Chiefs of Staff, Subject: 'Control of Information concerning a Special Operation,' 20 August 1942," RG 218, JCS 234, National Archives, College Park, MD, 1.

22 In the navy, Rear Admiral C. M. Cooke Jr., USN, Chief of Staff (Plans), "Memorandum (secret) for Admiral King, Subject: 'Security for TORCH Operation.' 21 August 1942." RG 218, JCS 234, National Archives, College Park, MD, 1.

22 The original proposal "Establishment of a Security Committee for Military Operations," 2.

22 Admiral King lost no time Joint Chiefs of Staff, "Directive: Security Control for Military Operations," 25 August 1942, RG 218, JCS 234/1, National Archives, College Park, MD, 1.

22 So Fairbanks's three-part sales pitch Fairbanks, *A Hell of a War*, 171.

24 So when all was Ibid., 272–273.

24 There wasn't time Quoted in Dwyer, *Seaborne Deception*, 7.

24 Soon the Beach Jumper base Ibid., 7.

25 Fairbanks continued to run Fairbanks, "Secret Memorandum for the Admiral, Subject: Special Operations—Summation report on (January 1943 to September 1944)," 1 September 1944, Command File World War II, Operational Archives, Naval Historical Center, Washington, D.C., 8.

26 Division 17 Dwyer, *Seaborne Deception*, 15.

28 But on this night The account of the Battle of Sandy Hook from the National Defense Research Committee, Office of Scientific Research and Development, Division 17, Section 17.3, Bell Telephone Laboratories, Inc., New York, NY, "Sonic Deception: The Reproduction, Transmission, and Reception of Deceptive Sounds," 15 December 1944, 2–3. Courtesy Darrel D. Rippeteau.

28 The timing was propitious For details of the Battle of El Alamein, see Montgomery, *El Alamein to the River Sangro* (London: Hutchinson & Co., Ltd., 1948), 44–45.

CHAPTER TWO
Hilton Howell Railey—The P. T. Barnum of Deception
1942–1944

30 *I seek a permanent connection* Hilton Howell Railey, Col., USA (Inactive), "Résumé," 19 October 1946, 6. Courtesy Darrel D. Rippeteau.

30 *They would usually make* The account of bootlegging Scotch based on several sources, especially Darrel D. Rippeteau, Col., USAR (Ret.), interview by author, 10 July 2001. I have fleshed out the details to show a "typical" booze run.

30 **The winter of 1943–44** *The New York Times Index, Year 1944* (New York: New York Times, 1945), 1658.

31 **In the vast meadows** Account of his service from Thomas M. Schwerin, interview by author, 10 July 2001. Mr. Schwerin reports that it snowed every single day in April 1944 at Pine Camp.

32 **And like Fairbanks** Hilton H. Railey, *Touch'd With Madness* (New York: Carrick & Evans, 1938), 14. Details of Railey's prewar life come from this memoir, unless otherwise noted.

33 **The minimum age** Ibid., 47–49.

33 **Railey was a member** For details of Railey's work for Admiral Byrd, see Richard Evelyn Byrd, Rear Admiral, USN (Ret.), *Little America: Aerial Exploration in the Antarctic, The Flight to the South Pole* (New York and London: G. P. Putnam's Sons, 1930), 11, 25–26, 373, 377; quote 26.

34 **At the end of that debacle** Railey, *Touch'd With Madness*, 197–198.

34 **When he recovered** Railey, "Memorandum for General Phillipson, 14 March 1942, requesting active duty," with cover memorandums of endorsement by Charles C. Blakeney, Col., G.S.C., President, Planning Board, 20 September 1943, and Robert E. Gaskins, 2d Lt., Signal Corps, Adjutant, Army Experimental Station Fort Hancock, NJ, 5 January 1944, 2. Courtesy Darrel D. Rippeteau.

34 **Railey was an impresario** Railey, "Memorandum for General Phillipson," 2.

35 **"One of the things he liked to do . . ."** Account of Rippeteau's service from Rippeteau, interview by author, 10 July 2001.

36 **His was an oddly effective** The account of Railey's lectures and accounts of their service from Rippeteau, interview by author, 10 July 2001; James Barrett, interview by author, 7 September 2001; and Edward W. Gilmore, MD, interview by author, 7 September 2001.

36 **"In August, 1920 . . ."** Railey, *Touch'd With Madness*, 55.

37 **Some who knew** Ibid., 40.

37 **"I hate institutions . . ."** Ibid., 302. Information about Railey's drinking from a variety of sources, including his own memoir; Rippeteau, interview by author, 10 July 2001; James V. Barrett, interview by author, 7 September 2001; Dr. Edward Gilmore,

interview by author, 7 September 2001; and Richard M. Syracuse, interview by author, 9 December 2000.

37 **Railey treated his "boys"** Railey, "Morale of the United States Army, an Appraisal for *The New York Times*," 29 September 1941. Military History Institute Library, Carlisle Barracks, PA, 12.

38 **In 1940, already anticipating** George C. Marshall, H. H. Arnold, Ernest J. King, (with foreword by Walter Millis), *The War Reports of General of the Army George C. Marshall, Chief of Staff; General of the Army H. H. Arnold, Commanding General, Army Air Forces; Fleet Admiral Ernest J. King, Commander-in-Chief, United States Fleet and Chief of Naval Operations* (Philadelphia and New York: J. B. Lippincott Company, 1947), 64–65.

38 **So reported *Life*** The account of the morale crisis from Maj. Stephen D. Westbrook, USA, "The Railey Report and Army Morale, 1941: Anatomy of a Crisis," *Military Review*, Vol. LX, June 1980, No. 6, 12–13.

38 **In stepped Arthur Hays Sulzberger** Arthur Hays Sulzberger, "Letter to Secretary of Defense, 2 April 1954," 1. Courtesy Darrel D. Rippeteau.

39 **"The men feel they are . . ."** Railey, "Morale," 33.

39 **It was difficult to create** Lieutenant General Walter Krueger, commander of Third Army, quoted in Railey, "Morale," 133–134.

39 **Morale-building in** Railey, "Morale," 139.

39 **"Now it is obvious . . ."** Ibid., 182; italics are Railey's.

39 **Sulzberger, for whom** Sulzberger, "Letter to Secretary of Defense," 1.

39 **Railey recommended stationing** Railey, "Recommendations," appendix to "Morale," 2.

40 **Though he'd already** Railey, "Memorandum for General Phillipson," 1.

40 **In short order** The book that emerged from Railey's new duties: *What the Citizen Should Know About Civilian Defense* by Walter D. Binger and Hilton Howell Railey (New York: W. W. Norton & Co., 1942).

41 **Thus Railey was sitting** For this and all specifications of the sonic equipment, see National Defense Research Committee, "Sonic Deception: The Reproduction, Transmission, and Reception of Deceptive Sounds."

42 **After a few months** Date of activation of AES from Robert E. Gaskins, Lt., Adjutant, AES, "Sonic Deception" (top secret report prepared for the information of a Secret War Department Mission), 22 September 1944, seven pages, copy twenty-nine of fifty, 1, courtesy Darrel D. Rippeteau; Railey, "Résumé," 1.

43 **Railey alludes** Railey, "Résumé," 2.

43 **Sergeant William D. Railey** Army Experimental Station, "Merry Christmas 1944—Pine Camp, Army Experimental Station," Roster of AES personnel, cour-

tesy Darrel D. Rippeteau; Hilton Howell Railey II, interview by author, 20 August 2001.

44   **Later in the war** The information on ASTP and the quote from Stephen E. Ambrose, *Citizen Soldiers: The U.S. Army from the Normandy Beaches to the Bulge to the Surrender of Germany, June 7, 1944–May 7, 1945* (New York: Simon and Schuster, 1997), 274–275.

45   **When Colonel Blakeney** Charles C. Blakeney, Col., GSC, President, Planning Board, "Memorandum for Commanding General, Operations Division, War Department; Subject: Promotion of Lt. Col. Hilton H. Railey 0-127454, 20 September 1943," 1. Courtesy Darrel D. Rippeteau.

47   **Pine Camp had been founded** All statistics about Pine Camp and Fort Drum from "History of Fort Drum" in "Fort Drum Economic Impact Statement, Fiscal Year 1999," prepared by the Installation Business Office, Fort Drum, NY, 2000.

48   **The AES men** Gilmore, interviews, 26 March 2001 and 7 September 2001; Barrett, personal interview, 7 September 2001.

48   **In the spring of 1944** Figure for ROTC officers and general army strength from Marshall, *The War Reports of General of the Army George C. Marshall, Chief of Staff; General of the Army*, 24.

49   **Another ROTC officer** The account of background, military service, and meeting Railey from Richard Syracuse, interviews by author, 14 September 2000 and 19 December 2000.

52   **In fact, it's not only possible** National Defense Research Committee, "Sonic Deception: The Reproduction, Transmission, and Reception of Deceptive Sounds," 42.

CHAPTER THREE
Casting Call for Camoufleurs
1942–1944

53   *Deception is an art* Letter to Maj. Gen. Lowell Rooks, U.S. Army, undated, quoted in Dwyer, *Seaborne Deception: The History of U.S. Navy Beach Jumpers*, ix.

53   **Hal had the same** Details of background and service of Harold "Hal" Laynor (born Levinsky), from Gloria Laynor, interview by author, 8 December 2000. The name change took effect while he was in the service, but for clarity he is referred to as Laynor throughout.

55   **On another day** Details of background and service of Vic Dowd from Victor Dowd, interview by author, 19 January 2001.

56   **Dowd was first assigned** Details of service of Sollohub and the 84th cadre from Julian V. Sollohub, Col., USA (Ret.), personal biography and interview by author,

13 July 2001; Roosevelt's warning from Robert Breckinridge, *The New Science of Protective Concealment* (New York: Farrar & Rinehart, 1942), 219.

56 **Bill Blass had visited** Details of Blass's service and background from Bill Blass, interviews by author, 18 June 2001 and 22 August 2001.

57 **William Flemer III—son** Details of Flemer's background and service from William Flemer III, interviews by author, 21 March and 7 August 2001.

59 **The mystery was solved** "Fort Meade Soldier-Artist Carves Thirteen-Foot Bust of President," *Fort Meade Post Enterprise* (undated), 1.

59 **Blass stood six feet** George A. Martin, interview by author, 8 August 2001.

60 **Blass was assigned to B Company** Before the battalion shipped out, some of the older men such as Martineau were released from service, new recruits were added, and men were promoted or shifted around. Thus Levinsky wound up in D Company and Dowd became a sergeant, and so on.

61 **The other companies** 603d Engineer Camouflage Battalion, "Seasons Greetings," Christmas 1942 dinner menu and roster of 603d Engineer Camouflage Battalion. Courtesy Richard Morton and Julian V. Sollohub.

61 **"A lot of these guys . . ."** Ed Biow, interview by author, 27 March 2001.

61 **During basic training** Details of Shilstone's background and service from Arthur Shilstone, interviews by author, 27 February 2000, 19 June 2001, and 22 August 2001.

62 **Ellsworth Kelly took** Details of Kelly's service from Ellsworth Kelly, interview by author, 3 August 2001.

63 **So he wrote to the adjutant** James C. Boudreau, Director of Pratt Institute, gives the Fort Meade camouflage battalion contact name for students in a letter to Richard H. Morton, 1 July 1942.

65 **Fort George G. Meade** Details of Fort Meade from *About Fort George G. Meade, Maryland* (The Chesapeake and Potomac Telephone Company of Baltimore City, 1943), and Robert S. Johnson, Director, Fort George G. Meade Museum, interview by author, 1 August 2001.

65 **The athletic director** Martin Sonnenfeld, interview by author, 12 July 2001.

67 **In fact, a number of the camoufleurs** Ambrose, *Citizen Soldiers*, 266–267.

67 **One of the more flamboyant** Details of De Terey's background from *Flat-Top*, Newsletter of 603d Engineer Camouflage Battalion at Fort George G. Meade, MD, Vol 1, No. 6, 17 September 1943, 7; his boast as it appeared there: "I have had everything in my bed except a 2d. Lt. and a snake." Later version from Robert Dahl, interview by author, 6 August 2001.

68 **Jim Laubheimer, a Baltimore** The shooting-range incident and details of service from James B. Laubheimer, "Pop Pop Went to War" (unpublished memoir), 8–9, courtesy James B. Laubheimer; and interview by author, 8 May 2001.

69 **When the Romans** Siege of Syracuse story cited in Guy Hartcup, *Camouflage: A History of Concealment and Deception in War* (New York: Scribners, 1980), 11.

69 **The British had** Details about khaki uniforms from Ibid., 12.

69 **A small, wiry** Richard Meryman, "A Painter of Angels Became the Father of Camouflage," *Smithsonian*, April 1999, 116–125: other details of Thayer from several sources, including Meryman's excellent article.

69 **In the 1890s,** Gerald Handerson Thayer, "The Concealing Coloration of Animals, New Light on an Old Subject (an Essay on the Question of How, and to What Extent,—Not Why,—Animals Are Concealed by Their Colors) with Pictures from Photographs and Paintings," *Century Magazine*, Vol. LXXVI, 249–261: 251.

70 **As the great powers** Quoted in "A Painter of Angels Became the Father of Camouflage," 9.

71 **Dazzle soon attracted** Quoted in Roy R. Behrens, *Art and Camouflage: Concealment and Deception in Nature, Art and War* (Cedar Falls: North American Review, University of Northern Iowa, 1981), 45.

71 **And somehow the peculiar** Statistic from Behrens, *Art and Camouflage: Concealment and Deception in Nature, Art and War*, 45.

72 **The French experiment** André Ducasse, Jacques Meyer, Gabriel Perreux, *Vie et mort des Français, 1914–1918* (Paris 1962), 510–511, quoted in Stephen Kern, *The Culture of Time and Space 1880–1918* (London: Weidenfeld and Nicolson, 1983), 303.

72 **Camouflage could be hazardous** Hartcup, *Camouflage: A History of Concealment and Deception in War*, 19.

72 **Naturally, the French** Makeup of French camouflage corps from Behrens, *Art and Camouflage: Concealment and Deception in Nature, Art and War*, 41.

72 **Georges Braque, whose** Quoted in Behrens, *Art and Camouflage: Concealment and Deception in Nature, Art and War*, 41.

73 **Pershing wanted** Details on composition of World War I camouflage corps from Hartcup, *Camouflage: A History of Concealment and Deception in War*, 17–19; 29.

74 **"I was not a desk commander,"** Details of flattop construction from *U.S. Army Field Manual 5–20: Engineer Field Manual: Camouflage* (Chief of Engineers, 1 June 1940), 10–23.

74 **The enlisted men held** "Swing Mauls, Axes," *Flat-Top*, Vol. 1, No. 5, 8 July, 1943, 1.

74 **After a few months of classroom** *Flat-Top*, Vol. 1, No. 5, 8 July, 1943, 2.

76 **His troops were sorry** Richard Morton, "603d Engineer Camouflage Battalion: Formation and Training, 1942–1944" (unpublished), 1.

76 **Sollohub considered Fitz** Details of service of Louis D. Porter from Porter, interview by author, 11 April 2001.

76   For diversion, they *Flat-Top*, Vol. 1, No. 5, 8 July, 1943, 2; quote from Harold J. Dahl, letter to Mrs. Anna M. Dahl, 17 January 1942.

77   Once the Combined Chiefs Details of the situation in the ETO, the Cover plan COCKADE, and General Devers's role in establishing the 23d HQ Special Troops from "Cover & Deception Report, ETO (Top Secret, Copy 3 of 6): 'Cover & Deception Synopsis of History' " (forwarded 11 December 1944 with critique by Col. John H. Bevan, London Controlling Section Offices of the War Cabinet, London), RG 319, National Archives, College Park, MD.

78   A top-secret War Ibid., 3.

78   Fortunately, a second deception Ewen Montagu, *The Man Who Never Was* (New York: J. B. Lippincott and Co., 1954)

78   On board the USS *Monrovia* Account of Patton's meeting with Fairbanks from Fairbanks, *A Hell of a War*, 182.

78   The long, bellicose message Text of Patton's message from Fairbanks, "Amphibious Assault: A History of the U.S. Navy's Participation in the Invasion of Sicily," microfilm, n.d., Section 8–4 of the microfilmed historical narratives, Operational Archives, Naval Historical Center, Washington, D.C., 35.

80   The result: "This study recommended . . ." Cover and Deception Report ETO (top secret): "Cover & Deception Report, ETO (Top Secret, Copy 3 of 6): 'Cover & Deception Synopsis of History,' " 3. There is a great deal of folklore surrounding the creation of the 23d HQ Special Troops, including purported secret meetings between Roosevelt and General Marshall. The record indicates that planning for the unit took place at a much lower echelon, as was routine for all special units designed specifically to meet the new missions of World War II, according to the established military hierarchy of responsibility—as the ETO report makes clear.

80   In order to give it the best Ibid, 3; Fox and Flemer, *Official History of the 23d Headquarters Special Troops*, 3.

81   All the pieces were coming Ibid., 1–3.

CHAPTER FOUR
Artists of Razzle-Dazzle
January–May 1944

82   *The essence of successful* "Establishment of a Security Committee for Military Operations," memorandum from the Psychological Warfare Branch, MIS, to Joint U.S. Staff Planners, cover letters by A. H. Onthank, Secretary, and R. L. Vittrup, Secretariat, 2 May 1942, RG 218, JCS 234, National Archives, College Park, MD, 1.

82   *At last, Lt. Col. Cliff Simenson* Details of Simenson's career and activities from Clifford G. Simenson, Col., USA (Ret.), interviews by author, 29 August 2000, 16 September 2000, and 20 November 2000.

85 **Camp Forrest was named** Details of the camp and Tullahoma from *This Is Camp Forrest*, 1943, 5–11.

85 **He wasn't just splitting** U.S. *Army Field Manual 90–2: Battlefield Deception*, HQ-TRA DOC, 3 October 1988, 1–38 to 1–41.

85 **Colonel Harry L. Reeder** Details of Reeder's career from Fox and Flemer, *Official History of the 23d Headquarters Special Troops*, 2.

87 **"All Trulys are tall . . ."** Jeanne Truly Davis, correspondence with author, 22 December 2001.

87 **Truly had started out** Details of Truly's life from Davis, *Truly Family: Descendants of Hector Truly; Allied Families: Key and Whitney; Glimpses of Mississippi: 1800–1900*, Jeanne Truly Davis 2000, 28, 67, and 96.

87 **Simenson was also lucky** Details of Frederic E. Fox from Hannah Fox, interview by author, 7 August 2001; Simenson, interviews by author, 29 August 2000, 16 September 2000, 20 November 2000; and Syracuse, interviews by author, 19 December 2000.

88 **It was the day after New Year's** Account of the Battle of Princeton from Fox, "The Deception Team: War and Football Are Getting Trickier," 1–3; and Don Higginbotham, *The War of American Independence: Military Attitudes, Policies, and Practice, 1763–1789* (Bloomington and London: Indiana University Press, Wars of the United States Series, 1971), 165–171.

89 **Fox loved the story** *Webster's New World Dictionary*, Deluxe Second Edition, 1979.

89 **First, it had a focus** Six criteria for a successful deception from Joint Chiefs of Staff, *Joint Doctrine for Military Deception*, Joint Pub 3-58, 31 May 1996, TRADOC, 1-3.

89 **"All deception begins . . ."** William A. Harris, Col., GSC, Chief of Section; Ralph M. Ingersoll, Lt. Col., GSC, Plans Officer; and Hanford W. Eldridge, Maj., AC, Intelligence Officer; for Special Plans Branch, G-3, 12th Army Group, "Informal Report to Joint Security Control; Part I: Appreciation of Deception in the European Theater," Washington, D.C., 25 May 1945 (top secret), RG 319, National Archives, College Park, MD, 3.

90 **Fifth, it was *timely.*** Ibid., 3.

90 **In addition to identifying** U.S. *Army Field Manual 90-2: Battlefield Deception*, 5–15; Eric Ambler, *Send No More Roses* (London: Weidenfeld & Nicolson Limited, 1977), 62, quoted in Ibid., 1–10.

91 **Washington's audacious ruse** Ibid., 1–10.

91 **"The deception story,"** Ibid., 1–29 and 4–13.

92 **1. Who must hold** Ibid., 4–12 and 4–13.

92 **To fool the enemy** Criteria for a successful deception story from Joint Chiefs of Staff, *Joint Doctrine for Military Deception*, Joint Pub 3-58, 31 May 1996, A-2.

93 "One does not conduct . . ." *U.S. Army Field Manual 90-2: Battlefield Deception*, 4-1.

94 And Cornwallis's own Ibid., 1–33.

94 Targets, like a con man's Ibid., 1–7.

95 To achieve plausibility Criteria which follow from Joint Chiefs of Staff, *Joint Doctrine for Military Deception*, IV-5 to IV-8.

97 Current doctrine confirms *U.S. Army Field Manual 90-2: Battlefield Deception*, 1–1.

98 Bill Blass and Bob Tompkins Details of Blass and Tompkins from Robert R. Tompkins, interviews by author, 21 December 2000 and 27 December 2000.

99 They had been well Harold J. Dahl, letter to Lou Dahl, undated.

99 Fred Fox had made Frederic E. Fox, letter to Hannah Putnam Fox, 30 April 1944.

99 Ellsworth Kelly remembers Travel and embarkation details and accounts of combat operations from Fox and Flemer, *The Official History of the 23d Headquarters Special Troops*, 4; Kelly, interview by author, 3 August 2001.

CHAPTER FIVE
Deceptive Fidelity—The Sonic Campaign
1944

100 *What you got was a panorama* Roy T. Tucker, Col., USA (Ret.), interview by author, 8 September 2001.

100 *Under cover of night* Scenario and quote dialogue from *Sonic Deception*, War Department Miscellaneous film #1151, produced by Army Pictorial Service, U.S. Army Signal Corps, 1945, script by Darrel D. Rippeteau, Capt., USA.

103 Walter Manser, a slightly Background and service of Manser from Walter Manser, interviews by author, 14 September 2000 and 8 September 2001.

105 So they decided Correspondence relating to this concept quoted in and details of the project from Dwyer, *Seaborne Deception*, 15–16.

105 His accomplice, Vincent Mallory Ibid., 16.

107 "Thus, military acoustical . . ." Details about *presence* and the new speakers from M. D. Fagan, ed., *A History of Engineering and Science in the Bell System: National Service in War and Peace (1925–1975)* (New Jersey: Bell Telephone Laboratories, Inc., 1978), 225–226.

107 The device had originally From Allen Koenigsberg, "The Seventeen-Year Itch," lecture delivered at the U.S. Patent Office Bicentennial in Washington, D.C., 9 May 1990.

107 Bell Labs, working National Defense Research Committee, "Sonic Deception:

The Reproduction, Transmission, and Reception of Deceptive Sounds," 12–13. Other details of the "junior heater" system from the same report.

109 **The Doppler effect** National Defense Research Committee,"Sonic Deception: The Reproduction, Transmission, and Reception of Deceptive Sounds," 18.

112 **Major Charles Williams** Initial number of troops and later details of embarkation from Syracuse," Notes of 3132 Signal Service Company Special (unpublished), 1, courtesy Richard M. Syracuse; Table of Organization and full-strength numbers from Ivan R. Miller, Maj., AES, "Sonic Warfare: The Sonic Company—Organization, Equipment, Employment" (top-secret report for the information of a Secret War Department Mission), 23 September 1944, ten pages plus supplements, 1 and appended figures 1–4. Courtesy Darrel D. Rippeteau.

112 **In a matter of minutes** Details of the sonic equipment and usage from National Defense Research Committee, "Sonic Deception: The Reproduction, Transmission, and Reception of Deceptive Sounds," 7–16 and 44–69.

113 **Sonic operator Harold** Solder repair and details of service from Harold W. Flinn, interview by author, 8 September 2001.

113 **But there was a second** Gaskins, "Sonic Deception," 2.

113–114 ***There were two old maids*** Limerick (which seems to be missing a line) from Gilmore, interview by author, 7 September 2001.

114 **"The sound level . . ."** National Defense Research Committee, "Sonic Deception: The Reproduction, Transmission, and Reception of Deceptive Sounds," 17; following data all from the same report.

115 **For instance, they noted** Miller, "Sonic Warfare: The Sonic Company—Organization, Equipment, Employment," 2.

115 **In practice, the sonic** Miller, "Sonic Warfare: The Sonic Company—Organization, Equipment, Employment," 3–4.

115 **The AES engineers** Fagen, ed., *A History of Engineering and Science in the Bell System*, 227.

117 **One of those warriors** Details of Brown's background and service from William W. Brown, interviews by author, 14 September 2000 and 8 September 2001.

117 **The remainder, Brown's** Sonic mission described in Miller, "Sonic Warfare: The Sonic Company—Organization, Equipment, Employment,"4.

118 **By late spring one important member** Details of Walker's experiences as a chemical officer from John Walker, interviews by author, 8 September 2001 and 6 December 2001.

120 **When the word came** Barrett, interview by author, 7 September 2001.

121 **Railey's boys had trained** Railey comment from Manser, interview by author, 8 September 2001.

CHAPTER SIX
Dress Rehearsal at Stratford-upon-Avon
May–July 1944

122 **If all the knights** Richard H. Morton, letter to Mr. and Mrs. Leon S. Morton, 17 May 1944.

122 **The USS *Henry Gibbons*** Sailing details from John W. Arnett, ed., "The Ghost Army Days of Walter Wendell Arnett" (unpublished, 1998), 9, courtesy Dr. John W. Arnett and Richard H. Morton; and from Fox and Flemer, *Official History of the 23d Headquarters Special Troops*, 4–5.

122 **While the escort Corvettes** Laubheimer, "Pop Pop Went to War," 17.

122 **The troops, as usual** Details of service of Richard H. Morton from Morton, interview by author, 7 May 2001.

123 **Many of the guys** Laubheimer, "Pop Pop Went to War," 16.

123 **Fred Fox followed** Frederic E. Fox, letter to Hannah Putnam Fox, 8 May 1944.

124 **He befriended Capt. Tom** Ibid.

124 **Fox had already assumed** Frederic E. Fox, letter to Hannah Putnam Fox, 25 May 1944.

124 **Rounding the coast** Laubheimer, "Pop Pop Went to War," 17.

124 **On the night of May 15** Ibid.

124 **Shilstone was struck** Details of service of Arthur Shilstone from Shilstone, interview by author, 19 June 2001.

125 **Albert Edward, Prince of** Elizabeth Hamilton, *The Warwickshire Scandal* (London: Pan MacMillan, 2000; first published by Michael Russell Publishing, Ltd., Norwich, 1999), 111. All details of the scandal from her fascinating book.

126 **Fox, the scriptwriter** Frederic E. Fox, letter to Hannah Putnam Fox, 16 May 1944.

126 **"We are living in tents . . ."** Richard H. Morton, letters to Mr. and Mrs. Leon S. Morton, 21 May 1944 and 16 July 1944.

127 **A mile down the Kineton** Details about wartime Wellesbourne from Elizabeth Hamilton, ed., *Wellesbourne at War 1939–1945* (The Wellesbourne, England, Village Society: Stephen England, Elsie Grant, Alan Griffin, Elizabeth Hamilton, Rety Harrison, Robin Harrison, Dennis Heath, Eric Herwin, Nancy Little, n.d.).

127 **Walter Arnett, the cartoonist** Arnett, ed., "The Ghost Army Days of Walter Wendell Arnett," 12.

128 **Even the gentry** Hamilton, ed., *Wellesbourne at War 1939–1945*, 1.

128 **The Special Troops** Frederic E. Fox, letter to Hannah Putnam Fox, 16 May 1944.

128 **The Special Troops were not** Lady Elizabeth Hamilton, interview by author, 23 February 2001.

129 **Still, catering to F.** Iris Irwin, letter to the author, 11 May 2001.

129 **The Americans were impressed** Harold J. Dahl, letters to Mrs. Anna M. Dahl, 29 May 1944, 22 May 1944, 1 July 1944.

130 **"The feeling over here . . ."** Harold J. Dahl, letter to Mrs. Anna M. Dahl, 7 July 1944.

130 **Lieutenant Colonel Olen J. Seaman** "Cover & Deception Report, ETO (Top Secret, Copy 3 of 6): 'Cover & Deception Synopsis of History,' " 6.

131 **Many of the troops** Guy Hartcup, *Camouflage: A History of Concealment and Deception in War* (New York: Charles Scribner's Sons, 1980), 53–58.

131 **Walter Arnett from headquarters** Details of Arnett's service in Swansea from Arnett, ed., "The Ghost Army Days of Walter Wendell Arnett," 12–13.

131 **Three years earlier** "The city's bleakest nights at the hands of Hitler's air force," "Swansea's Three Nights' Blitz," *South Wales Evening Post*, 10 February 2001, 2.

132 **Before long, on the billiard-felt** There is some disagreement about when the 603d actually received its pneumatic dummies. The *Official History* mentions briefly that the men trained with them at Camp Forrest, but no veteran interviewed recalls seeing one until Walton Hall.

132 **Now that the equipment** Richard H. Morton, letter to Mr. and Mrs. Leon S. Morton, 28 May 1944.

132 **To exploit the enemy's** Wooden bomb tale recounted in *U.S. Army Field Manual 90-2: Battlefield Deception*, 5–12.

132 **Their signature props** Ibid., 5–1.

132 **The pneumatic rubber** Specifications of pneumatic equipment from "Cover & Deception Report, ETO (Secret): Exhibit '9,' 'Report on Pneumatic Dummy Equipment,' 15 September 1944, Headquarters Twelfth Army Group," RG 319, National Archives, College Park, MD.

134 **At the end of May** Details of WWI tank camouflage from Hartcup, *A History of Concealment and Deception in War*, 21–22.

136 **But by the time Walker** Fox "(before LETTER #19)." *Dear Hannah / Dear Fred*, wartime letters of Frederic E. Fox and Hannah Putnam with explanatory prefaces by Fox (unpublished), courtesy Rev. Donald H. Fox and Hannah Putnam Fox.

CHAPTER SEVEN
Seeing the Elephant
June–July 1944

139 ***Seeing the Elephant*** During the American Civil War, the expression old hands used to describe a new recruit's first experience in battle was "seeing the elephant."

139 **The adjustment from man** Fox and Flemer, *Official History of the 23d Head-quarters Special Troops*, 3.

139 **As a privileged member** Frederic E. Fox, letter to Hannah Putnam Fox, 28 May 1944.

139 **As both a writer and actor** Frederic E. Fox, letter to Hannah Putnam Fox, 25 May 1944.

139 **But hardly had Fox** Frederic E. Fox, letter to Hannah Putnam Fox, 13 May 1945.

140 **His lighthearted, offhand** "Enemy Order of Battle in the West as at 6 June 1944" in "Cover & Deception Report ETO, Exhibit '6': 'Operations in Support of Neptune' (F) Results," RG 319, National Archives, College Park, MD.

140 **At Eisenhower's headquarters** Additional details of Operation TROUTFLY from Fox, "The Deception Team: War and Football Are Getting Trickier" (unpublished manuscript), 29 pages, Frederic Fox papers, Box 99, Dwight D. Eisenhower Presidential Library, Abilene, KS, 7–8.

141 **Ground troops quickly** Frederic E. Fox, letter to Hannah Putnam Fox, 17 June 1944; details and quotes from action with the 82d Airborne from Fox "(before LETTER #19)." *Dear Hannah / Dear Fred*.

142 **"It is very noisy . . ."** Frederic E. Fox, letter to Hannah Putnam Fox, 12 June 1944.

142 **Fox was a little** Frederic E. Fox, letter to Hannah Putnam Fox, 23 July 1944.

143 **Yet it was beautiful** Frederic E. Fox, letter to Hannah Putnam Fox, 17 June 1944.

143 **More heartbreaking than** Ibid.

143 **"As soon as the plane lands . . ."** That American tanks drove over their own men in an effort to get up the beach is reported by *Boston Globe* correspondent Iris Carpenter, quoted in Nancy Caldwell Sorel, *The Women Who Wrote the War* (New York: Arcade, 1999), 227.

144 **Twenty-four litters** Details of surgical evacuation from Sorel, *The Women Who Wrote the War*, 247.

145 **"The jerk was probably . . ."** Paul Fussell, *Wartime: Understanding and Behavior in the Second World War* (New York: Oxford University Press, 1989), 80.

146 **Probably no other unit** Fox and Flemer, *Official History of the 23d Headquarters Special Troops*, 6.

146 **The little, curious details** Laubheimer, "Pop Pop Went to War," 20.

146 **Once they got** Ibid, 21.

147 **Laubheimer motored in** The account and quotes of the nighttime journey from Laubheimer, "Pop Pop Went to War," 22–24.

148 **The Special Troops practiced** Harold Laynor, letter to Gloria Laynor, undated.

149 **And like the others** Harold Laynor, letter to Gloria Laynor, 23 July 1944.

153 **The D-Day invasion** For details of these and other D-Day foul-ups, see Fussell, *Wartime*, Chapter 3, "Someone Had Blundered."

154 **In evaluating the effectiveness** James W. Snee, Lt. Col., Cavalry, Commander (Armored Force), "Comments on Operation 1–4 July 44, by Lt. Colonel Snee, Armored Force Officer" (top secret), 4 July 1944, RG 407, SPHQ-23-0.3, National Archives, College Park, MD, 1.

154 **Snee's colleague at** E. W. Schroeder, Lt. Col., Cavalry, "Comments on Operation 1–4 July, by Commander CCR," 4 July 1944 (top secret), RG 407, SPHQ-23-0.3, National Archives, College Park, MD, 1.

155 **After the operation,** Fox and Flemer, *Official History of the 23d Headquarters Special Troops*, 8.

155 **Fox and the others** "Cover & Deception Report, ETO (Top Secret, Copy 3 of 6): Exhibit '8,' 'Tactical Operation "D," ' 6 Sept. 1944, H. L. Reeder, Col. Inf. Commanding," RG 319, National Archives, College Park, MD.

155 **Never shy about** Here and elsewhere quoted from Fox, "Memorandum 11 July 1944," RG 407, SPHQ-23-0.3, National Archives, College Park, MD.

156 **Some of the dummy** Fox, "The Deception Team: War and Football Are Getting Trickier," 9.

156 **"Since the enemy . . ."** Fox and Flemer, *Official History of the 23d Headquarters Special Troops*, 8–9. Further details of Special Troops doctrine from both *Official History* and Fox's memorandum of 11 July 1944.

157 **"Fred was always . . ."** Hannah Putnam Fox, interview by author, 7 August 2001.

157 **Colonels, too, were** George Rebh, Gen., USA (Ret.), interview by author, 16 September 2000.

CHAPTER EIGHT
Bad Show at Brest
August 1944

162 *The valuable lesson* David Mure, *Master of Deception*, 81–82, quoted in *U.S. Army Field Manual 90-2: Battlefield Deception,* 1–15.

163 **Their journeys toward Brest** Fox, "The Deception Team: War and Football Are Getting Trickier," 10.

163 **The "special angel"** Quoted in "Ingersoll: Pen vs. Sword," *Newsweek*, 20 July 1942, 28.

163 **Fox picked up his orders** Fox, "The Deception Team: War and Football Are Getting Trickier," 11.

164 **"When they saw trucks . . ."** Ibid., 11.

164 **Already the Special Troops** Harold J. Dahl, letter to Mrs. Anna M. and Lou Dahl, 8 August 1944.

164 **At Coutances,** Laubheimer, "Pop Pop Went to War," 29.

165 **They traveled on** Richard H. Morton, letter to Mr. and Mrs. Leon S. Morton, 7 August 1944.

165 **He formed the habit** Richard H. Morton, letter to Mr. and Mrs. Leon S. Morton, 21 August 1944.

165 **As they turned** Harold J. Dahl, letters to Mrs. Anna M. and Lou Dahl, 15 August 1944 and 8 August 1944.

166 **"Please send me also . . ."** Harold J. Dahl, letter to Mrs. Anna M. and Lou Dahl, 8 August 1944.

167 **August 1944 was a chaotic** For an excellent and full account of the confusing post-invasion situation in Normandy, see Ambrose, *Citizen Soldiers*, especially Chapters 1–3.

168 **All told, about a hundred thousand** Figures from Ambrose, *The Supreme Commander: The War Years of General Dwight D. Eisenhower* (New York: Doubleday, 1970), 477–478.

169 **"The principal and ultimate . . ."** Fairbanks, *A Hell of a War*, 232.

169 **Since shipping out** Ibid., 176.

170 **John Steinbeck, then** John Steinbeck, "Ventotene," from *Once There Was a War* (New York: Viking, 1958; first serialized in the *New York Herald Tribune* June–December 1943), 165.

170 **By the time of ANVIL** Silver Star citation from "Commander Douglas Elton Fairbanks, Jr., U.S.N.R.," Command File World War II, Operational Archives, Naval Historical Center, Washington, D.C., 2; quote from Fairbanks, *A Hell of a War*, 232.

170 **The invasion target** Ibid., 233.

170 **On August 17** Legion of Merit Citation from "Commander Douglas Elton Fairbanks, Jr., U.S.N.R.," 2.

171 **In the flurry of activity** Garrison estimates and American casualty statistics from Robert A. Miller, *August 1944* (California: Presidio, 1988), 216, 217, and 219.

172 **This division was not only inconvenient** Carl von Clausewitz, *On War*, ed. and trans. by Michael Howard and Peter Paret (New Jersey: Princeton University Press, 1976), 204.

173 **On August 20** Simenson, Commanding, "Report of Task Force Z, Operation BREST, 20–27 Aug 44 (top secret)," RG 407, SPHQ-23-0.3, National Archives, College Park, MD, 3.

173 **If the Germans could** Fox and Flemer, *Official History of the 23d Headquarters Special Troops*, 12.

174 **In the morning twilight** Memorandum from Headquarters 709th Tank Battalion, "Summary of Operations, 01 to 30 November 1944," published in Dale Adams Hughes, *331 Days: The Story of the Men of the 709th Tank Battalion* (Arizona: D. A. Hughes, 1980), B-32. In late November 1944, while checking his platoons, Perry would disappear in the Hürtgen Forest, missing in action, presumed killed.

174 **Meanwhile, thirteen miles east of Simenson's** Details of operations of Task Force Y from John W. Mayo, Lt. Col. Field Artillery, Commanding, "Report on Operation of Task Force Y (Brest) (Aug 231900–261400) in Support of Elements of 2d Inf Div Arty, 29 August 1944 (secret)," RG 407, SPHQ-23-0.3, National Archives, College Park, MD.

178 **Simenson controlled his** Simenson, "Report of Task Force Z, Operation BREST, 20–27 Aug 44," 4.

178 **As the first program** R. W. Rushton, Maj., Infantry, G-3 Special Plans Branch, "Special Signal Instructions, 23 August 1944," and Major Rohr, "Radio instructions for team to 29th Div. 24 August 1944," RG 407, SPHQ-23-0.3, National Archives, College Park, MD.

178 **An observer for** Bill W. Padan, Capt., Field Artillery, Asst. G-3, "Memorandum to Chief of Staff, 2d Infantry Division, 24 August 1944," RG 407, SPHQ-23-0.3, National Archives, College Park, MD, 1.

178 **"It was mutually agreed . . ."** Lt. Col. Simenson, Commanding, "Report of Task Force Z, Operation BREST, 20–27 Aug 44," 4.

179 **At nightfall, D Company** Account of Task Force X from H. L. Reeder, Col., Infantry, Commanding, "Reports on Operations Involving Special Troops. (Operation BREST 20–27 Aug 44) to Commanding General, Supreme Allied Expeditionary Force, G-3 Division Forward, 6 September 1944 (top secret)"; Oscar W. Seale, Capt Inf Arm'd, Commanding, "Task Force 'X'—Operational Report for Period 230715 Aug–260115 Aug, 1944 (secret)"; Cyrus H. Searcy, Col., GSC, Chief of Staff, Headquarters VIII Corps, "Report on Results of Deception Operation at BREST" to Commanding General, 12th Army Group, 11 September 1944" (top secret); and James W. Snee, Lt. Col., Cavalry, Commanding Task Force "A," "Report on Operations at Brest Period 20–27 August 1944 (top secret), 29 August 1944," all RG 407, SPHQ-23-0.3, National Archives, College Park, MD.

179 **Tompkins had already** Quotations from Tompkins, "World War II Diary" (typescript of three-by-three-inch fifty-six-page diary, typed by Ethel Blass, July 1945), courtesy Robert R. Tompkins, 3.

181 **Orders seemed to** Seale, "Task Force 'X'—Operational Report for Period 230715 Aug–260115 Aug, 1944," 5.

182 **Simenson concurred, in** Simenson, "Report of Task Force Z, Operation BREST, 20–27 Aug 44," 5.

182 **At 8:30 P.M., Seale** Charles R. Williams, Maj., Signal Corps, Commanding, "Report of Sonic Operation (Task Force 'X') BREST 23–26 Aug 44," RG 407, SPHQ 23-0.3, National Archives, College Park, MD, 4.

183 **Snee, whose approved plan** Snee, "Report on Operations at Brest Period 20–27 August 1944 (top secret), 29 August 1944," 3.

184 **The cost was high** The initial figure reported by Seale, "Task Force 'X'—Operational Report for Period 230715 Aug–260115 Aug, 1944," 1: ". . . five light tanks of this company were knocked out prior to 1800, 25 Aug." One of the five actually overran a dug-in German emplacement and fell into it, thus immobilizing it. Figures here are taken from Hughes, *331 Days: The Story of the Men of the 709th Tank Battalion*, which includes complete after-action reports by Capt. Thomas C. Perry, commander of D Company, 18–19; B-16.

185 **After the sonic operation** William A. Harris, Col., GSC, Chief of Section; Ralph M. Ingersoll, Lt. Col., GSC, Plans Officer; and Hanford W. Eldridge, Maj., AC, Intelligence Officer; for Special Plans Branch, G-3, 12th Army Group, "Informal Report to Joint Security Control; Part I: Appreciation of Deception in the European Theater; Part II: Possibilities for Employment of Deception in the Pacific; Part III: Research of Deception Results, European Theater; Part IV: Officers with Cover and Deception Experience, European Theater," Washington, D.C., 25 May 1945 (top secret), RG 319, National Archives, College Park, MD, 4.

185 **It was an old lesson** *U.S. Army Field Manual 90-2: Battlefield Deception,* 1–31.

186 **Lieutenant Colonel John Mayo** Mayo, "Report on Operation of Task Force Y (Brest) (Aug 231900–261400) in Support of Elements of 2d Inf Div Arty, 29 August 1944 (secret)," MD, 2–3.

186 **On Saturday, with the attack** Tompkins, "World War II Diary," 3.

187 **"We were always in trucks . . ."** Jack Masey, interview by author, 3 April 2001.

187 **He fell for the ruse** Searcy, "Report on Results of Deception Operation at BREST to Commanding General, 12th Army Group, 11 September 1944 (top secret)," 2.

CHAPTER NINE
Hold That Ghost Line
September–October 1944

189 *"Deception is common sense . . ."* Quoted in *U.S. Army Field Manual 90-2: Battlefield Deception,* 3–1.

191 **"It was a charming . . ."** Fox, "The Deception Team: War and Football Are Getting Trickier," 12. Other details about SIDECAR from Fox and Flemer, *Official History of the 23d Headquarters Special Troops,* 14.

191 **While they waited** Fox, "The Deception Team: War and Football Are Getting Trickier," 13.

192 **It must have been a prodigious** Details of "Cognac Hill" from Fox and Flemer, *Official History of the 23d Headquarters Special Troops,* and *Hold That Ghost* (Universal, 1941); Fox mistakenly reports the title of the film as *Ghost Breakers,* the title of a Bob Hope–Paulette Goddard romantic comedy also made in 1941.

192 **Apparently, the cache** Frederic E. Fox, letter to Hannah Putnam Fox, 7 October 1944.

192 **Hal Laynor wrote** Quotes from Harold Laynor, letter to Gloria Laynor, 4 September 1944.

193 **For the first time** Harold Laynor, letter to Gloria Laynor, 1 September 1944.

193 **Harold Dahl shared** Harold J. Dahl, letter to Mrs. Anna M. and Lou Dahl, 3 September 1944.

193 **Fox lost no time** Frederic E. Fox, letter to Hannah Putnam Fox, 11 September 1944.

194 **Shortly after leaving** Frederic E. Fox, letter to Hannah Putnam Fox, 2 November 1944.

194 **Richard Morton, like most** Richard H. Morton, letter to Mr. and Mrs. Leon S. Morton, 10 September 1944.

195 **He toured the city** Morton quotes from Richard H. Morton, letter to Mr. and Mrs. Leon S. Morton, 17 September 1944.

195 **Dahl continued to be** Harold J. Dahl, letter to Mrs. Anna M. and Lou Dahl, 19 August 1944.

196 **At last in Paris** Harold J. Dahl, letter to Mrs. Anna M. and Lou Dahl, 31 October 1944.

196 **Laynor had dreamed** Laynor quotes from Harold Laynor, letter to Gloria Laynor, 24 September 1944.

198 **Midday, a village** Impersonation based on account by Fox, "The Deception Team: War and Football Are Getting Trickier," 15.

199 **Likewise, by now** Frederic E. Fox, letter to Hannah Putnam Fox, 7 October 1944.

199 **Operation BETTEMBOURG** Details of Operation BETTEMBOURG from "Cover & Deception Report, ETO (Top Secret, Copy 3 of 6): Exhibit '8,' 'Tactical Operation "D," ' 6 Sept. 1944, H. L Reeder, Col. Inf. Commanding," which contains the operational Journal, as well as reports by Capt. Oscar M. Seale, Lt. Col. James W. Snee, Col. Harry L. Reeder, Col. Clifford G. Simenson, Lt. Col. Edgar W. Schroeder, Maj. Charles H. Yokum, Capt. Robert R. Hiller, Maj. David H. Bridges, and map overlays; RG 319, National Archives, College Park, MD.

199 **To the south, after** Fox and Flemer, *Official History of the 23d Headquarters Special Troops*, 15.

201 **And of course** Fox, "The Deception Team: War and Football Are Getting Trickier," 15.

202 **"By this time . . ."** Laubheimer, "Pop Pop Went to War," 31.

202 **Laynor also was** Harold Laynor, letter to Gloria Laynor, 1 September 1944.

202 **Like many of the guys** Harold Laynor, letter to Gloria Laynor, 24 September 1944.

202 **Dave Wynshaw remembers** Wynshaw's experiences from David Wynshaw, interview by author, 11 July 2001.

203 **"Civilians in nearby villages . . ."** Seale, Commanding, "Operational Report for Period 151830 Sep–222215 Sep 44 (top secret)," RG 407, SPHQ-23-0.3, National Archives, College Park, MD, 1.

203 **Two civilians were spied** David H. Bridges, Maj., Field Artillery, S-4, "Summary of Special Effects for BETTEMBOURG Operation 15–22 Sept 1944 (top secret)," RG 407, SPHQ-23-0.3, National Archives, College Park,. MD, 1.

203 **France had been friendly** 23d Headquarters Special Troops, "Journal of Operation Bettembourg (top secret), 16–25 September 1944," RG 407, SPHQ-23-0.3, National Archives, College Park, MD.

204 **"We're the only outfit . . ."** Tompkins, "World War II Diary," 4.

204 **"We should have moved . . ."** Ibid., 5.

205 **Intelligence also reported** Fox, "The Deception Team: War and Football Are Getting Trickier," 15.

205 **Tompkins recorded** Tompkins, "World War II Diary," 4.

CHAPTER TEN
Can You Hear Me, Luxembourg?
October–November 1944

206 *Colonel Reeder assembled* Reeder's speech from Laubheimer, interview by author, 8 May 2001 and "Pop Pop Went to War," 33.

208 **On September 25** Fox and Flemer, *Official History of the 23d Headquarters Special Troops*, 16.

208 **"The Germans have painted . . ."** Frederic E. Fox, letter to Hannah Putnam Fox, 24 October 1944.

209 **The men climbed** Laubheimer, "Pop Pop Went to War," 32.

209 **The mattresses, though** Arnett, ed., "The Ghost Army Days of Walter Wendell Arnett," 17.

209 **Patton recognized the critical** General George S. Patton Jr., *War As I Knew It* (Boston: Houghton Mifflin, 1995), 156.

210 **Laynor wrote to** Harold Laynor, letter to Gloria Laynor, 7 October 1944.

211 **In Luxembourg, Nazi** Richard H. Morton, letter to Mr. and Mrs. Leon S. Morton, 28 September 1944.

211 **In time, the Special Troops** Annie Michel, "A Letter From Luxembourg," *The Stars and Stripes*, Friday, 1 December 1944, 1.

212 **Laynor was among** Quotes from Harold Laynor, letter to Gloria Laynor, 7 October 1944.

212 **The signal operators** Fox, "The Deception Team: War and Football Are Getting Trickier," 17.

213 **"One measure of success . . ."** Ibid., 17.

213 **A second operation, VASELINE** Details of Operation VASELINE from Fox and Flemer, *Official History of the 23d Headquarters Special Troops*, 17.

213 **Though not assigned** Tompkins, "World War II Diary," 6.

214 **Laynor wrote to** Harold Laynor, letter to Gloria Laynor, 7 October 1944.

214 **George Vander Sluis** Harold J. Dahl, letter to Mrs. Anna M. and Lou Dahl, 1 October 1944.

214 **On October 17** William U. Hooper, Maj., CE, Executive Officer, "Memorandum 17 October 1944."

215 **ELSENBORN (November 3–12) was** Details on Operation ELSENBORN from Fox, "The Deception Team: War and Football Are Getting Trickier," 17–19.

215 **But the Hürtgen itself** For details of the battle, I am indebted to the authoritative account by Charles Whiting, *The Battle of Hurtgen Forest: The Untold Story of a Disastrous Campaign* (New York: Orion, 1989).

216 **"We began to get** Fox, "The Deception Team: War and Football Are Getting Trickier," 17.

216 **A captured German** Ibid., 19.

217 **The other two Special Troops operations** Paraphrase from Patton, *War As I Knew It*, 97.

217 **DALLAS (November 2–10) would** Details of Operation DALLAS from Fox and Flemer, *Official History of the 23d Headquarters Special Troops*, 19–20.

217 **"Squads alternate firing . . ."** Tompkins, "World War II Diary," 6.

219 **So Simenson had no** The *Official History* maintains that no sonic projection took place because of the planned crossing of the 95th. However, several eyewitnesses report that some sonic programs were projected and then shut down. Fox, principal author of the history, was in Elsenborn during the period of CASANOVA, perhaps the only time he was not an eyewitness to an operation.

219 **Patton visited the 90th** Patton, *War As I Knew It*, 172.

220 **The Special Troops** Tompkins, "World War II Diary," 7.

220 **Meanwhile air raids** Harold J. Dahl, letter to Mrs. Anna M. and Lou Dahl, 5 November 1944.

220 "It hadn't been reduced . . ." Frederic E. Fox, letter to Hannah Putnam Fox, 2 November 1944.

221 **On November 15** Frederic E. Fox, letter to Hannah Putnam Fox, 16 November 1944.

221 **Dahl was pleased** Harold J. Dahl, letter to Mrs. Anna M. and Lou Dahl, 16 November 1944.

221 **They had all hoped** Harold Laynor, letter to Gloria Laynor, 17 December 1944.

221 **Dahl bought a violin** Harold J. Dahl, letter to Mrs. Anna M. and Lou Dahl, 25 November 1944.

223 **As the commotion** *Luxemburger Wort*, 23 November 1944, 1.

223 **The troops were treated** Frederic E. Fox, letter to Hannah Putnam Fox, 23 November 1944.

224 **A week prior to Thanksgiving** Fox and Flemer, *Official History of the 23d Headquarters Special Troops*, 21.

CHAPTER ELEVEN
The Long, Cruel Winter
December 1944–January 1945

227 **KOBLENZ had started off** Details of Operation KOBLENZ from Fox, "The Deception Team: War and Football Are Getting Trickier," 19–22.

227 **"On the other side . . ."** Fox, "The Deception Team: War and Football Are Getting Trickier," 20.

232 **The futility of the Ardennes** Frederic E. Fox, letter to Hannah Putnam Fox, 29 December 1944.

232 **As the battle raged** Details of Operation KODAK from Fox, "The Deception Team: War and Football Are Getting Trickier," 23.

234 **The violent clash going** Frederic E. Fox, letter to Hannah Putnam Fox, 29 December 1944.

234 **Not long after** Tompkins, "World War II Diary," 9.

234 **The drive was typical** Harold J. Dahl, letter to Mrs. Anna M. and Lou Dahl, 1 January 1945.

235 **They'd also managed** Harold J. Dahl, letter to Mrs. Anna M. and Lou Dahl, 24 December 1944.

235 **Laubheimer wrote later** Laubheimer, "Pop Pop Went to War," 38.

236 **Morton recalls, "Enough . . ."** Richard H. Morton, letter to Mr. and Mrs. Leon S. Morton, 24 December 1944.

236 **Fox spent Christmas Eve** Frederic E. Fox, letter to Hannah Putnam Fox, 24 December 1944.

236 **That evening he found** Frederic E. Fox, letter to Hannah Putnam Fox, 5 February 1945.

237 **"Verdun is a depressing . . ."** Fox and Flemer, *Official History of the 23d Headquarters Special Troops*, 23.

237 **Laubheimer wrote, "There . . ."** Laubheimer, "Pop Pop Went to War," 30.

238 **New Year's Eve** Fox and Flemer, *Official History of the 23d Headquarters Special Troops*, 23.

239 **"Jerry just came in . . ."** Tompkins, "World War II Diary," 10.

240 **"He as well as Phil . . ."** Account of Pelliccioni's death and quotes from Flinn, correspondence, 12 November 2001.

241 **The operation, at least** Fox and Flemer, *Official History of the 23d Headquarters Special Troops*, 24.

241 **The Special Troops scarcely** Ibid., 25; details of Operation L'ÉGLISE, Ibid. 23–24; and Fox, "The Deception Team: War and Football Are Getting Trickier," 23–24.

241 **After five days** Ibid., 24.

242 **This was likely** It is also possible that Railey didn't appear at the front until February 13–14 for Operation MERZIG. In either case he didn't stay very long.

243 **The weather finally broke** Fox and Flemer, *Official History of the 23d Headquarters Special Troops*, 26.

243 **On the day the Germans** Frederic E. Fox, letter to Hannah Putnam Fox, 17 December 1944.

243 **"Well I saw more snow . . ."** Richard H. Morton, letter to Mr. and Mrs. Leon S. Morton, 16 February 1945.

243 **Despite an occasional spree** Frederic E. Fox, letter to Hannah Putnam Fox, 2 February 1945.

244 **For a time, it** Fox and Flemer, *Official History of the 23d Headquarters Special Troops*, appendix V.

244 **The winter of 1944–45** Russell Weigley, *Eisenhower's Lieutenants: The Campaign of France and Germany, 1944–1945* (Bloomington: Indiana University Press, 1981), quoted in Ambrose, *Citizen Soldiers*, 393.

244 **"It will take me years . . ."** Harold J. Dahl, letter to Mrs. Anna M. and Lou Dahl, 21 November 1944.

CHAPTER TWELVE
The Deadliest Show
February–March 1945

245 **And Truly stood out** Truly's daughter, Jeanne Truly Davis, recalls that her father was a stickler for wearing the proper uniform and is surprised at Wynshaw's recollection of his wearing sneakers—such a breach would have been very out of character. Davis, interview by author, 22 December 2001.

249 **About a week later** Quote and details of Operation MERZIG from Fox and Flemer, *Official History of the 23d Headquarters Special Troops*, 27.

249 **To hold the Panzers** Ibid., 27.

249 **While the sonic cars** Frederic E. Fox, letter to Hannah Putnam Fox, 2 February 1945.

249 **Back in their billets** Harold J. Dahl, letter to Mrs. Anna M. and Lou Dahl, 3 February 1945.

249 **As usual they** Ibid.

250 **Weary from the muddy** Harold J. Dahl, letter to Mrs. Anna M. and Lou Dahl, 3 March 1945.

251 **Dahl was struck** Harold J. Dahl, letter to Mrs. Anna M. and Lou Dahl, 25 March 1945.

251 **They were also seeing** Harold J. Dahl, letter to Mrs. Anna M. and Lou Dahl, 23 March 1945.

251 **But this time** Fox and Flemer, *Official History of the 23d Headquarters Special Troops*, 28.

252 **Immediately, on March 11** Details of Operation BOUZONVILLE from Fox, "The Deception Team: War and Football Are Getting Trickier," 24–25.

252 **"Leave Briey at 7:30 . . ."** Tompkins, "World War II Diary," 11.

252 **Fox's old friend** Fox, "The Deception Team: War and Football Are Getting Trickier," 24–25.

253 **On March 12, Tompkins** Tompkins, "World War II Diary," 11.

254 **The jeep that passed** Fox, "The Deception Team: War and Football Are Getting Trickier," 24.

255 **He had last seen** Fox, letter to Barbara Wells, 17 May 1945.

255 **Writing many years** Fox, "The Deception Team: War and Football Are Getting Trickier," 24.

255 **The artillery didn't** Tompkins, "World War II Diary," 11.

255 **Worse was to come** There is some disagreement in the record about whether the lethal shelling of the convoy took place on March 12 or 13. Since the operation

began about 3:00 A.M. on March 11 and lasted thirty-three hours, and the shelling occurred as the outfit was leaving the area, it seems most likely that it happened on March 13.

256 **In the first published** Quoted in Henry J. Boyanowski, "Ghost Army Fools Foe in Neatest Trick of the War," *Worcester Daily Telegram*, 4 October 1945, 1. Messina was a signalman, and it remains a mystery how he knew all the details about the "Big Picture" as he relates them in the article—or how the War Department censor passed it in the first place, as is claimed in an editorial introduction. His account does not square with other eyewitness accounts, none of which claims the vehicles were moving—and certainly not *into* Saarlautern.

256 **Tompkins had pulled** Tompkins, "World War II Diary," 11.

256 **"I had already experienced . . ."** Quotes from Harold A. Laynor, "Pain (A True Short Story)," 8 May 1947 (unpublished), courtesy Gloria Laynor.

259 **More than a month** Harold Laynor, letter to Gloria Laynor, 22 April 1945.

260 **In the hospital** Harold Laynor, letter to Gloria Laynor, 25 March 1945.

260 **When he was well** Harold Laynor, letter to Gloria Laynor, 16 April 1945.

260 **And despite the soft** Harold Laynor, letter to Gloria Laynor, 16 April 1945.

CHAPTER THIRTEEN
Grand Illusion
March 1945

263 **The Allies had battled** For details of the battle of the Rhine, I am indebted to Allen, *One More River: The Rhine Crossings of 1945*; Ambrose, *Citizen Soldiers: The U.S. Army from the Normandy Beaches to the Bulge to the Surrender of Germany June 7, 1944–May 7, 1945*; Breuer, *Storming Hitler's Rhine: the Allied Assault: February–March 1945*; and Montgomery, *Normandy to the Baltic—Victory*.

264 **Ralph Ingersoll, the Special Plans** Ralph Ingersoll, *Top Secret* (New York: Harcourt Brace and Company, 1946), 298–309.

267 **The orders from Ninth Army** 30th Infantry Division, "Annex #1 to G-2 Periodic report No. 282, 30th Infantry Division, Deception Measures for Operation 'FLASHPOINT' (secret), 26 March 1945," RG 407, SPHQ-23-0.1, National Archives, College Park, MD, 1.

267 **"Finally," according to** Ibid., 1.

269 **Embedded within EXPLOIT was** Merrick H. Truly, Lt. Col., Infantry, "Revised Plan for Employment of 23d Sp Trs Operation 'EXPLOIT,' 13 March 1945," RG 407, SPHQ-23-0.3, National Archives, College Park, MD, 1; details of Operation VIERSEN from above document and from Fox and Flemer, *Official History of the 23d Headquarters Special Troops*, 29–31, and appended "Digest of Operations" section XXI: Viersen.

269 **The back end of** J. W. Snee, Lt. Col., Cavalry, "Plan for Employment of 23d Sp Trs Operation 'Exploit,' 11 March 1945," RG 407, SPHQ-23-0.3, National Archives, College Park, MD, 1.

270 **For realism, Ninth Army** J. E. Moore, Brig. Gen., GSC, Chief of Staff, Ninth U.S. Army, "Cover Plan, Operation FLASHPOINT, 10 March 1945," RG 407, SPHQ-23-0.3, National Archives, College Park, MD.

271 **To direct such a** Simenson, "Operational Memorandum No. 6 (VIERSEN, top secret), 19 March 1945," RG 407, SPHQ-23-0.3, National Archives, College Park, MD.

271 **A directive was issued** M. G. Winget, Maj., CE, Executive Officer, "Engineer Plan for Operation EXPLOIT, 17 March 1945," RG 407, SPHQ 23-0.3, National Archives, College Park, MD, 1.

272 **Intelligence reports from** Joseph Kelly, Maj., G-2, "Estimate of Enemy Intelligence Capabilities (top secret), 19 March 1945," RG 407, SPHQ 23-0.3, National Archives, College Park, MD, 1.

273 **Simenson ordered: "All . . ."** Simenson, "Operational Memorandum No. 3 (VIERSEN, top secret), 19 March 1945," RG 407, SPHQ-23-0.3, National Archives, College Park, MD.

273 **There was even** V-mail was written on a special one-sided form, then photographed onto microfilm, which was then transported at a savings in weight and space, to be reproduced and delivered at the destination. Occasionally the larger, unmicrofilmed forms were sent.

274 **Whether it was Fox** Quote and signal details from Charles H. Yokum, Maj., Sig C, Sig O, "Report of Signal Operations VIERSEN, 17–24 March 1945, 23d Headquarters Special Troops" (top secret), RG 407, SPHQ 23-0.3, National Archives, College Park, MD, 2.

275 **5. Ninth Army Traffic** Ibid., 3.

275 **Typical traffic just a** Radio traffic quotes from 23d Headquarters Special Troops, "Traffic Control Net Script, 23d Headquarters Special Troops, 18–25 March 1945," 5, RG 407, SPHQ-23-0.3, National Archives, College Park, MD.

275 **Fox, in charge** Fox, "The Deception Team: War and Football Are Getting Trickier," 27.

275 **When not riding** Frederic E. Fox, letter to Hannah Fox, 25 March 1945.

276 **Fox had written the program** Fox, "Memorandum (secret)11 July 1944," RG 407, SPHQ-23-0.3, National Archives, College Park, MD, 1.

276 **Over the past couple** Radio traffic quotes from 23d Headquarters Special Troops, "Traffic Control Net Script, 23d Headquarters Special Troops, 18–25 March 1945."

277 **At Anrath, Simenson's** Simenson, "Report on Operation VIERSEN, 79th Inf Div

Phase, 17–24 Mar 45 (top secret)." RG 407, SPHQ-23-0.3, National Archives, College Park, MD, 2.

281 **Sergeant Jimmy Laubheimer** Details of Laubheimer's duties from Laubheimer, "Pop Pop Went to War," 41.

283 **Then the Germans** Joseph Kelly, "Summary of Enemy Activity XIII Corps Sector (top secret) 15–27 March 1945," RG 407, SPHQ 23-0.3, National Archives, College Park, MD, 1.

283 **Each night, single** Joseph Kelly, "Estimate of Enemy Intelligence Capabilities (top secret), 19 March 1945," 1.

283 **The design of** Edgar Schroeder, Lt. Col., Commanding, "Report of Operation VIERSEN, 30th Inf Div Phase, 18–24 Mar (top secret, 1945)," RG 407, SPHQ-23-0.3, National Archives, College Park, MD, 2.

284 **Fox was captivated** Fox, "The Deception Team: War and Football Are Getting Trickier," 26.

284 **In fact, things** Joseph Kelly, "Summary of Enemy Activity XIII Corps Sector (top secret) 15–27 March 1945," 2.

284 **The American patrols** Ibid.

285 **"In the whole range . . ."** Von Clausewitz, *On War*, 86.

285 **"Optimism is generally . . ."** Frederic E. Fox, letter to Hannah Putnam Fox, 25 March 1945.

287 **The crossing at Wesel** Casualty figures from Ambrose, *The Supreme Commander*, 626.

287 **By daylight on March 24** Tompkins, "World War II Diary," 12; reference to 83d Corps is enigmatic—probably XIII, the corps zone in which they were operating.

288 **And as G-2 Kelly reported** Joseph Kelly, "Summary of Enemy Activity XIII Corps Sector (top secret) 15–27 March 1945," 2.

288 **Three weeks after crossing** Capture figures from Ambrose, *Citizen Soldiers*, 454.

289 **Ingersoll glowingly chronicled** Ingersoll, *Top Secret*, 292.

289 **Fox reported just** Fox and Flemer, *The Official History of the 23d Headquarters Special Troops*, 29.

289 **He wrote his bride-to-be** Frederic E. Fox, letter to Hannah Putnam Fox, 25 March 1945.

289 **For once, Reeder** Harry L. Reeder, Col., Commanding, "Report of Operation VIERSEN, 17–24 March 1945 (top secret), 7 May 1945," RG 407, SPHQ-23-0.3, National Archives, College Park, MD, 1–2.

289 **"Were the above . . ."** 30th Infantry Division, "Annex #1 to G-2 Periodic report No. 282, 30th Infantry Division, Deception Measures for Operation 'FLASHPOINT' (secret), 26 March 1945," 2.

290 "This operation was . . ." Reeder, "Report of Operation VIERSEN, 17–24 March 1945 (top secret), 7 May 1945," 2.

290 **Special Plans Branch** Harris et al., "Informal Report to Joint Security Control, Part I, Subject: Appreciation of Deception in the European Theater," 6.

290 **A more personal kudos** Account from Charles Kizina, interview by author, 7 September 2001.

291 **For the first time** William H. Simpson, Lt. Gen., U.S. Army, Commanding, "Commendation to Commanding Officer, 23d Headquarters Special Troops, Twelfth Army Group, 29 March 1945," RG 407, SPHQ-23-0.1, National Archives, College Park, MD, 1.

CHAPTER FOURTEEN
Striking the Set
April–August 1945

295 "*. . . don't saddle your folks . . .*" Army Services Forces, "Lecture on the Safeguarding of Military Information to Be Included in Orientation Lecture Given at Separation Centers, Text No. 2, 1945," 4.

298 **Harold Dahl pulled** Harold J. Dahl, letter to Mrs. Anna M. and Lou Dahl, 17 May 1945.

298 **Hal Laynor was** Harold Laynor, letter to Gloria Laynor, 9 May 1945.

298 **A Japanese patrol** "Julian V. Sollohub, Lt. Col., USA, Citation for Silver Star Medal, 7 May 1945," courtesy Julian V. Sollohub.

298 **Like the other officers** Frederic E. Fox, letter to Hannah Putnam Fox, 25 May 1945.

299 **Even with the war** Frederic E. Fox, letter to Hannah Putnam Fox, 20 May 1945.

300 **On 6 June 1945** Frederic E. Fox, letter to Hannah Putnam Fox, 10 June 1945.

300 **After the Rhine campaign** Fox and Flemer, *Official History of the 23d Headquarters Special Troops*, 32.

300 **Part of Signal Company,** Ibid., 32.

300 **The 23d Headquarters** Sequential quotes from Frederic E. Fox, letter to Hannah Putnam Fox, 25 March 1945.

301 **The Nazis, abetted** Sequential quotes from Frederic E. Fox, letter to Hannah Putnam Fox, 25 March 1945.

302 **The habit of hush-hush** Harold J. Dahl, letter to Mrs. Anna M. and Lou Dahl, 6 June 1945.

303 **If Fox ever visited** Frederic E. Fox, letter to Hannah Putnam Fox, 1 May 1945.

303 **Headquarters Company was** Account from Arnett, ed.,"The Ghost Army Days of Walter Wendell Arnett," 23.

303 **"Incidentally," Laubheimer** Laubheimer, "Pop Pop Went to War," 45.

303 **Ingersoll, who had** Ingersoll, *Top Secret*, 294.

303 **"Here are all the things . . ."** Sequential quotes from Richard H. Morton, letter to Mr. and Mrs. Leon S. Morton, 22 March 1945.

304 **Dahl had similar** Harold J. Dahl, letter to Mrs. Anna M. and Lou Dahl, 23 April 1945.

304 **Tompkins reacted with** Sequential quotes from Tompkins, "World War II Diary," 13.

305 **The following day** Tompkins, "World War II Diary," 13.

305 **"They were strange . . ."** Laubheimer, "Pop Pop Went to War," 44.

306 **Even before the end** Richard H. Morton, letter to Mr. and Mrs. Leon S. Morton, 28 March 1945.

306 **The whole unit** Sequential quotes from Fox and Flemer, *Official History of the 23d Headquarters Special Troops*, 33.

308 **Soon the Special Troops** Fox and Flemer, *Official History of the 23d Headquarters Special Troops*, 35.

308 **Gloria Laynor tells** Account and quotes from Gloria Laynor, interview by author, 8 December 2000.

311 **Most of them came** Laubheimer, "Pop Pop Went to War," 55.

312 **The experience caused** Richard H. Morton, letter to Mr. and Mrs. Leon S. Morton, 29 May 1945.

314 **A 1978 report** Mark Kronman, "The Deceptive Practices of the 23d Headquarters Special Troops During World War II," Aberdeen Proving Grounds, MD: Tactical Operations Analysis Office, U.S. Army Materiel Systems Analysis Activity, 1978. Military History Institute Library, Carlisle Barracks, PA, 50.

315 **The 23d was not planned** Sequential quotes from Harris et al., "Informal Report to Joint Security Control; Part I: Appreciation of Deception in the European Theater," 6.

315 **Colonel Harry L. Reeder** Harris et al., "Informal Report to Joint Security Control; Part IV, Subject: Officers with Cover and Deception Experience, European Theater," 1.

316 **Harold Dahl wrote** Harold J. Dahl, letter to Mrs. Anna M. and Lou Dahl, undated, 1945.

318 **The closing page** Kronman, "The Deceptive Practices of the 23d Headquarters Special Troops During World War II," 51.

318 **Railey sent a telegram** Hilton H. Railey, telegram to General Ingalls, chief signal officer, 1 November 1945.

318 **The secret equipment** Office of the Chief Signal Officer, "Plans for Closing the Army Experimental Station," Tab A: "Equipment to Be Forwarded to the Signal Corps Engineering Laboratory, Bradley Beach, New Jersey, 20 August 1945."

318 **In a special ceremony** "Col. Railey Honored in D.C.," *Pine Post*, Vol 6, No. 6, September 30, 1945, 1.

319 **Gaskins, his wartime** Robert E. Gaskins, interview by author, 13 April 2001.

319 **In April 1945,** Quoted in Fairbanks, *A Hell of a War*, 253.

319 **As they prepared** Sequential quotes from Army Services Forces, Lecture on the Safeguarding of Military Information to Be Included in Orientation Lecture Given at Separation Centers, Text No. 2, 1945, 5.

320 **Some of them heard** Sequential quotes from Army Services Forces, "Lecture on the Safeguarding of Military Information to Be Included in Orientation Lecture Given at Separation Centers, Text No. 1, 1945," 2 and 1.

320 **Fox tried for years** Fox, "The Deception Team: War and Football Are Getting Trickier," 4.

321 **Dahl alerted his family** Harold J. Dahl, letter to Mrs. Anna M. and Lou Dahl, undated, 1945.

321 **The camoufleurs did stage** Harold J. Dahl, Galerie Bradtke program for "Exhibition of Oil, Water Colors, and Photos of Luxembourg Countryside" by artists of the 603d Camouflage Engineers, 23 February–1 March 1948. Courtesy Robert Dahl.

Index